Arming the Nation for War

Arming the

Nation for War

Mobilization, Supply, and the American
War Effort in World War II

Robert P. Patterson

Edited by Brian Waddell
With a Foreword by Robert M. Morgenthau

Legacies of War / G. Kurt Piehler, Series Editor

The University of Tennessee Press / Knoxville

The Legacies of War series presents a variety of works—from scholarly monographs to memoirs—that examine the impact of war on society, both in the United States and globally. The wide scope of the series might include war's effects on civilian populations, its lingering consequences for veterans, and the role of individual nations and the international community in confronting genocide and other injustices born of war.

 Copyright © 2014 by The University of Tennessee Press / Knoxville.
All Rights Reserved. Manufactured in the United States of America.
Cloth: first printing, 2014.
Paper: first printing, 2024.

Library of Congress Cataloging-in-Publication Data

Patterson, Robert Porter, 1891–1952.
Arming the nation for war: mobilization, supply, and the American war effort in World War II / Robert P. Patterson; edited by Brian Waddell ; with a remembrance by Robert M. Morgenthau. — First edition.
    pages cm. — (Legacies of war)
Includes bibliographical references and index.
ISBN 978-1-57233-872-2 (hardcover)
 1. Industrial mobilization—United States—History—20th century.
 2. World War, 1939–1945—Logistics—United States.
 3. World War, 1939–1945—Economic aspects—United States.
 4. United States—Armed Forces—Supplies and stores—Management.
 5. United States. War Department—Procurement.
 6. World War, 1939–1945—United States.
 7. Industrial mobilization—United States—Evaluation.
 8. Patterson, Robert Porter, 1891–1952.
 9. World War, 1939-1945—Personal narratives, American.
 I. Waddell, Brian, editor.
 II. Title.
 III. Title: Mobilization, supply, and the American war effort in World War II.

D769.2.P38 2014
940.54'1273—dc23
2013039697

For Sarah, Julian, and Emma

    and

To Garry Clifford

Contents

Foreword	
Robert Porter Patterson: A Remembrance	xi
Robert M. Morgenthau	
Preface	xvii
Introduction: Robert Porter Patterson and World War II	xxv
1. A Nation without Arms	1
2. The Slow Beginning	15
3. Airplanes Take Five Years	43
4. A Changing Nation	67
5. Altitudinal Goals	89
6. An Offensive Begins	123
7. Alaska, Australia, the Persian Gulf	143
8. Assault in Force	163
9. The End in Europe	181
10. Concentration East	205
Epilogue: Industry, Science, War, and the Future	215
Notes	229
Index	303

Illustrations

Following page 134

Judge Patterson in Uniform at Plattsburgh, New York, July 7, 1940
Patterson as the New Assistant Secretary of War, October 23, 1940
Patterson, Under Secretary of War
Office of the Under Secretary of War
Patterson with ex-General Motors Head General William S. Knudsen
Patterson with Rifle
Patterson Firing a Light Machine Gun, August 21, 1942
Citation Winners, December 1942
Patterson with Wife Margaret Christening the SS *General William A. Mann*, July 18, 1943
Patterson Visiting the 104th Division, Camp Carson, Colorado
Patterson Greeting Black Soldiers at Fort Huachuca, Arizona, June 1944
Patterson Visiting the hones and Laughlin Steel Corporation, Pittsburgh, Pennsylvania, November 2, 1944
Patterson Shaking Hand with General MacArthur in New Guinea, 1945
Editorial Cartoon by C. K. Berrymann
Patterson Inspects an American Red Cross Unit, Japan, January 9, 1946
Patterson Testifying at the War Profits Hearing of the Senate Special Investigating Committee, July 9, 1946
Article Covering Patterson's Death, January 1952

Foreword

Robert Porter Patterson: A Remembrance

Robert P. Patterson—federal judge, secretary of war, decorated hero of World War I, a respected leader of the Bar, and a Republican admired and promoted by Democrats—was my first boss in civilian life. Although my tutelage was cut short—I had the privilege of working with him for just four years—Judge Patterson served as the model for much of my work and life that followed.

Our relationship began fortuitously. After World War II, when I was finishing up an accelerated two-year course at Yale Law, I was eager to gain experience in the law, but also to enter public service. In the winter of 1948, as I began to make the rounds of the major New York firms, most of my interviews ended abruptly when I revealed an interest in public service. One hiring partner, as he showed me out the door, said, "I want associates who will work late at night so that I can go home for dinner and, perhaps, think about public service." By the time I reached Judge Patterson's firm, Patterson, Belknap and Webb, I realized that I would not likely be hired if I talked about my public service ambitions. When I got my interview, though, I got lucky. The only lawyer I spoke to was Judge Patterson. The judge, as I soon learned, was a great believer in public service. I was not sure when I started working at Patterson, Belknap that I wanted to be a lawyer, but under the guidance of the judge, I knew I had made the right choice.

○ ○ ○

On July 28, 1940, an urgent message arrived at 6th Company, Business and Professional Men's Training Camp in Plattsburgh, New York. Addressed to "Trainee Patterson," the telegram had come from Washington, D.C., asking Patterson to serve as the assistant secretary of war. At forty-nine, the judge had served a decade on the federal bench, earning renown for his simplicity, brilliance, and fortitude. Patterson was just finishing KP duty when the offer came. "They could get a better man," he told a fellow trainee. "But if they want me, I'll accept."

A decorated veteran of World War I, where he survived some of the bloodiest fighting in France, Patterson had grown up in rural Glen Falls, New York. His grandfather was an Irish preacher, a Methodist who traveled the villages and towns of northern New York and Vermont. His father was a lawyer well known upstate, twice serving as the district attorney of Warren County. Educated in the local public schools, Patterson worked in the post office downtown, and in the fall of 1908 enrolled in Union College. He went on to Harvard Law, where he took the first class taught by Felix Frankfurter, and became the editor-in-chief of the *Law Review,* finished first in his class, and was elected the class marshall. He graduated *cum laude* in 1915, joining the famous New York City firm of former Senator and Secretary of State Elihu Root: Root, Clark, Buckner and Howland.

Even before the "guns of August," Patterson would reveal his eagerness to serve. In 1916, he enlisted in the New York National Guard, serving as a private in the Mexican Border Patrol. Within a year, he had entered the first Officer's Training Camp at Plattsburgh, graduating in August 1917 as a captain of the 306th Regiment, 77th Infantry Division. Within months, he was in France. Assigned to Company F, 306th Infantry Regiment, he fought in the Oise-Aisne and Meuse-Argonne offensives—earning two citations for gallant and meritorious service "in utter disregard of personal danger." Near Bazoches, France, on August 14, 1918, Captain Patterson, along with two noncommissioned officers, completed a daylight reconnaissance operation behind enemy lines. Far outnumbered, they surprised an enemy outpost and destroyed it. In 1919, Major Patterson came home—with a Purple Heart, Silver Star, and the Distinguished Service Cross for "extraordinary heroism under fire."

In the 1920s, as he rose in the law, Patterson gained a national reputation. He helped found his own firm and twice turned down a chance to return to Harvard Law as dean. In the summer of 1930, Patterson was named to the federal bench, succeeding Thomas Day Thatcher in the Southern District of New York. By 1939, President Franklin D. Roosevelt had promoted Patterson to the U.S. Court of Appeals, Second Circuit. Roosevelt's court-packing defeat was still fresh, but Patterson's appointment brought only praise. He was that rare political figure—a Republican so staunchly independent and undaunted by patronage that both parties could embrace him.

As the horizon darkened in Europe, Patterson was among the first to foresee the coming of war. He also foresaw the inevitability of America's entrance into the war. In the summer of 1940, eager to serve, he returned to Plattsburg. With so much of the country deeply isolationist, Roosevelt searched for avenues to advance the country's military preparedness. The president's old friend Grenville Clark, a prominent Republican lawyer and partner in the firm that employed Patterson as an associate, suggested that Roosevelt name Henry Stimson secretary of war—the prewar title for the head of the War Department. Stimson was admired by both parties, but was seventy-three years old. He would need a young deputy. Once again, Clark had a candidate: his former associate.

Patterson would leave private practice to help lead a War Department mired in internecine struggles and uncertain of its future course. Yet, as under secretary of war, he would do as much as any American, civilian or military, to ensure America's victory. He helped reform and unite a vast organization that took the lead in preparedness. The department soon became a place, as he writes in this remarkable account of his efforts, where his staff "would never do more than admit that 'the impossible takes a little longer.'" Mobilization plans existed, but the Congress had not yet declared a national emergency. Raising an army of 3.5 million men and equipping them on an accelerated schedule, Patterson faced tall odds. But he helped pull off the feat. Before he was done, Patterson had spent $100 billion, an unheard-of amount in those days. He oversaw all fronts of domestic production, from laces for the GIs' shoes—the very shoes that he wore long after the war had ended—to the production of the atomic bomb.

When Stimson resigned in September 1945, President Truman named Patterson the new secretary of war. The appointment masked another story. Judge Patterson's résumé never mentioned it, but at the time there was also a vacancy on the Supreme Court. Truman recognized the judge's brilliance and offered him the job—Justice Owen Roberts's seat. The appointment was even announced. But Walther Reuther called Truman and objected to McCloy becoming secretary of war, so Truman said to Patterson, "You're going to become Secretary of War and then get the next vacancy."

Judge Patterson never let his regret be known. In 1947 Truman hoped to appoint Patterson as the first secretary of defense. But only days before the act was created, Patterson quit the cabinet. After seven years in the War Department, he did not wish to assume a position that he had helped create. "Never," wrote Truman, "have I accepted a resignation with more poignant regret." The judge returned to New York City. Time and again his name was floated for high office, whether mayor or senator. Truman offered to reappoint him to the Court of Appeals, but Patterson chose to go his own way. He returned to the law. In 1948 he joined Chauncey Belknap and Vanderbilt Webb to create Patterson, Belknap and Webb.

o o o

Nearly from the day I joined the firm, we worked together on every case. I was honored to sit at his knee; Judge Patterson was in much demand as a trial and appellate lawyer. He had cases in the Second, Third, Fourth, Sixth, and Eighth Circuits, as well as the Supreme Court of the United States and a number of the district courts outside of the Southern District. I not only saw a truly outstanding lawyer at work, but I also learned about integrity, independence, professional responsibility and commitment to the highest standards of the legal profession. We traveled everywhere together. On the road, he used to reminisce frequently about Emory Buckner, who had been his first mentor at the old Root, Clark law firm. Buckner had been a great U.S. attorney for the Southern District of New York, and Patterson told me a number of stories about Buckner, which stimulated my interest in becoming a U.S. attorney. Patterson spoke not only about Buckner's legal abilities but also about his concern for the welfare and training of young lawyers and his independence and integrity as United States attorney.

Working for Judge Patterson was an extraordinary learning experience; his integrity, independence and infectious love of the law remain with me to this day. I worked for the judge during the age of Senator Joseph McCarthy, and the judge took on loyalty cases when other lawyers were reluctant to do so. But he had an aversion to tax cases. He ardently believed that taxes were the price we paid for civilization and that our democracy was dependent upon voluntary compliance.

Above all, Judge Patterson was a man of modesty and honesty. He refused to accept special treatment and had no tolerance for those who did. His idea of a good meal was to go to the automat and have the baked beans and a hot dog. Together, they cost three quarters. Once, on a work trip to California, the client—Twentieth Century Fox—had arranged for us to stay in the presidential suite of a Beverly Hills hotel. The judge took one look at the luxury accommodations and said, "Please, take me to a regular room."

○ ○ ○

On the afternoon of January 22, 1952, Judge Patterson, at age sixty, was in Buffalo to meet with a new client. He and I always traveled together. But the judge had recently been retained to represent the United States Steel Company in a matter before the U.S. Supreme Court, and I told him that I could not go to Buffalo with him and get a draft of the brief in the case to him in time. I stayed behind in New York City. That was the only trip he took in which I did not accompany him.

The weather was poor that day and visibility low. American Airlines Flight 6780, on which the judge was returning home from Buffalo, had just begun a landing procedure when it crashed in a neighborhood south of Elizabeth, New Jersey. All twenty-three people onboard the Convair CV-240 were killed.

The law, and the country, had lost a great man. The *New York Herald-Tribune*, four years earlier, had aptly summed up Judge Patterson's gifts. In war and peace, he had been, an editorialist wrote, "an example of the public-spirited citizen." Judge Patterson had combined the work of a jurist with that of a soldier, and in both has shown courage, high intelligence, and a devotion to democratic principles. Too often, as Burke said, law sharpens the mind only to narrow it; and the military career, even more frequently, leaves those who have pursued it a preoccupation with force to the exclusion of ideals. Mr. Patterson has not only escaped these perils, but has added to his many services the stamp of his special integrity and distinction.

My own time with Judge Patterson was too brief. On that very sad day in the winter of 1952, I lost a friend and an extraordinary role model. Yet we had enjoyed a wonderful relationship, and even in death he remained a rare guide. When I became U.S. attorney and later district attorney for New York County, my experiences with Judge Patterson stood me in good stead. He had taught me that when you give responsibilities to young lawyers and treat them like equals, they will do their level best to live up to that confidence. He also taught me that when you do what you think is right, people will, by and large, respect you for it. In my naval career and nearly six decades as a prosecutor, I met many wonderful men and women. I can think of no one, though, whom I have more admired.

ROBERT M. MORGENTHAU

Preface

Robert Porter Patterson was one of the central figures during one of the most important periods of modern United States history. And yet, despite being the subject of a comprehensive biographical study that focuses primarily on his wartime service, his contribution to the U.S. victory in World War II and his continued service after the war have been too easily forgotten. This neglect may have to do with his quick departure from the Washington scene after serving an important stint as secretary of war after the war and his early tragic death in an airplane crash in January 1952. Unlike many of the other prominent figures who were "present at the creation"[1] and continued to exercise outsized influence on the development of the Washington establishment and postwar foreign policy, Patterson seemed to be content to relinquish the trappings of power and settle back into his prewar legal livelihood.[2] And now, sixty-plus years after he wrote it and stashed it away—seemingly forgotten to history—we have this document that assesses the issues of home-front mobilization and battlefield supply during World War II in Patterson's authoritative voice.

It is very rare to have a first-person, richly informative manuscript of this nature pop up out of the blue after being buried for so many years, and I knew that the document had great historical significance because of who wrote it, and because of the context—mobilizing for victory in World War II and creating the postwar national security state—within which it was written. The manuscript I was given was typewritten on War Department stationary and marked "SECRET," which would mean that it was written before the end of Patterson's tenure as secretary of war in 1947.[3]

The manuscript was discovered in 1969 in a file drawer in Patterson's law firm, Patterson, Belknap, Webb, and Tyler, by then associate Robert D. Sack (now a federal judge for the United States Court of Appeals, Second Circuit). Judge Sack walked it two doors down to his colleague, Robert P. Patterson Jr., who filed it away, not realizing its importance at the time. He came across the manuscript again while going through old file boxes as he was moving to a new apartment in 2006, and realizing finally what it was, he began the effort to get it published. His sister Virginia Patterson Montgomery, Patterson's youngest daughter, took over this effort, and contacted my colleague at the University of Connecticut, J. Garry Clifford, about the possibility of editing the manuscript. Garry in turn thought that I would be perfect for the task, and we met with Virginia early in the summer of 2009. As it turned out, Virginia showed us another manuscript that her father had written about his World War I battlefield experiences, and that manuscript has now been published with Garry as the editor.[4] I was greatly intrigued about the later manuscript, having written two books on the subject of World War II mobilization, and in 2010 the University of Tennessee Press agreed to publish both of Patterson's manuscripts.

As luck would have, as I was working on the nine chapters I was given (which were assumed to be the entire original manuscript), Virginia contacted me about the discovery of two more chapters. Virginia had been scouring old boxes in her brother's attic looking for relevant materials and photos to accompany the World War I memoir and there discovered two final chapters of the World War II manuscript. This was serendipity at its best. These had been originally found in file drawers at Patterson's old law firm in 1974, sent on to her brother by the office manager of the law firm, Ed Lampe, and promptly filed away separate from the rest of the original manuscript. And, so, because of Virginia's diligence, we now have the two final chapters, which round out the narrative with a focus on the defeat of Japan (chapter 10) but, even more important, provide Patterson's vision and recommendations for the future (the epilogue). The epilogue seems to demonstrate why Patterson wrote the document in the first place: as a warning for future mobilizers and as a prescription for the postwar organization of war preparation.

Given Patterson's prominence within the national administration during the years 1940–47, it is remarkable that we now have this recently discovered manuscript that covers his entire wartime service. The perspective of the manuscript is unique. It is not a "kiss-and-tell" memoir seeking to settle scores or to divulge personal anecdotes about official Washington. Patterson was clearly not a man who would go in for any type of after-the-fact axe grinding or self-promotion. Instead, his manuscript offers a serious and informative review of the many home-front mobilization issues, while also providing a careful overview and analysis of the battlefront supply issues that he and the army faced in the different theaters of the war. As he notes in his epilogue, "Until one goes through the experience, it is almost impossible to grasp the appalling technical difficulties of industrial mobilization."[5]

His purpose, then, far from offering simply an entertaining personal memoir, is the serious business of reviewing the myriad problems encountered on the domestic mobilization front combined with the logistical difficulties of supplying the different theaters and battlefronts of the war. The manuscript is important for the way it covers so much of mobilization effort in so many different areas of the home front and the far-flung battlefronts. Here Patterson has pulled together the production effort and the incredible feats of logistics and supply of the battlefront into one compelling narrative. He reviews the "technical difficulties" involved in these areas quite extensively based on his first-hand experience and provides insights and anecdotes that bring these issues alive for the reader. As he notes, "Ours was a logistical victory unusual in the annals of war,"[6] and reviewing this dimension of the Allied victory is one of the reasons Patterson wrote this document.

Throughout the manuscript Patterson provides specific examples of the problems encountered and the way that solutions were found. He develops in this way a running commentary on the main issues of mobilization and supply to impart the lessons he learned during the war. As he notes toward the end, "[T]he breath-taking display of power with which we closed hostilities in Europe must not allow us to forget that we had a terribly close call at the start. Nor can we afford to forget that it took nearly five years from the moment when danger threatened until we reached the pinnacle of our strength in the field. Destiny was generous of time, more generous than we deserved. We cannot count on such generosity again."[7]

This concern for learning the war's lessons seems to be the key reason he wrote this manuscript—to alert both his contemporaries and future mobilizers of the strenuous efforts required in so many different areas to successfully bring America's industrial might to bear on the battlefields of World War II. As he notes, "It detracts in no way from the skill and heroism of those who landed on the beaches on June 6 to say that the successful invasion of Normandy began several years earlier and that the first skirmishes took place in those offices and factories where preparations were made for the immense mass of materiel which, both on the ground and in the air, provided the sinews for this extraordinary victory" (see page 191, this volume). He remains intent, throughout the manuscript, on explicating and conveying the ways that he and others dealt with the thorny issues they confronted. And he does so with the immediacy of someone who was there from the very beginnings of the mobilization effort right through to the creation of the national security state in the postwar years. In fact, as is clear especially from the final chapter, Patterson very likely wrote the manuscript as a contribution to the postwar debates on the future of the military establishment and as a companion document to the National Security Act of 1947. He seems determined not to let the mobilization-and-supply experience simply pass into history but rather to rescue this incredible effort for posterity as a stern admonition on how difficult mobilization and supply proved to be. And he was here continuing his Jeremiah-like sermons about the perils of unpreparedness.

The manuscript thus reads in part like a catalog or registry for the lessons Patterson learned during the war for the edification of those, he feared, were becoming complacent in the immediate aftermath of the Allies' victory. His manuscript is a testament to remind his contemporaries of how close the margin of victory really was. "When I look back across those crowded five years," he notes, "it sometimes seems a miracle to me that we won the war."[8] As his biographer, Keith E. Eiler reports, Patterson "found it necessary, from the moment the war ended, to caution against a precipitous collapse of U.S. military power." Patterson remembered all too well that the "interwar years were . . . marked by extreme forms of pacifism, isolationist foreign policies, and scandalous neglect of the armed services. The thought that such patterns might recur in the far more dangerous world of A-bombs and guided missiles was a prospect too unsettling to contemplate."[9]

In this sense, the manuscript is in no way a triumphal victory lap, though given the picture it paints of the many different problems that were surmounted it certainly could be so. Rather, Patterson provides a very frank and candid perspective of the difficulties in managing the procurement, logistical, and supply operations of the war. Though on one level the manuscript seems written as a manual of sorts to help speed the learning curve of future mobilizers, it seems clear that it reflects Patterson's need to remind those busy building the new postwar framework for national security of the huge effort that the recently ended conflict required for victory. Since we would never again be without a permanent military presence at the heart of American government, he need not have worried: with the National Security Act came a permanent preparation for war that included strategic and logistical planning, war gaming, a military-industrial complex, and a nation kept on the edge of its seat in expectation of war.

Even before its publication, Patterson's manuscript has sparked controversy. Former New York District Attorney Robert M. Morgenthau and law professor Frank Tuerkheimer use an episode that Patterson relates to buttress their arguments in a piece titled, "How FDR Helped Save Jews of the Holy Land."[10] Patterson reports that President Roosevelt ordered in mid-summer 1942 a rushed shipment of three hundred Sherman tanks and one hundred howitzers to British General Bernard Montgomery's forces, who were facing annihilation in Egypt after a decisive defeat at Tobruk. If British forces fell, the entire Middle East—and especially Palestine—would be vulnerable to the declared Nazi policy of exterminating Jews. British Prime Minister Winston Churchill was visiting President Roosevelt at the White House when Tobruk fell to Rommel's forces, and when asked what the United States could do, Churchill requested that Roosevelt supply the tanks and other armaments needed to replace the munitions lost with the Tobruk defeat. And Patterson writes about this incident and how they were able to get these munitions to Montgomery's forces. As it turned out, Montgomery defeated the German forces in October and November 1942 at El Alamein with the help of the American-supplied munitions, and, as Morgenthau and Tuerkheimer argue, thereby "Helped Save Jews of the Holy Land." Reaction to this argument was swift, as Jonathan S. Tobin wrote in *Commentary*[11] magazine a short piece titled, "FDR Didn't Try to Save Middle East Jews." And this rebuttal led to an exchange in *Commentary* and even an editorial in the *New York Sun*.[12] It seems likely that the publication of Patterson's full manuscript might well provoke further discussions of controversial wartime decisions and their long-term implications.

Patterson wrote everything out in long hand, a manuscript that would have then been typed up by his long-serving secretary, Lucille Mundy. The typescript contained a few hand-written corrections by an unknown editor and one note signed "TSA," which must be the initials of Troyer Steele Anderson, a Patterson special assistant who was also a historian with the army and who authored a typescript monograph that covered the history of the under secretary's office from 1920 to 1941. I made only a few changes to Patterson's language so as to retain his voice, but added full names to those individuals whom Patterson mentions, and corrected any misspellings. Minor punctuation and formatting changes were also made to enhance readability. I found myself researching many of the topics Patterson covers, topics with which I was very familiar in many cases, but also many that were new to me. I have provided in my notes commentary based on what subsequent scholars and even some participants in these events have written about the story that Patterson relates.

I would like to acknowledge the reviews of the manuscript provided by Mark R. Wilson and John Whiteclaw Chambers II. Both of these distinguished historians offered substantive and perceptive comments about the importance of the Patterson manuscript. They both also provided detailed comments on my contributions that proved helpful and very welcome. Scot Danforth of the University of Tennessee Press was always ready with advice and support. Gene Adair, who copyedited the manuscript, also deserves a note of thanks for his efforts. Virginia Patterson Montgomery, Robert Patterson's daughter, was very eager to see this manuscript find a wider readership, and so provided strong support for my efforts. She followed my progress closely and answered any questions I had as they came up. And, as noted, she also dug through her brother's attic boxes and came across the final two chapters of this manuscript. I know the importance of this project to her and to Robert Patterson's other children. My father, David M. Waddell Sr., joined the Army Air Corps right out of high school in the summer of 1941 and served throughout World War II in the Pacific theater with the 22nd Bomb Group. I talked to him frequently while working on this manuscript about his memories from the Pacific theater and the larger war effort. And I owe a great debt, yet again, to my colleague Garry Clifford, who steered me into this project. Garry avidly read the chapter drafts and my notes, pointing me to new sources and correcting any mistakes he found. He provided great advice and a careful editing hand in helping me finalize the introduction. Of course, any remaining errors are mine alone. Last, I dedicate my efforts to my wife, Sarah, and our two children, Julian and Emma.

Introduction

Robert Porter Patterson and World War II

> We must never forget that, if we have another war, it will be nearly won, or nearly lost, on the industrial front before a shot is fired. That front deserves, and must have, in the years of preparation as well as in the months of conflict, the greatest efforts and the ablest minds that the nation can command. If we fail there, we fail everywhere, in combat, and in all those pursuits of peace which depend upon the successful maintenance of our national security.
> —Robert P. Patterson

Patterson's Service in Outline

Described in a 1942 *Saturday Evening Post* article as "The Toughest Man in Washington," Robert Porter Patterson began his World War II service in late July 1940, seventeen months before the United States formally entered the war. President Franklin D. Roosevelt appointed him to the position of assistant secretary of war under the new secretary of war, Henry L. Stimson, a Republican who had himself been appointed just a few weeks earlier. Patterson entered into his new post at the moment when the Congress had just passed, at Roosevelt's insistence, an enormous new munitions program, for which Patterson now had central directive responsibility. At the end of his first two years at the War Department, the *Saturday Evening Post* declared, he had spent "more than $46,000,000,000," noting, "No man in history ever before expended such money."[1]

Patterson's job title changed with new legislation in December 1940 to that of Undersecretary of War, a nominal change that left his authority intact but placed him more directly under Secretary of War Stimson. His job changed more substantially after the attack on Pearl Harbor, as a subsequent U.S. Army command reorganization divested him of direct personal authority over procurement and supply. But with this shift in command authority, Patterson found himself freed from the often-overwhelming day-to-day administrative details so that he could attend to the broader issues of industrial mobilization, procurement, and supply as the key War Department spokesman. His responsibilities remained extensive. As his direct superior, Secretary Stimson, later wrote, "Probably no man in the [Roosevelt] administration was more ruthlessly determined to fulfill his assignment than Patterson." He became during the war the War Department's official representative on the War Production Board, the War Manpower Commission, and the Committee for Congested Production Areas. Beginning with his direct responsibility for the pre-war army expansion programs of 1940–41, and continuing from his powerful position as the army's paramount civilian representative, Patterson played an outsized role in the enormous domestic industrial mobilization for World War II. As J. Garry Clifford reports, "An informal poll conducted after the war ranked Patterson second only to Army Chief of Staff General George C. Marshall as the person most responsible for America's victory over the Axis powers."[2]

The effort to carry out America's mission as the Allies' "arsenal of democracy" meant sorting out the government's role, especially regarding the civilian-military division of labor, in many areas. These areas included converting the civilian economy to war production, vastly expanding the industrial base, figuring out financing and ownership of the necessary new war plants, and controlling and overseeing expanding military procurement. The mobilization effort also meant overcoming material shortages, determining access to scarce raw materials, overcoming manpower shortages (and, for Patterson, pushing hard, albeit unsuccessfully, for national service legislation), controlling prices and profits, assessing the feasibility of the massive military orders (that is, whether uncontrolled military orders would overload the economy as they had in World War I), scheduling production of the many competing items, and planning for reconversion to peacetime production. Where there were few tensions and conflicts between President Roosevelt and his top military commanders throughout the war, civil-military relations in the area of mobilization and procurement were marked by the most intense domestic controversies of the war period. And Patterson inserted himself into the middle of these controversies as a stalwart defender of army prerogatives and army procurement needs. For Patterson, it was a matter of keeping faith with the common soldier, the GIs. As his biographer, Keith E. Eiler, notes, Patterson "was persuaded that no effort should be spared in reciprocating their trust and promoting their welfare."[3]

In recognition of Patterson's wartime service and achievements, President Harry S. Truman offered him a choice after the war to serve either on the U.S. Supreme Court or to build on his wartime experience by becoming Henry Stimson's replacement.[4] Asking only where he was most needed, he became the nation's secretary of war, where, with his navy counterpart, James Forrestal, he helped hammer out the National Security Act of 1947, one of the most important pieces of legislation in the nation's history. He finally left government service in 1947, after turning down President Truman's offer to become America's first secretary of defense. Certainly, there were few men who touched American history as indelibly as did Robert Patterson during his period of public service. Patterson's importance during one of the most critical moments in modern U.S. history is clear. As Eiler puts it, "'Fighting Bob' Patterson" was a "tough-minded, hard-driving, former federal judge who served throughout the emergency and beyond, and whose contributions to victory were, in the opinion of those who best knew his work, comparable only to those of the army's chief of staff, George C. Marshall, and of the president himself."[5]

Patterson's Pre–World War II Career

Patterson came from a modest background, growing up in the small Hudson River city of Glens Falls, north of Albany, and attending the small liberal arts school Union College in Schenectady, New York. After excelling at Harvard Law School, Patterson was recommended by one of his professors, Felix Frankfurter, to the partners of a small New York City law office that featured two men intensely interested in military affairs: Elihu Root Jr., whose father had been secretary of war and secretary of state under President Theodore Roosevelt, and also a U.S. senator who supported a preparedness movement to ready the United States for war with Germany after World War I began; and Grenville Clark, who would become an important mentor, promoter, and close associate for Patterson and who had, with Root, been one of the founders in 1915 of the famous, privately organized Plattsburgh Business Men's training camp in Plattsburg, New York, a city in the northern part of the state. In late 1915, Clark had also become a founding member of the Military Training Camps Association; that organization began agitating for a new round of preparedness in the wake of the Nazi blitz against France and the Low Countries in May 1940.[6]

Once in New York City, Patterson joined the old 7th Regiment of the New York National Guard and found himself near the Mexican border for six months in 1916 after President Woodrow Wilson mobilized the guard in response to revolutionary activity in Mexico. It was here, while serving as an ordinary private, that Patterson gained his first appreciation and sympathy for the plight of the common foot soldier. Released from this service and finding the United States soon at war with Germany, Patterson volunteered for the officer-training course at the Plattsburg camp in May 1917 and was subsequently commissioned a captain in the infantry. Arriving in Europe in May 1918, Patterson's unit waited until August to be sent to the front, whereupon Patterson was cited for "gallant and meritorious" conduct on his first night of action. A few days later, he earned the Distinguished Service Cross for his actions along the Vesle River near the small French town of Bazoches and later the Silver Star during the bloody Meuse-Argonne offensive that helped end the war. After the war, Patterson maintained close personal ties with the "doughboys" under his command, who in turn considered Patterson "their hero, model, and protector."[7]

After the war, Patterson returned to Root, Clark but then left to form a small firm with two friends from Harvard Law. After ten years of law practice in New York City, Patterson was appointed by President Herbert Hoover in 1930 to a judgeship on the United States District Court for the Southern District of New York. And then, in March 1939, with nine years' experience as a federal district judge under his belt, Patterson, a Republican, was appointed by President Roosevelt to the United States Court of Appeals for the Second Circuit in New York. Finding himself less interested in appellate law than in presiding over court cases, Judge Patterson grew more distracted from his judicial duties after the outbreak of another war in Europe. In the wake of the Nazi offensives against the Low Countries and France in the spring of 1940, Patterson wrote the War Department to request that he be recommissioned for active duty in the infantry. Although the War Department turned him down, noting his age of forty-nine, it would not be the last time he sought to return to active battlefield duty during World War II.[8]

The country's lack of serious preparedness activity and the seemingly entrenched public hostility to involvement in another European war greatly worried Patterson. As Eiler notes, "The possibility that war would come to an almost completely unprepared and essentially defenseless America obsessed him." (Indeed, his fear that the United States would allow its military preparedness to lapse again, as it had during the interwar years, was undoubtedly his principal motive for writing the manuscript published here.) Patterson was not alone in this sentiment. His mentors and now close colleagues Felix Frankfurter and Grenville Clark began to focus on preparedness themselves. Clark spearheaded a revival of the Plattsburg training camps movement, which would successfully promote the nation's first peacetime military draft leislation. Patterson, an old Plattsburger himself, readily joined Clark's effort to revive the camps and agitate for selective service legislation. When President Roosevelt reneged on a scheduled meeting with Clark concerning a peacetime draft, Clark instead went to see his old friend Felix Frankfurter, now a Supreme Court justice and Roosevelt confidant. Clark and Frankfurter agreed that a key obstacle holding up decisive domestic action in the burgeoning global crisis was the ineffectual leadership at the top of the War Department.

On the one hand, the secretary of war, Harry Woodring, was a midwestern traditionalist who stood firmly in support of neutrality and nonintervention. On the other, his assistant secretary, Louis A.

Johnson, proved to be exceptionally aggressive in attempting to prod war mobilization forward by using his independent powers under the 1920 National Defense Act. The resultant feuding became increasingly public and weakened the War Department at a critical time. It proved difficult for Roosevelt to simply jettison Woodring in the run-up to war because of the raucous support the former Kansas governor elicited from isolationists in Congress, and it had always been difficult for Roosevelt to part company with his top appointees. Clark and Frankfurter regarded unified War Department leadership as imperative in readying America for war, and they hatched a plan to replace Woodring and Johnson with a new team comprising Henry L. Stimson and Robert P. Patterson.

Stimson possessed sterling credentials, having served as secretary of war under William Howard Taft, an artillery officer in the First World War, governor general of the Philippines, and secretary of state under Herbert Hoover. Moreover, as a Republican, Stimson could provide immense cover for Roosevelt during a very controversial political venture: the president was positioning himself for an unprecedented third term in the midst of the growing international crisis. Of course, Clark and Frankfurter first had to gain the assent of Stimson and Patterson, but once they did so, Frankfurter went to work on Roosevelt, who proved very amenable to what was being proposed. It helped that Stimson, himself an ex-Plattsburger, was an outspoken advocate of rearmament, aid to the Allies, and some form of selective service. Frankfurter pressed his case relentlessly in the ensuing weeks, but it was the sudden collapse of France in mid-June, combined with news reports about Stimson's public address on the need for universal military training, repeal of the neutrality laws, and all-out aid to Britain and the free French, that convinced Roosevelt that Stimson was the one he needed to head the War Department. At the same time he offered the post to Stimson, he offered another Republican, Frank Knox, the GOP vice presidential candidate in 1936, the post of navy secretary.

The other shoe—appointing Patterson—did not drop right away, however, and for an awkward few weeks Johnson stayed on as assistant secretary. While Stimson continued to pester Roosevelt about the situation, Judge Patterson, meanwhile, headed back to the Plattsburg camp as a forty-nine-year-old private to study manuals and complete the drills and physical training that were part of the Plattsburg course. It was there, on July 13, 1940, that Patterson, after washing out garbage cans on K.P. duty, finally received word that the Senate Military Affairs Committee had acted affirmatively on his nomination to be assistant secretary of war. On the spot, as newsreel cameras recorded it, he was promoted from Private Patterson to Assistant Secretary of War Patterson. After years of acrimony, the nation finally had a unified team at the top of the War Department; Roosevelt soon expressed his delight: "Bob Patterson is a grand fellow and I think the War Department has become a happy shop again."⁹

Patterson as Assistant and Then Under Secretary of War

The job of assistant secretary was not simply one of helping the war secretary in his myriad official duties. Rather, the assistant secretary possessed independent powers of his own over industrial mobilization, military procurement, and military supply. These duties and powers were spelled out clearly in the National Defense Act of 1920, a product of congressional concerns about the army's dismal performance in organizing procurement and supply for World War I. Not one American-made plane, for example, had seen service on the Western Front in 1918. Congress wrote the law specifically to place a civilian in charge of army procurement and supply matters. Patterson had his own independent office, staff, and set of responsibilities. The 1920 act established the position of assistant secretary of war with the authority for procurement and industrial-mobilization planning and for oversight of the independent army supply bureaus.

Although the assistant secretary of war's office remained small between the wars, its staff nonetheless became the center of planning for procurement and industrial mobilization, producing a series of industrial mobilization plans beginning in 1930. The office therefore carried with it a great deal of potential authority. As army historian John D. Millett notes, "the Assistant Secretary's responsibility for economic planning made him potentially more important than many cabinet members, possibly even more important than his chief [the secretary of war]." The assistant secretary's independent authority is what led to the tensions between Stimson's and Patterson's predecessors. But any possibility of such tensions recurring was removed when Stimson persuaded Congress in December 1940 to amend the 1920 act so as to place the procurement and planning responsibilities under the direction of the secretary. Stimson then delegated Patterson's authority back to him, but the cosmetic change ensured a unified civilian-command system. With this alteration Patterson's title changed from assistant to under secretary of war, and he continued his duties as before.[10]

Patterson seemed an odd choice for the job in that it had always been assumed that an industrialist would handle the assistant secretary's duties. Patterson did, however, bring to the job an unequalled sense of purpose. He understood fully how vulnerable and unprepared the U.S. military was at this point, with the army capable of deploying maybe five under-equipped divisions compared to the more than two hundred that the Germans already had in the field. As Patterson notes at the very beginning of the manuscript, "The National Guard, at its forthcoming maneuvers [in 1940], would train with stove-pipes and beer cans labeled mortars, and with trucks certified to be tanks by placards."[11] The Congress had just passed a huge new Munitions Program on June 30, 1940, committing $6 billion—"an amount almost equal to total [army] expenditures . . . for the . . . years from 1922 through 1940"—and it was now Patterson's responsibility to spend that money quickly and efficiently. Patterson found himself with primary responsibility for acquiring the weaponry and supplies not only for the United States but also eventually for its Soviet, British, and Chinese allies. Of course, a series of civilian agencies and administrators began operating in 1940 to assist Patterson and the military services in organizing the home-front industrial mobilization. But because civilian authority in production, procurement, and supply grew slowly and unevenly, Patterson was forced to assert forcefully his own authority during this prewar period. And, inevitably, civil-military tensions accumulated because of the developing scramble for mobilization authority, leading, for instance, to clashes over the use of the priorities power and over army contracting.[12]

Patterson emerged as a key figure during the prewar months because the nascent civilian mobilization agencies remained weak and divided until after Pearl Harbor. His single-minded determination, combined with his new position as the "crucial link between the army and the nation's economy, and as the War Department's principal contact with other mobilization agencies," served to catapult Patterson suddenly into the top ranks of wartime leaders. His position also "placed him on a hot seat between the War Department and the watchdogs of Congress," where he spent many hours testifying to the problems and issues related to army mobilization. When Patterson arrived in Washington, the Office of the Assistant Secretary of War (OASW, later the Office of the Under Secretary of War [OUSW]) was still focused on its planning activities since procurement had not yet taken off. Patterson's arrival greatly accelerated the process. The planning activities of the OASW included keeping an inventory of industrial plants that could be used for arms production, maintaining estimates of military needs for critical materials, and identifying sources for these materials and the industrial facilities that produced them. OASW also planned for the coordination of priority controls (that is, who would get preference in obtaining scarce materials) among the army, navy, and foreign governments, and studying and coordinating key matters such as labor supply, electric power, transportation, and machine tools.[13]

Once on the scene, Patterson reorganized his office to elevate procurement, production, and delivery of munitions to central importance, given the new munitions program passed by the Congress. In July 1939, the OASW had employed 78 officers and civilians, a number that had increased to 181 by the time Patterson arrived. By November 1941, Patterson's office mushroomed to 1,136, including 257 officers and 879 civilians. Patterson had to build a capable staff almost from scratch by recruiting talented civilians, choosing primarily lawyers instead of industrialists with practical experience about the economy. He had to innovate constantly to make his jury-rigged system perform ably enough for the enormous job at hand. The job must have seemed overwhelming, especially for someone without the industrial or managerial experience expected for the position, even more so as spending on munitions leapt from $1.3 billion in 1940 to $7.5 billion in 1941. What he lacked in experience, however, he made up for with sheer dogged determination. And his goal was simply to push forward as quickly as possible the acquisition of necessary arms, equipment, and supplies. This included converting civilian industry to military production and financing the expansion of the nation's industrial plant. Speed seemed a natural and urgent goal, and the legal talent that Patterson attracted to his office knew how to push through procurement contracts rapidly, despite the preexisting hurdles placed on peacetime army contracting. But lacking detailed knowledge of how the economy worked meant that these orders could easily throw the economy out of balance; this had been a central problem during World War I as rushed orders led to bottlenecks.[14]

Patterson soon enough encountered the problems caused by over-contracting, but he thought that growing raw material scarcities and production bottlenecks could best be solved by asking for more civilian sacrifice. On the one hand, Patterson identified deeply with the troops because of his own World War I experience, and he took it as his personal responsibility that they get everything they needed. As he responded to critics who noted the great production achievements of the home front: "We do not ask our boys in combat to do an 'adequate' job; we ask them to do their best. We can do no less." Eiler reports that "[n]ever for a moment forgetting his own wartime service in the infantry, he suffered in constant solidarity with the suffering G.I.'s." Patterson even "regularly wore GI shoes—the sturdy, high-cut footwear of the infantry—on social occasions and in the office as well as at home and in the country."[15] On the other hand, it seemed to Patterson that civilians were never doing enough, and—even worse—seemed never willing to sacrifice enough for the war effort. "Business as usual" prevailed at a time when Patterson was convinced that the nation needed a more Spartan ethos. In this sense, he more fully embodied the military's outlook and perspective than most other mobilizers.

In fact, he fully identified with the military perspective on most of the wartime controversies that soon plagued the mobilization effort, distrustful in many cases of his counterparts in the civilian-mobilization agencies.[16] Repeatedly, Patterson called for more stringent measures to deal with striking workers and shortages that interfered with the war effort. As a biographical sketch noted in 1942, "A stern Jeremiah, [Patterson] dutifully ranged the country, calling civilians to repent their slothful indifferences to the country's plight." One of his colleagues commented, "If needful, Patterson would commandeer every motorcar not used in the war effort, impose short rations on civilians and put every able-bodied man not a war worker into uniform tomorrow." And as Eiler relates, "Looking out from the windows of his office in the War Department, an angry under secretary [Patterson] chafed at the sight of constant bumper-to-bumper traffic on Constitution Avenue, much of it obviously unnecessary or even frivolous. Trucks bearing heavy cargoes of soft drinks became especially infuriating symbols of self-indulgent irresponsibility. Journalists . . . soon began referring to him as "Judge Seven-Up," a sobriquet that was to last throughout the war."[17]

Patterson once grew so dispirited by what he saw as the lack of public commitment to the war effort that he tendered his resignation to Stimson so that he could return to active duty in the infantry. Stimson talked him out of it and noted in his diary: "He [Patterson] told me his reasons why he wanted to go into the Army. He felt that the country was not up to the war spirit and that it needed an example to show the importance of the work [yet to be done], and that he wanted to go into the Infantry for the purpose of making that demonstration and showing that example." Stimson, who had himself served as a fiftyish artillery officer during World War I, wisely vetoed the idea.[18]

This all-out commitment comes through in the manuscript at many points, although it is not the central point of Patterson's narrative. For the prewar period, when he had the greatest personal responsibility for procurement and industrial mobilization, Patterson shows more interest in providing an informed first-hand discussion of the problems involved in implementing the huge new army procurement program. He dispassionately reviews the technical complexities associated with spending the huge amount of money in an atmosphere of ingrained army timidity about spending large sums of money. He notes the public complacency about the war in Europe and frank distrust of war preparation while the country was still not officially at war. He recounts how firms (with the automobile industry foremost among these) sought to avoid military orders now that their civilian business was booming again, and how this fickle attitude was reinforced by the business community's continuing distrust of Roosevelt because of the New Deal. And he reports how entire raw-material industries (with steel and aluminum being key examples) refused to expand their capacity because of exaggerated fears of overexpansion.

Patterson had to overcome entrenched army procedures involving the letting of contracts. He did so by pressing for the end of competitive bidding, a time-consuming process. And he innovated with cost-plus-fixed-fee contracts, letters of intent, public financing for plant expansions, and the speeding up of tax amortization for private investments, along with V-Loan programs that provided government guarantees of private loans to army contractors. He explains how prewar British and French orders played a key role in preparing American industry for the much larger orders that were coming. And he reports how expanding civilian production continued, throughout 1940 and 1941, to consume huge percentages of critical materials that were growing scarcer by the minute.

Significantly, in his concern over burgeoning civilian production (especially of autos and refrigerators), he had allies in the civilian-mobilization agencies, especially men such as Leon Henderson, who moved between the civilian-mobilization agencies before becoming the wartime head of the Office of Price Administration. And Henderson was not alone among those "all-outers" in the civilian agencies agitating for reduced civilian production, especially in automobiles. Patterson mentions this fact, as well as his concern, shared by many civilian mobilizers, that a large part of the problem lay in the army's own institutional reticence in thinking big and becoming more assertive in proposing a much larger set of requirements. Of course, many in the civilian agencies went on to complain that once the war began military requirements rose too quickly all at once, creating problems of feasibility, shortages, and bottlenecks.

Patterson concludes his discussion of the pre–Pearl Harbor period in this way: "[W]e must not forget that the basis for the tremendous outpouring of munitions with which we overwhelmed our enemies in the closing stages of the war was laid before December, 1941. Had we not done what we did in the eighteen months before that date, there would have been no D-Day in 1944, nor any V-J Day in 1945."[19] This is not boastful triumphalism. Rather, as is clear from his narrative, Patterson is deliberately offering a warning about how long it took to get ready for mechanized combat operations in the industrial era, and how difficult it was to move those supplies to beachheads all over the world and on to the combat units fighting in every possible terrain.

Army Reorganization and Patterson's Wartime Service

Despite Patterson's successes in directing the army's huge new procurement programs, the continuing organizational incoherence of army supply operations and overall dysfunctions of army command led to his office being folded into a new overall command structure after war was declared. Patterson comments in the manuscript about these dysfunctions, how he had to supervise eight separate supply arms, including Ordnance and the Quartermaster Corps, and how each of these entities reported not only to him but also to Gen. George C. Marshall as army chief of staff. As Patterson laments: "There was no one to pull their various demands together and make sure that a clear and consistent over-all picture was presented to each of us."[20]

The 1920 National Defense Act had been designed to resolve the problems of command and supply that had hamstrung army efforts in World War I. But the dual command structure that Congress created—the General Staff as a central command post and the OUSW in charge of procurement and economic mobilization—led to crossed and confused lines of authority that actually reinforced the independence of the army's procurement bureaus. Both Marshall and Patterson found themselves bedeviled by their management task, and Marshall especially became so overwhelmed by the minutiae of his command that he could not focus on the larger strategic and logistical matters that were his primary responsibility. The army reorganization in March 1942 was meant to bring order and coherence to the system by creating three separate commands—one each for the ground forces, the air forces, and the service forces (including procurement, supply, and logistics)—leaving the General Staff, and Marshall as chief of staff, free to provide general coordination and overall command.[21]

Prior to the reorganization, Patterson's office remained in charge of procurement and industrial mobilization matters. But Lt. Gen. Brehon B. Somervell, placed in charge of the General Staff Supply Division (or G-4) in November 1941, began to plan the transfer of Patterson's staff and responsibilities to his own military command.[22] When Somervell learned that General Marshall was set to announce a reorganization plan, he pressed to include in it a reorganization of the army's supply functions that shifted Patterson's staff and responsibilities to his own military command in order to unify supply operations. Patterson was deliberately left in the dark concerning the plan; in fact, he was alerted to it only immediately before it was presented to President Roosevelt. Hence, Patterson "was practically faced with a choice of accepting a fait accompli, or delaying the much needed reorganization." The final plan worried Patterson's staff since a military officer would acquire his authority, thereby disregarding the key lessons of World War I concerning needed civilian oversight of military procurement practices. Patterson, always the loyal soldier, considered only minor changes to the proposed plan and happily went along with it.[23]

Roosevelt established the new army organization through executive order and the new command structure began operations in March 1942. Somervell became the commanding officer of the new Service of Supply (its name was changed to the Army Service Forces within a year), and his new command absorbed most of the power and responsibilities of Patterson's office. Patterson retained some oversight responsibilities but was left with only a handful of aides, some of whom complained that the under secretary was being cut out of the chain of command on a number of key issues. Patterson himself remained primarily concerned about Somervell's personality. Millett relates that Patterson "admired Somervell's dynamic personality but was somewhat worried about future relations with him" since "he had experienced at first hand General Somervell's brusqueness which could and did antagonize people." Nonetheless, Patterson's office was next door to Somervell's, ensuring that they would work closely together. And they shared the same uncompromising outlook in aggressively promoting army needs, the all consuming issue for Patterson.[24]

It can be said that with Somervell's elevation, Patterson actually gained stature by becoming the principal spokesman for the War Department, as the army's public voice on the War Production Board and on high-profile controversies that continued to mark domestic mobilization. Somervell excelled as a manager of a large, complex organization, and Patterson was thereby freed from the numbing details of procurement and supply to focus on the larger issues of home-front mobilization and battlefront supply. It is this larger vision that he projects so vividly and persuasively in his postwar manuscript.[25]

Patterson certainly kept busy. He was an active participant in all major issues of domestic mobilization, including the feasibility of army requirements, material control and production scheduling, control of manpower and the continuing issue of national service legislation, and the shortages of gasoline and rubber. He became especially embroiled in the controversy over the speed of reconversion from war to civilian production that began in 1943. Patterson refers to these issues often in his narrative, but he is not interested in simply rehashing the wartime battles along the Potomac. Indeed, Patterson, who was so forceful in fighting to prevent any premature reconversion steps out of fear that any diminution of production for war would lead immediately to greater battlefield losses, recognizes in hindsight that domestic production problems were not the cause of supply shortages at the European front. As he writes, "[It was a] fact that the only serious setback we received in our great offensive came when, not lack of production, but insuperable difficulties in the way of moving supplies forward as rapidly as the Army moved, forced us to give the Germans a breather that enabled them to take position in their frontier defenses." He also notes that "German soldiers captured when the Italian campaign ended complained bitterly that American artillery tactics permitted us to fight a 'cheap war' with a maximum of supplies and a minimum of human sacrifice."[26]

This account of plentiful supplies and problems with moving supplies to the front jibes with the historical record—there were no production delays caused by reconversion talk, and any battlefield shortages had to do with the lack of transportation or bottlenecks at the fronts themselves. But at the time, Patterson and the head of army supply, Brehon Somervell, engaged in an all-out public campaign to paint any talk of reconversion as likely to prolong the war and endanger soldiers' lives because workers were supposedly deserting their war work for work in plants producing civilian goods. As Patterson acknowledges later, "It was our position in the War Department that we were not willing to save dollars at the risk of lives. Furthermore, we had a faith in the capacity of the nation to readjust its industry to peace, even if the start was somewhat delayed, which made us feel that the needs of readjustment did not require risking the prolongation of the war by a single day."[27] This intense commitment to winning the war as quickly as possible with the fewest American casualties was Patterson's mantra.[28]

Concluding Notes

In his memoir, Patterson presents a comprehensive overview of the entire experience of World War II mobilization, including issues of production, technological change, and the problems of supply in each combat area. In short, he tells us how and why we won the war as quickly as possible. His likely goal was to fully impress his countrymen and his fellow governmental leaders with the herculean efforts that ensured the Allied military successes. Patterson conveys with his review of the World War II mobilization experience the all-important lesson of being better prepared for all-out total war the next time around. For reasons both past and present, such preparation would have been for Patterson a great necessity.

On the one hand, Patterson is only too well aware that the United States was not prepared for World War II, and he states again and again that we were lucky this time to emerge victorious. On the other, he relates in his final chapter how the nature of war had changed with the introduction of the new weaponry that collapsed time and space—atom bombs, long-range bombers, jet aircraft, and the like—resulting in much less time to prepare for the next war. As he notes, "I agree just as heartily with the view of Gen. ["Hap"] Arnold [commanding general of the Army Air Forces in World War II expressed just after V-J Day": 'Projecting our thoughts into the future results in sobering thoughts of the potentialities of air power. ... Next time, our American potential may be destroyed without giving us time to arm and take the offensive, unless we are adequately prepared. It is easy to lose the peace after the war has been won.'"[29]

As Stimson's postwar successor as secretary of war, Patterson worked very closely with his navy counterpart during the war, James Forrestal (who had been assistant secretary of the navy and later the navy secretary) to ensure that the nation acquired a permanent readiness capability. Together they led the intense negotiations that culminated in the creation of a postwar military establishment. Besides the issues of demobilizing the huge military machine of World War II and initiating the process of desegregating the army, the battles over military unification and creating the national security state would be Patterson's main focus and legacy as war secretary. And it is within this context of both the rapid demobilization of the wartime army and the creation of a new national security apparatus that he revisited his wartime experiences.

Patterson remained for the most part uninterested in what he saw as the parochial concerns of Forrestal and the navy admirals, who feared mightily that unification meant the downgrading of the navy as the nation's premier service in favor of the aggressive advocates for a large postwar air force. Nonetheless, navy plans also differed from army plans in recognizing that any new postwar military establishment involved much more than uniting the services into one organization to reduce the duplications and waste of the war years. Forrestal and the navy sought a comprehensive rebuilding and reorientation of the entire national government in order to integrate the military services, intelligence and foreign policy, economic and industrial mobilization, and science and technology into a single postwar national security establishment. Forrestal's Holy Grail was nothing less than a full-scale reconstruction of the national government around the needs of national security so as to place military needs and the permanent preparation for war at the heart of the national governmental enterprise.[30]

From Patterson's warnings about the future, especially in the conclusion to his manuscript, it seems clear that he agreed with Forrestal's larger agenda to maintain continuing military mobilization. Like Forrestal, Patterson advocated a permanent preparation for war and for uniting the forces of science, industry, and the state behind an ongoing military establishment. His public statements demonstrated the degree to which he shared Forrestal's concerns regarding the Soviet Union. As he told one audience in 1949, "The hard truth of the matter is that we have face to face, confronting us . . . a set of men who have within their grip the resources of a powerful nation, who are fired with the ambition of world rule, a tenet of their creed ever since they came into power, a set of men who have utterly no scruples as to how they gain that end." And he testified to Congress during the hearings over the National Security Act of 1947 that, because of the rapid technological developments in military weaponry and given the growing Soviet threat, the United States now faced a time of "total war" and as a result could no longer base the "nation's security . . . on one organization in peace and another in war."[31]

His manuscript can in this sense be seen as making a case for the necessity of continuing the mobilization task into the postwar period. He argues directly in his last chapter that other nations (the Soviet Union goes unnamed here) would learn from the just-ended war, and would put in place their own institutional mechanisms uniting science, technology, and military preparedness, and that the United States would need to be ready for this hostile new world. So, besides the valuable look back at the mobilization effort for World War II, we are able to see Patterson's contribution to the debates over the postwar direction of the United States.

In this manuscript we hear from someone very close to postwar developments articulating fears about losing America's wartime military capabilities. For Patterson, the issue was one of warning his contemporaries about the very quick demobilization of its military ranks, its military-scientific and military-industrial connections, and its organizational capacities built during the war for mobilizing the nation's economy for war. Patterson envisioned a future mobilization that would take a similar form to the one that he and his cohorts had just completed, where major industries and communities would have to transition to war production from their peacetime pursuits. This task would require maintaining an established planning capacity and some kind of continuing skeletal mobilization set-up that would sustain the process of engagement with major firms and industrial centers around the nation. The National Security Act provided for such a continuing mobilization capacity when it authorized a National Security Resources Board (NSRB), a Munitions Board, and an Office of Scientific Research and Development (OSRD). The NSRB was to plan for military and civilian mobilization, link the military services to their corporate contractors, and, in the event of a war emergency, become the main operating agency. The Munitions Board would integrate and balance the needs of the three services. And the OSRD would connect the military services to scientific research in industry and the nation's universities.

Patterson himself was very pleased with this extensive new military establishment. As he notes in his last chapter, "In these new instrumentalities we have, not only a structure for peace-time industrial preparedness, but the framework for a war-time structure. It is an enormous advance upon anything we have had previously."[32] Ironically, however, he need not have worried about the need for a massive mobilization effort because future conflicts—the "limited" wars of Korea and Vietnam—would not resemble the total wars of World War I and World War II. The United States has never again had to mobilize to the degree it had mobilized in those previous conflicts. Nonetheless, the United States did indeed achieve a level of permanent mobilization and preparation for war that Patterson, in this manuscript, advocated but at this point (1947–48) did not foresee. The ongoing Cold War provided the impetus. In fact, as historian Ernest R. May has concluded, "[T]he main business of the U.S. government had become [by the early 1950s] the development, maintenance, positioning, exploitation, and regulation of military forces."

As Michael Hogan puts it, "[N]ational security concerns became the main common currency of most policy makers, the arbiter of most values, the key to America's new identity."[33]

Little did Patterson realize the extent to which the industries providing military hardware would become for the most part an entirely separate economic sector of the nation's economy (the ACE sector—aerospace, communications, and electronics). There would never again be a need to mobilize the entire economy or the full panoply of the nation's industrial firms for military production. Military production would become a separate and continuing sector in its own right, indeed one that President Eisenhower would later decry as the "military-industrial complex." So Patterson need not have feared that we would slip back to the unpreparedness and peacetime habits of our prewar days, forgetting the need for military preparedness. It may well be that Patterson perceived these changes taking root and creating a very different environment than had existed before and immediately after the war, and thus decided his manuscript was no longer needed. In fact, as he was to proclaim in 1949, "The risk of war is always a real one when a restless dictator is on the loose. . . . On the other hand, we have a sound military establishment. . . . We have a sound foreign policy. . . . We have the asset of a productive economy with an industrial plant far and away beyond anything that Soviet Russia can hope for. . . . Those assets, if wisely managed ought to give us a very substantial margin against the outbreak of war in the foreseeable future."[34] Perhaps for the reason that it might seem redundant in the heightened Cold War atmosphere of 1947–50, Robert Patterson decided not to publish his wartime narrative after he finished it. We are fortunate to have it now, however, more than sixty-five years later.

At a time when few are asked to sacrifice or serve, when we pursue tax cuts during times when our troops are in harm's way and foreign military adventures are paid for on credit, and when few of our leaders who urge interventions abroad have ever served in combat, Patterson's call for shared sacrifice and some kind of universal national service may sound quaint and outmoded. Yet, in the context of today's debates about deficits and the drive to reduce the tax burden on wealthy Americans at the same time that we have seen a much greater burden on the diminishing number of Americans who volunteer for our armed forces, it is refreshing to be reminded of the degree to which an earlier generation of leaders had placed nation ahead of partisan politics, self-promotion, and personal wealth.

Patterson wrote when the demands of American global leadership necessitated some degree of continued military mobiliztion. Instead of a return to isolationism and demobilization, which Patterson feared, the nation was rapidly whipsawed into acceptance of such a large degree of militarization that former Allied commander and outgoing President Dwight D. Eisenhower warned in his 1961 farewell address that "the potential for the disastrous rise of misplaced power exists and will persist." Even two decades removed from the collapse of the Soviet Union, we remain as a nation unable to come to grips with the need to scale back our military might and balance our national security needs with other pressing domestic concerns. Patterson wrote to remind his fellow Americans of the need for a national reckoning, which in his time meant pressing for continuing military preparations and resisting the past history of severe military cutbacks. Given Patterson's example of willing and dedicated service and sacrifice, and given his own regularly voiced concerns about the need to share the burdens of war as widely as possible in solidarity with the troops in the field, I can only believe that he would be greatly disheartened by the turn we have made as regards the great burden placed on a small number of troops in the past decade. And he would be at the forefront of calling for a new reckoning, one that would emphasize the pillars of shared sacrifice, broad responsibility, and dedicated public service that he brings to this manuscript written some sixty-five years ago.

Chapter 1

A Nation without Arms

To some Americans, Europe still seemed far away in the spring of 1940, and Japan appeared almost as remote as the moon. True, when Hitler had marched into Poland the previous fall, and France and Great Britain had gone to war in support of their pledges, the President had proclaimed a limited emergency. The authorized strength of our Army had been increased from 174,000 to 235,000 men, with an additional 235,000 in the National Guard.[1] But by straining to the utmost, we could not actually have put into the field more than 75,000 troops—five modern divisions. Even those divisions would have been seriously handicapped by a lack of sufficient up-to-date equipment. The National Guard, at its forthcoming maneuvers, would train with stove-pipes and beer cans labeled mortars, and with trucks certified to be tanks by placards.[2]

To anyone who looked realistically at the situation which then existed in both Europe and Asia, these grave imperfections in our military preparedness were alarming to an extreme degree. Hitler had been industriously preparing for war since the moment he came to power in 1933. Only belatedly did France and Greet Britain initiate steps to match the vast and carefully concealed arms factories which had been created in Germany to support the army and air force which were being built in defiance of the Treaty of Versailles. How great Hitler's power was by the spring of 1940 was not precisely known, but it had been enough as early as September 1938 to make the western democracies unwilling to try conclusions with him at that time. An accurate understanding of the processes of industrial mobilization would have told us that the German margin was likely to be greater, rather than less, eighteen months later, in spite of the belated efforts of Hitler's intended victims to overcome the German head start. The lull before the storm that struck in the spring of 1940 was full of warnings for those who cared to look, warnings of German strength and of the weakness of those who stood in Hitler's path. And the brief, but utterly decisive, Polish campaign of the previous September had demonstrated once again that bravery alone cannot compensate for inferior weapons.

At the same time, across a wider ocean, and in less sudden but equally decisive fashion, the steady advance of the Japanese in China was pointing to the same moral, and also jeopardizing the American position in the Pacific. For those who took counsel with the facts, rather than with their hopes, it was becoming increasingly clear that Japan had embarked upon a course of action which it could not complete without forcing us to ingloriously abandon policies which we had supported for more than half a century, and which it could not halt without bringing disaster upon the Japanese military junta.

Yet, in spite of these grim but undeniable facts, many Americans in high places continued to insist that slight basis for alarm existed. They said that the United States must keep out of war. Business could not afford an increase in the national debt, so they declared. As late as May 2, 1940—a week before Germany invaded the Netherlands, Belgium, and Luxembourg—a very influential American national business organization resolved that all defense financing must be "on a pay-as-we-go basis."[3] A few Americans were even so foolish as to hint that the President, in pointing to the perilous situation, was trying to scare the country into giving him a third term in the White House.[4] These elements who decried alarm did not seem to realize that business—and, indeed, all American life—as they knew it would cease to exist if the Axis won the war.

Other Americans were indifferent because they could not believe that our nation was vulnerable to the dangers which threatened other nations. Was not the United States the wealthiest nation on earth, and with its wealth able to do whatever it really set its mind to? An armada of airplanes, they seemed to believe, would spring into existence if the nation was actually threatened. They had no idea how long it takes to transform money into weapons. But we learned before long, as James B. Reston wrote in his *Prelude to Victory,* "that you cannot stop a tank with a thousand dollar bill or even with a large unexecuted authorization bill."[5]

It is strange, at first sight, that a nation like ours should have shown such unawareness of the elementary facts of national security. Of all nations we were the most advanced mechanically, the most ready to turn to the machine to solve the problems both of the individual and the community. In almost every aspect of civilian life, Americans were quick to recognize that inferiority in equipment was likely to be a fatal handicap. It would have been natural to expect that, in the matter of national defense, we would have been equally determined to be superior in equipment. A reluctance to have large numbers of men under arms in time of peace was understandable, in the light of our national tradition, but the reluctance to provide adequate arms for those men, or to prepare adequately for placing arms in the hands of those we would call to the colors in the hour of peril, was less comprehensible.[6]

It was not that the history of our own previous wars had misled us. In our two great modern wars up to that time, the Civil War and the First World War, superiority in equipment and supply had played decisive roles.[7] Once hostilities were begun, every effort was made to utilize to the full the advantage which machinery can give. But between wars we seemed to forget, and to hark back to the earliest days of the Republic when we won our independence in spite of inferior equipment.

Americans are inveterate optimists. The illusory peace of 1918 would last, they felt, forever. They turned their minds away from war or preparation for it. Although men like General Tasker H. Bliss warned us that the World War of 1914–1918 had let loose forces in the world which would not be quieted in a generation, few Americans took such warnings seriously.[8] Even the unmistakable signs that all was not well with the postwar world failed to shake our complacency. We agreed reluctantly that it was not going to be as good a world as we had hoped, but few considered seriously the possibility that, before the men who fought in 1917 and 1918 had grown old, our Nation would face a far greater peril than that which threatened it in the days of their youth.[9]

Even the War Department was guilty of some share in that complacency. In those years of peaceful hope, when appropriations for national defense were cut to the bone, it was difficult even for the professional soldier to think in terms that bore any resemblance to the actualities with which the Second World War was to ultimately confront us. Far-seeing vision was curbed by acute realization of how little could be done at the moment, and "What do we need" had to yield precedence to "What can we get?"[10]

Nevertheless, a start was made. Even in those early postwar years of optimism and lethargy, there were some who did not forget how critical had been the problem of producing weapons in 1917–1918. They remembered vividly how little we had understood in advance the tremendous industrial operations necessary to equip a modern army and maintain it in the field. They recalled the perilous confusion which had resulted from lack of coordination in military procurement, the destructive competition between the various procurement branches, the lack of knowledge of where to go to get the necessary work done, the waste of both time and money which lack of previous planning entailed. They also remembered the dangerous dislocations of the national economy which a flood of war orders had caused, the overloading of some plants and the failure to use others, the shortages of vital materials, the congestion of transportation, the lack of skilled labor, and the thousand and one other difficulties which emanated from the necessity of turning our vast and complex industrial system sharply away from its normal objective of consumer production toward the new objective of production for war.[11]

These few who both remembered and looked ahead also recalled how, when a breakdown of war production threatened, salvation came in the nick of time from the skill with which Bernard M. Baruch and the War Industries Board broke up and brought under control the economic congestions of modern war, and with which Assistant Secretary of War Benedict Crowell brought order into the procurement of supplies for the Army. They resolved neither to forget the dangers which had almost paralyzed our war effort nor to lose the advantage of the hard-won experience which had finally brought us success.[12]

To these few who realized that modern war is a thoroughly integrated effort of the entire nation, we are indebted for not having to face the Second World War with as little industrial preparation as that with which we faced the First. Through their efforts, the Congress in 1920 enacted Section 5a of the National Defense Act, which placed upon the Assistant Secretary of War the responsibility for coordinating War Department procurement and preparing plans for industrial mobilization. In 1922 the Army and Navy Munitions Board was set up to coordinate Army and Navy procurement, and in 1924 the Army Industrial College was founded to train officers in the complex tasks of military procurement and industrial mobilization. Thus, before the experience of the First World War was swamped in the rising tide of indifference and complacency, a framework of industrial preparedness was established in the War and Navy Departments.[13]

In the years that followed, much valuable work as done by these new agencies. Great numbers of industrial plants were surveyed with an eye to their availability for the manufacture of arms during an emergency, and they were then allocated to one or another of the several procurement branches. Studies were made of the adequacy of raw materials and the other economic sinews which war production on a vast scale would require. These studies led in 1930 to the creation of an industrial mobilization plan, which was thrice reissued in amended and improved form during the succeeding nine years. Thus, for the first time in our history, we approached a major war with both some concept of its industrial requirements and a plan for meeting them.[14]

Unfortunately, the amount of actual preparation which had been achieved by the eve of the Second World War did not measure up to the pioneering genius of those who created the framework of preparation. The responsibility for this disappointing result cannot be laid at any one door. Some of it must be assigned to the War Department itself, some of it to other agencies of government, and no inconsiderable part to the nation at large.

In the War Department, the major difficulty was that of winning adequate recognition for the new responsibility with which the Assistant Secretary of War was charged. It was natural that the ablest officers should aspire to lead the combat forces. Toward the realization of this ambition, service in the field of industrial preparedness was usually regarded as something of a detour.[15] Thus it was difficult to secure for this work the ablest of the young officers, although there were some notable exceptions to these limitations. The most outstanding of these was General Dwight D. Eisenhower himself, who both graduated from the Army Industrial College and spent a period of duty in the Office of the Assistant Secretary.

Certain of the rivalries and jealousies which inevitably afflict any great organization also worked against the fullest development of the new organization for industrial mobilization. The officers assigned to these novel duties owed a previous obligation to, and frequently felt a primary loyalty toward, some older branch of the service. They worked faithfully but lacked the stimulus of feeling that the success of their careers hinged upon this particular job. At the same time, the modest rewards of government service and the lack of general interest in industrial preparedness made it hopeless to attempt to secure competent men from the business world to undertake these tasks in time of peace.

The same lack of interest stood across the path of cooperation with other agencies of government. Probably the War Department was a little remiss in not seeking that cooperation more energetically, but it is dubious whether it could have been secured, even if sought. Absorbed, as the majority of government agencies were, with the pressing domestic problems of the inter-bellum period, industrial preparation for war seemed at best remote, and at worst sinister.

But, even had conditions in the War Department and in the other agencies of government been more favorable, the attitude of the public would almost certainly have prevented the adequate development and use of the new organization for industrial mobilization planning. A few elements in the business world were cooperative, but most of the public—business or otherwise—was simply indifferent. Those who were not indifferent were, unfortunately, hostile. The moment the War Department published its first Industrial Mobilization Plan, a barrage of criticism was directed against it. This criticism came mostly from two groups: first, the pacifist group which was opposed to all preparation for national defense, and secondly, a group which mistakenly suspected that the plan was a mask behind which selfish business interests planned to utilize war as a means to dominate the national economy.[16] Although this charge was grossly unfair, and based usually upon only a most superficial examination of the Industrial Mobilization Plan, it was nevertheless highly successful in blocking the full development and implementation of the War Department's plans. It was hopeless to seek the legislation necessary to put the plans in legal form, ready for full and instant use when an emergency came. Although it is true that there was some ineptitude in the War Department in handling the public relations aspect of this novel phase of national defense, the major difficulties were probably beyond control, in view of the then-existing state of public opinion. But an understanding of why full preparation was impossible did not make this failure any the less unfortunate.

Possibly, even had public support left nothing to be desired, the results would not have been altogether adequate. To convert a group of army officers, trained to lead armies in the field, into economists and industrial managers of sufficient skill to handle the almost unbelievably complex problems of a war economy was almost too much to ask. Perhaps the only justification for attempting to do so was the fact that the job had to be done and no other agency was willing to undertake it. It is also true that the plans, as made, failed by more than half to envisage the magnitude of the armed forces we would have to put in the field and on the ocean when war came. But the magnitude of the coming holocaust was something which few people foresaw, and the Army's industrial planners were chiefly criticized at the time for overestimating the numbers of men who would have to be placed under arms.[17] In spite of the fact that there were many faults in the men who made the plans and in the plans themselves, it seems a fair judgment to say that the plans were better than could reasonably have been expected under the circumstances and that, had they been carried out as their designers intended, much time and danger might have spared.

But war is not a contest for an improvement prize, nor a race in which the less capable contestants receive handicaps proportionate to their inexperience. It is a race from scratch, a grim contest in which Fate takes no account of how much you have increased your strength, but asks only how it compares with the strength of your enemy on the day of battle. In effect the Second World War began in 1933 when Hitler came to power and began to gather the raw materials and build the factories which were to support his plan of aggression. And from that year we began to fall behind, become month by month relatively less ready to meet the danger which was gathering both across the Atlantic and across the Pacific.

In order to realize how greatly our defense position was deteriorating, even when we effected some belated improvement in our absolute strength, we must understand how the time factor works in industrial mobilization. The public realizes that the act of summoning a million men to the colors does not create an army, that many months must elapse before the men can be brought together, organized, trained, and equipped, and that during the first few months of this preparation the newly-recruited soldiers are of little more immediate use than if they were still in civilian life. The obvious external differences between civilian and military life, the uniform, the moving of men from their homes to camps, the familiarizing them with completely new techniques and a new way of life—all remind the public that something new is being done which takes time before it can become effective. And, in spite of an unrealistic minority which refuses to face this difficulty,[18] good sense and recent experience have taught the majority of Americans that it takes time to train an army.

Unfortunately, the public was not equally aware that it takes time—much time—to convert a peaceful industry into a war industry. Part of that defective realization came from the fact that only in the very recent period had industrial mobilization on a vast scale become indispensable to success in war. Part of it came from the fact that the external appearance of an industry engaged in the manufacture of munitions is not appreciably different from that of an industry engaged in the manufacture of the goods of peace. The plants and machinery look almost the same at least to the inexpert eye. The workers wear no uniform to indicate the character of their tasks. Subject to very minor regulations for security purposes, they operate in the same fashion as in time of peace. They work under the same foremen and arrange terms of employment through the same unions. If they find shortages of housing and facilities when they come into new areas of defense industry, the inconveniences are not different in quality from those experienced in boom districts of peacetime industry. For these and many other similar reasons, the complexity of the conversion of industry to war is hidden behind a continuity of external appearances. It was therefore not surprising that the public tended unconsciously to assume that our unequalled industrial plant could be converted to war production without the long delay that was obviously unavoidable when millions of civilians were turned into soldiers and these individual soldiers welded into an army. The production of munitions was expected to expand rapidly within a few weeks after the government decided to act. And thus it was believed that, with only a slight delay, we could begin to catch up with any rival whom we had allowed to get a head start.

Unhappily, this was the direct opposite of the truth. In spite of the previous existence of an immense industrial establishment, the early months of industrial mobilization are less productive of weapons than the early months of training are of soldiers. In part, this is a consequence of an essential difference between a soldier and a weapon. Under certain emergency conditions even partially trained troops can have some military value. War has frequently seen occasions where troops not yet ready for full field operations have held defensive positions or served as replacements alongside seasoned veterans. A price is always paid in excessive casualties, but results can sometimes be achieved.

But a half-finished weapon is no more useful than a weapon not yet begun. I recall that one day during the early months of our war production effort, I stated with satisfaction to Bernard M. Baruch[19] that in July we would have completed so many hundred bodies of a new tank. "When will the engines be ready?" asked Mr. Baruch. "In August," I replied. "Then you will have no tanks until August," he said. "And when will the guns for these tanks be ready?" he continued. "In September," I answered. "Then you will have no tanks until September," he remarked. "And when will the fire control apparatus for these guns be ready?" he inquired. "Not until October," I confessed. "Then you will have no tanks until October," he said. And he was right. From his profound experience he knew what some of us who were then new to the task were occasionally tempted to forget, that a potential weapon was, for military purposes, still no weapon at all until all of its essential parts had been completed, assembled, and tested.

And the same thing can be said of factories for the production of munitions. In the intricate, mechanized, assembly-line system of modern production, no process can be completed until every piece of machinery needed for the various stages of manufacture is ready and in place. When everything is ready and production begins, the rate of output is amazing, but it is often a long and difficult job to get the necessary machinery in place. This is especially true because of the fact that special machine tools are required, tools of complicated design which have to be custom-built for these particular requirements.

For these and other reasons associated with the technical complexity of modern industrial processes, the tooling-up stage of war production is abnormally long.[20] Although such items as uniforms and shoes, which require only slight adjustments of existing machines, can be produced on a large scale at relatively short notice, many months must elapse before even a trickle of new production can be secured in those complicated machines of war which dominate the battlefield of today.

Our experience and that of our allies and our enemies shows that during the first half of the period needed to convert peaceful industry to war production, the increase in the production of finished weapons of the more complicated sort is relatively insignificant. In the third quarter of the preparatory period, the rate begins to rise rapidly, but actually more than half of the expansion in actual production takes place in the last quarter of the period.

The import of these facts for us during the half-dozen years before the war was ominous, although few realized it at the time. During the years when many comforted themselves with the belief that there was something ludicrous and unsubstantial about Hitler's regime, the Nazis and their industrial allies were pushing forward through the slow, early stages of war production.

The evidence that they were not as yet producing many weapons blinded the world to the fact that they were preparing the plant from which a little later would pour forth a flood of weapons of the most modern design. The democracies dozed complacently in what they thought were the safe shelter of their superior industrial plants and a moderate stock of still somewhat serviceable equipment left over from the First World War. The volcano of enemy war production which was soon to engulf their complacency rumbled distantly, but as yet the flow of lava—or weapons—suggested to the superficial glance only an eruption of moderate intensity.

When Great Britain and France, in the late thirties, awoke with a start to the magnitude of the danger which had arisen, the German industrial preparations were already so far advanced that the final, and tremendously productive, quarter of German industrial mobilization was certain to arrive before the democracies could get past the early, and largely unproductive, stages of industrial preparation. The tardiness of the democracies, which enabled the Germans to reach their last quarter of industrial mobilization before Great Britain and France had reached their half-way point, made war inevitable. It gave Hitler a year or more of overwhelming advantage which could not be snatched from him during that period, nor be regained subsequently if he failed to utilize it when first presented. Hitler was not a man to let slip so unique an opportunity, and he did not.

The United States was even tardier than France and Great Britain in awakening to danger and taking steps to overcome it.[21] We viewed with alarm, to be sure, the rise of the Nazis to power, but a large segment of American opinion refused to believe that this could involve, at least at any early date, military danger for us. Even those who did not share the common illusion that Hitler's regime could not last, too often failed to foresee the rapidity with which German armament would be reconstructed. They also put too much faith in the strength of Great Britain and France, forgetting how rapidly the immense power of 1918 could vanish in the face of technological innovation and a false sense of security.

Behind this comforting curtain, which hid us from reality, we dawdled through the mid-thirties. Domestic problems were pressing and, at close range, it seemed to most that there were more important things to do with our money than to create armaments. Undoubtedly this smugness was accentuated by our recollection of the First World War, when the firm resistance of the French and British armies gave us time to build up our munitions plants and to put our new armies in the field. It scarcely seemed possible that Hitler, starting almost from scratch in 1933—at least we so believed—could achieve what the long-prepared armies of the Kaiser had never been able to do and destroy the British and French armies before we could get assistance to them, if in the end we decided to provide assistance.

Not until about 1937 did we begin to wake up at all seriously to the problem facing us, and begin to realize that if war came in Europe we would find ourselves sadly lacking in the sinews of war, unless we took prompt steps to overcome our deficiencies. The nation owes a debt of gratitude to my predecessor as Assistant Secretary of War, Mr. Louis Johnson,[22] and to the group of officers who assisted him, for the initiative they took in getting up the momentum of industrial preparation. In quantitative terms, what they did seems small when compared with the vast efforts into which we threw ourselves a few years later. But the increase in our preparatory efforts was radical in terms of what had previously been done.

In a certain qualitative sense, it was even more important. The slowest and outwardly least productive phase of any great defense effort is the opening one. We cannot do things until we know what to do or until we have the organization with which to do them. Information must be gathered, administrative organizations created or enlarged, and new personnel recruited. During the three years before the fall of France, we achieved some of this preliminary work. We added little in terms of finished munitions, and not a great deal in terms of armament plant ready for use; but we did gain some momentum, and we learned to see our problem more clearly than before.

Certainly weeks, and perhaps months, were saved in 1940 because of the steps—modest though they were—which were taken during this preliminary period.

But, in doing justice to those who started the ball rolling and to the willingness of Congress to appropriate larger sums for military preparation than had ever before been appropriated in time of peace,[23] we must not forget that our preparations were terribly inadequate when measured against the magnitude of the crisis which was soon to strike us. This was as true in the realm of the preparation of industry for war as it was in the realm of the preparation of troops. We had, to be sure, an unequalled industrial plant, but nearly all the definite steps needed to convert it to war purposes remained to be taken. A modest program of educational orders, involving the expenditure of only a few million dollars, had at last been authorized after several years of pleading by the War Department. With these orders a few manufacturers were given an advance view of the problems they would have to face in the production of some of the more difficult items of military equipment. We took steps to renovate and enlarge our arsenals. And—probably most fortunate of all—we initiated several months in advance of the major crisis a sharply expanded airplane program which led to the creation of new capacity. We also began, belatedly and on what was ultimately to prove far too modest a scale, the stockpiling of a few critical materials.[24]

We also gained further momentum, undoubtedly, by the placement of French and British orders for arms after the modification of our Neutrality Act in 1939 made this possible.[25] This led to the creation of new arms-manufacturing capacity that we were not yet quite ready to create for ourselves. However, this was not pure gain, for when we started to place our own heavy orders late in 1940, we found an appreciable amount of the capacity we had originally planned to use already taken up in producing weapons for the nations whose efforts on the battlefield were giving us time to arm. Under the circumstances, we could not afford to interfere with the production they so desperately needed, but the fulfillment of our own plans was somewhat delayed by the necessity, in a good many cases, of finding alternative sources of supply.

Thus a start, an important start, was made. But the sum total of our preparations was small. It would have been very meager even in the war production terms with which we became familiar at the time of World War I. It was fantastically small in terms of the as yet uncomprehended demands of World War II. We were, in truth, very largely a nation without arms. And we were without arms at a moment when war had developed a reach and striking power such as the world had never seen before.

Chapter 2

The Slow Beginning

Although war began in Europe in September 1939, American opinion was terribly slow to grasp its full implications. At first there was a flurry of excitement and apprehension, enough to make possible the modification of the Neutrality Act, but public concern soon began to wane. We convinced ourselves that the sudden collapse of Poland was attributable more to the weakness of Poland's armament and the vulnerability of her strategic position than to the excellence of the German army. The long weeks—which soon became months—of inaction which followed persuaded us that Hitler dared not throw his armies against the fortified positions of the French and British. Even the destructive war in the air, which it had always been supposed would be unleashed against the cities of Britain and France the moment hostilities began, failed to materialize. We did not know then, as we have learned since, that the Blitzkrieg in the west was originally planned for the fall of 1939 and was only postponed at the eleventh hour.

Instead, we concluded that the stalemate which we contemptuously dubbed the "Sitzkrieg" was an evidence of German weakness, of either lack of adequate resources for seeking a decision in the rest, or a political fear of asking the German people to accept the sacrifices in blood which we assumed the attempt to secure a decision would entail. Thus the alarm of the previous September, inadequate though it was, subsided. The public—at least a large section of it—deluded itself into believing that Hitler had already found himself with more than he could handle, and that he would probably be brought down by the superior economic weight of his opponent without the sanguinary fighting in the field which had characterized the First World War.[1]

This fond illusion was jolted when Hitler invaded Denmark and Norway at the beginning of April 1940 and scattered to the winds a month later when the Anglo-French front collapsed with a suddenness and finality that would have been thought impossible before the event. Within two weeks of the German onslaught, their troops stood on the shores of the Straits of Dover, and less than a month later the last French resistance had collapsed. No active opponent of the Nazis was left on the continent of Europe, and in the west there was not even a potential opponent. Only Great Britain still stood in the west, and she was largely without defense, except for her navy and her small but expert air force. In sober realism it seemed but a matter of a few weeks until the Germans would be ready for their next, and final, spring across the English Channel.

This sudden disaster awakened American opinion as nothing previously had succeeded in doing.[2] The President went before Congress and demanded new and—as it then seemed—stupendous appropriations. He set a target of fifty thousand planes a year for the American aircraft industry, a goal far beyond our capacity in the months just ahead, but one which was ultimately far surpassed.[3] American opinion, jarred into a realization that the Atlantic might soon be dominated by a potential enemy, who would only wait a convenient moment to become an actual enemy, supported the President's program and Congress quickly voted the sums asked.

But it is a long path from the voting of an appropriation to the placing of a finished weapon in the hands of a soldier. Modern war cannot be supported by placing orders in the fashion of a shopper going into the retail market. It is a major operation of industry and finance, as well as of soldiers, sailors, and aviators. To prepare this major operation of our economy we had as yet done but little. To his great credit, Mr. Morgenthau,[4] through the Treasury Department, had taken steps to begin the more general development of the productive capacity needed by national defense, but these moves had begun only a few weeks before, and the existing departmental set-up could scarcely provide an adequate mechanism for initiating and

The Slow Beginning

controlling the vast changes which our economy was shortly to have to undergo.

At this juncture we sadly missed the Industrial Mobilization Plan which the War Department had prepared and had hoped to be able to use when an emergency arrived. Steps had been taken at the end of the previous summer, when it had become increasingly obvious that war in Europe was just around the corner, to review the plan and get it ready for early use. But this effort was halted by the delicate balance of domestic politics. When the President was only with difficulty persuading the nation to modify the disastrously rigid neutrality policy of the middle 'thirties, there was danger that such a frank recognition of the possibility of war would have been misinterpreted to indicate a desire for war. So the work of the War Resources Board, which had reviewed the Industrial Mobilization Plan, was buried.[5] With it went the opportunity to put into effect, in advance of the hour of extreme danger, the plans which the War Department had spent years in preparing for such a moment. Those plans were not perfect, and we can see now that in many particulars they fell short of our ultimate needs, but they would have been invaluable if they could have been put into operation early in the crisis. It is worthy of note that the changes we made in our procedures, as the emergency pressed more heavily upon us, very largely took the direction originally proposed by the Industrial Mobilization Plan, although not until after Pearl Harbor did we achieve anything like as thorough and balanced an organization as that would have provided us.[6]

When it became evident, in May 1940, that we would immediately have to embark upon a major defense production program, and that this could not be done successfully without some overall guidance for industry, the President revived the National Defense Advisory Commission and appointed William S. Knudsen, later Lieutenant General Knudsen, as production head.[7] When Mr. Knudsen arrived in Washington, he found a prodigious task awaiting him and the other members of the Commission. The most recent M-Day plan[8] was already out of date. The War Department, as he later remarked, was thinking in terms of an airplane and machine-gun war. He heard, as he took office, talk about landing craft. No specifications for large tanks were in existence. Fortunately, however, the situation with respect to small arms, ammunition, and explosives was somewhat better.

That it was so was largely the result of the foresight and energy of Maj. Gen. C. M. Wesson, who was then Chief of Ordnance.[9] General Wesson had taken full advantage of the legislation—sought for seventeen years by the War Department and finally passed in 1938—which permitted the award of educational orders to companies qualified to manufacture munitions. This program allowed for the design of the necessary tools and gave essential experience to management and skilled labor. Congress at first authorized the expenditure of $2 million annually for five years for these educational orders. The items first selected for manufacture in limited quantities were the gas mask, the 3-inch antiaircraft gun, the semiautomatic rifle, the antiaircraft searchlight, the forging of 75-mm shells and the machining of 75-mm shells. Two years later, Congress increased the appropriation for educational production to $14,250,000.

In the First World War, a year had elapsed before quantity production of ammunition had been obtained, while much longer delays set back mass production of artillery and other weapons.[10] The educational order program greatly reduced the required time. General Wesson also began the manufacture of machine guns, other small arms, and explosives at government arsenals. The Springfield arsenal started to make Garand rifles. The Rock Island Arsenal experimented with light tanks. It also gained some experience by Navy contracts for gunnery equipment. This alert planning by General Wesson made it possible for us to have stocks of all these necessities on hand by the time of Pearl Harbor. How much time would have been saved with respect to other items had the requests for appropriations for educational orders been granted when first asked cannot be precisely estimated, but it certainly would have been very substantial. In those critical months of 1940 and 1941, advances in production which may seem small, in the light of the quantities we ultimately produced, might have been of crucial significance.

But there was no certainty—in fact, at the time, it seemed that there was little probability—that our national defense could be made secure merely by armament production which could not mature for many months. The end of the summer might find the Germans in possession of Great Britain, and possibly of at least a part of the British fleet. We could not be sure but that we would have to defend our own shores before winter. Under that menace we enacted the Selective Service Act, although precious weeks slipped away between the initiation of the legislation and its final passage.[11] For the first time in our history, we began to prepare an adequate army before the actual initiation of hostilities, although in the summer of 1940, the probability that we would have to face direct attack within a few months seemed so great that "too little and too late" seemed more likely than foresight to be the description history would attach to our efforts.

But the Selective Service Act, although it promised to provide us the men for our defense, did not provide the arms. It became evident at once that we would be short, not only of sufficient equipment to enable these men to take the field as an effective fighting force, but even of enough to enable them to be trained in the most expeditious and effective manner. The situation in Europe made it clear that, even before the first selectee was chosen, we would have even less equipment. The survivors of Dunkirk began to come ashore on May 29, 1940. Behind them they left their tanks, their trucks, their artillery, and a good part of their lighter weapons. The British had virtually no reserves. They stood alone, unarmed against an enemy who was superbly equipped and separated from them by only a few miles of water. In this crisis the Prime Minister appealed to the President and asked whether any surplus arms in the United States could be shipped. Britain would arm the Dunkirk survivors and the Home Guard with anything that could be spared, and with these they would fight, as he told the House of Commons that week, "on the beaches . . . on the landing grounds . . . in the fields and in the streets . . . we shall never surrender . . ."[12]

The War and Navy Departments were immediately ordered to canvas their stocks. General Wesson, for the Army, reported in forty-eight hours that 500,000 rifles, 900 75-mm field guns, 130 million rounds of small-arms ammunition, and 100 million rounds of ammunition for the field guns, a few bombs, and some powder could be provided. To avoid complications under international law, possibly forbidding a neutral nation to sell arms directly to a belligerent one, the stocks were sold to the United States Steel Export Company for $37,619,556.60. That corporation promptly sold them to Great Britain for an identical sum. The first shipments sailed within a week after the contracts were signed. We kept modest stocks of small arms and ammunition for the new citizen army. More serious was the loss by the Army of ninety-three light bombers. They, too, were turned over to the French and were to have been delivered by the aircraft carrier *Bearn,* which was waiting at Halifax. But Petain asked for an armistice while she was at sea, and the *Bearn* was ordered to Martinique, where the planes rusted and became worthless. They would have been useful after Pearl Harbor.

This prompt dispatch, immediately after Dunkirk, of an appreciable fraction of our available arms and ammunition in this country, brought into sharp relief a grave strategic problem that affected our whole armament program in the months just ahead. The situation of Britain, from Dunkirk until well into the winter of 1940–41, was so precarious that it raised the question whether it was worthwhile to risk any of our precious store of arms—few as they were—in so hopeless a cause. Was sending them abroad not merely the equivalent of turning them over to the Germans? That would not add much to their already ample stocks, but it would drastically diminish our available equipment.[13] We could certainly make use of all that equipment for training; and, if the expected happened, we might need it before many months for the defense of this hemisphere.

The same dilemma presented itself in our early production plans after Dunkirk. Should we complete orders for the British, should we give their armament priority over ours, when in a few weeks there might be no more British resistance, at least in Europe? At this time, it must be remembered, British orders could not be filled without some cost to our own production.[14] Although at a later date the coordination of our own and British orders upon American industry was so well organized that one seldom got in the way of the other, that was not true in the early stages of the defense effort. Our production plans called for the use of factories the British were already using, and for materials and tools the British were either using here or wished to have shipped to them for use in their own factories. For many months the immediate military peril to the British Isles was so great that there was a definite possibility—for a time a probability—that everything we sent them would be lost. Small wonder then, that many in this country wondered whether support to Britain was not an investment that risked our own defenses unduly.

The decision of how much of our production to bet on the ability of Britain to survive, and how much to retain for our own direct needs, was one of the most difficult of the war.[15] Its critical character was well attested at the time of Pearl Harbor, when we found ourselves both committed to full industrial support to Britain—and by this time Russia as well—and also faced with a direct attack from the Japanese. When that moment of crisis came, our margin of security against direct attack was small. But that is also testimony to the fact that our allocation of armament was sound. In view of the critical situation in Europe, we could not afford to devote more to our own protection than was absolutely necessary. We did have enough, and the fact that it was just enough meant that nothing was denied our allies which could have been safely given them.

Although a wave of fear swept over the country with the fall of France, within a few months apathy began to return. The German invasion of Great Britain, which the public expected at first would follow immediately upon the extinction of the last French resistance, did not occur. The attack upon Britain from the air, spectacular though it was, yielded no apparent strategic results. The layman did not realize, nor was it safe at first to tell him, by what a narrow margin decisive success escaped the Germans. When the skies did not fall immediately, many Americans began to doubt whether the props had really been shaken. The weedy growth of normal routine began to hide the tender sprouts of our first alarm, and the drama of a presidential campaign conspired with business as usual to restore partially, although luckily not wholly, our complacency of the previous winter.

Fortunately Congress acted swiftly in the months after the fall of France. By the end of June, it made available a billion and a half dollars. The War Department, for its part, established a new and clearer objective for its supply program. It thought now in terms of equipping an army of a million men, of providing reserves of critical items for twice that many, and of building an armament industry capable of supplying a 4-million-man army. The cost was estimated at $5.9 billion, and by September Congress had appropriated almost four billion. This objective was, of course, very far short of what we would ultimately need; but in comparison with any previous tangible program, the increase was tremendous. Very probably it was at the point of transition between the previous program and this new program of the summer of 1940 that lay the critical moment of inertia which, in the organizational as well as the physical world, it takes the greatest amount of effort to overcome.

Our first problem was to transform appropriations into actual contracts. Millions of dollars voted by Congress looked impressive in the newspapers but they could not move a man nor turn a wheel for the actual production of weapons until contracts were made with the industrial firms that were to do the work. Under our peacetime procedure, formidable obstacles stood in the way of the prompt letting of contracts. Military procurement in normal times was dictated in large measure by a fear of abuses and the attendant fear of criticism. For this reason the law required that contracts be let by competitive bidding. This secured goods at the lowest price, and protected the War Department from the charge of favoritism toward certain firms, but it necessarily consumed a great deal of time. It also made it very difficult, in fact almost impossible, to distribute orders in such a fashion as to facilitate the well-balanced development of our armament industry. When one added to this the meticulous method of the Army in writing contracts, whereby each contract was checked and rechecked, it was obvious that the retention of normal contract methods would invariably cause several weeks' delay, and that not infrequently the delay would run into months.

Fortunately, the War Department was thoroughly aware of the need for shortening drastically the usual peacetime procedures and had prepared legislation for this purpose. Congress appreciated the need for measures which would both permit more speed and make possible a better-planned utilization of our industrial resources. It therefore enacted appropriate legislation early in July 1940. This legislation gave permission for the letting of bids without advertising, thus accelerating the award of contracts. It removed certain restrictions which had previously been imposed in the interest of better labor practices.[16] It also authorized the use, under certain restrictions, of what was known as the cost-plus-fixed-fee contract. As this type of contract played a very important part in our military procurement, especially in the early stages of our defense effort, it merits a word of description and comment.

One of the greatest difficulties connected with persuading manufacturers to accept munitions contracts was the vast uncertainty about the cost of producing some of the items. Many of the firms which we asked to accept orders had had no previous experience with items of the type they were to manufacture. Others, such as the aircraft companies, had had experience with small orders but none with costs under mass-production conditions. This uncertainty produced either a reluctance to bid, or a tendency to make the bid so high that it would cover the greatest conceivable cost. Either tendency was inimical to the defense effort.

This difficulty had appeared in the First World War and had been dealt with by an expedient which proved unfortunate. That was the cost-plus-percentage contract, whereby the contractor was allowed to take, as his profit, a certain percentage of his total cost. This offered a glittering temptation to pad costs in order to raise the amount of profit. The degree to which contractors yielded to this temptation became a national scandal. All those concerned in planning for the munitions program of the Second World War were determined to avoid a repetition of that unhappy experience, but it was equally necessary to devise a form of contract which would allow cost, as actually experienced, to enter into the final determination of price. This the cost-plus-fixed-fee contract did by setting a fixed fee, rather than a percentage of cost, as the rightful profit of the contractor.[17] The system was not without its loopholes through which some abuses entered, and it was always under suspicion. Nevertheless, it is difficult to see any other way in which the very real uncertainty about cost could have been overcome without accepting delay, which would have endangered our nation's defense. In the later stages of the defense effort, after industry had acquired experience with almost every conceivable type of military equipment, we were able to abandon the cost-plus-fee contract except in a few instances.

Another new device was developed to shorten the inevitable delay between the first steps toward the negotiation of a contract and the final signing of the contract. Under previously existing procedures, if a contractor spent money for tools materials, labor, or any other expense of production in anticipation of receiving a contract, he did so entirely at his own risk. If, for any reason, the contract was not finally signed, there was no way he could be reimbursed for his anticipatory expense. Therefore it was natural that most contractors would wait until the final signing of the contract before making any purchases or letting any subcontracts looking toward its fulfillment. Thus serious delay ensued.

This difficulty was obviated, in large part, by the letter of intent. As soon as the War Department, or other government agency concerned, decided that it was probable that a contract would be negotiated with a particular firm, it issued a letter of intent. This letter authorized the firm to spend immediately up to a certain sum in initiating the first steps toward the fulfillment of the anticipated contract. If, for any reason, the War Department finally decided not to go through with the contract, the contractor was reimbursed for any sums already spent. If, as was usually the case, the contract was finally completed, valuable time was saved.

This device was all the more necessary because of the tremendous pressure upon the War Department's contracting personnel. It was a stupendous task to work out all the details of the thousands of new contracts which had to be let. The task was all the greater because the majority of contractors had little familiarity with the peculiarities of governmental contract procedure, and because a large proportion of the War Department's contracting officers were new to the job, and were inadequate in numbers anyway. At times it was impossible to avoid a delay of months between the first approach to a manufacturing firm and the conclusion of a contract. Had there been no means of getting actual work under way during this interval, the certain result would have been both a dangerous delay in production and a careless drawing of contracts in a desperate effort to minimize that delay. Even as it was, we could not avoid delay, which caused some concern and brought down upon us criticism from those who did not fully appreciate the immensity of our task. Without these new devices, the delay and the criticism would have been many times multiplied.

But the removal, whole or partial, of many of these technical obstacles to the letting of defense contracts did not solve all our difficulties. In fact, it left one of the major difficulties practically untouched. This was the problem of persuading American industry to discard a large part of its usual business and accept defense orders instead. As we look back and see what happened during the subsequent five years, it may seem odd that this presented any difficulty, but at the time the difficulties were very real and very considerable.

The major difficulty at the outset was the fact that no one could say just how long our defense production, at the tempo at which we planned it, would last. If the national emergency lasted four or five years, then well and good. Then the manufacturer who turned to defense orders would produce enough to repay him for his original investment in new plant and new machinery. But suppose the emergency lasted only a year or two.[18] If Hitler collapsed, so vast an armament—at least so it seemed—would not be needed. Or he might make a negotiated peace with Great Britain which, although it would not spare us the necessity of having an armament greater than ever before in our peacetime history, would not require the expansion of our munitions capacity at the rate planned in the summer of 1940. In either of those two cases, the manufacturer who turned to munitions work might face the cancellation of his orders before his new plant had repaid its original cost. And, in the meantime, he might have lost his place in the highly competitive consumer market in which he had previously been engaged. That was indeed a very serious prospect, one to give pause to any company official as he contemplated what he would say to his stockholders in such an eventuality.[19]

The fact that civilian business was booming, under the impact of the war in Europe, made it even more difficult for the manufacturer to contemplate switching to munitions. He knew his way about in the field of his usual business, and that way at the moment promised to be lucrative. Why turn to something which he understood but little, in which his mistakes might be serious, and in which his profit would be limited by the various measures designed to keep the government from paying more than was necessary for purchases from industry? Small wonder that business hesitated, and that special measures had to be taken to overcome this hesitation. Although some of this hesitation undoubtedly sprang from motives that do not merit praise, perhaps the wonder is that there was not more hesitation. Certainly, without some of the special measures adopted in order to overcome the understandable fears of business, this hesitation would have been much greater and might have assumed very serious proportions.[20]

One of the most important of these measures was the tax amortization law. Under normal procedures it was not possible to amortize new plant, for tax purposes, in less than twenty years. A firm might actually amortize its plant more rapidly, but it could not write off annually more than 5 percent of the total of amortization in its tax return. Thus the cost of a more rapid amortization would have to come out of taxable profits.

Under the new tax amortization law, it was possible to allow annually for the depreciation of 20 percent of the original cost, of the defense plant, thus making possible full amortization of the plant within five years, a period which seemed somewhere near the approximate duration of the major defense effort. Thus the specter of unamortized plant—or plant amortized only by the use of profits from which the government had already taken a large fraction for taxes—was removed. A major part of the munitions plants built at private expense was accorded this special permission.

The administration of the tax amortization act was a story in itself. It presented unusual legal and administrative difficulties, complicated in the early stages by division of authority. There was also a temptation for any firm even remotely connected with defense to claim the privilege of tax amortization for its new facilities, and it was often extremely difficult to decide whether particular claims had merit. Those who carried the major responsibility in the administration of the law worked largely in an unexplored field, and we owe much to their resourcefulness.

It is impossible to calculate with any precision how great an influence the law had in speeding up the letting of contracts, for it is seldom possible to say, in specific cases, whether the absence of the law would have delayed or prevented the acceptance of a contract by the manufacturer. Nevertheless it seems a reasonable judgment that the tax amortization law, assisted by vigorous and intelligent administration, played a very significant part in overcoming the early reluctance of industry to enter wholeheartedly into the defense program.[21]

But even with this assistance, it became clear at an early point that private financing alone would not bring about a sufficiently rapid expansion of our munitions industry. The risk seemed too great. At this point the Reconstruction Finance Corporation stepped into the breach and extended credits upon a most liberal basis. Its subsidiary, the Defense Plant Corporation (DPC), made loans and authorized the building of factories of all kinds. After some experimentation, satisfactory contract forms were devised for the expansion of plant with the assistance of public funds. The plants thus built included aluminum and magnesium plants, synthetic rubber works, chemical factories, and a huge steel plant in Utah.[22] Some were operated on a fee arrangement directly for the government.

I remember a conversation with General Knudsen in which he told me of his cordial relationship with Jesse Jones, then head of the Reconstruction Finance Corporation (RFC).

"I call him up and ask for the money," the General explained. "He says, 'Yes, send me a covering letter.'"

This cordial and informal relationship extended down the line to the officials of the Defense Plant Corporation and lesser officials in the War Department. A telephoned request to the DPC was usually sufficient to start things moving. The legal formalities could be handled later, and in more leisurely fashion, without holding up the steps necessary for the actual beginning of construction.[23]

Time proved that still more financial assistance was needed. Many would-be contractors found it difficult to begin operations because they lacked ready funds for the purchase of necessary materials or machinery. To overcome the cautious loan procedures of the banks was a slow job, and meanwhile production waited. To get around this difficulty, advances of 30 percent of the value of the contract were made to prime contractors, but this did not apply to subcontractors. In 1942 an Air Force officer flew from California to tell us that a small company on the coast, manufacturing a part essential to all aircraft, could get no loan from its bankers. It had a big flow of orders but precious little in the way of assets. Unless helped immediately, it would shut down and endanger the whole air program. This was remedied by a Presidential order allowing the War Department to guarantee such loans. Thus the V-Loan program was launched. Before the war ended, a total of $9 billion had been loaned by private banks to contractors all over the country—the loans ranging from $400 to $1 billion. The War Department put a ceiling on interest charges and was paid a fee by the banks for guaranteeing the loans. We expected to lose money on this program, since the loans were primarily for production and risks were freely taken. Strange to say, we made a profit of $16 million.

Thus the government stepped in to assist in financing the expansion of munitions plants in cases where private finance either felt unwilling to take the risk, or was too slow in its procedures. About two-thirds of the facilities built in order to fill War Department orders were built with the assistance of government financing.

One of the most tremendous jobs faced by the War Department was the building up of its procurement organization. In time of peace, military procurement proceeds slowly and the administrative force needed to carry it out is not large. Now the first thing we needed, even ahead of those equipped to handle the technical side of production, was the men and the organization needed to organize and execute the War Department's business operations. We needed men with the legal and business skills greatly in demand in civilian business.[24] Unless we got them, the program would not move. But how were they to be secured? We could not draft youngsters and gradually teach them the necessary skills, as we were about to do under Selective Service for the military end of national defense. The men must be secured either from officers already in the Army, or from men in civilian life who already possessed the necessary skills.

How we got them is a long story.[25] Some had retained reserve commissions and could be called into service. Others, and before long the great majority, had to be brought in without the help of such a leverage. For them no flags were waved, and they were more often greeted by exasperation at technical complexities over which they had no control than they were by applause. Inevitably, there were some among them who were somewhat inept, and who perhaps found in government employment greater rewards than they had been able to win in private business. But the great majority were very capable and many of them made their contribution to our national defense at a considerable sacrifice. Among them were not only men of great patriotism, but also some men of very unusual ability. The nation owes more than it probably will ever recognize to these brilliant recruits to military procurement, and to the skill with which they devised ways and means to get round difficulties which had previously held us up. It owes an equal debt to that much larger group who had no chance to demonstrate brilliance but who carried on, with unflagging patience and under terrific pressure, the almost endless work of completing the details of contracts, authorizing loans, approving tax amortization applications, and carrying out many other types of administrative work.

One of our great problems in developing our administrative organization for procuring munitions for the Army was to decide how far to centralize and how far to decentralize operations. For quick action decentralization was the obvious answer. But, in an emergency such as that which hit us in 1940, more had to be considered than speed in detail. We had to build up our production system in such fashion that it would not get out of balance. We had to guard against congestion in one spot and a neglect of available facilities at another. We had to endeavor to see the whole process of production so that its several parts would mesh smoothly with each other. There had to be supervision in timing as well as in spacing. Clearly such supervision could be exercised only from a vantage point from which the whole picture could be seen. That point was usually Washington.

To meet these conflicting requirements, we pursued the course of centralizing policy and overall supervision, and of decentralizing detailed operations. We already had in existence regional procurement districts for the several Supply Arms and Services, of which the most highly organized was the district system of the Ordnance Department. These procurement districts handled most of the detailed work of letting contracts. They were required to send in for central approval in my office only those of such magnitude that they would influence the general balance of the production program, or those which called for use of one or the other of the various special contractual devices which Congress would not have authorized in normal times and over whose use therefore we were at least morally, if not always legally, obligated to exercise some special supervision. As time went on, and the program far outgrew anything we at first contemplated, it became necessary to delegate authority over the expenditure of ever-larger sums. When I first took office, great numbers of contracts for tiny amounts came to me for my signature. By the time we entered the war, I seldom saw personally anything not expressed in terms of millions.

Another problem that plagued us was the rival claims of big and little business for war contracts.[26] In the early stages, at least, the War Department tended to favor the awarding of contracts to the larger concerns.[27] We were much criticized for this, but in the majority of cases there were sound technical reasons for this policy. Our problem in the summer of 1940 was less one of planning the best ultimate utilization of all our industry than it was one of securing enough output at once to protect us, and the nations friendly to us, from immediate danger. Generally speaking, the large firms were best able to do this job for us. They usually had the best plants, the best engineers, and the capital with which to purchase materials and secure new machinery. Both their financial stability and their technical skill offered the best guarantee of ability to achieve both quality and speed of production. Of course, there were times, as was inevitable in such a tremendous and hasty effort, when favoritism crept in; but the technical arguments for giving the greater part of the business to the big concerns were so convincing that, even had no contracting office ever been guilty of partiality, the total result would probably not have been very different.

The Slow Beginning

It ought also to be noticed that, at first, the majority of the smaller firms were not eager to secure munitions contracts. They were aware of their own technical limitations. "What do we know about making bombs?" they asked. And they, just as much as the large concerns, had to take into account the business risk involved in switching to an armament program of uncertain duration. They, too, felt the magnetic pull of ample profits from familiar work which the upswing of business activity offered them.

Not until much later, for the most part after Pearl Harbor, did the attitude of small business reverse itself. Then, as we had to shut off materials from consumer industries in order to keep our munitions plants going, firms without defense orders were confronted with the prospect of having to shut down. To a large degree, the smaller plants found themselves in that category. Consequently, they soon came into Washington clamoring for defense contracts. We set up special agencies in the War Department to look for opportunities to steer munitions contracts in their direction. It must be admitted, however, that at this stage, when small business needed orders from the War Department more than the War Department needed the facilities of small business, our response to these requests lagged somewhat. Better, but never entirely satisfactory, results were achieved later on when we needed small business as much as it needed us.

Undoubtedly, had we been able to see our ultimate goal from the very beginning, and had we been able to make full preparation with that goal in mind, we could have arranged to bring small business into the picture systematically from the start. There can be no doubt that the national defense would have gained from such foresight. But in our early state of industrial unpreparedness and our uncertainty about ultimate objectives, it is not surprising that we proceeded in somewhat piecemeal fashion, and that our procedures were sometimes better calculated for surmounting the major hurdle which lay just ahead than they were for surmounting hurdles in the distance which we could not be sure we would be called upon to leap. We were also plagued, in planning the expansion of our munitions industry, by strategic limitations. When we began, we could not be sure but that the arms we expected to produce would have to be used for the defense of our own coasts. The General Staff therefore drew a line approximately two hundred miles from the coast and directed that, insofar as possible, defense industry be located back of that line. Appropriate machinery was set up to carry out this directive. In practice, however, the directive had to be very widely disregarded.[28] Because of the already existing location of American industry in the coastal areas, a strict adherence to the directive would have caused delays and inconveniences which would have constituted a more serious risk than the possibility of enemy raids upon our coasts.

Another factor, not serious at first but very important later on, which affected the location of war plants was that of congestion. There were obvious advantages in placing new plants near old ones. But as the munitions industry grew, the disadvantages soon outdistanced the advantages. It might be convenient for a gun plant to be near a steel mill, but the advantage quickly disappeared if the local transportation facilities were overtaxed, if there was not a sufficient labor supply in the neighborhood, and if there was not enough housing for new workers who had to be brought in. Just as some business firms took in more defense orders than they could handle rather than see the business go to a rival, so communities sometimes sought new defense industry beyond the real capacity of the community to accommodate it.[29] Even when a community was already overburdened, from the overall point of view, there was invariably some interest in the community which stood to gain—or thought it did—from a further influx of industrial activity. It was not an easy task, and one in which we never fully succeeded, to counteract this tendency to build new plants in regions already highly industrialized.

Another major problem which confronted us was that of labor relations.[30] The world crisis struck as at a moment when labor had just made very important gains, and when many believed that the momentum acquired ought soon to result in further gains. It was, therefore, not surprising that some of the leaders and friends of labor saw in the awarding of government contracts an opportunity to bring pressure upon employers who had hitherto succeeded in resisting the pressures available under normal conditions. And it was equally to be expected that some employers would see in the national emergency an opportunity to call a halt to labor's gains in the name of national necessity. Both sides put pressure upon the War Department, and both had to be resisted.

The most serious episode in this pushing in both directions was the endeavor of labor to force the exclusion from the award of defense contracts of all firms which did not meet certain standards in labor relations.[31] Had this endeavor succeeded—and it did have some measure of success for a few months—it would have brought about two unfortunate results. First, it would have forced us to deny contracts to some of the largest and best-equipped industrial firms in the country, firms which normally handled a very appreciable percentage of the nation's industrial production.[32] Secondly, it would have turned the War Department into an agency for enforcing labor policies of the government. Not only was the War Department ill equipped for such a task, but it would have forced the Department into the very middle of an intense political and economic controversy at the very moment when the Department particularly needed the support of all segments of American life.

The War Department, therefore, fought constantly to avoid being pushed into this unfortunate role. The Department realized, of course, that labor relations constituted one of the major problems of production, and it employed skilled personnel and eternal vigilance to forestall difficulty, where it could be seen in advance, and to terminate it quickly, where it could not be forestalled. But the attitude of the Department was that its interposition in labor disputes would be solely for the purpose of preventing disastrous interruptions of production. That interposition was always managed, insofar as possible, so as not to affect the permanent balance between the contending parties. That this was not an easy role to play can readily be understood, but any other role would have been more difficult, in the long run, and might have proved disastrous.

But it was not only in labor problems that normal peacetime objectives came into conflict with our defense needs. We had trouble with the big manufacturers when it began to become apparent that our defense orders could not be filled without some curtailment of civilian production.[33] In October 1940 General Knudsen addressed a convention of automobile and truck manufacturers in New York and told them they must subordinate 1941 model changes to the needs of the aircraft program. In December 1940 Walter Reuther offered his plan for the production of five hundred fighter planes a day within six months without interfering with normal motor schedules.[34] This was based on his contention that the industry was operating far below capacity. Instead of 3.5 million cars, he said it could turn out 8 million annually. Looking back, I am now inclined to believe that we should have given more serious consideration to the Reuther plan. But our pressing need was for bombers, not fighters. In addition, the Air Corps had decided in 1938 that the automobile manufacturers would serve as subcontractors, under the guidance of aircraft engineers with greater experience in that type of production. That decision was to be changed later.

The automobile manufacturers, approaching their record production of 1929, did not taper off until late in 1941. They were using materials, labor, and engineering in tooling up for 1942. Urgently needed die and tool makers were not yet shifted over to defense work. With the Japanese attack, however, Detroit needed no further urging. The automobile men converted far more rapidly than we had dared hope.[35]

Attention must also be called, in connection with the use of big industry, to difficulties we had in developing an adequate use of subcontracting. There was a tendency in some quarters to build new plant, at the expense of both time and money, rather than to subcontract as much as possible of the business provided by munitions contracts. Various motives dictated this reluctance. In some cases there was an understandable doubt whether smaller and less experienced firms would meet satisfactorily the difficult technical requirements contained in many of the contracts. In other cases, it must he confessed, there was a reluctance to see an expansion of plant by firms outside the prime contractor, an expansion which, it was feared, might affect the competitive market after the emergency was over. As a result of this reluctance, some companies took larger orders than they were at the moment able to fill with their own plant resources, and either let them pile up, or initiated their own plant expansions which, at the moment, could have been avoided by fuller subcontracting.

In the end, however, the loss was probably not as great as at first seemed likely. Our ultimate production goal was so much greater than anyone anticipated in 1940 and 1941 that new industrial plants, which were not really necessary for the fulfillment of the early limited goals, were fully needed for the achievement of our final objective. And in spite of our faults in this particular, it is doubtful that any other nation secured a greater increase of production, in proportion to its expansion of facilities, than did we. It is interesting to note that the Germans, when after Stalingrad they faced the need for greatly expanding their war production, did so in large measure through imitating American methods of fabricating parts in separate plants and assembling them in a parent plant.

Another difficulty that we faced was the fact that most of the firms which accepted munitions contracts also continued their usual civilian business. At times this undoubtedly led to a less vigorous pressing of defense production than would have been the case had these firms excluded all but munitions work. The British got round this difficulty during the war by directing certain plants to concentrate upon the civilian production which was deemed to be necessary, and directing all others to concentrate upon war production. To protect the plants assigned to war production from the loss of competitive position to the plants assigned to civilian production, the goods produced by the latter were in accordance with a standard pattern, and without any mark to identify them with the firm which produced them. Thus munitions orders did not have to compete, in the same plant, with goods which affected the position of the producer in the competitive civilian market.

There is much to be said for the British practice, but it was probably impractical for us to adopt it, in view of the fashion in which we built up our munitions production. Our first munitions program, great though it was by previous standards, was not of sufficient magnitude to justify such stringent measures as those adopted by the British. They were actually at war; we were only potentially at war. Until the great bulk of our facilities in certain fields were involved in war production, it was not feasible to abrogate the usual competitive procedures. And by the time that measure of absorption in war production had been achieved, we were already very much committed to the pattern of permitting firms to have both civilian and government business.

After Pearl Harbor we were compelled to convert some industries, such as automobiles and typewriters, 100 percent to war production, and require that the civilian community get along with the goods already produced. We were, however, better able than most countries entirely to forego certain types of civilian production because in normal times we were so much better equipped than any other country with all types of machine products. Consequently, our early compromise between the production of munitions and civilian goods did not prove as costly as, under slightly different circumstances, might have been the case.

The whole matter of the relationship between war production and private business is, of course, a fundamental problem of any mobilization of the nation's industry for defense. In some quarters there was a demand that the new munitions industry required by the emergency should be government owned and government operated. This demand was motivated largely by a belief that it was not proper that private business should profit from the national emergency, and it received some reinforcement from the reluctance shown in certain quarters of private business to go all out in the defense effort.[36]

It would, however, have been a grave error to refuse to make the greatest possible use of existing private firms and to endeavor instead to build up a vast new government-production system. American industry has an unequalled combination of skill and equipment. It would have been a very difficult, well-nigh an impossible, job to endeavor to withdraw the best of that skill and equipment from private industry and turn it over to a new, government-munitions combine.[37] We could not afford the time necessary for such a transfer, even had there been no other objection to it. The only way to get the best American industrial brains and machines promptly to work on defense orders was to give those orders to the firms which already employed the brains and machines, and which gave to their use the advantage of an experienced and well-tested business organization.

Furthermore, any attempt to exclude private business in favor of a vast, exclusively governmental munitions industry would have aroused intense controversy. The government can maintain arsenals for the production of its modest peacetime demands for munitions without influencing appreciably, one way or the other, the character of the American economy. But to build up, almost entirely on a government basis, the vast industry needed to fight a modern war would have had such vast and obvious implications for the future that the plan would have been the certain signal for a political battle of the first magnitude. We had serious difficulties, as it was, with the economic implications of using the existing industrial system with a minimum of amendment. To attempt what a large section of the country would certainly have regarded as an economic revolution would have risked delay that might well have proved fatal.

We had to meet the defense crisis with the United States as it was. It is my belief that our country as it was showed a superb adaptability to the needs of defense, once we awoke to the magnitude of the emergency. But whether I am right or wrong, whether we were well, or poorly, designed for defense, we had no option at the moment but to do our best with the system we had. So it will always be in national emergencies. If there is some feature about our national system that is gravely inadequate to national defense, it must be repaired in advance of an emergency, for when the emergency strikes there is no time for experimenting with the foundations of our industrial life.

From the very beginning, munitions orders from those who were eventually to be our allies played a large role in the American production picture. Assistance to Great Britain and France, whose valiant resistance gave us time in which to start building our own defenses, had been handicapped by the Neutrality Act. When war came in September 1939, the President had been forced to put an embargo on all arms shipments, and we found ourselves in the tragic position, for the moment, of being compelled by our own laws to refuse aid to those who were fighting our battles. Fortunately, in November 1939, the Act was amended to permit "cash and carry." With this opportunity, restricted though it still was, Great Britain and France in the first half of 1940 ordered eight thousand airplanes and thirteen thousand engines in the United States. They invested $84 million in new plants and plant extensions. In addition, they placed orders for over $100 million in machine tools on top of 138 million dollars' worth which they bought for the American manufacturers who were to produce their war goods.

These orders, and the outlay of capital required for filling them, benefited the United States even more than they did our future allies. They enabled our manufacturers to make a start toward getting the factories, the tools, and the skilled labor and experience needed for the five years ahead.[38] Although scarcely one hundred planes had been shipped to Great Britain when France surrendered, in due course, and with the further assistance of Lend-Lease, we were to make adequate repayment for the boost given our munitions industry. During the last half of 1940, foreign government orders for war goods were placed on a scale that then seemed enormous. The Dutch had lost their home territory, but they still had an empire in the East, and they were doggedly determined to defend it. They ordered $50 million of American products to that end. China, with loans of $75 million from the Export-Import Bank, wanted all kinds of arms. The British could no longer get supplies from Holland, Belgium, France, or the Scandinavian countries. The British Isles seemed almost certain to be invaded. The Suez Canal had to he defended. The Japanese, moving south into French Indo-China, would soon be in a position to strike at Singapore and the southwest Pacific. The true nature of the appalling years which lay ahead was revealed when Germany, Italy, and Japan agreed on September 27, 1940, to take action against the United States if we interfered in any way with their program of world conquest.

Between January 1, 1939, and June 1, 1940, foreign governments had ordered a total of $600 million in war materiel. In June 1940 alone, they ordered $800 million, and during the next six months of the year they sought an additional $1.2 billion. The British wanted planes at the rate of four thousand a month by the end of 1941. That confusion should grow out of all these demands was inevitable. In August 1940 the Joint Aircraft Committee, with representatives from the Army, the Navy, and the British Air Commission, was created with wide powers. Through its operations, British and American aircraft de-

The Slow Beginning

signs were harmonized. Weapons were exchanged. The 40-mm Bofors antiaircraft gun was adopted as standard for the Army and manufactured in large quantities. Other weapons were modified to meet the ideas of each nation's experts.

Aircraft engines constituted a bad bottleneck. Our Air Corps had developed the air-cooled engine. The British, however, had the Rolls-Royce Merlin, which had proved itself in combat. On request, Lord Beaverbrook readily agreed to issue a license for manufacture in the United States. On September 3, 1940, the Packard Motor Company was authorized to begin making three thousand of these engines for the United States and six thousand for the British.

Another problem was tanks. The British needed thousands, and so did we. Only one concern, the American Car and Foundry Company, was in production, and it was turning out only light types. Again American and British experts worked out a design for a medium tank, which came to be known as the General Grant. It probably should have been heavier, and the gun should certainly have had a wider field of fire. But at the time it seemed adequate. The War Department agreed to finance a $20 million tank plant at Detroit, to be operated by the Chrysler Motor Company. Other orders for tanks were placed with the Pullman-Standard Car Manufacturing Company, the Pressed Steel Car Company, the Lima Locomotive Works, and the Baldwin Locomotive Works. The RFC, that same month, lent $8 million to Continental Motors Corporation for a plant which would make six hundred tank engines a month. It is but a statement of certain fact to say that the British would have been pushed out of Africa in 1942, and that Egypt would have fallen and the Suez Canal have been captured by Rommel, had not those contracts been signed in September 1940. The engineers who designed those tanks, the American industrialists who supplied the management, and the workmen who built them are entitled to share in the credit for the survival of democracy. Thus, closely, in modern war, are production, strategy, and tactics connected.

By the fall of 1940, British dollars were running out. In September 1939, the British had about 4.5 billion in gold, dollars, and American investments which could be converted into cash. As the year drew to a close, the total dropped to $2 billion, of which $1.5 was already obligated by existing contracts. Of course, loans could have been made to Britain, as in the last war. But those had only resulted in difficulty and bitterness. Great Britain was fighting the battle as we struggled to prepare. Some other solution than loans in order to continue the flow of supplies was vital. At his press conference on December 17, 1940, President Roosevelt disclosed what he thought this should be.

Munitions orders from Great Britain, the President observed, were "a tremendous asset to American national defense because they automatically create additional facilities."[39] He spoke selfishly, he added, "from the American point of view—nothing else." Then the President told the correspondents that what he was "trying to do is to eliminate the dollar sign," and gave his now famous illustration of lending the garden hose to put out a neighbor's fire. At that time the President thought the hose would be returned when the conflagration ended, but this did not prove possible or desirable. Supplies of armament and food under the provisions of Lend-Lease, which grew out of the President's ponderings on that December day, made it possible for the Russians to stand at Stalingrad.

The year 1940 was one of accomplishments, but the accomplishments for the most part took the shape of laying foundations for later production. On the day that Petain became Premier of France, the United States had no more than five hundred tanks or combat cars—enough for one German armored division. Although we had nearly three thousand planes of all types, scarcely three hundred of them were fit to take the air in modern combat. Although, by previous standards, appreciable additions were made to our stock of munitions during the second half of 1940, the amount was tiny in comparison with our ultimate needs. At the end of the year, the President announced his intention to make the United States the "Arsenal of Democracy."[40] It was one of the fundamental strategic concepts of our ultimate victory over the Axis. And yet, in truth, even then our industrial preparation was only on a part-time basis. And so it remained for several months more. The motor industry turned out 3.5 million passenger automobiles in 1941—40 percent higher than the average 1935–1939 production rate—although every other industrial nation on earth had long since stopped the making of cars in order to produce airplanes, tanks, and guns. In 1940 we produced a monthly average of 226,000 electric refrigerators, and in 1941 the average rose to 296,000. We still thought we could defend ourselves with one hand and help ourselves to the delights of peace with the other.

Not only were we preparing on a part-time basis, but as yet we had no picture of the ultimate goal of our munitions production. What did the "Arsenal of Democracy" mean in terms of guns, planes, tanks, and ammunition to be produced, and in terms of the factories and raw materials needed to produce them? What would be the schedule for production, the manpower needs? To all these and other related problems we as yet had no answer, and without that answer it was almost impossible to plan production efficiently. Every time we enlarged our ultimate goal, we had to repeat laboriously thousands of processes—calculations, contracts, orders, and the like—which we might have accomplished in a single step had we known at the start just how far we were going to go and what we were going to need in order to get there.

The time and effort lost in these repeated edgings forward of our munitions program were increased by a timidity upon the part of military procurement officers inherited from peacetime. With so little money to spend on munitions in previous years, and the expenditure of that so jealously guarded, procurement officers developed an understandable reluctance to commit themselves to expenditures beyond what was needed by existing and fully authorized plans. They feared, too often, that the roof would fall in on them if they authorized expenditures with an eye to future needs which had not yet been fully approved. Thus, from top to bottom, there was a constant tendency to move cautiously, and it was very difficult to shake them loose from this hesitancy to which they had been trained through so many years in which they had been compelled to place financial caution ahead of military foresight.[41]

But the major cause of our inability to secure the efficiency of industrial planning that would have been made possible by a prompt specification of our ultimate goals ought not to be attributed either to the timidity of procurement officers, or to the tremendous difficulty, in 1940, of knowing how much of a military effort would be required to defeat the Axis. Rather, it was our uncertainty about the exact role we intended to play in the world crisis that most seriously handicapped wise planning. We could not, in 1940, begin immediately full production planning and operations for an all-out participation in the war by the United States, for our nation was as yet reluctant to believe that such a role would be required of it. Until the nation was far more ready for that role than it was in 1940, the War Department could only bridge very partially the gap between the military requirements for the defense of our own coasts and those needed to overthrow the Axis. The waste and delay involved in partial planning can never be avoided until the nation is willing to determine its role in any coming crisis far enough in advance to permit full planning at the time when industrial preparation must begin. That means that we must know, at least two years in advance of the climax of our efforts, the part we intend to play. Even had the War Department procurement authorities in 1940 been almost superhuman in energy and in the avoidance of error, their efforts would still have been handicapped by lack of authority to assume an objective comparable to that which events, a few months later, imposed upon us.

Chapter 3

Airplanes Take Five Years

When victory had been gained in Europe, General Eisenhower wrote,

> ... we had, above all, to be grateful to the work of the Allied air forces. Long before we landed in France, the heavy bombers had begun their task of destroying the centers of production on which the enemy relied.... Following the invasion these strategic blows at the heart of German industry were continued, and the task was also undertaken of cutting the supply lines which linked the factories to the fronts.
> Meanwhile the tactical aircraft, by their incessant bombing and strafing of the enemy before us in the field, broke his powers of resistance and prepared the way for the ground advances which struck towards the center of Germany. Those thrusts, moreover, were made with a rapidity which only the expedient of airborne supply could support. The overwhelming Allied superiority in the air was indeed essential to our victory....[1]

Thus the leader of the Allied forces in Europe testified to the decisive importance of the tremendous concentration upon airpower which President Roosevelt had enunciated when, in the spring of 1940, he called for the production of fifty thousand planes a year. It was a bold strategical innovation to devote so much of our strength to the air, and to stake so much on a strategic air force. Even the Germans, for all the vaunted prowess of the Luftwaffe in the early stages of the war, both designed and used that force predominantly as an auxiliary to the ground forces. That limited vision contributed to the German failure in the Battle of Britain. Our greater boldness of concept made the battle over Germany an unqualified success.

But it would not have been a success had not this bold decision—which was ultimately to devote about one third of all the production effort of the War Department into the aircraft program—been taken very early in the crisis. The mass production of combat aircraft takes longer than that of any other weapon used by the Army. Many people doubtless believe that the B-17, the B-29, the other bombers, and the swift fighters that wrecked Germany and Japan were modern in the sense that they were developed after Pearl Harbor. Such is not the case. An average of from five to seven years was required for the production of every type of aircraft used in this war. No plane was used in combat by the AAF which was designed after 1940. To put it another way, a minimum of five years passed before our new planes were designed, tested, and in mass production.

But time was not the only obstacle to the prompt production of masses of airplanes. Even five years would not suffice unless there was clear vision, and policy and organization based upon it. For the problems associated with the mass production of airplanes were enormous and frequently novel. They had plagued the belligerents in the First World War and were to prove equally stubborn in the Second.

Basic to the gap between design and production of war aircraft was the bitter controversy over the validity of air power. The outspoken convictions of Brig. Gen. William Mitchell resulted in the 1923 tests in which two obsolete battleships were sunk. But General Mitchell's demand that the bomber should be adopted as the basic weapon of national defense went unheeded.[2] As late as 1934, the then Secretary of War denounced the theory that armies or cities could be destroyed from the air. This was the "fantasy of a dreamer," he said. Any invader of the United States would be unwilling to "waste efforts in meaningless aerial bombardment," he added, and denied that the War Department General Staff was improperly minimizing the Air Corps.[3]

Such, it is safe to say, was the majority view both in and out of the Army in 1934, one against which the Air Corps had to make such progress as it could. The Navy, at about the same time, criticized proposals to develop bombardment aviation for coastal patrol. The Navy, it insisted, was the nation's first line of defense. Any extension of Air Corps activity to the protection of sea lanes would be an infringement upon the Navy's long-standing duties.[4]

The troubled history of the Flying Fortress, in which tens of thousands of young Americans exploded Goering's boast that the Reich would never be bombed, is an illustration of the difficulties with which the Air Corps had to contend. That history goes back to 1934. Gen. Douglas MacArthur, then Chief of Staff, declared in June of that year that the bombardment plane was the most important element in an air force. It made possible, he said, assault on the enemy in the rear of his armies and in his zone of interior. But this was the sole influential voice raised in support of heavy, long-range bombers. The Baker Board examined the general problem and saw no likelihood of danger from the air.[5] Obsolete geography still bemused us.

The air forces had a bomber in 1934, the B-10. It was twin-motored, slow, and of limited range.[6] Despite General Staff disapproval and lack of funds, the Materiel Division of the Air Corps in Dayton, Ohio, was working on plans for a four-engine monoplane bomber of radical design. This was the father of the Flying Fortress. The next year, Brig. Gen. Oscar Westover, Assistant Chief of the Air Corps, said that the Boeing B-17, although costing 75 percent more than the B-10, would have a vastly greater range. It could fly to Pearl Harbor. An even bigger ship would be designed, he promised, if the B-17 was a success.

In its tests the B-17 surpassed expectations.[7] More experimental heavy bombers were built. By 1938, however, it was clear that other nations were ahead of the United States in both bombers and fighters. By this time Gen. H. H. Arnold was running the Air Corps.[8] But even his vigor and persuasive salesmanship could not persuade the War Department to go ahead with an adequate production program. In October 1938 it expressed itself as aware of the needs of the Air Corps. But it was the firm belief of the Army that infantry divisions were the basic combat elements by which battles were won and enemy forces destroyed. The Air Corps would not be enlarged beyond extension of the other arms. By then, it is well to note, Ethiopia had been conquered with the aid of air power. Madrid had been bombed. Hitler had taken the Rhineland, Austria, and the western part of Czechoslovakia. Japan, Secretary of State Cordell Hull declared on September 21, 1938, intended to dominate half of the world by force.

A turn in our policy came when, in November 1938, Gen. George C. Marshall, the new Deputy Chief of Staff, gave unstinted support to Gen. Arnold.[9] And after the outbreak of the war in Europe, of course, the attitude of the War Department changed radically. But the cost of our delay was heavy, as we discovered when war came in the Pacific. The United States had less than fifty heavy bombers at its strategic insular outposts. The ones which were not destroyed on the ground fought superbly against overwhelming odds and showed the excellence of their design and construction. But quality was not an adequate substitute for the deficiency in quantity to which our previous hesitations in policy had exposed us.

But it was not merely in a deficiency of planes actually produced that we paid for these hesitations. In the late fall of 1940, about six months after President Roosevelt had ordered the production of fifty thousand planes annually, Robert A. Lovett, a New York banker, called on me. Mr. Lovett had been a naval flier in the last war and had retained a keen interest in air power. He had recently returned, he told me, from an inspection of our aircraft industry. Mr. Lovett's conclusions were ominous, and I asked that he put them in writing. Among other deficiencies, he had found "that the airplane manufacturers do not yet realize the size of their problem." They had "prejudices against mass-production because of their education along one line—custom built jobs."[10]

"This is a quantitative war," Mr. Lovett wrote. "The airplane industry has, so far, been qualitative."[11]

But this could be changed. A greater degree of standardization in models was possible. Many important parts, such as tail assembly units, outer wing sections, and engine beds, could be subcontracted. New plants could be separated geographically so that they would not, to the existing degree, bid against each other for labor. The automotive industry could be brought into the picture.[12]

Mr. Lovett also felt that some of the planes being produced were not suitable for war conditions. Landing gears were too light. Armament should be heavier; not enough fire power had been provided. Certain models, he wrote, "seem to have achieved a positive triumph of gadgets on the instrument panels." With respect to engines, the emphasis on the air-cooled types had been at the expense of liquid-cooled engines of sufficient power. Mr. Lovett pointed out that the United States had no airplane power plant which could compare with the German B.M.W. (Bayerische Motor Werke) 1,500-horsepower engine.

Mr. Lovett's foresight was publicly demonstrated two years later. Considerable criticism of American fighting aircraft was being voiced. Our fighters, it was said, were not equal to the Japanese Zero. Our B-17s were reported to be ill-adapted to their task in Europe. Because of this criticism, the Office of War Information (OWI) in October 1942 published an independent and objective report on the design and operation of our combat aircraft. The OWI declared most of our planes were excellent, but its criticisms paralleled those voiced almost two years earlier by Mr. Lovett. The report said:

> Some American warplanes are badly designed or ill-matched against the equipment of the enemy. Some planes now in action have definite deficiencies, ever within the purpose for which they were designed. . . . The country paid in blood and defeat for the determined blindness of its peaceful years. Even our bomber, performing superbly in retreat, could have done better if the past had given them a chance.[13]

The OWI also took note of the air- versus liquid-cooled engine controversy. The air-cooled type had been used by the commercial airlines and developed to a high state of efficiency, but it offered greater wind resistance. The liquid-cooled engine, streamlined and sleek, was a vital necessity for fighter and pursuit craft. Even by October 1942, the Allison, then the only type we had in mass production, had not caught up with British and German liquid-cooled engines.

This was one of our worst production problems in 1940, and for a time it endangered our whole fighter schedule. We had planes enough, but the Allisons were not coming off the line in sufficient numbers to power them. They were being manufactured by the General Motors Corporation, and I might cite this as an example of why, in the early months of the war, we had no choice except to turn to the nation's great industries. Had a concern weak in engineering or finances been in charge, it would certainly have gone to the wall. But General Motors sent its top-flight production men to the Allison plant, and in due course they eliminated the trouble. Later, we had the British liquid-cooled engine, the Merlin-Rolls Royce, which was manufactured in large quantities by the Packard Motor Company.

But to return to Mr. Lovett and his remarkable insight into aircraft mass-production problems which he manifested in the closing months of 1940. Like many other patriotic Americans, he paid for his foresight in calling attention to the deficiencies in our aircraft industry. He left private life and became, first, a special assistant to the Secretary of War and later Assistant Secretary of War for Air. His contribution was outstanding.[14] The Air Corps was not, in the fall of 1940, a well-integrated and smoothly functioning organization.[15] It was composed of young men brimming with enthusiasm. It had its share of zealots who believed that air power, alone and unaided, could win any possible war. Secretary Lovett contributed business management to talent and initiative. His guidance played a decisive part in making possible the overwhelming manifestation of superiority in the air whose share in our victory General Eisenhower so well described.

It was a tremendous task to take what was still in many ways an infant industry, and which was certainly one whose thinking and methods had never contemplated production on the scale now required, and build it up to the point where it could provide us the overwhelming strength in the air which our new strategy demanded.

New factory space, many times larger than that already in existence, had to be created. Scores of thousands of workers, who knew nothing of the structure of an airplane, had to be trained to their new tasks. It soon became evident that, if we were to reach our goals in time, we would have to enlist in aircraft production firms already established in other lines of manufacturing. The automotive industry contributed an essential part of total production. But we learned, after five years of all-out endeavor, that it takes from one to two years to bring auxiliary sources of production into the picture. Nine-tenths of the airplane bodies used in the war were produced by the already established aircraft industry, although largely in newly built factories.

It is again well to remember that our Allies held off the enemy for two years while we belatedly got ready, for we needed that long to build up our production of airplane engines. All of the engines used up to V-E Day in Europe and up to V-J Day in Japan were designed before 1941. Of course, improvements were made. Horsepower was increased in relation to size and weight, and various advances in details were incorporated in our latest models. But the Wright 3350, which propelled the B-29, the Pratt and Whitney 2200-C, which drove the P-47 fighter, and the Wright 1820 cubic inch, with which B-17s were equipped, were the result of designs which were inaugurated before we were at war.

The single greatest obstacle to the mass production of airplanes, after the revolution in thinking which it required, was the shortage of machine tools. I recall that General Knudsen, soon after coming to Washington, called on the President with tentative plans for expansion of the industry. Mr. Roosevelt asked him to estimate how many aircraft this great industrial country could produce. "As many as you want," said General Knudsen, "but it will take time." General Knudsen's boundless faith did not blind him to the difficulties. Machine tools were needed for nearly every war-manufacturing process. It became apparent in the fall of 1940 that a bottleneck would develop. By next summer, aircraft companies, ordnance concerns, government arsenals, and the Navy all were clamoring for tools. Furthermore, the demand for machine tools on the part of our Allies became formidable in its proportions.

The machine-tool industry, upon which this burden fell, is a peculiar one. It is composed of a number of quite small firms which ordinarily do nothing but make these tools. These firms employ a group of highly skilled workers, for the art of building machine tools is a difficult one. In normal times the demand for machine tools is sharply seasonal and the companies which manufacture them have to plan carefully in order to carry through slack periods the skilled workers their methods require. Hence, when the emergency came and haphazard orders were given to this limited number of manufacturers, they hesitated to expand at their own expense lest they be bankrupted by excess capacity in the postwar period. Delays were also caused by a reluctance to supply tools to manufacturers with uncertain credit rating. Since our munitions expansion inevitably brought into the field new firms whose credit reliability could only be guessed at, the difficulty caused by this hesitancy were considerable. During all the early months of our munitions expansion, this problem of machine tools dogged us, and it was evident in most other branches of production as well as in the aircraft industry. Strenuous endeavors were made to locate and put to work existing machine tools. Although this effort was attended with some success, it was impeded by the tendency of the owners of such tools to hoard them against the possibility of enlarged orders for their own plants. Not until early in 1942 did we devise a satisfactory solution to the machine-tool problem. At that time the government removed the hesitation of machine-tool manufacturers by underwriting maximum production on their part, thus making it possible for them to go ahead safely without waiting for orders from individual customers. A pool of machine tools was then established upon which any approved manufacturer could draw. This plan solved the machine-tool problem. The lesson should not be forgotten in any future emergency.

In spite of these and many other difficulties, and in spite of the fact that we started almost from scratch, in less than five years the United States spent $3.8 billion for aircraft plant and equipment and approximately doubled the rate of production which President Roosevelt had called for in 1940. When we remember the increased size of the planes produced in the later stages of the war, the record is even more remarkable. Order gradually emerged from the original confusion, although separate procurement by the Army and the Navy always hindered maximum production. But progress was made in overcoming this difficulty as well as the many others.

At first, manufacturers bid against each other for materials which were rapidly getting in short supply. In April 1941 the Joint Aircraft Committee was created.[16] The Army Air Forces (AAF), the Navy Bureau of Aeronautics, the Office of Production Management (later the War Production Board), and the British Air Commission were represented on it. At the same time, an Air Scheduling Unit (ASU) was established as a contact point between government war production agencies and the aviation industry.[17]

The assignment of ASU was to utilize all forms of industry to the utmost degree. A main part of its work was that of making certain that materials flowed smoothly to all plants. When a surplus of aluminum, for example, was discovered in one factory, it was transferred to another. Strategically located warehouses were stocked with supplies upon which manufacturers could call.

No form of warfare changes more rapidly than war in the air. That axiom applies not only to strategy and tactics but to the equipment employed. For instance, during the period in which the B-17 was our dominant heavy bomber, some fifteen hundred changes were made in the ship. And this was more or less typical, for some defect brought out by the rigors of campaigning, or some enemy improvement which it was necessary to match, brought incessant demands for the improvement of all types of materiel.

This presented a serious dilemma for those managing production. We could not afford to fight with inferior equipment, but every modification of designs already in production involved serious delay. So closely coordinated are all the processes of assembly-line production that, if it is decided to modify the turret on a bomber, the whole production process is held up until the modification has been accomplished. Hence the cry of those who used the planes in the field, for the very latest improvement was matched by a demand from the production people that they be let alone, lest their productions schedules be wrecked. It was difficult to know, in many instances, whether the introduction of some improvement in an item of equipment would compensate for reduced quantities of that item in the near future. Agreement was the more difficult because those in the field knew little of the problems of production, and because those in production were remote from the necessities of the soldier under fire.

Eventually a scheme was worked out which did as much as anything could to solve this dilemma. This was the creation of modification centers.[18] When it was decided that some improvement was necessary in an item already under production, instead of halting production while the necessary new tools and methods were inserted into the production set-up, production of the item as originally planned was continued. Then, after completion in accordance with the original design, the newly finished item was sent to a special plant where the particular detail that had become obsolete was removed and one of the latest pattern installed in its place. Thus the only expenditure of time and labor was that involved in making the actual modification. On the other hand, if the modification had been introduced into the original assembly-line process, all phases of the work subsequent to the point at which the modification was being introduced would have been held up because no work was coming through, and all phases prior to it would have been blocked, because work already completed could not be moved ahead and out of the way.

Although it will carry us beyond the pioneer phase of our war production program, to which we have confined ourselves so far, it may add clarity to our account of airplane production if at this time we take up some of its later problems. By the end of 1943, the Flying Fortress was technically obsolete, although it still scourged the Reich and the Luftwaffe. No further B-17s were ordered. More than a year before, a bomber with greatly increased range had been tested. This was the huge, super-secret B-29, which would carry the war to the Japanese mainland. An experimental model, the XB-29, was ready in September 1942 and was flown successfully. But following flights were accompanied by engine failure, fires, and other hazards. The XB-29 ended in tragedy, as had the first B-17 in 1935. It crashed, killing the test pilot and all the members of the crew. To suggestions that the project be abandoned, however, Assistant Secretary Lovett, General Arnold, and their staffs turned deaf ears.

Work on the bomber which was to become the B-29 had been begun in 1939. Even earlier, in 1937, Air Corps technicians had developed a pressurized cabin which would make it possible for the new ship to fly at unprecedented altitudes. The plane, it was specified, must attain speed in excess of 380 miles an hour at thirty-five thousand feet or higher, fly thirty-six hundred miles to a target, and then get back home. In June 1940 the Boeing Aircraft Company and the Lockheed Aircraft Corporation received contracts to build wind-tunnel models. But Lockheed decided to concentrate on fighters, and in August Boeing was authorized to begin work on two XB-29s. The cost would be somewhat more than $3.5 million.

Many problems arose to plague the engineers. That fall it was decided that the plane was too heavy for its wing area. Engines were not ready. Fire-control apparatus had to be developed. Many changes in design were necessary. But long before the first B-29 was completed, the AAF had authorized the construction of factories and other facilities. Secretary Lovett and General Arnold toured the country urging hesitant contractors to assume portions of the work. Crews were given preliminary training before planes were more than blueprints. Landing fields and runways were inadequate for so large a plane, but the Curtiss-Wright Corporation developed reversible-pitch propellers which enabled the B-29 to shorten its landing run by a considerable fraction.

On a test flight to England, the windows of the plane fogged so dangerously that new defrosting devices had to be installed. The first production B-29, as distinguished from the virtually hand-made preliminary models, flew in June 1943. The first to reach Karachi, India,[19] landed on April 2, 1944. Meanwhile there had been rigid tests at the Proving Ground Command, Eglin Field, Florida. It was found that the B-29 could fly from Eglin to the Bay of Fundy and return, roughly the distance from a base in India to Yawata, Japan. On June 5, 1944, Bangkok was raided. Ten days later came the raid on Yawata.[20]

It was all very dramatic. Again, it looked as though American daring and ingenuity had quickly solved another war problem. Actually, almost five years had elapsed between the inception of the idea and the dropping of bombs on Japan. Tens of thousands of designs and blueprints had been made. The AAF poured millions into new plants. The Boeing Company used over $50 million worth of government-owned plants. The Bell Aircraft Corporation produced B-29s in a $57 million plant. These sums do not include other millions spent for manufacturing major components of the plane. The Omaha plant of the Glenn L. Martin Company was switched from making B-26s to B-29s. Its cost was $22 million.

With the capture of island bases in the Pacific, the effectiveness of B-29 bombardments increased. Saipan was only seven hours and twenty minutes from Tokyo by air. Okinawa was only five hours and fifteen minutes distant.

"The combat efficiency of the B-29's was such," General Arnold has written, "that we were able to reduce Japan more economically than Germany."

It now appears certain that Japan would have been defeated without the atomic bomb, although at greater cost and not as quickly. Premier Prince Naruhiko Hagashi-Kuni has testified that by June 1945, following the B-29 incendiary attacks, the nation's capacity to continue modern warfare had been "disastrously undermined."[21]

At that time 854 of the huge ships were operating against Japan. By March 1946, had the war continued, the number would have increased to 2,000. Meanwhile, however, Project SILVERPLATE was underway at Wright Field. About six officers were in charge of the modification of the B-29's bomb bays so that it could carry and drop the atomic bomb.[22] The Martin B-29 plant at Omaha received a contract for making the necessary changes in forty-five airplanes. Not that many were needed.

The B-29 was approaching obsolescence, too. Far back in April 1941, the Douglas, Consolidated, and Boeing companies had been asked to submit designs for a multi-engine bomber which could fly 450 miles an hour and travel 12,000 miles with a bomb load of 4,000 pounds. This enterprise resulted in a contract with Consolidated for three B-36s. Again changes in design were found necessary. The experts had difficulty with engines and with excessive weight. Initial flights scheduled for June 1944 were postponed until September, then to December, then to June 1945. But success has at last attended this immense effort. The B-36, it is estimated, can fly 10,000 miles with 10,000 pounds of bombs; 4,000 miles with 71,000 pounds. Both loads are exclusive of fuel.

Tom Girdler of the Consolidated Company came to see me in the fall of 1943. He asked me if the war would last two more years. I said that I did not know, but we had to make our plans on the basis that it would last longer than two years. He then asked me if a saving on the deliveries of B-36s might help win the war. I thought that it might.

"Very well," he said, "give Consolidated an order for 100, and we will make deliveries nine months earlier. On this order for three that we have, I can't get subcontractors interested in making quick delivery of parts. But an order for 103 will stir them up. Don't do it, though, if you are sure the war will be finished within two years."

I gave the order for one hundred more B-36s.[23]

Equal, or worse, problems were faced in the production of fighters. This was particularly true when expanding operations forced us to look for a long-range escort fighter. At a meeting of the Combined Chiefs of Staff in March 1942, consideration was given to a message from Prime Minister Churchill asking for a force of one hundred bombers at the earliest possible moment for joint British-American attacks on Germany. This reinforced General Marshall's belief in the need for a heavy bomber offensive. The first units of the Eighth Air Force were already in England. But how pitifully small the Eighth then was is shown by the fact that four months later the United States had a mere 423 planes of all kinds based on England. On August 17, 1942, a total of 12 Flying Fortresses attacked the marshaling yards at Rouen. Much of our meager strength had, of course, been diverted against Rommel in the Mediterranean theater.

Medium and heavy bombers could make raids on occupied France, escorted by British and American fighters of limited range. But the raids which came later were of a different kind. They went far beyond the range of existing fighter escorts and, deep in the heart of

Germany, struck at the enemy's communications, his oil, and other war industries. I have always believed, in fact, that it was inaccurate to describe these attacks as raids: they were invasions. Thousands of aircraft and tens of thousands of men were involved. The Casablanca Conference approved the augmented onslaughts in January 1943. Their objective, it was decided, was "the destruction and dislocation of the German military, industrial and economic system and the undermining of the morale of the German people to the point where their capacity for armed resistance is fatally weakened."[24] We were to hear those words again and again.

But German morale was far from cracking as yet. Her fighter production rose from 512 in January 1943 to 1,243 in July, and bomber production from 674 in January to 743 in July. In May 1943, the Combined Chiefs of Staff approved the Eighth Air Force plan for heavier attacks on German communications and war industry. The first target was the aircraft factories. Some success was achieved. Fighter production dropped somewhat. On October 14, 1943, however, the Eighth Air Force learned that the Luftwaffe was still very strong indeed. One of many strikes on the ball-bearing industry, essential to the building of aircraft and many other war weapons, took place on that date. The target on this black day in the history of the Eighth Air Force was Schweinfurt in Western Bavaria. A force of 228 heavy bombers started. From the German frontier, because of the short range of our fighters, they flew unescorted to the target. The Luftwaffe was out in force. Flak was extremely heavy. The Eighth lost 62 bombers, with 138 more damaged. More serious, 599 airmen were lost, and 40 more came back wounded. The ball-bearing works were damaged, but the heavy losses caused postponement of another attack for four months. The Germans, with their amazing recuperative powers, had time to repair their plants.[25]

Such losses could not be allowed to continue. Both the AAF and the War Department realized that daylight bombing might have to be abandoned. Unescorted aerial invasions were too expensive. So, if they were not to be given up, fighter ranges would have to be increased. A project with this as its goal was already underway—the P-75 fighter plane. In September 1942, a year before the-ill-fated

Schweinfurt raid, the General Motors Corporation proposed the construction of a pursuit plane which could fly to any target in the Reich. But the P-75 proved to be one of those hoodoos which harass the leaders of every war. Delays in designing the new ship brought up the possible necessity of abandoning it. However, the Eighth Air Force bomber losses made long-range fighter escort essential. In July 1943, the building of twenty-five hundred planes at a cost of about $325 million was approved by the War Department. This was later reduced by $75 million, but by that time the delivery of the first production P-75 had been delayed until June 1945. All this was the result of deficiencies in experimental models. Of the twenty-five hundred P-75s ordered, only five were delivered, and two of these were destroyed in accidents. The whole experiment with this model wound up in failure, at a cost of perhaps $75 million.[26]

Yet even before the final failure of the P-75, it became evident that the AAF could not wait. The daylight attacks had to go on unless the high strategy of the war was to be changed. General Arnold therefore ordered the Air Technical Service Command at Wright Field, Dayton, Ohio, to increase fourfold the range of fighters already in use. At first sight this demand seemed fantastic. The P-47 could normally fly out only 150 miles and still have a chance of getting back. But by equipping this fighter with supplementary gas tanks, dropped on the return trip, the combat range had already been increased to 300 miles. What General Arnold ordered was a pursuit plane which could fly from England to Berlin, consume additional fuel in a dog fight if necessary, and return to base.

Thunderbolts, Mustangs, and Lightnings are small, compact ships jammed to capacity with ammunition, machine guns, radio equipment, and oxygen tanks. If the range was to be increased, still more oxygen would have to be carried. Yet sixty-five additional gallons of gasoline were squeezed into the wings of the P-47, which gave it a combat radius of 625 miles. The P-51 was modified by installing a tank behind the pilot's seat in the place of some radio equipment. The P-51 could now fly a total of 1,500 miles in addition to whatever fighting might be necessary en route to or over the target. These changes were rushed at modifications centers.

Under pressure from the AAF, aircraft manufacturers also made alterations. A later model of the P-38 had a combat radius of 850 miles after Lockheed had concentrated on the problem. Republic increased the radius of the latest P-47 to 1,000 miles. After February 1944, fighters accompanied bomber forces to targets everywhere in Germany. The greater range also brought about a change in tactics. Hitherto, fighters, if they had not dropped out of the mission, were charged only with defending the bombers. Now a primary duty was to pursue enemy aircraft and knock them out of the skies. The new tactics were demonstrated during the week of February 20–25, 1944. Almost seven hundred German planes were shot down. Four thousand tons of bombs were dropped on aircraft plants. Sometimes industrialists and engineers in the continental United States, indeed the belittled "chairborne" officers of the Pentagon and other War Department centers, were closer to the battle than it then appeared.

Building airplanes was one thing. Transporting them to the fighting fronts was another. Knocking down, crating, shipping, and then reassembling an airplane is a long and expensive business. But fighters, even with their increased ranges, could not follow the air lanes of the bombers and proceed under their own power. Shipping was short when our need for reinforcements was greatest. The problem was partially solved by building special superstructures on oil tankers. By the end of the war, 535 tankers had thus been altered and had carried nineteen thousand airplanes overseas. Other planes were delivered by aircraft carrier and even by Liberty ship.

Our greatest asset in the delivery of fighters was the base on Ascension Island, a volcanic spot of land in the middle of the South Atlantic. Before the war it had been inhabited only by a few employees of a British cable company. British engineers said it was impossible to build an airfield on its volcanic ash and steer hills. Yet a one-mile runway was constructed by the summer of 1942 so that pursuit craft could fly from Natal in Brazil, to Dakar, and then north to the battle lines. Wide-awake Field on Ascension Island also served as a refueling point for bombers and transport ships. At its peak use, an average of 27 planes a day landed there. In 1944, 10,000 planes were serviced with 12 million gallons of gasoline. We got the planes across. By the termination of hostilities, 94,180 combat and cargo planes had been flown or shipped overseas. Had all been sent by boat, together with fuel and other AAF materiel, 780 million cubic feet of shipping space would have been required. This does not include aircraft or materiel purchased by our Allies or supplied to them through Lend-Lease.

The importance of the system developed for moving airplanes overseas under their own power becomes even more evident when one thinks, for a moment, of the vast expenditure involved in packaging those war supplies that had to be shipped by boat. The public has little concept of the magnitude of the effort necessary to crate the instruments of modern war—which are at the same time huge and delicate—so that they can safely withstand handling, climate, and the other hazards of transport. At the height of the conflict, we spent $5 billion annually for packaging alone! When one considers that aircraft are both among the bulkiest and the most delicate of all forms of military equipment, the saving we secured by direct transport becomes more evident.

Mention has been made before of the rapidity with which types of aircraft change under conditions of modern war. Upon occasion the Army was not sufficiently alert in adopting new types and putting them into production. A simple case of this was the small, unarmed plane for liaison and observation. Crude types had been flown in World War I. In the interim, however, they were regarded as pleasure craft by military fliers. The prewar maneuvers of our growing army quickly demonstrated the fallacy of such thinking. Ground-air liaison was essential to the effective movement of large numbers of troops.

But disagreement on the type of observation plane best suited to this task set back production. I recall vividly that the Vultee Company began building a huge plane which looked like a sea gull. AAF officers told me that the Ground Forces had endorsed it. One virtue of the new ship was that it could land on restricted runways. It seemed to me, however, that lack of time forbade experimentation, and I suggested that small planes of the cub type should be used. Work on the larger plane was halted.

Soon the demands for these small planes were swamping us. In January 1942, four thousand planes were needed. The Civil Air Patrol, gallantly flying 600,000 miles a week in search of submarines, required more small planes. So did the underground forces in the occupied countries. Enough were finally available, but not on time. They took the place of the venerable and extremely vulnerable observation balloons. They were used by divisional, army, and corps commanders to watch the battle's progress. They could land almost anywhere. They rescued wounded from jungles and other inaccessible places.

The subject of extremely high-speed jet-propelled fighters is a much more complicated one. Criticism was frequently voiced by our pilots and crews because the United States did not get a jet-engined ship to the front in time for combat. Those who felt this way have a case, but they do not take into full account the problem of the AAF. The plan to wreck German industry, communications, and morale required bombers, which had to be protected by long-range fighters. Jet-propulsion did not permit a fighter to stay in the air long enough, at its excessive speed, for our strategic and tactical necessities. Germany, on the other hand, was defending her homeland. Jet-propelled fighters were perfectly suited for sudden forays against a bombing mission. The German ME-262 was in production in April 1944. It was, General Arnold reports, "Germany's great hope and, we must state frankly, the greatest threat to our bomber operations."[27] I am free to confess that the danger that this new weapon might threaten our control of the skies over Germany was our most serious worry in the closing weeks of the war in Europe.[28]

That it did not play a more important part is to be attributed largely to the fact that German strategy did not take into consideration the possible influence of this new plane upon operations. When Hitler made his stand in Normandy, and lost a large part of his army in doing so, he put matters to the touch in an area which could not be reached by the closely based ME-262s. Then, when in February and March 1945 Hitler chose to stand west of the Rhine, he gave up much of the advantage which his jet-propelled planes might have given him had he withdrawn his army and made his last major effort east of the Rhine. Had the major fighting been within the area of the most effective operation of the German jet-planes, our difficulties would have been serious, for our best fighters were no match for them. We were also beneficiaries of what General Arnold brands as Hitler's amazing decision to use the plane for bombing. He was told that it would carry a one-thousand-kilogram bomb, which it never could. The ME-262 accomplished nothing as a bomber. The few which attacked our air forces had been exempted from the bombing conception.

Tardy development of jet-propelled fighters in the United States was another of those calculated risks which must be taken in war procurement as well as in battle. We shipped two XBP jet-propelled fighters to England in 1944, but further testing seemed necessary. After V-E Day, strenuous efforts were made to get P-80s to the Pacific. Insufficient stocks of kerosene, which must be used for fuel, and lack of spare parts in the theater kept them out of the fighting.

Progress since the end of hostilities has brought us well up with the rest of the world in jet-propelled craft, and our present planes are far ahead of the German M-262. Doubtless nothing we have seen so far, however, compares with the jet propulsion of the future. Only unremitting vigilance, which means unceasing research by the Army, the Navy, the aircraft industry, and the universities of the nation, will keep us abreast of jet developments. Only if this is done, and if we are willing to spend freely on costly wind tunnels and the other equipment of scientific research, will the United States be even reasonably safe from attack by tomorrow's aircraft.

But it was not only in the building of combat aircraft that we met, and for the most part overcame, formidable problems of design and production. Not enough credit has been given to the achievement in airborne supply of personnel and materiel. We built 22,816 transport aircraft. The size of the airlines operated by the Air Transport Command and by the numerous service commands in the theaters may be realized when it is recalled that all of the commercial airlines in the United States owned only 358 ships in 1941. Every phase of the war, all over the world, would have been prolonged had it not been for these cargo craft and for the young men, denied the glory of combat, who flew them across every ocean and over other routes far more dangerous.[29] They had to fly in all kinds of weather, in ships which were heavily overloaded according to commercial standards. The casualties were many. In the India-Burma theater, airplane crashes accounted for more than half of all American deaths. Several hundred bodies still remain in the jungles of Assam and Northern Burma where they crashed on the route over the Hump to China. They are truly among the heroic "missing in action."

The Army Transport Command—or ATC—was our largest air-supply organization. First called the Air Ferry Command, it flew 6,937,300,000 passenger miles between July 1, 1942, and August 31, 1945. It carried 2,369,400,000 ton miles of cargo. But these staggering figures should not obscure the equally important work of the troop and service commands. They made possible the swift pace of modern war. They insured the success of the advance across France. Their "flying box-cars" also brought victory in Germany. During April 1945 alone, 1,500 IX Troop Carrier Command C-47s, assisted by heavy bombers altered for cargo, flew over 80,000 sorties. They delivered 60,000 tons of freight, including over 10 million gallons of gasoline, to the front. They landed on hastily built airfields, sometimes in pockets temporarily surrounded by the enemy. Outward cargo flights from France in the morning would return in the evening with thousands of wounded and liberated Allied prisoners.

Many other achievements stand to the credit of non-combat aircraft. They dropped agents of the Office of Strategic Services and armed services intelligence officers into occupied France, where they helped to organize the Free French resistance forces. Bulky C-47s made astonishing landings at night on short runways, without benefit of lights or radio, to bring out other agents. Food, ammunition, radio equipment, and other supplies were delivered by parachute to the underground in France and to Marshal Tito's forces across the Adriatic in Yugoslavia. Propaganda leaflets and newspapers were distributed. These planes brought out of Yugoslavia hundreds of American fliers who had been shot down in the Balkans and taken care of by guerillas.

Without the flying boxcars, China could not have remained in the war. The President, the Prime Minister, and the Combined Chiefs of Staff realized from the outset that the collapse of China might prolong the war by years. At the first anxious meetings in Washington in December 1941 and January 1942, it was realized that Chinese morale was dropping fast. The Burma Road, the only supply line to the Chinese armies from the Allies, was still open. But it was under constant Japanese air attack. Brigadier General (now Major General retired) Chennault's valiant Flying Tigers—the American volunteer group—had been shooting down Japanese planes for more than six months.[30] The struggle, however, was uneven. The supplies that reached China were only a trickle.

By the time of the Casablanca conference a year later, the Burma Road was closed. The President pointed out that even a small effort to help China would have important political results in that country. From 200 to 250 planes should be sent at the earliest opportunity. Five months passed. Mr. Churchill returned to Washington in May 1943, and the President reiterated his belief that aid to China must be sent immediately. It was not enough merely to tell that troubled nation that supplies would be given. Affirmative action must be taken, he said. The Prime Minister agreed but was pessimistic. The Burma Road could not be reopened until 1945, he thought. He did not believe that more than 20,000 tons a month could be carried over it. At the same conference, General Stillwell estimated that about 10,000 tons a month could be flown into China, although 3,700 tons was the record thus far. President Roosevelt said that he had never admitted that the ultimate figure would be as low as 10,000 tons.

The optimism of the President was justified. By the end of 1943, the lift over the towering Himalayas had been increased to nearly 10,000 tons a month.[31] When the Combined Chiefs of Staff met at Potsdam in July 1945, they were gratified to hear that 100,000 tons a month were being flown into China or moved by the reopened Burma Road. Fifteen Chinese divisions, trained by American officers and equipped with American arms, would be ready for combat by August.

The skill and courage of the airplane personnel who did this job merit the highest praise, but it is necessary to remember that their success could not have been attained had we not first accomplished a prodigious feat of airplane production, and of the production of the high-test gasoline and all the other auxiliaries of airplane equipment and operation. I do not want to belabor the point, but it is obvious that we could have helped China more swiftly and effectively—just as we could have helped the Soviet Union—if we had possessed in 1940 or 1941 a fraction of the production potential we enjoyed in 1944. In the first quarter of 1943, we were producing more than ten times as many airplanes, by weight, as in the first quarter of 1941. In the second quarter of 1944, we were producing twenty-five times as many. We actually had a surplus of airplanes, and we cut production back slightly. General Knudsen's forecast that we could make any quantity needed had been made good.

A word at this time about the future of our aircraft production may not be out of place. However great the expansion of commercial flying, no chance exists that so vast an aircraft plant can he kept in operation during peace. There is no need for it. How much of it, then, should be operated or kept on a stand-by basis so that, if war comes again, we shall be ready? Long before the end of the war, studies were begun so that Congress would have some data on which to base an answer to this all-important question. A subcommittee on Demobilization of the Aircraft Industry was created by an Air Coordinating Committee on which were representatives of the Army and Navy, the State and Commerce Departments, and the Civil Aeronautics Authority. The subcommittee made its report on October 22, 1945. Its recommendations were:

- That peacetime research and development of air weapons must not stop with experimental versions but must be thoroughly engineered and tested.
- That the minimum procurement must be three thousand military aircraft a year, with an airframe weight of at least 30 million pounds.
- That in order to insure the production of these planes, government-owned plants should be made available to the aircraft industry on favorable terms.

- That some of the existing plants, dangerously congested on both coasts, should be dispersed.
- That a reserve plant capacity of 26 million square feet should be maintained.
- That the armed services should maintain a reserve of 65,000 general-purpose tools.

"Everyone," the subcommittee stated, "is familiar with the peacetime maneuvers in which ground, sea and air units engage in simulated combat missions to maintain proficiency in organization, command, and tactical deployment. The type of preparedness for industrial expansion which we are recommending is the counterpart of these maneuvers and the purpose is essentially the same. It seems to us that because of the heavy reliance of the services on American industry, industrial maneuvers are just as essential as the familiar air, sea and ground application of tactics to typical calculations."[32]

The annual cost would be about $15 million. I am in wholehearted agreement with the excellent recommendations of the subcommittee on Demobilization of the Aircraft Industry. I agree just as heartily with the view of General Arnold expressed just after V-J-Day.

"Projecting our thoughts into the future results in sobering thoughts of the potentialities of air power in the light of the atomic bomb, radar, rockets, jet propulsion and unlimited other future developments," said the Commanding General of the AAF. "Article 45 of the World Charter places tremendous responsibilities on the Air Force for preventing future wars. This responsibility must be understood and supported by all Americans if the AAF is to perform its true role as the spearhead of American security. Next time, our American potential may be destroyed without giving us time to arm and take the offensive, unless we are adequately prepared. It is easy to lose the peace after the war has been won."

But, in order to treat the problem of airplane development in a single chapter, we have got ahead of the rest of our story. We must return, now, to the problems of industrial mobilization in the months before Pearl Harbor, months in which we were gathering speed but as yet were far from hitting on all cylinders.

Chapter 4

A Changing Nation

On New Year's Eve 1940, the rasping voice of Hitler proclaimed his certainty that 1941 would "bring consummation of the greatest victory in our history." At first sight his boast seemed justified. France had fallen; Great Britain, although uninvaded, was rocking under bombardment from the air; and few suspected that any power in Europe could halt the seemingly invincible German army. One of the very few rays of hope in that dark situation was the fact that the United States was beginning, although as yet on a small scale, to produce munitions.

But, if we were to have a thoroughly adequate munitions program, we had to know when, where, and against whom we might be forced to fight. Those questions could not be answered at the moment. The majority of our people still wished to remain neutral. And, in fact, we were still far from ready for war. About the only thing that could be decided at once in our munitions program was the fact that, in the war then being fought in Europe and in our military effort should we be forced into war, air power would play the decisive role. But the other aspects of our munitions objective, barring further clarification of political and military requirements, necessarily remained rather obscure. Even the enunciation of the concept of the "Arsenal of Democracy" did not determine automatically with what the arsenal should be filled. Something had to be done to give us a detailed picture of what might be required.

As a preliminary step in mapping our possible objectives, Maj. Gen. James E. Chaney and a group of sixteen American officers conferred with the British in London shortly before the end of 1940. The General and his staff had gone abroad in civilian clothes. The

President had instructed that they be called a "Special Observers' group."[1] Strict secrecy, they were told, would be maintained with regard to all functions except those of special observer. Later, if we entered the war, General Chaney and his fellow officers would be members of a military mission.

The first task of General Chaney and his colleagues was to appraise Britain's chances of survival in the critical months just ahead. If England was going to fall, it would be folly to send vast quantities of Lend-Lease supplies to the British Isles. On December 15, 1940, General Chaney reported that in his judgment an invasion would fail, that Great Britain would stand. This judgment was essential to our later plans.

From January 29 to March 27, 1941, a delegation of British Army and Navy officers worked together with us on what was called Plan ABC-1, which established a detailed pattern for offensive and defensive global war.[2] It must be clearly kept in mind, however, that these discussions in no way committed us to enter the war, or to go beyond what the nation at that time was willing to sanction. But the possibility that we might be forced into the war was so obvious that it would have been folly not to make contingent plans. And, in view of the circumstances of the war, it was impossible to make plans without discussing contingencies with the military and naval authorities of those nations to whom, if we entered the war, we would be allied. It was fully understood by the British, as well as by our representatives, that these discussions did not constitute a political commitment.

The agreement worked out provided that, if the contingency upon which the plan was based should become reality, the United States and the United Kingdom would call themselves the "Associated Powers" and would "collaborate continuously in the formulation and execution of strategical policies and plans which shall govern the conduct of the war...." The American and British leaders assumed "that when the United States becomes involved in war with Germany, it will at the same time engage in war with Italy. In these circumstances, the possibility of a state of war arising between Japan and an Association of the United States, the British Common Wealth and its Allies, including the Netherlands East Indies, must be taken into account."

ABC-1 further called for protection of American interests in the Western Hemisphere for the safeguarding of British possessions, including India, of the British Commonwealth of Nations. It was agreed that Germany was the "predominant member of the Axis powers" and that the "Atlantic and European area is to be considered the decisive theater."

"United States Army air bombardment units," the plan stated, "will operate offensively in collaboration with the Royal Air Force primarily against German military power at its sources."[3]

Of course, had our future enemies gained knowledge of ABC-1, they might have anticipated developments by starting war against us at once. That would have been awkward, for we were far from ready. But the need for this planning was so essential, if our military and munitions plans were to have coherence, that we had to take the risk. Without it, we would have had to build up our war plant without knowing which things came first. Fortunately, the secret was well kept.[4]

Then came Pearl Harbor. The Prime Minister of Great Britain hurried to the United States with his military, naval, air, and production advisers for conferences with the President and the American Joint Chiefs of Staff. They confirmed the basic assumptions of ABC-1. The defeat of Germany was given precedence over everything else. The Japanese attack had not changed this basic principle. Once Germany was out of the war, Italy would collapse and Japan would be defeated. The following program, it was concluded, would lead to victory:

- Protect centers of American war industry, and so achieve the armament program.
- Maintain essential supply and communication lines.
- Close the ring around Germany.
- Wear down and undermine German resistance by air bombardment, subversive activities, and propaganda.
- Continually develop offensive activity against Germany.

- Maintain, for the present, a defensive position in the East to safeguard vital interests and deny Japan access to raw materials.

Thus we gained some idea of the gigantic size of our production job. We had, in fact, been moving toward a more precise formulation of our objective in the weeks before Pearl Harbor, during which we worked on the preliminary stages of what came to be known as the Victory Program.[5] But, of course, even those plans which seemed stupendous when first advanced had to be enlarged after Pearl Harbor.

Mr. J. A. Krug, now Secretary of the Interior, who was at the close of the war chairman of the War Production Board, has summarized very well some of the reasons why production planning during war is complicated and difficult:

> Even after a production record had been built up and some measure of the adaptability of American industry was available, it was a difficult enough task to estimate operational and pipeline needs in a war which was being fought on four continents and on all the oceans of the world—a war in which needs for cargo ships depended on the degree of success of the enemy's submarines and torpedo planes, needs for bombers were subject to the efficiency of enemy fighters and anti-aircraft, needs for radio tubes could be suddenly skyrocketed by a lucky German bomb hit on a British tube factory. And, of course, production plans were constantly being revised by changes in models, designs, and specifications growing out of inventions and the lessons of battle experience.[6]

But we could not wait for direct experience to give us answers to these problems, for we had to have our answers at least a year or two before the moment of experience, since it took that long to build factories and get into production. We had to make decisions, relying in large part upon the theoretical soundness of our experts, months and years in advance of the day when events would prove them right or wrong. An interesting example of this concerned the manufacture of wire for field communications, and it is scarcely too much to say that the liberation of France was partly due to plans approved in March 1942 for building a copper wire factory in St. Louis.

Despite all developments in radio, wire is still essential to army communications. No other method of sending messages is so safe from interception as by telephone and telegraph. Signal Corps and Engineer Corps technicians hit all the beaches with combat troops and immediately begin laying the vital network. When the war started, our production of field wire was about 42,600 miles a month, and nearly all of this was going to England and Russia. In February 1942 General Knudsen authorized the expansion of facilities to make possible 120,000 miles a month. This, it appeared, would be adequate. It was—until the final requisition of supplies for D-Day. In May 1944 General Eisenhower called for 270,000 miles of wire! It would not have been available had not the St. Louis plant been in operation. By that time this one factory was producing 50,000 miles a-month—more than the entire capacity of the industry during the first quarter of 1942. The cost of the factory, $5 million, was trivial in comparison with its ultimate importance. But this factory would not have been available to meet General Eisenhower's needs had not General Knudsen authorized it more than two years earlier.

Because this wire was produced, the American armies had superior communication systems everywhere and effective military operations depend to an enormous degree upon adequate communications. It is essential to the teamwork of all arms. The men of the Signal Corps, often under the heaviest fire, laid the necessary lines and brought up the equipment. On the larger islands of the Pacific, telephone systems as large as those in many American cities were swiftly installed. But they could not have been had not the immense need for wire and other communication equipment been seen and provided for far in advance.

If a discussion of the many achievements of our munitions program even before Pearl Harbor makes it sound as if we made such rapid progress as to be soon out of danger, I want to warn the reader against such a conclusion. Nothing could be further from the truth. During the period of conversion and new construction, the production of actual munitions was a meager stream compared to the flood which safety demanded. It took us over two and a half years to reach top production, but in the first half of that period, we produced only a quarter of the munitions we turned out in the second half. Production in the last quarter of the period equaled that of the first three quarters. And meanwhile, the German munitions industry was in full swing.

There is a very important law of modern war in all this. Assume that two nations have identical production potentialities. One begins two years before the other, however. It is a great mistake to suppose that the tardy nation begins to catch up as soon as it sets out to overtake its earlier starting rival. The truth is that for the first part of the tardy nation's effort to produce weaponry to repair its earlier carelessness, it continues to lose ground. At that time it is only building its factories, whereas its rival is producing at full speed from factories which have just been completed. When the backward country is halfway through its program, the gap between its production and that of its more alert enemy will be much greater than when the tardy party first became aware of its danger and began to do something about it.

Not until the last quarter of the tardy nation's period of industrial mobilization will it begin to overtake its more alert rival. Thus, a late start in a race of armament production means, not gradually increasing relative strength, but ever-increasing weakness in comparison with the enemy until toward the close of the period needed for industrial mobilization. Only after new facilities have been built can the laggard nation gain in relative strength on the field of battle and, even then, only if it can survive eighteen months of increasing relative weakness without disaster. Fortunately for us, the Japanese did not strike until the period of our greatest weakness—that in which we were building many factories but producing few finished weapons—was almost over.

In fact, when I look back across those crowded five years, it sometimes seems a miracle to me that we won the war. But for some policies adopted and actions taken long ago, we might not have won, for the nation was not awake to its danger as it ought to have been in 1937 and 1938 when, as we can now see, full-speed preparation ought to have begun. In the mood of the nation between wars, it would have been so easy for the War Department to neglect the industrial mobilization planning that was actually undertaken and which, even if imperfect, saved us many months of time which, even if imperfect, we could not afford to lose. Or we might have neglected the advances in our manufacture of arms in the year or two before the outbreak of war in Europe, advances which, although very modest in quantity, were influential in overcoming inertia and providing original momentum.

It was also very fortunate that we took steps, inadequate though they were, to build up reserves of critical materials. In April 1938 Senator Elbert Thomas of Utah introduced legislation which provided for the acquisition of stockpiles of critical materials over a period of four years. The War Department had already listed thirteen strategical—the most urgent category—and twenty-six critical materials. It was also making studies of the available supplies of scrap iron and steel, of rock phosphates and other supplies without which modern war cannot be fought. This work, in cooperation with the Navy, was under the supervision of the Army and Nary Munitions Board.[7]

Senator Thomas's bill did not pass the Congress.[8] But that summer our eyes started to open. Hitler had seized Austria and would soon move into Czechoslovakia. Our government began to realize that the United States had long been a victim of an undeclared economic war. Germany had been working through cartel agreements and by control of patents to weaken America's feeble military strength still more. American production of war materials had been limited. Enemy agents, sworn to support Hitler, held important posts in ostensibly American corporations which actually were owned by Nazis.

"By economic penetration," reported the Treasury Department in June 1942, the Axis has opened an "unseen front" whose aim is enslavement rather than trade. We are faced with the fact that for years the activities of the Axis economic system have been directed with a single mindedness that is almost incredible toward the strengthening of Axis military might. For the Axis "business man", no transaction has been too small and no commodity too insignificant to escape attention.

By control of corporations, by accumulating stocks of raw materials, by carefully directed but unlimited bribery, by the use of force and the threat of force, and by any other methods which come to hand, the Axis has, for years, been carrying on an undeclared economic war. Throughout the world, the powerful I. G. Farben, Mitsubishi and similar interests have been plotting the downfall of free peoples who gave them an opportunity to prosper and grow rich by honest trade.[9]

I. G. Farben was, I might add, an integral part of the Nazi state.[10] It employed 300,000 workers. It had charge of producing synthetic rubber and gasoline, textiles, aluminum, explosives, and other essentials for Hitler's armed forces. This parent company sent executives to subsidiaries in the United States and other countries with orders to become citizens so that they could claim exemption from alien control legislation in event of war.

The battle against these economic weapons of the Nazis which, unless counteracted, might have done serious damage to our industrial mobilization, was carried on by many agencies: the Treasury, the Board of Economic Warfare, the War Production Board, the Federal Bureau of Investigation, the Department of Agriculture, the State Department, the Office of Strategic Services, the Alien Property Custodian, and others. Their duties took them all over the world—even into Nazi-held territories—and often were dangerous in the extreme.

The Treasury acted first, in April 1940, when Norway and Denmark were invaded. Both countries had large dollar and credit balances in the United States which Germany would now use, unless stopped, against Britain and France. So the funds were frozen. The process continued as the other countries of Europe were overcome. When relations with Japan became strained in July 1941, the funds of that country were also frozen. In less than a year, more than $7 billion in foreign assets of thirty-five countries were controlled by the Treasury.[11]

This had a positive, as well as a negative, bearing upon our industrial mobilization. Among the assets were many business enterprises. A year and a half before we began military operations, the Treasury Department started a careful scrutiny of all foreign-owned funds and other property. Actual enemy ownership was frequently hidden through Swedish, Swiss, Dutch, and even American dummies. But the Treasury's financial detectives tracked them down. By the morning of December 8, 1941, its agents were posted at all enemy-owned plants in the country, including I. G. Farben subsidiaries. Some of the concerns were shut down and liquidated. When useful for our production program, the Treasury put in new management. About one hundred "American citizens," several earning $50,000 a year, were dismissed. In due course the Alien Property Custodian's office, created to take over these functions from the Treasury, continued operations and frequently increased production.[12] We in the War Department were happy to agree in awarding the Army-Navy "E" to a number of these plants for their production records.[13]

The order in which the major problems of industrial mobilization hit us were as follows: first, tooling up—in which is included both the conversion of old facilities and the creation of new ones; second, getting into production—which includes "getting the bugs" out of a million and one unfamiliar production problems; third, shortages of materials; and fourth, shortages of manpower. It was with the first two problems that we were primarily concerned before Pearl Harbor. The major impact of the second two came after we entered the war, although the material shortages began to be felt in a number of directions even before then. Many of the problems connected with the conversion of old and the building of new facilities have already been discussed. It was a tremendous task to work through the multitudinous problems of detail which had to be solved before factories could rise from their foundations or new tools be put in place. But by Pearl Harbor we had made tremendous progress. It is estimated that roughly one-third of all the facilities created by the War Department during the entire period of the emergency had been authorized by this time, and that nearly a fourth had been completed, or were at least in partial operation. By the same date, not more than one-twentieth of all the munitions we were to create had been produced. Thus the facilities program was far in advance of our record in the production of finished munitions.

As events turned out, it was wise that we put so much of our effort into new facilities at the start. The military successes of the Axis in the closing weeks of 1941 and the early months of 1942 were not the only successes our enemies gained. The original superiority of the Axis over Great Britain and Russia in the production of munitions had disappeared early in 1941. But with the acquisition of new resources in freshly conquered territory, and with an intensification of German production when it became apparent to the Nazis that they were facing a long war, Axis production surpassed that of Great Britain and Russia before the close of 1942 and remained ahead for more than a year.

Had other things remained equal, this would have given the Axis a second chance to win the war, a chance not now based upon surprise, but rather upon a prolonged superiority in the output of munitions. That the Axis did not, in fact, have this chance is attributable to the rapid rise in American production. And the rapid rise in American production at a time when we were still suffering new setbacks in battle is attributable to the broad scope and rapid progress of our pre–Pearl Harbor facilities program. In the weeks when our forces on land and sea were still struggling desperately to slow the enemy's advance, our newly created munitions factories were being completed and brought into production.

Largely because of that fact, the Axis did not enjoy the many months of superiority in the field and in the factory which, at the beginning of 1942, it at first sight seemed likely to have. In an interval so brief that it astonished the world, we passed from the defensive to the counteroffensive. Our enemies were given no time to consolidate the gains they had won by the shock of their first onslaught.

Well before the end of 1942, we had regained the initiative.[14] This would not have been possible but for the broad scope and prompt execution of our original facilities program.

The problem of getting production under way in facilities converted or newly built cannot be measured in percentages, or in millions of dollars. It called for the expert analysis and skillful solution of literally millions of problems of detail, problems connected with new machinery, new personnel, new methods. The great majority were solved by the men on the spot, by the self-reliant workers and supervisors whose ingenuity and willingness to assume responsibility constitute the greatest asset of American industry. But sometimes the problems could not be settled by the men on the spot, because they did not command the resources or the necessary authority. Some of them came up to my office, where, in the early stages of the program, there was a Production Division to follow the progress of production and solve problems that could not effectively be solved at a lower level.

In this matter of breaking production bottlenecks, General Knudsen, both before and after he came to the War Department, rendered invaluable service. He was always happiest when visiting some plant that was in difficulties, where his vast experience with production and his uncanny genius for putting his finger on the spot that was causing the trouble, solved more problems than the record will ever show. If there was something wrong in the set-up of the assembly line, his eye spotted it. If materials—some crucial part, for example—were missing, he more often than not knew where it might be secured. Without General Knudsen, and many others like him,[15] we might have suffered months of delay in getting our new facilities into effective operation. That delay, at such a critical moment, might have lost us the war.[16]

It was probably a surprise to a considerable section of the American people to discover, before we had gone very far into our munitions program, that we were suffering, and would soon suffer much more seriously, from a shortage of materials. So accustomed had we been to take comfort in our apparently inexhaustible resources that few of us realized that we are a "have-not nation" in many things needed for war. As we began to arm, we found ourselves short of manganese, nickel, chromium, tungsten, and vanadium which we had imported from Latin America, Canada, Turkey, Africa, and China. We had to have more platinum for smokeless powder, and the principal sources of supply were in Colombia, Canada, South Africa, and the Soviet Union. Without bauxite from South America, we could not continue building our air fleets. Government agents scoured the world for these materials, not only for our own use but, through preclusive buying, to keep them from reaching the Axis. In March 1942 our situation with respect to mica was desperate. Mica is used in radio and radar equipment, for aircraft magnetos, for fire control apparatus, and for many other instruments of war. Only 15 percent of the quality mica needed was produced in the United States. We had to have 333,000 pounds a month of high-grade block mica for 1943—five times the peacetime requirement. Nearly all this had to be imported from Brazil, Argentina, and India, and we did not have ships enough to bring it here even if it was produced.

Officers of the Board of Economic Warfare (BEW)[17] undertook to stimulate production. Ships of the Air Transport Command stopped at Karachi for Indian cargoes of the precious mineral. Two hundred thousand pounds a month came by sea and air from India, and 80,000 more monthly from Brazil. Our needs were met. No lack of radio sets marred our communications. The radar devices made possible through these mica supplies were used in every engagement in the war. They made possible the development of night fighter tactics over Italy and Germany.

Tantalite, also used for radio and radar and as a catalyst in the production of synthetic rubber, had to be obtained in Brazil, the Belgian Congo, and other remote countries. Quartz crystals, without which no walkie-talkie or other radio set can operate, are mined by natives in the Brazilian hills. BEW men encouraged them to work harder and we got enough crystals. Rotonone, a non-poisonous insecticide, is vital for certain domestic bean and pea crops. We normally imported it from the Far East, but stocks were also available in Peru and Brazil. The Chinese rotonone had been shut off by Japanese action in March 1942, and the pea and bean crops were in danger. Fifty tons, however, were flown from South America.

The margins were often narrow, but we obtained these and other scarce commodities from all quarters of the earth. Global warfare has an economic as well as a military significance.

But it was not only in materials we had to import from overseas that we suffered shortages. Even with the familiar metals it became evident that we would be short, both because of the unprecedented demands of this unprecedented war, and because we continued far too long to waste machine tools, steel, aluminum, and other vital things in the production of refrigerators, automobiles, washing machines, and other useful but not, at the moment, necessary items.

Steel, of course, was basic. It was needed for nearly everything. We at first suffered from over-optimism about our supply. The steel industry assured us that, when available capacity was utilized to the full, all our needs could be met. Then, ingot production reached capacity in May 1943. We were abruptly confronted with the estimate that the 1941 deficit would be 1.4 million tons and that we would be short 6.4 million tons in 1942.[18]

Aluminum supplies were critical from the beginning of the emergency. In 1938 capacity in the United States was only 300 million pounds annually. As the air program was constantly enlarged, both in number of planes and in airframe weight, requirements rose astronomically. Between July 1, 1940, and the end of 1941, we built 23,228 airplanes of all types, weighing 94,959,000 pounds. In 1944 we built 96,359 planes with a weight of 965,108,000 pounds—three times the prewar aluminum capacity of the nation. But by then our ingot capacity was 2.3 billion pounds per year. However, this figure was not reached until we had overcome infinite difficulties, all the way from exploring the possibility of new processes to finding ways and means to circumvent the submarine menace which was interfering with our importation of bauxite via the Caribbean.[19] It was a complicated and confusing thing to have to endeavor to secure military supplies, on the scale on which we needed them after the summer of 1940, while the civilian economy was still allowed to operate almost without restriction. The services, in spite of precautions, competed with each other and with purchasing agents from abroad. Contracts were signed and orders placed with often no real assurance that they would be executed and delivered. Officers in the Army and Navy, as well as the patriotic civilians who hurried to Washington to help their country, worked under terrific pressure. Tempers were sometimes strained beyond reason.

In all this the imperturbable good humor of General Knudsen, not to mention his standing in industry, was one of America's greatest assets in those early days of confusion. During one of the many aluminum shortages, the Secretary of War and the Secretary of the Navy conferred with General Knudsen. They told him drastic action was necessary.

"It can't be so bad as all that," said the General, looking at a sheet of paper. "See, I have an order here from the armed services for 20,000 aluminum chairs and 20,000 aluminum tables."

Another time the subject under discussion was copper. Domestic production of refined copper was a mere 70,000 short tons in 1939. It had increased by 185,000 tons at the end of 1942. But until large imports had been secured, copper remained critical. In the face of that, at a conference called to consider ways and means of getting more copper, General Knudsen read from a Navy requisition demanding three hundred brass cuspidors.

"Can't the sailors spit out to sea?" he asked.

Both of these cases, the one of aluminum tables and chairs and the other of brass cuspidors, do not illustrate human absurdity as much as they do the tremendous administrative task of getting into war production. In normal times, there were sound reasons for using aluminum and brass in those specifications. But, in the face of all the other work which had to be done during the crisis, no one had got round to altering the specifications of these items so as to take into account the existing shortage. Hence when some junior officer or civilian official found himself called upon to order the necessary fittings for some new ship, these were the only specifications he found available and already approved.

The shortage that struck us most suddenly, and with what, for a time, threatened to be calamitous, was that of rubber. There had been some apprehension about rubber months earlier, and some steps had been taken to build up a modest stockpile. But for reasons which are still the subject of controversy, this effort had not progressed far.[20]

In our then prevailing tendency to underrate the military power of Japan, we probably did not really take seriously the technical possibility that we might be cut off from the natural rubber of southeastern Asia and the East Indies, not for weeks, but for the duration of the war.

When the dreadful truth became known, it was obvious that we were up against a major danger. We could not fight the sort of mechanized war which we planned with the meager stocks of crude rubber in the country at the time of Pearl Harbor. We would need synthetic rubber on a vast scale. But accustomed, and financially able, as we had always been to purchase as much crude rubber as we needed, we had not pushed the development of synthetic rubber with the vigor shown by the Germans, who had known for years that they would need it. We had many technical problems yet to solve and many disputes over method to settle. To make matters more difficult, these disputes were not confined to technical quarrels between rival schools of chemists and engineers, but became enmeshed in the rivalry of economic groups. The grain producers insisted we employ methods that used alcohol, and the oil producers with equal vehemence extolled the superiority of methods based upon the use of petroleum. It was one of the many great services which Mr. Bernard M. Baruch rendered to the nation that, under his chairmanship, a committee studied this problem and made sound recommendations.

Before the rubber problem was solved, however, a method was employed of which I always disapproved, no matter whether it was employed for rubber or any other difficult item of war. This was to set up a special organization for pushing the rubber program, an organization substantially independent of the controls applied to other aspects of the war production program and endowed with what almost amounted to an overriding priority. Undoubtedly this brought great vigor into the synthetic rubber program. Unfortunately, however, synthetic rubber does not stand by itself. It had to compete very directly with our program for aviation gasoline, since both depended primarily upon petroleum.[21] It seemed to us in the War Department, who were acutely aware of the vital need for pushing the bombing attack upon Germany just as rapidly as possible, that aviation gasoline deserved at least equal, and probably superior, consideration. Certainly it would have been better to have these technically interlocking programs come for a decision on their claims to a superior who had equal authority over both.

The rubber issue was the more irritating to us in the War Department because of hesitation elsewhere in effecting the greatest possible economy in the use of rubber in civilian activities. Admittedly, the nation had become extraordinarily dependent upon the automobile for its daily business transportation, but it was equally true that an immense amount of unnecessary driving, which can only be called joy-riding, was taking place. Only very reluctantly, and at first in very partial fashion, was gasoline rationing adopted in order to save the tires of the nation for essential use.[22]

It was obvious very early in our production effort that some method would have to be devised to apportion out, in the way best calculated to serve the public interest, those materials which were in short supply; otherwise, they would quickly disappear from the market. Those who already had adequate supplies, or who could afford to pay very high prices, would have them. Other producers, with equally important jobs to do, would have nothing. That would have meant chaos.

The War Department had, of course, studied this problem carefully in its industrial mobilization planning and had favored a system of allocations. By such a system the available supply of some scarce material would be apportioned out to various producers, in accordance with a central determination of the need of each producer, in order to bring about a balanced plan of production. No one would get all he wanted, but everybody who was doing anything important would get something. Producers might find themselves slowed down, but never stopped. Unfortunately, in the face of the gradual, and business-as-usual-plus-defense-production policy of the first months of the crisis, the allocations system was thought to be too drastic. In its place there was adopted a system of priorities. By this system, when a manufacturer was doing important defense work, he was given a priority upon the available supply of a scarce material. After he had taken what he needed, what was left was offered to those without priorities.

This worked reasonably well so long as there was an ample supply for all defense needs, and only non-defense production had to go without, although even then it sometimes produced a tendency for those with priorities to hoard against the possibility of more serious shortages in the months ahead. But the system got us into immediate and serious difficulties as soon as defense demands rose to the point where they alone could not be satisfied with the available supply. Then it became necessary to introduce various categories of priorities, so that items considered more difficult or more important could have precedence over the others. This, however, was an open invitation to hoarding. Even where it did not lead to that, it really was of little benefit to our national defense to have those with first priorities produce all they had contracted to produce, and then have those with lesser priorities fall far short of their assignments because, by the time they had access to rare materials, all but a small and insufficient quantity had been preempted by those who held the top priorities.[23]

Under these circumstances, the moment any priority holder began to get less than he wanted because the holder of some higher priority had been there first, he began a battle to have his priority lifted. He usually won it. But, the moment the originally favored manufacturer found that someone else had climbed up on level terms with him, he in turn set out to recapture his advantage. And he usually did so through the creation of a super priority, and then of a super-super priority. There is no telling to what fantastic lengths this game of priority leap-frog would have gone had it been allowed to continue indefinitely. It did continue too long, but before we had been at war many months, it became apparent, as the War Department had long been pointing out, that this first method was impossible. Late in 1942 we adopted the Controlled Materials Plan, a thorough system of allocating scarce supplies, and from that time on distribution followed a sensible pattern. The new system did not, of course, end shortages: only production or importation of the deficient materials could do that. But it did provide that, in accordance with a central scheme for evaluating the importance of each item in the defense program, each manufacturer got that share of a scarce material which it was to the best interest of the whole program that he should have at the moment.[24]

At the same time that we were doing our utmost to build factories to produce guns, tanks, planes, ammunition, trucks, and the thousands of other items of equipment with which an army fights the enemy in the field, we also had to provide housing, roads, mess halls, and many other facilities for the new citizen army that was being created as a result of the passage of the Selective Service Act of 1940.[25] Sites of land as large as ninety by forty miles had to be found for maneuvers. The building of cantonments, which had to be pushed in great haste because delay in passing the Selective Service Act left us only a few weeks before the onset of winter, brought some confusion and waste, much of it unavoidable but not all. However, by November 1941 the Quartermaster General had completed cantonments and training grounds for 1.3 million men and had built ten hospitals with a capacity of 10,400 beds.

Concurrently, the Quartermaster General began work on seventeen new supply depots within the country and in our foreign possession. Construction started on forty-two new plants, to be owned and operated by the Army, at which were to be manufactured TNT and other explosives, small arms, ammonia, tanks, armor plate, nitrates, and other necessities. They were over half completed by Pearl Harbor. The Chief of Engineers, at the same time, was building twenty-one airfields at home and on the bases where Great Britain had granted us rights in return for the overage destroyers. These projects were under way in Trinidad, Bermuda, and Newfoundland.

Meanwhile, the new Army was growing and taking shape, but at this stage it was far from the significant force which finally overthrew our enemies. The maneuvers it held in Louisiana in the fall of 1941 were the largest in American history. But, when they ended, Lt. Gen. Leslie J. McNair said that both leadership and discipline were bad but that the principal deficiency had been lack of ammunition.

Many soldiers had never been able to fire their guns. Few had been able to qualify as marksmen because there was not enough ammunition for them to practice with.

Meanwhile, in spite of the German failure to invade Great Britain, the situation was growing steadily blacker. Greece had been conquered by the spring of 1941. Total submarine sinkings reached more than 5 million tons in April.[26] On Sunday, June 22, the German armies attacked the Soviet Union to the accompaniment of almost universal American predictions that another victory for Hitler would shortly follow.

The President continued his warnings of danger. The United States faced, he said, "a world-wide crisis of truly desperate intensity." A few days later, he proclaimed an unlimited emergency and announced that any necessary action would be taken to insure the delivery of munitions to Great Britain. When Russia was invaded, the President declared, despite opposition, that the United States would give all possible aid. Frozen Russian credits of $30 million were immediately released.

United States Marines landed in Greenland in April 1941 to protect that strategic point from Axis attack, and in Iceland in July. The Navy instituted patrols along their supply routes, and bloodshed was not far off. After the U.S.S. *Greer,* a destroyer delivering mail to Iceland, had been fired upon, the President issued his "shoot on sight" order. On October 15, Nazi submarines damaged the destroyer *Kearney* and sank the *Reuben James.* Only 44 men in the crew of 120 were rescued. Hostilities were close, but the apparent enemy was Hitler. The public did not grasp the full meaning of the southward march of Japan toward Thailand.

Although there were many who felt deeply alarmed by developments throughout the world, the nation as a whole did not react adequately to the growing danger. Leon Henderson of the Office of Price Administration asked for a 50-percent cut in the manufacture of automobiles, light trucks, and refrigerators in the next six months, but 600,000 cars were scheduled for the period August–October 1941. Secretary of the Interior Harold Ickes warned of gasoline shortages on the eastern seaboard by winter. In May a test blackout in Newark, New Jersey, had created a "mardi-gras atmosphere" in the crowded, downtown streets.

Lack of concern, in fact, seemed to be the dominant public mood in the months before Pearl Harbor. A degree of defeatism existed too. Armchair strategists pointed to the impossibility of effective American participation in the war. Some grew specific in their warnings. They said that an army of 8 or 10 million would be needed and that such a mighty host could not be trained in less than five years. Others declared it would take just as long to build the ships with which to transport the armies to Europe. Such attitudes—encouraging, as they did, an unwillingness to sacrifice civilian consumption to defense needs—undoubtedly contributed to the shortages of materials which plagued us until 1943.

The gap between goods on order and goods on hand can be dangerously wide. For all our efforts during the better part of two years, the United States Army was weak indeed on December 7, 1941. It consisted of 1.6 million men, 27 partly trained and equipped infantry divisions, 4 armored divisions, 2 cavalry divisions, and about 200 air squadrons more or less complete. Only 7 divisions were sufficiently hardened to go overseas. Shipping was lacking to send many more. The Quartermaster General had been able to obtain clothing and other housekeeping items for the Army, but the stocks of guns and ammunition were far from adequate even for training purposes. We had only 16,000 tons of bombs, in comparison with more than 1.4 million tons dropped by the Army Air Forces alone before the collapse of Germany. The Army had 450 million rounds of small arms ammunition, less than was fired in two months by the infantry in France. We had fewer than 500 radar sets, no airplane landing mats, few tractors. Munitions production in December 1941, except for aircraft, was only $450 million as compared with $2.1 billion, the peak, in March 1945.

How incredibly the situation changed was revealed when President Roosevelt, Prime Minister Churchill, and Marshal Stalin met for their first conference at Tehran on November 28, 1943. After a report on the military situation in Europe and in the Pacific, discussion turned to the invasion of France, then scheduled for May 1944. Marshal Stalin said that his experts agreed that Northern France was the best place for the cross-channel blow at Germany. It must be expected, he said, that the Germans should fight like devils against the attack. Mr. Churchill gave the confident reply that the Allied forces would consist of 19 United States and 16 British divisions. They would be twice as strong as the German ones, and 1 million men would land in France in 1944.

The Prime Minister's estimates proved to be conservative. On February 4, 1945, the heads of the three great countries met again at Yalta. France had been liberated and Germany invaded. General Eisenhower's armies were massed to cross the Rhine when the weather permitted in March. This time Marshal Stalin asked whether his co-leaders were certain that they had enough tanks. His own forces had used up nine thousand in the most recent offensive, he warned. General Marshall gave assurance that the Allied forces had almost 10,000 tanks in the European theater. They also had 4,000 heavy bombers. When the Allied forces crossed the Rhine; 4 million men, fully equipped, were on the European continent.

The contrast between this and our armament on the eve of Pearl Harbor is striking. But we must not forget that the basis for the tremendous outpouring of munitions with which we overwhelmed our enemies in the closing stages of the war was laid before December 1941. Had we not done what we did in the eighteen months before that date, there would have been no D-Day in 1944, nor any V-J Day in 1945. Whether our hard-pressed Allies could have waited another year or eighteen months for our assistance is, to say the least, problematical. We undoubtedly ought to have done more than we did before Pearl Harbor, and by not doing so we ran great and needless risks. But it is not unlikely that final victory hinged on what we did do.

Chapter 5

Altitudinal Goals

The Prime Minister of Great Britain was again at the White House in May 1943, his third visit since Pearl Harbor. The war picture was brighter now. The North African campaign had ended in victory after a year of planning and fighting. But the leaders of the United States and Great Britain remembered vividly the dark days and hours of less than a year ago, when Tobruk had fallen, 25,000 British soldiers had been captured and utter and final disaster in the Near East seemed likely at any moment. It might have involved the loss of the war.

Gen. Brehon Somervell, Lt. Gen. Leroy Lutes (his successor as head of the Army Service Forces), and their staffs will never forget that danger-laden summer of 1942. General Lutes was then director of operations of the ASF. On June 27, he was summoned to a conference in his chief's office. General Somervell ordered him to have 300 Sherman (M-4) tanks and 100 howitzers, mounted on tank chassis, ready for shipment to Cairo on July 12. They would have to take the long route, 20,385 nautical miles, around Cape Horn and up through the Red Sea to Suez.

The order was an almost impossible one, even for an organization which would never do more than admit that "the impossible takes a little longer." But the fate of the whole war was at stake. Rommel had driven what remained of the British Eighth Army to El Alamein in Egypt, only seventy-five miles from Alexandria. British and American planes covered the retreat and saved it from degenerating into a rout. But the British had lost 80,000 men. They had sacrificed vast stocks of materiel, and this was a battle of supply, with the Axis enjoying far shorter lines from Italy.

The United States did not have 300 tanks ready for shipment. This was part of the penalty for making 3.5 million automobiles and more than an average number of refrigerators the previous year. It was part of what had to be paid for putting only 15 percent of the national income into production for the war, which was now so precariously close to ending in defeat.

The Sherman tanks had to be requisitioned from camps where they were needed for training armored divisions. Maj. Gen. L. H. Campbell, Chief of Ordnance, telegraphed ordnance depots and the few factories where tanks were in production. They were to rush work on any near completion.

All manner of complications developed. Sand filters had to be installed because the tanks were to be used for desert fighting instead of, as originally intended, for maneuvers in the United States and the contemplated invasion of France. Engines had to be equipped with new cooling devices. Canvas breech covers were cut and sewn by Philadelphia tailors. To General Lutes's office came scattered reports. He would get 56 tanks from Toledo. The Pullman Company could supply 17, the Fisher Body Company 77. Somehow, by July 12, the 300 tanks and the guns were on board fast merchant ships. The total lift was 38,000 tons. Six days later, General Lutes received word that one of the ships had been torpedoed. He had to find 75 additional tanks and self-propelled weapons as well as ammunition. He found them, and on July 28 they were shipped on a sea train, a vessel built to carry railroad and other rolling stock. It made the hazardous, seventy-day voyage unescorted and reached Suez one day ahead of the convoy.

The tanks and howitzers were only a fraction of the supplies sent around Cape Horn or, by the British, over the 10,000-mile route south of Africa. Bombers flew from the United States. Aircraft carriers steamed to the African coast, where fighters took off from their decks. For his forthcoming battle, Gen. (now Field Marshal) Sir Bernard Montgomery had, including the Shermans, about 900 tanks. He had 25,000 trucks and 90 American 105-mm self-propelled guns.

The weight of the Arsenal of Democracy was now tipping the scales of war. On October 23, 1942, General Montgomery struck at

Altitudinal Goals

El Alamein. Ten days later the British broke through, and Rommel began the retreat eastward that had no turning. In a week the combined American-British forces landed in French North Africa.

The day of victories was dawning, but as yet our efforts were on a very minor scale compared with those which lay ahead. That we could take the offensive at all in 1942 was the result of the repeated demands by the President for war production, and of the early efforts to implement those demands which I have already described. The President had revealed his policy at a press conference on December 20, 1940. It was, he said, to "ask for twice as much as you expect to get." This lay behind his order the previous summer for 50,000 airplanes.

Naturally, when he set these lofty goals, there was skepticism, both inside and outside the government. We in the War Department must concede that in some cases we did not fully appreciate the industrial potential of our country. Neither did the heads of the other services. Mr. Krug is correct in his statement that war production for 1942 was originally set at $28 billion when $40 billion was possible. But this estimate was lifted drastically when the President set new production goals on January 6, 1942. He ordered that 60,000 planes be built within the year. In 1943 the goal was 100,000. Forty-five thousand tanks were to be made in 1942, and 75,000 in 1945. Antiaircraft gun production was set at 20,000 for 1942 and 35,000 the following year; merchant ships at 8 million deadweight tons in 1942 and 10 million in 1943.

This was "incentive scheduling" on a level never before imagined. It was calculated that the cost in 1942 would be $60 billion and, in 1943, $100 billion. The goals could not be met. Actually, war goods to a total of $44 billion were turned out in 1942 and $63 billion in 1943. However, if many billions short of the objective set by the President, the achievement should be compared with the $1.5 billion spent for plant and munitions in 1940.

This practice of incentive scheduling, so spectacularly employed by President Roosevelt, presents very serious problems in the management of industrial mobilization. Probably, under the then-existing circumstances, it was justified. As a nation we were tempted to walk into war with one hand in our pocket, and were perhaps ready to persuade ourselves that what could be done by the one free hand was the limit of our possible effort. The President's bold formulation of goals that few had dreamed of shocked us out of that contentment with half-measures. There could be no doubt that we would have to go into the job with both hands if we hoped to come anywhere near producing all that he asked.

But there is also a drawback in assigning production goals beyond the technical capacity of a nation to attain them. Theoretically, if the overall goal is too high, the program as a whole falls short by whatever is the difference between the proposed objective and what is practical, but all aspects of the program have been stimulated to greater effort than would otherwise have been generated. In practice it does not work that way, for a war production program—and least of all a hastily constructed one like ours—is never in balance. Some items can be produced easily, because of abundant materials and because the machines and the skills needed to produce them closely resemble machines and skills of which we make abundant use in peacetime production. Others, however, demand machines and skills, and frequently materials, for which we have only a very modest need in time of peace. Production of this type cannot be stepped up rapidly.

What happens, then, when we set incentive goals which go beyond our total industrial capacity? For items of the program similar to items of peacetime production, it is not difficult to attain the goal set. Men with but very little retraining, machines with but very little adaptation, and factories with but modest additions are all immediately set to work and the objective is triumphantly achieved. But what happens to items that are not familiar, that require new skills, new machines, often new factories, and frequently increased stocks of rare materials not normally produced in this country? It takes time to secure all these things, time to plan, time to build, and time to train. And then, when this planning and building and training have finally been mapped out, what do we find? That men, machines, and materials have already been preempted by those phases of the production program that required little adaptation and were, therefore, ready to go to work at once. It then turns out that the abundant production of the easy items is blocking, and blocking very badly, production of the difficult items. It amounts, in a sense, to turning the priority system upside down and giving priority, not to the hard items, but to the easy ones.

The confusion that arises from this is not difficult to imagine. A war program is a balanced program. It is useless for an army to have abundant planes if it has no tanks, or ample air frames if there are no engines to go in them. No such elaborately coordinated mechanism as a modern army, navy, or air force can operate effectively unless it has adequate quantities of all the essential items it needs. Gasoline is not a substitute for ammunition, nor rubber tires for guns. Even though it is true that no military force ever enters a campaign without some deficiency, there must be substantial balance in the essential things. Otherwise the campaign is certain to bog down at some point.

Nor is it the military forces alone that must have balanced equipment. The forces of production need a similar balance. They have weapons of production in the shape of generators, pumps, electrical wiring, and thousands of other things which are needed to make a factory work. War production demands them in greatly increased quantities, and often in unusual sizes and designs. The absence of any one of them may force a factory 99 percent complete to stand idle. Perhaps the materials and labor which enabled the contractor who put up the frame of the factory to boast that he completed his job ahead of schedule, actually served to prevent the factory coming into production on schedule because, having been tied up immediately in an easy job, they were then not available for the more difficult job that could not then be begun promptly. Thus an excessively high objective may result, in the end, in less production than would a more modest one.

We began to run into this danger within a few months after Pearl Harbor. No longer hesitant about the exact scope of our part in the war, we pushed with enthusiasm toward goals that only a mathematician could fully comprehend. Before long, however, some of our experts began to warn us that we were in danger of getting badly out of balance, and that the final result might be less production than a more modest overall objective would bring. We were loath to accept this warning, for our need seemed limitless, and we had just come to realize how much we had previously underestimated our industrial capacity. Now that we at last agreed with the economic experts who had told us a few months before that we were setting our sights too low, it was somewhat bewildering to learn from the same source that we had now set them too high.[1]

But they were right, and before long we began to cut back our objectives. We accepted the fact that war production, like the classic description of politics, is "the art of the possible." Just how high our production could go under perfect conditions of management it is impossible to say. Had we possessed, from the very beginning, a thoroughly adequate system of production controls, we could doubtless have pushed our production figures to a higher point than any we ever achieved.[2] But the half-way fashion in which we advanced into industrial mobilization, for reasons already discussed, denied us a really adequate system of control at the moment when we most needed it, that of the most rapid acceleration of our expansion.

One very important field in which our production program threatened to get out of balance was in the building of new facilities. We were undoubtedly saved because we pushed the facilities program, even where necessary at the expense of the immediate output of munitions in the months before Pearl Harbor. Acutely conscious as we had become of the fact that we could not produce until we had tooled up, the weeks just after Pearl Harbor witnessed a flood of authorizations for new facilities. Two-thirds of all the War Department facilities created during the crisis were initiated subsequent to the Japanese attack, and the great bulk of them came during the three months that followed it. Again we had to be reminded that we were in danger of overdoing one vital item of our program at the probable expense of the others. Again we were reluctant to recognize this,[3] for nearly everyone charged with a particular job could see where a new facility would come in handy, and convenience very easily grew up into necessity. But we soon had to recognize the necessity for balance, and to realize that men and materials used in building facilities would not be available for producing finished munitions. So we cut back our facilities program and imposed strict controls upon the creation of new facilities, to ensure that we did not spend precious effort in building new factories to do work that could be distributed to plants already in existence.[4]

Although, in the weeks just after Pearl Harbor, we were formulating altitudinal goals for our war production, this was also the period in which we felt most nearly the penalty of too little and too late. Supplies were needed for the defense of the British Isles, for the bases defended by American soldiers in Greenland and Iceland, for the Philippines, for Australia and New Zealand, for China, and for Russia under terms of the agreement with Marshal Stalin. If materiel was shipped to one beleaguered place, it could not go to another in equal peril. Almost everywhere we were forced upon the defensive. American and British experts were forced to the reluctant conclusion that Allied forces could not fight their way into North Africa, that only a peaceful occupation was possible. In the Pacific, it seemed that the best we could hope for was some time to slow the Japanese, and that many months must pass before we could really stop their advance.

"The first victory we have to win," Mr. Churchill cabled the President only two months before the invasion of North Africa, "is to avoid a battle."[5]

Of course, the production picture was not entirely bad and, in fact, in comparison with what it had been a few months before, it was good. We were turning out three times as many tanks and combat vehicles as a year before, five times the guns of all types, nine times the ammunition. Landing craft, however, were nonexistent except for some boats which were utterly inadequate for the amphibious engagements which would have to be staged. We were doing little to develop rockets or jet-propelled aircraft. The worried Joint Chiefs of Staff, in almost daily session to devise ways and means to strike back at our enemies, had no illusions about how weak we were in the winter, spring, and summer of 1942. There was more truth than paradox in Mr. Churchill's cable.

We were shortly to see the way in which democratic nations, if they fail to prepare adequately for war, may be forced into foreign policies which are repugnant to their citizens. We had to appease Vichy and the infamous Laval.[6] The Chiefs of Staff considered asking the President and the Prime Minister to make a political approach to the French. Maj. L. T. Gerow reported at a February meeting of the military leaders that Secretary of State Cordell Hull had expressed apprehension that France might turn over its fleet to Germany, and that American consuls and observers might be evicted from France and North Africa, where they were gathering vital information. Relations with Vichy had to be maintained.

This was but one of many well-nigh insoluble problems. The basic need, said General Marshall in January 1942, was to move, in a single month, men and supplies which would normally take three months. But where were they to be sent? New Caledonia, the French colony in the far-off South Pacific, was essential to the holding of Australia. But Gen. H. H. Arnold, commander of the AAF, said that he did not have bombers and fighters to send there. Besides, New Caledonia ought not to have priority over Samoa and Fiji. If those air bases were lost, bombers could not be flown to Australia, and the Dutch East Indies would be conquered. A hard decision, but the correct one, was made. General Marshall said that a convoy of 21,800 men would sail from New York for the Far East on January 20. Ten thousand were earmarked for Caledonia, where they landed without opposition on March 12. In order to do this, the Chief of Staff added, an Iceland convoy was cut from 8,000 to 2,500 men, and reinforcements to Northern Ireland from 16,000 to 4,000. Supplies to Russia would have to be slashed by 30 percent, and this was in addition to existing deficiencies in the amounts promised.

The protests from Russia were prompt and vehement. But protests came from every direction. From General MacArthur on Bataan arrived word of desperate shortages. The crushing success of Japan in the Philippines and the East Indies forced the modification of basic strategy. At first it had been hoped that an invasion of Europe could be staged in 1942 or 1943. Sending convoys to Australia made this impossible. Twenty-five cargo vessels, which might have carried supplies for the British or reinforcements for the hard-pressed army in Africa, were diverted from the Red Sea to the Pacific. At a meeting of the Joint Chiefs of Staff on March 3, 1942, General Marshall reported that thirty United States divisions had been fairly well trained during a period of a year. They had, however, only half the needed equipment. Not more than fourteen divisions could be maintained overseas. Added to all these difficulties was the cutting of the Burma Road, and Axis submarine and air activity, which was causing cruel losses among the ships plying the northern route to Murmansk. Admiral of the Fleet Sir Dudley Pound revealed in April that ice conditions were the worst in a quarter century. At the moment, he said, sixty-five vessels were waiting in Iceland for the next convoy. The sinkings would certainly be heavy.

In one way or another, directly or indirectly, nearly all of these difficulties were tied up with the fact that we did not yet have enough war production. We needed more trained men, to be sure, but we needed equipment even more, both for operations and to train the men. If the need is great enough, use can be made of men whose training is not quite finished, although the price in extra casualties and diminished effectiveness is high. But there is no such thing as using equipment that is three-quarters finished. So far as use is concerned, it doesn't exist until it is fully completed. For all the tremendous outpouring of munitions a few months ahead, when the hour of greatest danger struck, we were equipment poor, and things which we desperately needed to do could not be done because we had not the supplies or transportation with which to do them.

It is greatly to be regretted that the American people could not have been told the full story at the time. Had it been possible to do so, I am sure many of our production difficulties would have been greatly diminished. The manpower problem would probably have been handled more adequately, and there would have been no strikes.[7] The American people were sometimes given an overly optimistic picture for two reasons: first, because the Japanese did not know the full damage they had inflicted on the Pacific fleet or the true extent of our weakness—and we did not propose to tell them. The second reason, I am afraid, is inherent in human nature. The leaders of our armed services, military and civilian alike, are inclined to emphasize victory and minimize defeat. I know that the Army must plead guilty to this tendency. Perhaps the American propensity, as manifested in peacetime, to demand the scalp of the coach as soon as his team has lost two or three games is not without some responsibility for the unwillingness of military leaders to confess their mistakes publicly.

Now that we were at war, and pledged to unprecedented levels of war production, the control of the civilian economy became a pressing issue. The measures taken before Pearl Harbor had been very tentative and half-hearted. The Office of Price Administration, having no legal power, had been attempting to regulate prices by voluntary agreement, but the cost of living had risen 11 percent by the close of 1941. On April 27, 1942, the President submitted to Congress his seven-point program which called for heavy taxes, ceilings on goods and rents, stabilization of wages, control of farm products prices, rationing of scarce commodities, and limitation of credit and installment buying. The program, although not nearly so drastic as those employed by the other belligerents, did contribute powerfully toward concentrating public energy on the war. Taxes were heaviest in our history—about $123 billion were collected between December 1, 1941, and the end of hostilities—but this was only 40 percent of the cost of the struggle. Only partial success, too, marked repeated attempts to reorganize the civilian war-production agencies. The abandonment of the original Industrial Mobilization Plan had left us to wander through a rather unhappy series of improvisations during the pre–Pearl Harbor period. The first agency set up to supervise defense production was the National Defense Advisory Commission (NDAC).[8] It was not really a commission at all, but rather a group of experts in various phases of the problem facing us, each one of whom was directly responsible to the President. Neither singly nor collectively did its members have any real authority, and certainly none proportionate to the critical task they were called upon to face. They did the best they could, and often they rendered extremely valuable service, but they had no chance of achieving real adequacy.

There can be little doubt that some measure of the friction which developed between the armed services and the various civilian agencies engaged in the war-production job grew out of the inadequacy of this original set-up. The War Department's Industrial Mobilization Plan had called for the establishment, at the beginning of a national emergency, of a strong civilian board to supervise all aspects of war production. As soon as that board could be got into operation, the War and Navy Departments proposed to hand over to it practically all of the broader control over the national economy, and to confine themselves largely to the more limited task of the direct procurement of munitions.

But, when faced with the inadequate set-up and authority of the National Defense Advisory Commission, the armed services almost inevitably found themselves compelled to push into areas in which they had originally not expected to intrude, in order to get things done. Naturally this led, before long, to charges that the Army and Navy were trying to dominate the civilian economy. Inevitably, when we found things that needed to be done but would not be done unless we pushed hard, we sometimes pushed too hard, or in the wrong places. That led to resentment and resistance. This, in turn, aroused suspicion that not all was being done that could have been done, and charges that the military were out to dominate the national economy were countered by accusations that some of those in the civilian agencies had more of a weather eye out for the interests of their peacetime employers than was appropriate under the circumstances.[9]

There was, of course, a slight measure of truth in both accusations. But the great bulk of the friction grew out of the inadequacy and uncertainty of the original set-up. In administration, as in other media, nature abhors a vacuum, and when it rushes in to fill the empty space, stormy currents are likely to arise. They were the result, however, chiefly of energetic and public-spirited men reaching out to do jobs that needed to be done, only to find that other men, of equal energy and loyalty, were seeking to put their hands to the same task-because no one had indicated clearly where responsibility lay.

Furthermore, if at times the Army and Navy felt they could handle some civilian aspects of industrial mobilization better than they were at the moment being handled by civilians, it is equally true that there were those on the civilian side who aspired to take from the armed services their historic procurement functions and place them in the hands of a civilian organization.[10] The aggressors were not all in one camp. But it would be a mistake to emphasize as much as some have done the amount of this friction, or assume that it seriously hampered the production of munitions. Administrative squabbles of the sort which arose always make good copy for the newspapers, and perhaps a certain reverence for those who had to take responsibility in the field demanded psychological compensation in greater attention to the infirmities of those responsible for phases of the defense program not directly related to combat.

However that may be, it was a long while before we got an administrative set-up that was at all adequate. By the end of 1940, it became evident that the National Defense Advisory Commission would not do, so it was replaced by the Office of Production Management. This was a two-headed affair with—as he then was—Mr. Knudsen and Sidney Hillman, the labor leader, as joint chairmen. But it had no real powers, even though it was stronger than the NDAC, and the two-headed control was confusing. The picture was scarcely clarified when, eight months later, the Supply, Priorities, and Allocation Board was set up with authority that could scarcely be kept distinct from that of previous and still existing agencies. Not until after Pearl Harbor, and the announcement of altitudinal production goals, did the President create the War Production Board and appoint Mr. Donald Nelson as chairman.[11] At that time General Knudsen accepted an army commission and became Director of Production in the office I then held, that of Under Secretary of War. As has been mentioned before, in that capacity he became the nation's outstanding troubleshooter for production problems. He flew 250,000 miles, and visited twelve hundred plants in all parts of the United States. The B-29 bomber, for example, could not possibly have operated against Japan as soon as it did but for General Knudsen's skill in handling some of its very difficult production problems.

But even the creation of the War Production Board did not give us the full system of coordination that we needed. There were still too many agencies concerned with production, stockpiling, procurement, and other related problems. Even after the War Production Board was created, there remained a tendency to proliferate special agencies to handle problems, as when the War Manpower Commission was set up as a separate agency. Confusion was inescapable. The continuation of this centrifugal tendency made it necessary, finally, to create the Office of War Mobilization in October 1944, in order to provide an agency which could settle disputes between the various agencies whose fields of authority overlapped. This brought a marked improvement, and did give us something which approached the concept of the original Industrial Mobilization Plan, that of having all war production activities report to one man who was responsible for overall coordination. But even the Office of War Mobilization was not a full answer, for its role was too much that of the adjudicator of disputes, and too little that of the originator of policies, to provide an entirely adequate top leadership. However, it is interesting that, through many improvisations and detours, necessity finally forced us back to the concept of industrial mobilization which the War Department had stated clearly in its prewar plans. It was a striking vindication of the insight of the men who did that job.[12]

As for the War Department, its organization was a long way from perfection or even adequacy as it faced the most tremendous task in its history. This was as true of its logistical as it was of its combat functions. The logistical function was divided among eight supply and eight administrative services. The supply services each reported to the Chief of Staff [Gen. George S. Marshall] on strictly military matters and to me as Under Secretary of War on matters of procurement. The Chief of Staff in particular, to whom the various combat arms as well had to report, found it an almost insupportable burden to have to deal directly with so many agencies. Under war conditions, it consumed time he could not afford to spare.

Another difficulty in the existing set-up was the fact that each of the supply arms, Ordnance, Quartermaster Corps, etc., reported to two superiors, the Chief of Staff, and myself. There was no one to pull their various demands together and make sure that a clear and consistent overall picture was presented to each of us. If there was inconsistency between the picture the supply services presented to the Chief of Staff and that which they presented to me, as Under Secretary, there was no mechanism to make it apparent until each of us had acted and thus, perhaps, quite inadvertently precipitated a conflict of policy.

On March 9, 1942, the President reorganized the War Department. In place of the several arms and services there were substituted three commands, the Army Air Force, the Army Ground Force, and the Army Service Force (ASF),[13] although the last of the three for a few months bore the name of Service of Supply until the nomenclature was changed to avoid confusion with service of supply in the theaters. The ASF was made responsible for supply and service activities for the whole War Department, except for the AAF. Thus, if there was a conflict between the requirements of supply in the field—matters formerly handled by G-4 of the General Staff, and the needs of procurement (matters formerly handled directly by my office)—the conflict was worked out in the headquarters of ASF before the matter was presented either to the Chief of Staff or to me for approval. We could thus be sure that we were approving—or disapproving—the same thing. General Somervell, as commanding general of ASF, had the formidable assignment of organizing, expanding, and operating the new supply organization.

The new system worked far better than the old one, but there was still room for improvement when the war ended. One failure was in not establishing identical supply and distribution systems in all of the overseas theaters. When we had not one but many overseas theaters, and each in competition with the rest for supplies, it was confusing and detrimental to wise apportionment to have different systems in the theaters. Another shortcoming lay in inadequate and inefficient methods for controlling stocks. Supply information sent back to the United States was often inaccurate. The cigarette shortage which so shook the United States in 1944 turned out to have been caused in part because the European Theater of Operations failed to include in their reports the cigarettes en route or on board ship. It was also a not infrequent thing to receive duplicate requisitions for goods already shipped.

A much more serious flaw which the reorganization left was independent procurement by the AAF and the Navy. The AAF was given the right to contract for "items peculiar to the Air Forces," but nobody knew precisely what this meant, and it was interpreted in the broadest possible way. Duplication was inevitable and continuous, although it did not, happily, occur so frequently in the overseas theaters as in the United States. Here at home the AAF even had its own hospitals. It produced and distributed its own training films, although a large, costly, and efficient motion picture unit had been established in the Signal Corps. The Air Forces often dealt directly with the War Production Board and other civilian agencies. No sane reason can be offered for operation by the AAF of separate repair facilities, communications systems, and mortuary procedures. The AAF even sold its own surplus coal.

I had questioned the wisdom of separate procurement by the AAF when the reorganization scheme was first presented to me, and I did what I could as Under Secretary of War to minimize the confusion and added cost by designating ASF staff divisions to supervise a number of common activities such as cancellation and contract renegotiation. But effective cooperation such as that achieved between the ASF and the Army Ground Forces was never universally achieved with the AAF.

It has long been my conviction that the Army and Navy should be brought into a single defense department. This unification, now happily achieved,[14] seems to me essential to the future safety of the nation. Reasons for it can be gleaned from almost every page of the history of the recent war, but it can be justified on the issue of production and supply alone.

It is true that, even without unification, we saw some magnificent examples in the field of cooperation between the Army, the Navy, the Marines, and the Coast Guard. Unfortunately there were far fewer examples of similar cooperation in procurement. Both the War and Navy Departments were to blame. By long-standing custom they had been wholly independent, each responsible only to the President as Commander-in-Chief and to Congress. Each had its own warehouses, hospitals, repair shops, medical services, and messes. Each had its differing procurement systems and price policies. The Army's Air Transport Command operated separately from the Naval Air Transport Service. Bitter jealousy frequently arose.[15]

It took almost three years of our most perilous war to change this at all. Even then, the separation of nearly all facilities was maintained. A large number of makeshift committees were established, most of them under the Joint Chiefs of Staff. Among them were such organizations as the Army-Navy Petroleum Board and the Army-Navy Selective Service Commission. There was also the older and more permanent Army and Navy Munitions Board, which had sometimes been very active and had at other times lapsed into quiescence. Some progress toward coordination was made. But at the end of the war, both the Army and Navy had separate supply lines running everywhere. Thousands of different items which might have been standardized for each service remained different, some in minor, some in major degree. The Army and Navy still had their own conflicting and duplicating systems for military justice, finance, security, personnel, supplies, transportation, and other operations.

The cost of this duplication cannot even be estimated. It seemed as though some progress had been made when the Navy agreed to allow the Army's Ordnance Department to buy most of its powder. But even this did not work with complete harmony. Ordnance arranged expansion of the New York Ordnance Works at Syracuse for the manufacture of ammonium picrate, a pressed powder used in naval guns. But the Navy, without notifying the Army, built a factory at Lansing, Michigan, for producing the same powder. The Syracuse facilities, although ready for operation, were not needed, and thus $14 million was wasted.

The salty curses of the Navy were trained on the Army's Corps of Engineers, on the other hand, because it had cornered the nation's lumber supply, so that no other agency of the government could get the lumber it needed. The Engineers, as it happened, were without malice in this case. Finding their method of purchasing lumber antiquated, they had substituted a new system which was so superior that it quickly got control of the existing stocks.

The history of this episode is illuminating. One of the first lumber procurement jobs of the emergency was the purchase of 200 million feet for four Army cantonments. In attempting to buy this, the Engineers used 300,000 sheets of paper in soliciting bids. Over 250,000 prices were submitted. Thirty accountants worked day and night trying to compile data on which awards could be made. Then, twenty typists did nothing but write out telegrams. It quickly became evident that this system was impossible and that, if the training camps were to be built in time, better methods would have to be devised.

The first improvement was the holding of auction sales in all parts of the country. Lumbermen offered specific sizes of their product. Contracts were let within ten minutes. The Army built the camps, but the nation was drained of lumber. To assure more equitable distribution in the future, the Central Procuring Agency of the Lumber Branch, Corps of Engineers, was created. The Navy, the lumber industry, and other government agencies concerned had representatives on it. By the middle of 1943, the branch was buying twenty thousand carloads of lumber a month for the Army, the Navy, the Maritime Commission, the War Shipping Administration, the Defense Plant Corporation, and thousands of contractors. It was an excellent demonstration of the sort of cooperation which was possible. Unhappily, it had few imitators.

Difficulties with radar equipment may also be cited as an example of Army-Navy friction. The Navy's interest, quite naturally, was in a set for search at sea. It was bulky and heavy. The AAF wanted lighter, smaller sets for strategic bombing. During 1944 and 1945, we bought about 20 percent of our sets through the Navy, and the larger sets were packed in such a way, for the Navy, that about 5 percent of the equipment was of no use to the Army. The loss from this was about $12 million. Procurement by a single unit for all branches of the Army and Navy would, of course, have made impossible such absurd and costly errors.

It is important, now that unification of the services has been achieved, that maximum advantage be taken of the opportunity it presents to eliminate costly duplication in procurement. In spite of unification it will still be easy, unless serious attention is devoted to the matter, to allow the old wasteful methods to persist. Procurement offices do not have to be in different departments to be unaware what each other is doing, or to cling to their own methods even if they are so aware. It will take vigilance and initiative, high and low, to secure full use of our new opportunities. So great are the material demands of modern war—or even of adequate preparedness for war—that we cannot afford to tolerate overlapping and waste at any spot where it can be avoided. Pride in past prerogatives ought not to be equated for a moment with the national safety.

But lost motion in procurement, because of rivalry and duplication by the Army and Navy, although serious, was far from the most serious problem that faced us in the months after Pearl Harbor.

Shortages of materials, which we had felt even before the Japanese attack, grew worse for a while, and some of them remained with us to the end. Within a few months, however, expanding production of steel, aluminum, and other items, together with the improved methods of allocation, eased our shortages. But there was one thing we could not expand beyond a certain definite limit: that was manpower. We could enlarge mines, open new blast furnaces, and by better methods and more vigorous operations step up the production of materials often by as much as two or three times. But we could not create new men or women. It was simply a question of utilizing what we had, and of doing so at a time when nearly 12 million of our best workers were being taken away for service in the armed forces.[16]

The manpower needs of our war production program were prodigious. In 1939, the year after Munich, between 1 and 2 percent of the national factory workers were in munitions production. By 1944 this had risen to 57 percent. The total labor force of the country climbed in five years from 54.1 million to 64 million. The number of women in factories doubled. The average workweek climbed from 37.7 hours in 1939 to 45.2 in 1944.

When it finally became evident that there was going to be a shortage of manpower, a scramble began to recruit and hold labor. This began fairly early in certain classes of skilled labor, but by the time we approached peak production, the competition for workers was almost as keen in the unskilled categories. Inevitably, there was waste and hoarding. The harassed contractor, under pressure from the Army to turn out the goods, was inclined to get as many skilled mechanics as he could find. Once he had secured them, he saw no reason, for instance, to release scarce toolmakers during a momentary slump in production. He would need them later, and if he let them go, he knew he had small chance to get them back. Furthermore, thanks to the cost-plus-fixed-fee contract, if that was what he had, the government was paying their wages. Of course, gross cases of such manpower hoarding were not common. But almost every contractor was subject to almost irresistible temptation to indulge in a little of it, and to feel that the importance of his product for the national defense justified him in holding on to workers who might prove irreplaceable.

Even the Armed Services were guilty too. By repeated examination of its needs, the ASF was able, in the two years between June 1943 and June 1945, to reduce its operating personnel by 225,000, despite a 30-percent increase in workload. This was partly the result of increased efficiency, as more experience was gained, but it is also true that in the first months of the expansion, too many people were hired. It will probably never be possible to say just how much waste and hoarding of manpower there was, for the subject is fraught with too many complexities to submit to precise analysis. But it is undoubtedly true that the public came to believe that the waste was serious. This belief was a serious deterrent to the prosecution of the war. It made men skeptical about the manpower needs of both the armed services and industry. On one hand it produced opposition to the creation of military forces of adequate size, and on the other it stood across the path of adequate legislative and administrative measures to deal with the manpower problem in war industry.

Probably the fundamental difficulty in handling the industrial manpower problem was the fact that we were using a totally different method from that employed to solve the manpower problem for the armed forces. For the latter we took men, by the authority of the nation, and assigned them to the spot where they were most needed. We undoubtedly at times misjudged the need at particular spots, but subject to the imperfections of our judgment, need was the only criterion, and command, based on careful appraisal and planning, was the method by which need was supplied.

We started out on a very different basis in the use of industrial manpower. In the early days, and to some degree throughout the whole crisis, we relied upon inducements which would appeal to the individual worker to take the necessary man or woman to the right spot. Inevitably, then, those inducements had to be to a large degree financial. If we suffered from a grave deficiency of workers in a particular industry, the thing to do was to make the job financially more attractive.

Of course, I do not mean to suggest that higher wages constituted the only inducement that took people into particular war plants. Thousands worked at inferior wages because they were doing the job they had always done and which had become a habitual part of their lives. Others accepted lesser wages in order that they might remain in the communities in which they already lived, where they had friends, owned homes, and enjoyed the intangibles that add to the value of life. Thousands of others disregarded financial advantage and accepted lower-paid positions because it was explained to them that the nation needed them in these jobs. But, after due allowance is made for all these factors, an appreciable portion of our manpower, if it was to be moved, had to be moved by greater financial inducement. Unless we could offer such an inducement, it was difficult to effect an increase of the labor force in any particular spot.

For a while, this method of moving labor about did not get us into serious difficulties for, at the start of the national emergency, we still had large numbers of unemployed to whom the offer of employment at prevailing wages was an inducement to move to the spot where they were needed. But, as our war production expanded, and the normal labor force was depleted by the induction of men into the armed services, this cushion was taken away from us. If every time we needed to add to our labor supply at a certain point, we were to raise wages there, we would soon be caught in a vicious spiral of inflation. Furthermore, the raising of wages would not draw merely the right workers in the right numbers, from among those who could be spared from the jobs with which they had previously been occupied. It would, instead, draw any and all, and almost certainly pull key workers away from tasks to which they were essential.

To us in the War Department, such a method of maneuvering manpower seemed too crude, too hit and miss, to meet the peculiar and rapidly shifting requirements of war industry. By constantly unsettling the wage and price structure, it served as a provocation to conflict between management and labor, and by exercising a general inflationary influence, it both added uncertainty to our contractual relations with munitions producers and created an upward pressure on the price ceiling, which was almost certain to have, as it actually has had, a strongly inflationary effect in the immediate, postwar period. For these reasons many of us thought that the proper solution to the increasingly acute labor shortage lay in fairly rigid work controls such as those employed in Great Britain, Canada, Australia, and New Zealand. The Austin-Wadsworth Act was designed to achieve a somewhat similar control here. I urged the passage of the Act because, as I said in 1943, I felt that it would "mitigate the loss of life on the fighting front,"[17] since any improvement in our system of war production was certain to hasten the end of the war and reduce casualties.[18] That is still my belief. Men had been drafted for the Army and Navy. The government had the power to requisition any property needed for the war. Management could be ordered to engage in any war activity the government saw fit to demand of it and, if proved unfit, be removed. Profits were controlled by renegotiation.[19] It did not seem unreasonable to subject manpower to controls which would insure taking labor to the spot where it was most needed and keeping it there so long as the need lasted.

To many, however, the Austin-Wadsworth bill seemed alien to the democratic principles for which the war was fought. Others had doubts whether the measure would be properly administered—and I can say that to a certain extent I shared their misgivings. But the main reason for the failure of the bill, I think, was the public conviction that manpower was being wasted. Servicemen wrote home about fellow soldiers idling in cantonments. Reports of labor hoarding in shipyards, arsenals, and factories were published, and some were true. Labor, still sensitive from the bruises of its recent struggle for better conditions, feared lest the bill hide some dark plot of employers to snatch away the recent gains. For all these reasons, Congress refused to pass the needed legislation and the makeshift system continued until the end of the war.

The essence of this makeshift system was an endeavor to steer people into the jobs where they were most needed by making it difficult for them to take new jobs where they were less needed. Thus we sought to limit shopping around for higher wages, and also to prevent the enticement of workers away from critical production by employers who might command greater financial resources. But this system did not permit us to take direct steps to put the right man in the right place. He might not be in the place where he was most needed, but if he chose to remain where he was, we had no way of moving him. We could not move him in the direction we wanted unless he first chose to move of his own volition, or unless the work he was previously engaged in came to an end. Even then, if he chose to remain unemployed, there was nothing we could do unless he had been exempted from the draft on the ground that his services were essential to war industry.

Fortunately, no major breakdown in the labor supply occurred, but the crises were repeated. In the closing stages of the war, when our production system was in full cry, it was seldom that we needed vast numbers of new workers in spots where they were not available. More often what we needed was a few workers of unusual skill for expert jobs, or of unusual ruggedness for jobs involving very heavy strain. But these jobs, although requiring but a tiny fraction of our total labor supply, often had a tremendously significant role in our whole production program. As often as not, they involved the production of some critical item without which the work of many thousands of workers upon some related items might be rendered useless. For example, we were threatened in the summer of 1941, with a grave copper shortage because of a deficiency of workers in the mines. Such a shortage would have laid a paralyzing hand upon almost every aspect of the production of arms and combat equipment, so much so that it was necessary to release twenty-eight hundred miners from the Army. Many other such instances occurred, and serious damage was at times only avoided by the narrowest of margins.

Until April 1942 the War Production Board and its predecessors handled manpower. Then the War Manpower Commission was created. It has always seemed to me that it was unfortunate, in dealing with a problem so intricately tied up with all the other problems of war production, to separate more sharply, as was done in this case, the responsibility for the control of manpower from the overall responsibility for the control of war production. As a situation such as manpower becomes tighter, what is needed is not a more separate treatment but a better coordinated one.

Of course, the fundamental difficulty facing the newly created Manpower Commission was the one already referred to, the fact that it was compelled to use almost entirely voluntary methods in getting the right number of workers to the plants where they were needed. Training courses were begun. Every effort was made to provide housing, although it was far from adequate. Contracts were withheld, whenever possible, from sections of the country where the labor supply was short. But certainly our experience with manpower controls in the recent war ought to leave us in no doubt that better, and probably more drastic, methods will have to be employed in another emergency.

One interesting and novel device employed to improve labor utilization was the labor-management committee, which grew out of a drive for increased production by the War Production Board and other agencies in the spring of 1942. At first, both labor and management viewed the new committees with suspicion: the former on the ground that the plan was a disguised speed-up, the latter because it was afraid of interference with management by the workers. However, the plan was endorsed by the United States Chamber of Commerce and the National Association of Manufacturers on the management side, and by Philip Murray, of the Congress of Industrial Organizations, and other leaders on the labor side. On the whole, it worked well. The War Department agreed to the setting up of similar committees in its arsenals and installations. The committees worked to conserve manpower, cut down absenteeism, establish car pools, and make awards for suggestions which increased production. Accident prevention, health preservation, housing, and worker morale were among the subjects handled. Through the committees, more than 6 million suggestions were turned in for reducing turnover and absentee rates and for increasing plant output.

The winning of a war demands peace on the labor front. From this point of view, the Second World War came at a rather difficult time for the United States. The prewar years of depression and uncertain recovery had produced rapid changes in employer-employee relationships, changes which had not yet had time to settle and which some regarded as having gone too far and others as having gone not far enough. Furthermore, labor itself had split into rival camps,[20] and jurisdictional problems hovered on the heels of every negotiation over conditions of employment. The possibility of serious trouble was very great, and it was certain that conflict on this front would set loose controversial passions of wide extent.

Perhaps, in looking backward, we ought to congratulate ourselves that we ran into as few storms as we did. The no-strike pledge of December 23, 1941, with the heads of unions with a membership of

11 million was an achievement of inestimable value, and no responsible labor leader violated it. But there were many wildcat strikes, nonetheless, and many were potentially dangerous. Some were caused by delays of the War Labor Board, which was swamped with cases, in settling wage and other disputes. Some came from honest disagreement over cost-of-living statistics. Others, for which there was no excuse, came from jurisdictional disputes between rival unions.

The evaluation of the importance of work stoppages as a result of strikes and lockouts is not an easy one. On a quantitative basis, the loss in man-hours was microscopic: in January 1941, 1.1 percent of the total; January 1942, 0.6 percent; January 1943, 1 percent; January 1945, 0.3 percent. The loss from absenteeism and industrial accidents was far greater. Labor Department statistics show a total of 6,725,000 worker casualties of whom 37,600 were killed, 200 disabled for life, and 4,500,000 temporarily incapacitated. The dead in industry almost equaled our dead in battle during the First World War.[21]

Nevertheless, this was a case where quantitative figures did not tell the real story. Even when absenteeism was at its worst, no factory was ever stopped by it. Whatever the factory was producing still came off the assembly line, although in reduced quantities. And, as absenteeism was in some measure or other a universal phenomenon, the balance between various items of production was seldom drastically upset by this one factor alone. The total effect, in generally reduced production, was of course serious, but it simply meant, in most cases, somewhat reduced production all along the line.

Stoppage as a result of strikes, however, was often quite a different matter.[22] Frequently these strikes hit, or threatened to hit, industries whose production was small in total quantity but was essential to the functioning of many other aspects of the production program. And because this quantity, although vital, was small, sometimes the nation's entire supply might depend upon one or two factories. Thus a single strike, involving perhaps only a few hundred workers, might tie up hundreds of thousands of workers in plants which could not operate without the product made by the few hundred. Hence, statistics of man-days lost in strikes never constituted a thoroughly accurate picture of the damage done, and at times there was almost no relationship between them and the real harm done to war production.

The broader responsibility in the field of labor relations, of course, did not lie with the War Department. The War Labor Board, under William H. Davis, and the Office of Price Administration were charged in January 1942 with the responsibility for keeping wages and prices as equal as possible. Out of their deliberations grew the "Little Steel" formula—15 percent increase in pay over January 1941. Since we were not willing to follow the suggestion made by Mr. Baruch, that wages and prices be frozen for the duration of the emergency, these hard-pressed agencies undertook the extremely difficult task of seeing to it that any changes which had to be made should creep instead of gallop, and that income and purchasing power should not get out of alignment. In view of the difficulties they faced, and the modest authority with which they were endowed, they merited more credit than the general public has as yet been willing to bestow upon them.

The responsibility of the War Department in the field of labor relations lay in the timely discovery of possible interruptions of its production by strikes, in heading them off by informal intervention when that could be wisely attempted, and in bringing the danger promptly to the attention of the appropriate authorities where more formal preventative measures were necessary. An organization in my office, under the supervision of Mr. Edward F. McGrady, a man who brought to his task long experience in the labor movement and the respect of all parties, did valiant work to forestall difficulties and to limit the extent of those which could not be prevented. Only one who was a constant witness of the skill, patience, and, where necessary, firmness with which Mr. McGrady and his assistants dealt with a succession of dynamite-laden problems can appreciate the amount of trouble and loss they enabled us to avoid.[23]

There was developed during the national emergency one device to prevent work stoppages which brought heavy burdens upon the War Department which we did not relish, but which I think we assumed with notable success. This was the plant takeover.[24] It became evident even before we entered the war, that in some cases a disastrous stoppage of work could not be avoided if it were left to management and labor to deal directly with each other. In a number of such eases, the government stepped in, took over the plant, and for the time being placed itself in the position of management. By this device the plant could be kept going without, for the moment, either labor or management surrendering the points for which they had been fighting. When, with the extra time thus made available, the disputing parties reached an agreement, the government withdrew and returned the plant to management. A number of very critical work stoppages were prevented by this procedure.

When such takeovers took place, some department of government was called upon to assume the detailed administrative responsibility. Partly because so large a part of our war production was under War Department contract, and partly because of the confidence felt in the integrity of Army officers and War Department officials, a great many of these cases were turned over to the War Department.[25] We never welcomed the burden and felt, in most cases, that it ought not to have been placed upon us. It took us into work which was outside our normal experience—for this was far more than a policing job—and it placed heavy burdens upon the time of men who already had more than they could do to handle duties more logically connected with the military organization. But we did the job, and did it well.

In some cases the work was not difficult, for both labor and management were glad to accept this escape from their immediate impasse. In such cases the running of the plant was scarcely affected. The same plant officials did the same production jobs as before. In some cases, however, cooperation was refused, and then it required great caution and judgment to secure a satisfactory result. But experience was a rapid teacher, and before long we had built up procedures and developed a group of experienced officials, both military and civilian, who knew how to spot and avoid the many pitfalls in this delicate operation.

But our vulnerability to strikes in critical plants, and the care we took to prevent them, must not be allowed to create the impression that the American worker during the war was constantly on the verge of downing tools and going on strike. The opposite was the case in the great majority of instances. The workmen of America, whether organized into unions or not, labored long and hard under trying conditions. They were frequently far from their homes and families. They had to contend with crowded transportation systems, bad housing, and lack of recreational facilities. Secretary of Labor Lewis B. Schwellenbach estimated in 1945 that by remaining on the job on important holidays, labor "had put in more than five times as many man-days of work as were lost through strikes and lock outs during the first six months" of 1945.

Labor often acted swiftly to help solve some sudden emergency of production. Two weeks before the German breakthrough in December 1944, a grave tire shortage developed. Tires were needed for cars, trucks, aircraft, and heavy guns. A $155 million expansion program was authorized, and the United Rubber Workers agreed to work seven days a week for 120 days. The Army agreed to furlough thirteen hundred tire workers. The program had to be curtailed at mid-point because of a dwindling supply of carbon black, but 300,000 more tires were produced in the last quarter of 1944 than in the third.

In September 1942, land was acquired in Tennessee for the community to be called Oak Ridge, where would live about seventy-five thousand people employed—although they had no idea what they were doing—on atomic fission.[26] Among other workers needed for this phase of the Manhattan District project were carpenters. William L. Hutcheson, president of the United Brotherhood of Carpenters and Joiners of America, agreed to assist in recruiting non-union craftsmen, although all we could tell him was that the job was vital to the war. Union meetings could not be held for security reasons, but dues were collected by the contractor.

Not one of our production goals could have been reached without the women of the United States. This was true even in the production of tanks, armor plate, artillery, and other heavy war goods which could not be handled by women. By entering the light industries, they released men for the heavier work. During the first six months after Pearl Harbor, most American women seemed to be skeptical about the real necessity for their help, although hundreds of thousands had already taken war jobs. A government survey showed that less than a third believed that the success of the production program depended on them. They shared the general complacency whose traces were not entirely swept away by our original disasters. By V-J Day, however, between 18 and 19 million women, an all-time record, were working. For the first time, more married than single women were employed.[27]

All this required sweeping social adjustment and was in many aspects far from desirable. They left their homes and children to fend for themselves during most of the day. In the Northwest, working mothers drove eighty to ninety miles a day from their rural homes to the shipyards. The United States was dotted with trailer camps. The rising curve of juvenile delinquency was unquestionably accelerated by the absence of mothers in war plants, and of fathers in the Army and Navy. The situation was ameliorated somewhat by foresighted employers who provided nurseries and childcare centers. The government established three thousand similar centers, and many city and private welfare agencies took similar action. It should be noted that fewer of these women, who could ill be spared from home, would have been needed in war plants had Congress approved the Austin-Wadsworth bill.

As the labor situation grew acute in 1943, energetic campaigns urged women to enter war work. If they knew how to use a sewing machine, they were told, they would be useful on airplane parts. If they had done fine embroidery, or had made jewelry, they could learn to assemble time fuses, radio tubes, and control instruments for airplanes and submarines. They learned. In such intricate operations as assembling time fuses, only 2 percent of the employees at Army arsenals in 1939 were women. By 1942 the percentage had been almost exactly reversed.

Management and the Army learned too. It was with extreme misgiving that old-time officers permitted women, some of them looking like debutantes or school girls, to test antiaircraft and other guns at our various proving grounds. I shall never forget my own shock when, on a visit to Aberdeen, I saw a motherly lady wearing a bandanna and slacks banging happily away testing guns. But their record was good. Their innate womanly caution prevented accidents. The patience which enabled them to excel men in intricate hand or machine operations made it possible for them to work longer hours.

The sudden entry of millions of American girls into war plants had its problems, of course. The War Manpower Commission appealed to a young Hollywood actress, whose trade-mark was a blonde lock over her right eye, that she was endangering feminine war workers who were imitating her. She readily changed her hair-do when she realized that other locks, blonde or brunette, might catch in the machinery.[28] Occasionally a foreman or personnel manager felt it necessary to issue a solemn warning that too-tight sweaters were playing Hitler's game. In the main, however, American women and men worked together sensibly. The forebodings of the pessimists were seldom justified. One apprehensive aircraft manufacturer discovered this when the first group of two hundred girls had finished their training period and were ready to go out into the plant. He told them that they had nothing to fear from the men, who were seasoned, experienced veterans, most of them family men.

"Listen, mister," called out a girl in the group, "Don't worry about us. We've handled men before."

Also essential to our achievements in production were the skill and hard work of the American Negro. In four years after April 1940, the number of employed Negro men and women rose by almost 1 million. Far more important than this total, however, is the degree to which Negroes qualified for higher-paid positions. They were trained in the aircraft industries, shipbuilding, sheet metal work and welding, automobile production, machine shop operation, and other essential occupations. Many became foremen and inspectors. During a four-year period, about 500,000 Negroes successfully completed the training courses.[29]

Every conceivable source of labor was converted to war. The unfortunate men and women imprisoned in state and federal penitentiaries were not lacking in patriotism. They frequently agreed to work longer hours, without increase of the meager pay they were receiving. About 130,000 inmates of one hundred state prisons, working six and sometimes seven days a week, produced textiles, canned food, twine, and other war goods in 1943 with a value of $10 million. The Prison Industries Branch of the War Production Board provided equipment when needed and stimulated increased production. The value of goods manufactured per convict rose from $1,465 in 1939 to $5,300 in 1943. Marines fighting in the Pacific used sixty-five-foot wooden boats built by men in penal institutions. The lame, the blind, and the otherwise physically handicapped also helped to fill the constantly increasing demand for labor. To many of them, the war brought a usefulness and a purpose in life which they had never known before. As a nation proud of being progressive, however, we can find no satisfaction in the children who left school and went to work by the hundreds of thousands. Over 225,000 small girls, under fourteen years of age, were added to the labor force. It is all too probable that a large percentage of them, along with their brothers, will never return to school, but will spend their lives under the burden of this handicap. If the United States had been more alert between 1931 and 1941, it could have won the war without imposing this penalty on its children.[30]

In commending American workers for their part in war production, we must not lose sight of the great achievement of American management. It was management's task to design, experiment with, and develop the materiel needed by our fighting forces: to lay out the production lines; to obtain or devise the machine tools; to train the workers. This task American management performed most admirably. The measure of its success is shown not only by the fact that we achieved our goals, but also by the fact that, in spite of the constant drain of the best workers into the fighting forces and the necessity of training hundreds of thousands of new workers, either women or men under or above the prime age for labors, our production per worker improved steadily to the very end of the crisis.

As a matter of fact, the way of life for which we were fighting was, in the last analysis, the secret of our success both in the field and in the factory. Those priceless qualities of initiative, flexibility, willingness to assume responsibility, and confidence in one's fellows which spring from our free institutions worked constantly and decisively in our favor at every level of the battle of production, just as they did in every armed clash with the enemy. We did not so much save democracy: we were saved by it. And that was true in spite of the fact that some of the imperfections of democracy exposed us to needless peril at the beginning of the crisis.

It may not be fully recognized yet that our war production program brought about a stupendous social transformation in this country whose full consequences it is still too early to appraise. It produced one of the greatest migrations of history. The Bureau of the Census estimates that over 15 million civilians left their homes between December 7, 1941, and March 1945. Some went only short distances, but many others moved thousands of miles. The trend was predominantly westward. The Pacific Coast gained 1.2 million new residents. The South lost about 900,000 to the Far West, and the East 500,000. All in all, the South probably lost 1.6 million of its residents, who left to take the better jobs beckoning them in the North. Some of the immediate consequences of this migration manifested themselves in the nationwide housing shortage, which is still with us. What deeper and more permanent consequences may ensue from our industrial effort during the war only time will reveal. Certainly, in our management of the production program, we utilized the American industrial structure, insofar as possible, as we found it, and we returned it to civilian use, insofar as we were able, in the condition in which we took it over. But no economic organism can go through so tremendous an experience without change, and doubtless the years ahead will reveal transformations which we did not plan, and which, as yet, we sense only dimly.

It ought also to be noted that, in a sense, the unprecedented volume of American war production produced a new theory of military tactics. The older fire doctrine was expressed by the command which has come down through history from Bunker Hill: "Don't fire until you see the whites of their eyes." And, as a nation, we have always had the pioneer's pride of marksmanship, even when we were not, as at Bunker Hill, embarrassed for lack of ammunition. And this belief in making every shot count, and in firing only at what you can see, had not disappeared from our Army at the time it began training for World War II, even though there was at no time any serious danger of a shortage of small-arms ammunition, and even though motor transport adapted to cross-country work had relieved the soldier of many of the limitations which used to limit the amount of ammunition he could fire in battle. So we spent long hours on target practice, with the result, sometimes, that we deterred our men from firing at all when in combat, because they could rarely see a target.

Fortunately, our military leaders had little patience with the older, more conservative training methods by which troops were taught that they should never fire blindly, but only at specific targets. Our policy, even though it was resisted by some of the less progressive elements, was to provide enough guns and ammunition so that whole areas could be saturated. In this connection it is interesting to note that German soldiers captured when the Italian campaign ended complained bitterly that American artillery tactics permitted us to fight a "cheap war," with a maximum of supplies and a minimum of human sacrifice. Lt. Gen. Karl Thoholte, regarded as the ablest of the Nazi artillery commanders, told our intelligence officers on May 15, 1945:

> The United States practice of firing to saturate an area has been criticized adversely by many German officers because they have witnessed at one time or another the firing hundreds of rounds, not one of which caused a German casualty. The fact that the United States had a huge supply of ammunition as compared with Germany made it profitable to saturate an area now and then just to prevent enemy action and pin him down. However, if the Germans had had an equal amount of ammunition, the United States artillery would have been required to choose targets more judiciously.

The late Gen. George S. Patton, Jr., realized clearly the importance of the new fire tactics based upon an abundance of ammunition. I remember conversations with him, in my office at the Pentagon and on trips of mine to the European theater, in which he vigorously criticized the use of rifle ranges in training infantry.

"When armed with that wonderful weapon, the M-1 rifle," he said on one of these occasions,

> the ground soldier can fire about forty rounds a minute He should keep on firing, whether he sees anything or not. He should fire as he advances, about a round to every two or three steps.
>
> We are now certain that the whistle of these bullets, the bits of branches shot from trees and the flying earth and rock demoralize the enemy. His own small arms fire dwindles. Rather often, in this war, the tradition of target training caused the men to hold their fire until they saw targets. Instead, they should have kept firing at the probable location of the enemy. It is always better to be extravagant with ammunition than with lives.

In view of the controversy in which we were involved at the time of the adoption of the Garand rifle, this testimony by General Patton was gratifying. Conservatives had criticized us for giving up the reliable old Springfield, with which the very best soldier could scarcely exceed fifteen shots a minute. Others had criticized us for not adopting a rival make of semiautomatic model. Events demonstrated both the soundness of our judgment in replacing the old bolt-action rifle, and the accuracy of our appraisal of the controversial Garand. Even beyond the field of fire tactics for infantry and artillery, it was our general theory of war to overwhelm the enemy with materiel.[31] It saved American lives, countless numbers of them, in individual actions. It also saved lives because, determined to suffer no shortage in supply which we could prevent, we sent so much to the men in the field, once our production was at full blast, that it was seldom that our operations were delayed because of supply defects. This was very important when our major counteroffensives against both Germany and Japan began. It meant that, once we had dealt the enemy a heavy initial blow, we did not have to pause while supplies were produced for a second blow, and thus give the enemy a chance to recover and get set once more. How important this was is shown by the fact that the only serious setback we received in our great offensive came when, not lack of production, but insuperable difficulties in the way of moving supplies forward as rapidly as the Army moved, forced us to give the Germans a breather that enabled them to take position in their frontier defenses. There would probably have been many more such breathers, and many more reverses such as the Battle of the Bulge, had our production plans not been designed on such an ample scale. It took tremendous military and naval skill to finish the war in such a short space of time after our major offensive began. But that skill would not have sufficed for so quick a victory had we not decided to take no chances with the adequacy of our supplies. And the quick victory is almost always the cheap victory, cheapest in dollars and cheapest in lives.

For that reason we are proud, not only of our ability to achieve altitudinal goals, but also of the fact that we set them so high. Untold thousands of American young men are back with their families today because we did so. For the whole world, in truth, the lingering horror of war was shortened by the magnitude of our production.

Chapter 6

An Offensive Begins

Because our output of munitions was not far enough advanced, only a few blows were possible during the first half of 1942. The Navy made its hit-and-run attack on the Japanese islands in the Gilberts and Marshalls on January 31. A task force struck at Wake and at Marcus in March. In May and June, the Navy successfully fought the far greater and profoundly decisive actions of the Coral Sea and Midway.

The first vague hopes that an invasion of France would be possible in 1942 faded when Japan continued her conquests, when Tobruk fell, and when the Soviet Union met severe reverses in the Crimea. In July 1942 a meeting of great importance was secretly held in London. General Marshall, Admiral King, and the late Harry Hopkins discussed the difficult alternatives with Prime Minister Churchill. Some operation to relieve the pressure on Russia and on Great Britain was mandatory.[1] One possibility, debated for weeks, was finally discarded. This was Operation SLEDGEHAMMER. It called for a quick assault against the French Coast some time in 1942, ahead of schedule. Some six divisions would be needed if SLEDGEHAMMER was to have any hope of success. But we lacked landing boats and nearly everything else for such an attack. Strategy had to wait upon production.

An invasion of North Africa was selected as a last resort. It would draw heavily upon troops and equipment which were being built up in England, and a major invasion of France would be delayed until 1944. General Eisenhower preferred a cross-channel attack if any offensive was to be attempted in 1942, but Operation TORCH had its advantages. Axis forces were concentrated on the struggle on the eastern front. A successful invasion of Africa might draw some German divisions from Europe and thus lessen the pressure upon the Russians. It would also make possible air bases to protect Mediterranean supply lines. If the Germans were ejected from North Africa, very valuable results would be gained. The Mediterranean, hitherto pretty much of an Italian lake, would be opened and an immense saving in shipping be effected. Gen. Brehon Somervell[2] estimated it would be nearly 2 million tons in five months.

The President and the Prime Minister agreed on the North African attack in July 1942. Planning for the arduous undertaking began at Norfolk House in London and at the old Munitions Building in Washington on July 18. Mr. Churchill, knowing that Britain had aroused the enmity of the French by firing on part of their fleet in 1940, urged that the invasion should appear as American as possible. It was hoped this would soften any possible resistance. To that end, he suggested the appointment of General Eisenhower as Supreme Commander. Admiral Sir Andrew Cunningham would serve as Naval Commander-in-Chief.

The problem of secrecy was vital and difficult.[3] The operation was extremely precarious, and if the Axis leaders learned of the impending blow, they would almost certainly be able to repel it. Thus relatively few officers knew that North Africa was the general target and fewer still precisely where the landings would be made. The Joint TORCH Planning Committee was instructed to work on covering plans for attacks on other Axis territory. At times it seemed impossible that troops could be trained, supplies manufactured and delivered, and convoys assembled without a leak.

We now know that we succeeded in keeping hidden our first great offensive of the war. A digest of interrogations of Axis prisoners discloses that the Germans observed a large increase of shipping at Gibraltar toward the close of October. However, even when one huge convoy of eighty vessels was seen in the straits, the German High Command did not envision a systematic landing in French North Africa. It suspected, rather, an invasion of Southern France or reinforcements for Tunisia or Libya. The failure to occupy Tunis, which stemmed from this misunderstanding of our intentions, was to prove fatal to the Germans.

Differences of opinion between the British and Americans on the strategy to be followed delayed the planners in London and Washington. The American Chiefs of Staff desired, in addition to the Mediterranean attack, an Atlantic invasion which would protect our supply lines in event of hostile action by Spain. The British opposed the dividing of the Allied forces. Precious time was lost while these disagreements were settled in favor of a two-pronged invasion. The date was postponed from October 1 to the early part of November.[4]

Our supply services were forced to face the utmost difficulties in preparing for the invasion.[5] The Army Service Forces[6] (ASF) was not informed about TORCH until July 27. By August 5 the troop basis, which is required before the nature and quantity of the equipment and supplies can be decided, had not yet been drawn up. The following day, orders came to equip three infantry and two armored divisions, in addition to certain antiaircraft units, and to do it by September 5. A normal time schedule for such an assignment would have allowed at least three months.

The original conception of TORCH had been that troops and supplies would sail from the British Isles southward to Casablanca, where the forces would split, the British continuing on through the straits. But supplies in the United Kingdom proved inadequate. They had been sent there for a cross-Channel operation and for the defense of England. Furthermore, vast tonnages had been improperly stored and labeled and could not be disentangled for this new demand upon them.[7] Not enough service troops had been sent abroad to handle the munitions. In spite of the fact that a supply line from Britain to North Africa, shorter by thousands of miles and less subject to submarine attacks, was greatly preferable to the long route from the United States, Britain simply could not meet the logistical demands. Ultimately, one task force, under the command of Gen. George S. Patton, Jr., was trained and equipped in the United States.

The separation of staffs in London and Washington contributed to the confusion which marked this first offensive.[8] Messages and letters were lost or garbled in transit. Shipments were frequently sunk and had to be duplicated hastily from stocks which were rarely adequate. In Washington, despite all the appeals of the United States Civil Service Commission, stenographers were still at a premium, and this additional obstacle to efficiency plagued the planners of TORCH.

"Work on this operation," noted one of them on September 14, "is being delayed from one to two days by lack of stenographic help. As the stenographers who are available continue to be overworked, this situation is expected to become worse."

Doubtless there was too much paper work. The Army was still fighting a gigantic Blitzkrieg with methods inherited from days when operations were small and leisurely. Before the war ended, the ASF was able to eliminate 125,000 time-honored forms which until then had had to be filled out, copied, checked, initialed, signed, and then checked again. But, even with the most rigorous pruning of procedure, the administrative detail remained stupendous.

The immense size and diversity of demands of this war can be illustrated by a few selections from an order given by General Lutes to his staff on September 11, 1942. Among the items on this single requisition for TORCH were: 3 fifteen-ton ice plants; $500,000 worth of tea, sugar, and cotton goods with which to pay native labor; 6 cold-storage units with chemicals; 500,000 board feet of assorted lumber; 18 cranes of assorted sizes; 4 steam hammers with boilers and hose; 10 miles of two-inch and 10 of four-inch pipe; 50 miles of four-inch gasoline pipeline, complete with all pumps, fittings, and tankage; 6 water purification units; special tools for laying and repairing 50 miles of railroad; 3 sets of diving equipment; 80,000 yards of black-out cloth; 2,500 barrels of cement; 200,000 square feet of screening; 1,000 sheets of corrugated iron; 2,000 sheets of plywood; 200 sixty-foot piles. All mechanical items were to be accompanied by sufficient spare parts, fuel, and lubricants to last forty-five days. Just a look at this single order, a microscopically tiny fraction of all the supplies required, will show what an immense variety of things must be both produced and transported in order to carry out a modern military operation.

From October 1 to the end of December 1942, a total of 1,250,000 measurement tons (roughly half a long ton) went to the United Kingdom, Gibraltar, and Africa. New problems arose daily. On September 17, it developed that 17 million gallons of gasoline would have to

An Offensive Begins

be dispatched on dry cargo vessels, because Axis submarine operations had created a shortage of tankers. Nothing comparable had ever been attempted. The gasoline had to be poured from tank cars into 1 million five-gallon cans and 225,000 fifty-five-gallon drums. Unless the operation was kept secret, it might tip off the coming offensive to Axis agents. Tank cars were assembled at Atlanta, and a force of trusted civilians hired. Within two weeks the 17 million gallons of gas were awaiting a convoy at an Atlantic port.

Even greater demands were made of the supply services in the weeks after the invasion. In January 1943 General Marshall and General Somervell were in Casablanca for the conferences between the President and the Prime Minister. The Chief of Staff learned that American troops were rapidly wearing out their shoes on the rough African terrain, although three pairs per man had been supplied. So, he cabled the ASF to ship 400,000 additional pairs within three days. This was a mere detail in the 653,300 measurement tons of cargo dispatched that month.

On January 27 General Somervell, after conferring with General Eisenhower, notified the ASF by radio that a supplementary convoy with 230,000 tons of almost everything under the sun must sail within twenty days. It included 5,000 two-and-one-half-ton trucks, 2,000 one-ton trailers, 72 forty-ton tank transporters, 8 locomotives, 136 railroad cars, 400 dump trucks, 40 P-38 planes, 30 tractors, 20 twelve-cubic-yard scrapers for building airports, 12,000 tons of coal, and 7,000 pounds of candy, cigarettes, and other PX supplies.

"The convoy will sail on February 15," Maj. Gen. W. D. Styer notified General Somervell, "but next time, if you want us to ship the Pentagon, give us a day or two more."

The problem of moving these supplies, especially when the demand came on short notice, was stupendous. But they could not have been moved unless they had first been produced. It was critical, in TORCH and other operations, to be able to fill unexpected requirements of vast dimensions and infinite variety, and to do so almost at once. Many times our campaigns would have bogged down had these demands not been met, and it would have been a costly process to get them started again. Even with the best of planning by the commander and his staff, all the needs of a campaign cannot be precisely foretold. That we produced enough to make it possible to meet promptly these unpredictable demands was an essential feature of the American system of war.

One surprise that affected our supply problems was the fact that we learned rather tardily that Operation TORCH was to be far more than just an occupation of friendly territory. It was, instead, to be a campaign of movement, with heavy losses in men and materiel, which changed the whole supply problem. From a supply point of view, the summer and fall were filled with problems new to the relatively inexperienced officers who were grappling with them. And on the military side, the venture seemed so hazardous that its abandonment was considered. Even General Patton, a man not easily alarmed, was concerned by reports that enemy troops near Casablanca, where he was to land, greatly exceeded his own strength. He was also worried by the lack of suitable beaches and by the high and fickle tides.

The American and British planners worked together in harmony, despite the many problems which arose. The system for keeping track of supplies in the United Kingdom came close to breaking down. This led to duplicate, and sometimes triplicate, shipping of many supplies, some of them critical.[9] Differences developed over the number of cargo ships each country should supply for the convoys. Both nations were short of coal, and discussions over the quantities to be furnished by each consumed precious time. Additional confusion arose over a task force to be held in readiness for two months after the first landing against the possibility that Germany might occupy Spain.

Problems arose as to allocating responsibility for the maintenance of the different Task Forces once operations had begun. It was finally arranged that the Western Task Force would from the first be equipped and maintained from the United States, and that the Central Task Force, although at first maintained from the United Kingdom, could later be supplied from the United States.[10]

One great difficulty was the unloading of ships.[11] General Patton found, during rehearsals at the Navy's Amphibious Training School at Solomon's Island, Maryland, that only two of his booms could lift heavy combat vehicles. Each boom could discharge only one fifty-ton tank lighter per hour, and he had 120 lighters on board.[12] Thus the best possible time in which the convoy could be unloaded, providing the run from ship to shore and back took only two hours, was three days. Would the French coastal batteries, if the French resisted, permit such a performance? Or would so cumbersome an operation escape annihilation from the air?

Lack of sufficient escort vessels proved the final difficulty. This is another example of the limiting influence of supply on strategy. The original hope had been to conquer Tunisia with its naval and air bases in twenty-eight days after the landings. But the escort vessel situation had been serious since the beginning of the War. At a meeting of the American British Combined Chiefs of Staff in June 1942, Admiral King reported an order from the President for an accelerated program; some 150 new vessels were scheduled for delivery by the first of the year. But not enough were ready for TORCH. On September 27, the ASF presented to General Eisenhower one of those dilemmas which rack the sleep of military commanders. The Navy could not escort all the cargo ships which were ready. Either the size of the Western Task Force must be cut from 167,000 to 100,000 men, or half its equipment, principally vehicles, would have to be left behind. This also applied to the convoys being mounted in the United Kingdom. The decision was to use the maximum personnel, so the trucks and other vehicles were not taken.

The British forces landed without serious difficulty in the Mediterranean and turned east in order to begin the Tunisian campaign. But the roads were bad. The railroad was a single-track line with worn-out rolling stock, and little of that. It was to be May 1943—not twenty-eight days—before Tunisia had been cleared of Axis troops.

A principal reason for the delay was the necessity for leaving vehicles behind in the United States. The movement of troops and supplies was slowed down. The campaign proved once more that combat forces are almost wholly dependent upon their lines of communication. Sending maximum quantities of soldiers and equipment at the expense of service troops and motor transport had been a mistake, and the campaign could be pressed to a successful conclusion only after this mistake had been corrected.

But the original difficulty, of course, was the failure to plan early enough for a sufficient quantity of escort vessels. Thus we lost valuable time, supplies, and men because production planning was not closely enough linked to strategy, because we did not secure an accurate estimate of our need for escort vessels in time to have them ready for the day when they were needed. The event demonstrated again that production must be the first step in the implementation of a military plan.[13]

There had been additional supply difficulties at home before General Patton's convoy sailed from Hampton Roads, Virginia. The elaborate and efficient staging installations which would be used to embark millions of young Americans for their great adventure at a dozen ports had not yet been built. Confusion extended to the handling of troop and freight trains. One time a search had to be made through 690 cars on sidings before certain necessary equipment could be found. At the last minute, a fully loaded ship developed engine trouble. The entire cargo had to be transferred to another ship.

But the Patton convoy sailed, nonetheless, on October 24 and followed a zigzag course across the Atlantic, dodging the submarine wolf packs, to its rendezvous off Gibraltar with other units of the Western Task Force, which sailed from England. The ships from the United States carried almost 35,000 men, 728 tracked vehicles, about 5,500 other vehicles, and 97,000 tons of assorted cargo, to make up a total of 239,000 measurement tons.

The soldiers on board the convoys converging on North Africa carried a new weapon, in the use of which they had received no training. This was the secret anti-tank rocket, familiarly called the bazooka.[14] Need for some effective way for the foot soldier to stop tanks had been clear from the time of the invasion of Poland. The old conception that artillery or other tanks were enough to do the job had been invalidated by the rapid thrusts of the German panzer divisions.

Experts of the Ordnance Department began work on a new weapon early in 1941. Among the seemingly insuperable difficulties was the heavy recoil of guns firing shells large enough to pierce tank armor. So, rockets equipped with a new type of explosive head, the shaped charge, were substituted. A small amount of explosive, so shaped, could blow a hole in the toughest tank armor. Although tests could not be held until May 1942, they were sensationally successful. By June 20,000 bazookas were in production. Up to May 1945, almost 500,000 had been made.

They first saw action in North Africa and initial reports of their value surprised even those who had been most optimistic. One soldier knocked the turret completely off a tank at seventy-five yards. A detachment of ten enemy tanks surrendered because, as its commander explained, it had seemed to be in direct range of 105-mm guns. In later campaigns the bazooka was used against pillboxes, Japanese caves, and all kinds of emplaced positions.

Debarking from an armada of seven hundred transports, cargo ships, and naval vessels, the American-British forces began the assault on French North Africa on the morning of November 8. Algiers and Oran capitulated within two days, but the French Navy at Casablanca continued to fight until November 11, while American representatives wrangled with Admiral Darlan and other French Navy and Army leaders. Darlan then ordered all resistance to cease and that the French forces begin war against the Axis.

TORCH was, however, far from a smooth operation. Landing craft hit the beaches miles from their assigned points because of faulty navigation. East of Casablanca heavy swells damaged landing craft. The "invaluable DUKW's,"[15] as General Eisenhower has described them, which were later to be used by the thousands in all amphibious operations, were still unavailable because of Army and Navy reluctance to adopt an untried vehicle.

In the initial landing, equipment losses were unexpectedly light except in radio and other Signal Corps supplies, and a supplementary shipment of seventeen hundred tons of these was rushed to General Eisenhower within three weeks. But shipping losses inevitably mounted as the African campaign continued. By March 1943 thirty-six vessels were useless, twelve of them through enemy action, and the rest because they had collided or run aground. In one case a ship carrying $5 million in radio equipment for the Eighth Air

Force was sunk. Yet, by April 30, 1943, almost 5 million measurement tons had been floated to North Africa by the American supply forces and 3.5 million tons by the British.

The military situation remained critical until April 1943. Hitler occupied the rest of France and thereby secured its Mediterranean Coast. He sent reinforcements into Tunisia. General Eisenhower estimated, on December 6, 1942, that the enemy forces in Tunisia numbered thirty thousand men, and he considered that an Allied retreat might become necessary.

In all truth, the Allied invasion of North Africa had been done on a shoestring, largely because, in the existing state of our munitions production, we could not do more. And, even in those aspects of supply where our stocks were more ample, we often bumped into some other deficiency, such as that in escort vessels, which cancelled the value of our sufficiency in other things. The following May, at his meeting with Mr. Churchill at the White House, the President observed that 200,000 casualties had been suffered in the campaign and that the number might have been greatly reduced had Tunisia been captured on schedule. In future operations, he added, there must be no underestimate of the strength which we needed to mount a successful assault.

Without the unhampered use of French roads and railroads—without the effective fighting of the Free French armies—the casualties would have been heavier still. But at the start the Free French were virtually without weapons. The American-British Chiefs of Staff at first considered equipping them with stocks captured in Libya. However, the arming of the French on a large scale in 1943 and 1944 was possible only because the ASF, in originally planning its supply program, had included a ten-division strategic reserve of weapons of all kinds. From this reserve the French secured the arms with which they made such an effective contribution to victory.

The railroads in North Africa presented a serious problem. Until American equipment arrived, the Rail Division of the Office of the Chief of Transportation in North Africa operated the Chemin de Fer du Maroc and connecting lines. The right of way was undamaged, but the engines were "comical contraptions of a dinky one-horse variety," as a Transportation Corps historian wrote, while the boxcars were constructed to "provide minimum capacity with maximum construction." Air-brake hose had been removed from the freight cars to be used on passenger trains, so braking had to be done manually by Arabs. When ordered to move fifty-four thirty-two-ton tanks to the front, the GI railroad men had to build new floors on the flat cars so that the tanks would not fall through. First, however, they had to scour the countryside for lumber. Hardware merchants were awakened at midnight and asked to turn over nails they had been hiding from the Germans.

Some picture of the difficulty of the supply problem might have been gained by watching the convoys as they arrived after the invasion. The port at Casablanca had not been damaged nearly as much as were later such ports as Naples, Cherbourg, and Antwerp. Yet the French battleship, *Jean Bart,* lay battered and helpless, blocking two berths.[16] Other French ships burned and sank at their piers. Several smaller vessels were submerged in the harbor. But the work of cleaning up was done swiftly. On November 18, D-Day plus 10, the men of the Sixth Port of Embarkation (Mobile) arrived to handle the supporting convoys. They slept in pup tents in open fields and ate K-rations. Few were professional longshoremen. They were inexperienced in the use of winches and other port machinery. The first convoy unloaded by the 1,800 men of the Sixth Port had 60,000 tons of cargo, including 2,600 vehicles. The second consisted of 25 ships with 130,000 tons. The job at Oran was even bigger. That port handled 1.4 million long tons in the first seven months of TORCH as compared with 843,000 tons in Casablanca.[17]

When the President and the Prime Minister met at Casablanca on January 15, 1943, the Allied forces in North Africa numbered 320,000 men. They were supported by a rising weight of materiel which would soon, despite the reverses immediately ahead, make the outcome inevitable. In March 831,000 measurement tons reached North Africa; in April, 1,370,000. In May, the month of the German surrender, the total was a little over 1 million tons, because cutbacks had become possible. Between D-Day and June 30, 1943, 75,000 vehicles were unloaded and 450,000 American soldiers disembarked.

When the war in Europe ended, our intelligence officers questioned German and Italian prisoners of war regarding Axis supplies and reinforcements in the Tunisian campaign. At no time, they estimated, had more than eight hundred men a day been shipped or flown in. Not more than forty thousand tons of supplies had been received in any month, they thought. Our weight of materiel was at least 20 to 1.

Without that advantage we would not have won. It took superb organization to assemble, transport, and disembark such quantities of supplies and equipment in the face of very unfavorable conditions. But even before that, we had to produce it. Many of the hazards we ran stemmed from the fact that we did not produce more at an earlier date. Our final success we owe to the fact that we planned our production on generous lines, and were determined that our troops, when they entered battle, should enjoy an overwhelming superiority in materiel.

Judge Robert P. Patterson in uniform at the Business and Professional Men's Camp at Plattsburgh, New York, July 7, 1940, shortly before being appointed assistant secretary of war. (Acme photo.)

Patterson as the new assistant secretary of war, October 23, 1940. (*New York Herald Tribune*)

Robert P. Patterson, under secretary of war, official photo. (U.S. Army)

Official photo of the Office of the Under Secretary of War. Patterson is seated at center, with William S. Knudsen to his immediate right. (National Archives)

Robert P. Patterson with ex-General Motors head and then General William S. Knudsen. Date and location unknown. (U.S. Army)

Patterson with rifle. Date and location unknown. (U.S. Army)

Under Secretary of War Patterson firing a light machine gun at Fort Leonard Wood, Missouri, August 21, 1942. (U.S. Army)

Citation Winners, December 1942. Donald M. Nelson, chairman of the War Production Board, and Patterson examine the Citation of Individual Production pins. (*Left to right*) Stanley Crawford, RCA Manufacturing Company; Nelson; Edwin Curtis Tracy, RCA Manufacturing Company; Patterson; and an unidentified individual. (Library of Congress)

Patterson with his wife, Margaret, christening the SS *General William A. Mann,* July 18, 1943, at Kearney, New Jersey. (Patterson family photo)

Patterson visiting the 104th Division under the command of General Terry Allen, Camp Carson, Colorado. (U.S. Army photo)

Patterson greeting black soldiers of the 92nd Division at Fort Huachuca, Arizona, June 1944. (U.S. Army photo)

Patterson visiting the Jones and Laughlin Steel Corporation, Pittsburgh, Pennsylvania, November 2, 1944. (Newman-Schmidt Studios)

Patterson shaking hands with General Douglas MacArthur in New Guinea, 1945. General William S. Knudsen stands to their left. (Library of Congress)

As the Caissons Go Rolling Along

Editorial cartoon by C. K. Berryman depicting armed forces unification. *Washington Evening Star,* December 21, 1945.

Patterson inspects an American Red Cross unit in Japan with Col. Fred H. Stoll, January 9, 1946. (U.S. Army photo)

Patterson testifying at the War Profits Hearing of the Senate Special Investigating Committee, July, 9, 1946. (Acme photo).

New York Herald Tribune article covering Patterson's death and funeral, January 25, 1952.

Chapter 7

Alaska, Australia, the Persian Gulf

War in the Pacific was one war, fought in many far-distant theaters. Every part of each theater was related, directly or indirectly, to all the others. The Pacific War started in 1941 with Japan close to victory. It ended with Japan's unconditional surrender three and a half years later. Her navy and most of her merchant fleet had been destroyed, and so had the effective part of her air force. But the Japanese army was still strong. It numbered 4.6 million men—110 infantry and 4 armored divisions. Why, then, had this powerful and arrogant nation been forced to admit complete defeat?

The answer is found in that part of the science of warfare called logistics, which means the equipping, supplying, and transporting of armed forces. The fatal predicament of Japan becomes clear if we look at her position in the Pacific in July 1945, just prior to V-J Day. The area of Japanese control extended, in theory, from the Kurile Islands west and north to Karafuto and the coast of Siberia. She controlled, in theory, the Japan and the Yellow Seas, the East China Sea, the eastern coast of China, the South China Sea, the island of Hainan, and southward to the Dutch East Indies. Far to the east, the Japanese had garrisons in the Marshall and Caroline Islands.

A complete collapse of logistical capacity made false the theory of Japanese control of any part of this empire.[1] What remained of her shipping was subjected to air and sea attack. More than 2 million troops were scattered through Manchuria, Korea, China, French Indo-China, Sumatra, Java, Borneo, Formosa, and in the Pacific Islands. The island garrisons were close to starvation and were utterly without offensive capacity. The others were living off the land, but were unable to strike at United Nations forces.[2]

The position of the United States, logistically, was not as desperate in 1941 as was that of Japan in 1945. But it was bad enough. Our huge air fleets existed only as bauxite—aluminum ore—and we did not have enough of that. We did not have shipyards, let alone ships, in which to build the naval, transport, and cargo vessels we needed. The Army was growing, but it lacked equipment. That is why war in the Pacific was one war. We could not ship oil to Alaska because of the critical shortage of tankers. We could not send supplies or reinforcements to the beleaguered Philippines. Three months after Pearl Harbor, the United States Maritime Commission predicted that the shortage in deadweight tons of shipping would rise from 900,000 to 6.2 million in a year. Not until November 1943 did the United Nations replace, through new construction, the shipping losses incurred since the beginning of the war.[3]

The United States had to support communication lines to every part of the world, a total of 86,000 miles. We did not have sufficient merchant ships to ply them or escort vessels to patrol them. It was 5,410 nautical miles from San Francisco to New Caledonia and 6,193 to Brisbane. The route from Los Angeles to Calcutta was 12,163 nautical miles; from Hampton Roads to Bombay, 11,392 miles. It was 12,000 miles from Hampton Roads to the Persian Gulf. Meanwhile submarine and air attacks on United Nations ships caused losses of 183,000 gross tons in November 1941, 513,000 tons in December, and 552,000 tone in January 1942.

Even before Pearl Harbor, it was clear that, if war came, supply would be perhaps our most critical problem. Two months before the Japanese attack, as the war clouds darkened, it was estimated that not more than 855,000 gross tons of shipping would be available should the need arise for an emergency operation somewhere overseas. With this, perhaps fifty thousand troops could be shipped and maintained. During 1942 it was thought seventy thousand per month could be moved. That presented a gloomy outlook for the support of our overseas possessions, some of which were practically in the backyard of our probable enemy.

After December 7 Australia was made the main supply base of the South Pacific, at first in the hope that reinforcements could be sent to the Philippines. The War Plans Division of the General Staff had concluded late in 1941 that the Philippines could not long withstand the Japanese attack which seemed imminent. But prompt reinforcement, it felt, might "enhance the probability of holding Luzon, and, in any event, give a reasonable assurance of holding Manila Bay."[4] To this end, a number of ships sailed from San Francisco. At Hawaii they joined a small convoy under the protection of the cruiser *Pensacola*.

On November 27 the War Plans Division had sent a significant message to the commanding generals of the Hawaiian Department, the Caribbean and Western Defense Commands, and the American forces in the Far East. Paraphrased, it said:

> To all practicable purposes negotiations with Japan appear to be terminated with only the barest possibilities that the Japanese government might come back and offer to continue. Japanese future action unpredictable, but at any moment hostile action possible. United States desires that Japan commit first overt act if hostilities cannot be avoided. Prior to hostilities, undertake such reconnaissance and other measures as are deemed necessary.[5]

Upon receipt of this warning, the commanders of the convoy decided to sail a southwesterly course instead of the usual one close to the Japanese mandated islands. It is well they did, for while the convoy was at sea, a second radio message on December 7 said: "Japan started hostilities; govern yourself accordingly."

The convoy would have been easy prey for any marauding Japanese, for with the exception of the lone cruiser, it was practically defenseless. Five of the eight ships had no guns at all, and the armament of the others was trifling. The only hope was that, assisted by the constant scouting of the four reconnaissance planes of the *Pensacola*, contact with enemy forces could be avoided. Fortunately it was, and the convoy, meanwhile having received orders to proceed to Australia instead of the Philippines, reached Brisbane safely.

This was the vanguard of the 150,000 Americans who would be rushed to the defense of Australia and New Zealand by June 1942.[6] The first duty of General Barnes, senior officer with the convoy, was to get as much as possible of his modest store of supplies to the Philippines. But it was soon apparent that little, if any, would reach General MacArthur's forces. The ships had been loaded by peacetime standards, and had to be completely unloaded before the most acutely needed equipment could be found. Parts essential to the firing of the A-24 bombers' guns were never located and had to be flown from the United States. They arrived too late, after General MacArthur had withdrawn to Bataan.

No better luck attended dispatch of the rest of the cargo. The Army transport *Holbrook*, and a Dutch vessel, the *Bloemfontein*, which were the fastest ships of the convoy, made ready to sail for the Philippines. But the master of the *Bloemfontein* balked at the dangerous voyage, and went to the Dutch East Indies instead. And it soon became evident that there was no port left in American hands at which the *Holbrook* could dock.

Everything possible, even at this late date, was done to relieve the Philippine forces. Three submarines managed to bring into Mindanao a million rounds of .30-calibre ammunition. General MacArthur refused to admit that the blockade could not be broken. He was "professionally certain," he said in the middle of January, that small boats could get through. Even if the losses were high, the tonnages brought in would alleviate the situation somewhat. Moreover, he added, the people of the Philippines would never comprehend why the United States could not run the blockade in the Pacific when it was doing so successfully in the Atlantic. An attempt, at least, must be made.

So a search was made for small boats with daring crews and skippers. Few were found with stomachs for such a hazardous enterprise. The use of even these was held up for a while by War Department red tape which stood in the way of the prompt transfer of the funds needed to pay these crews. Finally, six small ships left for the Philippines, but only three of them got through. Planes and submarines brought in a few more supplies, but the total was not enough to affect the final outcome.[7]

The fate of the democracies in the South Pacific now hung on our getting supplies to Australia, just as, at the same time, it would hang on supplying the British at Suez and the Russians via the Persian Gulf. Australia was not easy to supply or defend. Java fell and a Japanese attack and invasion from the northward seemed certain. The six-thousand-mile supply line to San Francisco had to be protected by a badly crippled Navy. Even if successfully protected, there were all too few cargo ships to ply it.

Supplying Australia would have been difficult even had enough convoys been able to move safely and swiftly. A third of its 7 million population lived in Sidney and Melbourne, far removed from the strategically important Darwin area in the northwest. The country's already small reservoir of manpower had been further drained by the Army and by essential industries. When ships arrived, they could not be unloaded on schedule because of the lack of stevedores. Many of the available dock workers were past their prime and could handle only five to nine tons per hour, compared to twenty-five tons by untrained American soldiers.[8] To relieve this difficulty, by March we had seventy-five thousand Negro troops on their way to Australia to assist the service commands.[9]

"The paucity of the service troops was so severe," states a report to me from the Southwest Pacific Theater,

> that from the time of the first operations which stopped the Japanese at Buna in the New Guinea jungle until the end of the war the great majority of service units, once committed in support of operations, worked without let-up or periods of rest, recuperation, and re-equipment.
>
> The shortage of these troops was so critical that in every operation it was necessary to employ a portion of the fighting troops to discharge ships, handle supplies, and perform other duties which kept them out of the fighting lines. During the phases following the capture of objectives, when facilities had to be developed to support future operations, combat troops which had captured areas

had to be employed to develop them. . . . These methods
. . . forced the employment of combat troops insufficiently
trained for the fighting they had to do. This caused a progressive wearing down and lowering of efficiency . . . to
the point of near exhaustion before the war was won.

Communications within the commonwealth were bad. Australia, which is about the size of the United States, has only 27,900 miles of railroad, and these are of four different gauges. No transcontinental line exists. The northwest coast, where the attack seemed likely, was not connected by rail with the north and west coasts. On top of all this came Japanese air raids. A raid on February 19 sank a destroyer, an Army transport, and a merchant ship. After Dutch Timor was captured on March 10, the raids came almost daily.

Attempts to supply Java from Australia had to be abandoned two weeks later. Of greater strategical importance was New Caledonia, the French possession off the east coast which was needed for the protection of our sea lanes and also as an air base. Furthermore, the island had important nickel, tin, chromium, and manganese deposits. New Caledonia was held by one company of Australian infantry and three thousand Free French, who had obsolete equipment. It was a tempting prize for the Japanese, who could have seized it without difficulty. To forestall this, an American expeditionary force was landed in New Caledonia on March 12, an added responsibility for the supply services in Australia.[10] This force later became the famous Americal Division, the only infantry division without a numeral. Again there was a shortage of stevedores. Troops had to be dispersed over most of the island, which had only four roads. American soldiers promptly started to operate twenty miles of narrow-gauge railroad and raised its capacity to three hundred tons a day.

The Southwest Pacific Theater, as reports which have since reached me show, continually suffered shortages which damaged fighting efficiency and unduly endangered the lives of American troops. Liberty ships had to be used as transports, although they were slow and unwieldy and unfit for such use. But we had to improvise as best we could for better was not at the moment available.

Loss of materiel through exposure to the elements was a further complication in Australia and New Caledonia. This ran as high as 25 percent for early shipments, and thus imposed a further strain both upon our production and our communications. Then, perishable goods were packed in wooden and tin containers to protect them from the heavy rain and humidity. Tanks were completely covered and sealed against damage by sea spray, at a cost of $160 each. Trucks were crated before being shipped. All this special care needed in shipment added greatly to our production problems, as well as to those of manpower, for both the materials and the labor needed for this especially elaborate packaging were tremendous.

This was a new and ugly kind of war in which storm, heat, and jungle diseases had to be fought as well as hostile troops. In no other war had millions of men been engaged in jungle fighting. To minimize disease casualties, principally from malaria, hundreds of scientists labored to improve existing remedies and to devise new ones. The menace of malaria was first felt during the defense of Bataan. When the surrender came, more than half the troops suffered from the disease. In the offensives to retake the Solomons and New Guinea, several divisions were at times out of action.

Quinine had been the traditional specific for malaria. It did not effect a cure, but it arrested the disease. The fall of Java in March 1942 cut off further quinine supplies. This centered attention on atabrine, on which research had started in Germany more than a decade ago. Atabrine soon proved superior to quinine, although its tendency to discolor the skin produced a hostile reaction to it among the troops.[11] And like quinine, it arrests rather than cures the disease.

So, research for a new drug went on simultaneously with efforts to check malaria at its source by draining swamps and using DDT. Before the end of the war, at the cost of several millions, several new drugs had been developed through the researches of Army and Navy doctors and of the members of the committee on Medical Research of the Office of Scientific Research and Development.

It may be difficult to think of the medical profession in terms of war production. Yet the problems faced by the Army Medical Department, especially in the Pacific, called for enormous production efforts in order to solve them. First, our surgeons, dentists, pharmacists, veterinarians, and medical technicians had to devise, discover, or improvise medicines, chemicals, equipment, and techniques which would combat foes more deadly than the Japs—the insects and diseases of the tropics. Then, when a cure or preventative was developed, medical supply houses, working closely with our Medical Department, had to provide supplies in usable quantities—often in the face of material shortages as serious as those confronting the manufacturers of planes and tanks. Penicillin and atabrine are only two of the near-miraculous developments of the medical profession in this war. Until atabrine was developed and produced in sufficient quantities for general use, ten times as many American soldiers were being incapacitated by malaria as by Jap bullets. In this war, despite the increased deadliness of weapons and the terrible terrain conditions, approximately ninety-six out of every hundred wounded men to reach an Army hospital survived. In World War I the death rate was about twice as high. Medical production was an important factor in this wonderful improvement.

The connection between supply routes to Australia, Suez, and the Persian Gulf, and those to Alaska may seem tenuous. But, whatever the case in time of peace, during a war this is certainly one world. The crusading Billy Mitchell had been among the first of the unheeded prophets to declare Alaska "the most strategic springboard for offensive warfare on earth." The United States had no interest in offensive warfare, however, and all we did was to take some slight defensive measures in Alaska.

I make the categorical statement that Japan would never have attacked Pearl Harbor had we established strong, offensive air bases in Alaska and down the Aleutian chain. The islands reach westward over 1,000 miles into the Pacific. Attu is only 720 miles distant from the northern end of the Kuriles, and 2,000 miles from Tokyo. The Japanese task force would never have steamed toward its December 7 target had the warlords of Japan known that we could instantly and effectively hit back at their homeland. I am assuming, of course, that in addition to building air bases in the Aleutians, we would have developed some such heavy bomber as the B-29 and also fighters with long ranges. I assume, further, that we would have perfected plans to supply them with adequate fuel and ammunition.

Credit for what progress was made in developing Alaska as an air base belongs to the Civil Aeronautics Authority (CAA) rather than to either the Army or the Navy. This was not the fault of the armed services. The CAA found it less difficult to obtain funds with which to build airports. Its activities in 1940 and 1941 were of inestimable value. Its program was not finished on December 7, but range and other communication facilities had been built. Airports on which work could now be rushed had been, at least, chosen and surveyed. However, if the Japanese had made their attacks on Dutch Harbor sooner than they did, it is quite likely that this base would have fallen. Luck was with us again. The attack was delayed until June 1942.[12]

When war came as 1941 ended, American eyes were opened to the significance of Alaska. This was not limited to air routes. The shortest sea lane from Japan to our Pacific Coast lay far from Hawaii; it ran through the Aleutians. A knowledge of the air distances from Fairbanks, slightly east of the central part of Alaska, dispelled the last doubts about the importance of this area. Fairbanks was three hours from Siberia. A modern plane could fly from it to New York, Tokyo, or Murmansk in fifteen hours; to London, Berlin, or Moscow in eighteen. It was five thousand miles shorter to Japan via Alaska than by going to San Francisco and thence to the Philippines.

The defense of Alaska was equally vital to the United States and to Canada. This had been recognized in July 1941 by the Permanent Joint Board on Defense, of which Fiorella H. LaGuardia was chairman. Essential to such defense was a highway linking Canada, through the Yukon, with Alaska. The Joint Board urged that surveys begin immediately, and subsequently the Secretary of War declared that "the construction of this highway now appears desirable as a long-range defense measure." Unfortunately, such had not been long the viewpoint of the War Department. The War Plans Division of the General Staff had declared in 1938 that "from a purely practical standpoint, the military value of the proposed Alaska Highway is so slight as to be negligible."

It was the job of the Navy as well as of the Army to defend Alaska. To fulfill its responsibility, the Navy began the construction of three bases in Alaska. Although the one at Sitka, far to the south, was nearly finished by December 1941, that at Kodiak Island was far from completion, and the combined air and submarine base at Dutch Harbor had barely been begun.

Two weeks after Pearl Harbor, Maj. Gen. J. L. DeWitt, head of the Western Defense Command, telephoned the War Department that the sea lanes to Alaska were in peril. He summarized a conference just held with Admiral Charles S. Freeman, Commandant of the 13th Naval District: "He has only five destroyers—three he is using in Alaskan waters principally to protect our shipping going up with materiel and food for the command up there, and two in Puget Sound. That is so puny that he is almost helpless to assist me in what I've got to do up there."

On January 3, 1942, General DeWitt informed the War Department that "there is not at the present time a single up-to-date fighting plane in the Alaska Defense Command." The total available air force consisted of twenty-three planes. For three or four weeks following Pearl Harbor, nearly every American ship leaving a West Coast port had been attacked by enemy submarines. Hostile submarine and surface craft had been detected off the coast and in Alaskan waters forty-one times, he added. The General's report was exaggerated, as it turned out, but it stimulated action in Washington.

The President on January 16 authorized surveys for the Alaska Highway. The route chosen extended fifteen hundred miles from Dawson Creek, British Columbia. The Army Engineer Corps did the job, with the valuable aid of the Public Roads Administration and the Canadian government. It was a tremendous task, for the road had to cross mountains and valleys, and to bridge rivers which compare with the Missouri and Upper Mississippi in size. Long sections of the road had to be built over that curious phenomenon of the north, permanently frozen ground.

The engineers moved forward first. Behind them came the civilian employees of the contractors to which the Public Roads Administration had assigned the task of building a pioneer supply route, first, and then a permanent all-weather highway. There were sixty-three American and eighteen Canadian contractors who employed more than fourteen thousand civilians. In the incredibly short period of six months a fifteen-foot gravel-surfaced road fifteen hundred miles long was opened to military traffic. Then work began on the permanent road.

This also was completed with remarkable speed. Construction required the building of 133 bridges, including a 2,130-foot suspension bridge across the Peace River near Fort St. John. The broken terrain required eight thousand culverts along the highway. Yet the road was finished, except for final touches on the bridges, in October 1943. The cost was not quite $140 million.[13]

Was this excessive? Alcan was built to aid in the defense of Alaska. Actually, its logistical influence was to be felt on the Russian front where, at approximately the time the pioneer road was finished, the Red Army was saving Stalingrad. Aircraft, delivered to the Soviet forces by the Alaskan route because Alcan existed, fought in the 1943 offensives mounted by Marshal Stalin.

Future operations by Russia were a major topic for discussion when the President, the Prime Minister, and their staffs assembled for the Casablanca conference in January 1943. The Allied leaders agreed that the supplies promised by the United Nations must be delivered, but they were thinking principally of transportation by sea. However, German submarine and air attacks continued to make this costly, and we did not have immediately available enough escort vessels appreciably to reduce the risk.

Mr. Harry Hopkins raised the question of an alternative. He had in mind routes through Alaska and by way of the Persian Gulf. This was ultimately done, and part of the credit must go to the Alaska Highway. The route had been chosen so that supplies could be transported to American and Canadian airfields. With the airfields thus serviced by the road, during 1943 over 2,700 airplanes, most of them for Russia, were ferried over this route. In 1944 the number increased to 3,273.

"Never has a road been so important to airmen," General Arnold testified.[14]

When work started on Alcan, Hitler was driving for the oil fields of the Caspian and Caucasus, and the outcome of the struggle, to put it mildly, was in doubt. It was possible the Russians might have to retreat to Asia, where they would then have faced the certainty of attack by Japan. In this case, the Alaska Highway would have been of profound importance in keeping Russia in the war. But this was not all. Apart from possible assistance to Russia, Alaska, supplied in the way that the highway made possible, was a threat to Japan. The enemy was never quite certain, until the blow came, whether our ultimate offensive would be launched from the Aleutians or from the south.

The significance of Alcan is closely interwoven with that of the Canol Project, which has been so energetically debated for more than four years.[15] The critics of this great undertaking to develop new oil reserves in northwestern Canada contend that Canol, if started at all, should have been abandoned when the Japanese menace began to subside somewhat in 1943. Those who hold that we should have stopped work on the project earlier than we did have their arguments, but I disagree with them. It is unthinkable that Canol should not have been attempted. Its cost about equaled that of fighting the war in 1944 for a single day. It was a military, not a commercial adventure. We were, as I said in June 1942, "daily taking greater chances." The invasion of the island of Kiska, I might add, probably cost between $150 and $175 million, yet nobody suggested that it should not have been staged just because the Japanese had escaped through the Aleutian fogs by the time the American task force landed.

We should have been more tactful in dealing with other government agencies as we prepared for Canol, even though neither the War Production Board nor the Petroleum Coordinator for National Defense, Mr. Ickes, had any actual jurisdiction over this military operation in a foreign area. But, as we were to ask the WPB officials to approve allocation of pipe and other materials, and as Mr. Ickes was closely connected with all phases of the oil shortage, it would have been better to have consulted them.

Canol, like Alcan, must be viewed in the large perspective of holding Alaska against Japanese invasion and as a possible base for offensive operations when American strength made them possible.[16] The purpose of Canol was to provide fuel for the trucks on the highway, for the aircraft operating on patrols off Alaska, for our own combat aircraft, and for the planes going to Russia. To be properly understood, it must be regarded as part of our whole communications and supply system in the Pacific Northwest area.

During peace Alaska's oil needs could be met by sending oil by sea from the California fields. But now that war had come, major obstacles arose to prevent this. One was the fact that California production had dropped from 292 million barrels in 1929 to 223 million in1940, and no important new wells were in prospect. To bring additional oil from Texas required a long haul in tank cars which were not available. Axis submarines, prowling the Atlantic, had taken a heavy toll in tankers, and we needed 250 more than we had. Between two and three tankers were being sent to the bottom for every new one built, and the losses were not repaired until the beginning of 1944.

Even had tankers and California oil been procurable, the passage to Alaska across the Gulf of Alaska was subject to Japanese submarine attack. In February 1942 General Marshall asked Admiral King whether, considering its current commitments and future ones, the Navy could "maintain, under all circumstances, uninterrupted communications for the United States forces in Alaska and insure the delivery of essential supplies to the civilian population."

"I can make no such categorical commitment," replied the Chief of Naval Operations.

Admiral King added, however, that while some ships might be lost, he believed that adequate supplies could be escorted to Alaska. The War Department could not rely on this uncertain forecast. Alaska, I must repeat, had to held at any cost. If it were conquered by Japan, the day would quickly come when land-based aircraft could bomb our concentrated shipyards in the Northwest as well as our equally concentrated aircraft industry on the Pacific Coast.

We were forced to the conclusion that additional sources of oil would have to be found. Moderate new resources would be enough because operations in Alaska, although of enormous strategic importance, would not be in great force. Early this same year, attempts were made to find oil in New Zealand, but drillings failed. How valuable it would have been had oil been struck there was indicated by the fighting in Guadalcanal in the fall of 1942. The American forces were twice stalled by gasoline shortages because the Japanese had made artillery hits on the small stocks on the island.

For more than twenty years, oil wells had been operating in the wilds of northwestern Canada, and the reserve was estimated at not less than 33 million, and perhaps as high as 100 million barrels. The oil had excellent qualities for use in Alaska since it would flow at temperatures of 70 degrees below zero. According to the most reliable estimates, the Norman Wells field, if developed, would produce about thirty-five hundred barrels a day.

The difficulty was in getting at the oil. Laying the pipeline over mountains and rivers, along with building the refinery and the pumping stations, constituted a task more formidable than the Alcan Highway. Knowledge of the area, and of the precise conditions which must be met, was sparse, but the difficulties were known to be very great. There was no time for other than hurried aerial surveys. A winter road one thousand miles long would have to be built down the Mackenzie River Valley, and thousands of tons of supplies floated down the rivers and across the Great Slave Lake during the limited season when navigation of these northern waterways was possible.

Crude oil was to be piped six hundred miles from Norman Wells to Whitehorse in the Yukon, on the projected Alaska Highway, where the refinery would be located. The gasoline and other fuel produced at the refinery was then to be piped to dockside at Skagway and to Fairbanks, and storage tanks would be erected at strategic points. The production and refining of the oil were to be managed by Imperial Oil, Ltd., which operated the existing Norman Wells development. It is a subsidiary of the Standard Oil Company of New Jersey. Such, in outline, was the Canol project.

General Somervell authorized the project on April 30, 1942.[17] The advance guard of Canol reached Edmonton at the end of May. Soon engineer troops arrived, among them Negro soldiers who labored with fortitude, skill, and industry despite the cold. The greater part of the labor had to be brought in from the United States. At the employment offices, the following sign was posted:

<u>THIS IS NO PICNIC</u>
Working and living conditions on this job are as difficult as those encountered on any construction job ever done in the United States or foreign territory. Men hired for this job will be required to live under the most extreme conditions imaginable. Temperatures will range from 90 degrees above to 70 degrees below zero. Men will have to fight swamps, rivers, ice, and cold. Mosquitoes, flies, and gnats will not only be annoying, but will cause bodily harm. If you are not prepared to work under these and similar conditions
<u>DO NOT APPLY</u>

This was no exaggeration, although no fatalities occurred because of the hazards of the Far North. The project proved that machinery of all kinds could be operated effectively in extremely low temperatures. But the difficulties exceeded those of building Alcan, and progress on Canol never met our hopes. The causes were many. Alcan had been given priority. Shortage of transportation and construction in such barren country contributed to the delays. The War Department had to face the risk, however, of a long and hard war. It could take no other course. By November 1942 we were reasonably certain that Norman Wells would reach the desired output of three thousand barrels a day. In fact, by March 1945, when the refinery was closed down, it had reached four thousand barrels a day and had produced a total of over 1.6 million barrels of crude oil.

Nobody will contend that the oil obtained from Canol was in great quantity compared with the huge needs of the war, but that is not the proper way to judge the project. There was not only a world oil shortage, but there were acute local deficiencies. One of these local deficiencies was on the Pacific Coast, and it is in the light of that, in part, that Canol must be judged.

The argument made against continuing to develop Canol is that Japanese sea power had already been broken and that Alaska was no longer in danger of invasion after the battle for Midway in June 1942. But naval warfare is subject to shattering reverses, and the fact that we did not suffer any such calamities does not mean that we ought not to have allowed for that possibility. The Joint Chiefs of Staff had to allow for every eventuality. Besides, the argument does not take into account an offensive against Japan from Alaska, or the value of the threat of such an offensive. It was not until August 1943, in the conference between President Roosevelt and Mr. Churchill of that month, that the specific routes of the advance on Japan were laid out. Even then, much had to be done and many stepping-stones conquered, before our forces could move over them. Changes in plan might still be necessary.

Our military situation had, of course, improved by June 1942. The Battle of Midway, which took place from June 4 to 6, will rank among the decisive engagements of history. The Japanese attack on Dutch Harbor on June 3 and June 4 was part of a master plan to cut off Alaska and seize control of the Central Pacific shipping lanes so that, later, the Hawaiian Islands, and possibly the Pacific Coast, could be seized. But rapid construction of an Army air base at Umnak, one hundred miles west of Dutch Harbor, thwarted the Japanese aspirations.[18] Surprised by the attack of land-based planes, the astonished Japanese retired down the Aleutian chain and occupied Kiska, Attu, and Agattu.

Although, for some mysterious reason, the Japanese did not strike again at Dutch Harbor, the closeness of the enemy forced a change in the plan for building Canol. The capture of Attu in May 1943 and the Japanese evacuation of Kiska in August renewed the demands that Canol be abandoned. General Somervell's hope that the work would be completed by that time had not been fulfilled. The need for service troops in ETO [European Theater of Operations] occasioned by the decision to invade Sicily and Italy brought a still lower priority for Canol. But, with some of the project already in operation, our answer to the abandonment proposal was that $50 million had already been spent and that all of this would be sacrificed if work was stopped.

We thought an additional $38 million would complete the job, but we were overly optimistic. The final cost was slightly in excess of $133 million.

In December 1943 Secretary of War Stimson pointed out that termination of Canol would not save more than $10 million and that nobody knew when the war would end. It would be "decidedly reckless" to deprive the nation "of all chance of realizing the far-reaching advantages which now appear to be possible from this development."

"The Joint Chiefs of Staff," he said, "have notified me that the completion and operation of the project . . . are necessary to the war effort. . . . In the light of that determination and of the events taking place throughout the world bearing on the possible strategic necessity of oil from this project, I am certainly not now prepared to say that the project which our military advisers have determined to be necessary shall be abandoned."

I fully agree. Nobody denies that millions were spent on Canol which might have been saved had we known that the war would end when it did, or had we been able to foretell the exact strategy which would bring victory. The dollars were expendable, just as were the dollars used for B-17s, which are now without value, or for delicate precision gauges which cost several hundred dollars to make and are now worth, as scrap, a few cents. Furthermore, in view of the advancing limitations of the world's oil supplies, the proof of the availability of extensive reserves in the Northwest may be of great value.

The heavy goods of war, such as tanks and artillery, could not be sent to the Soviet Union by way of Alaska. Although small tonnages moved across the Pacific, on Russian freighters, to Vladivostok, the only significant routes before the opening of the Black Sea ports in the summer of 1944 were those by Murmansk and the Persian Gulf. The first was terribly exposed to enemy attack, and the second was terribly long. Plans to supply Russia through the Persian Gulf, by the Iranian State Railway and by truck, began before the United States entered the war. A mission under Col. Raymond A. Wheeler was authorized to proceed to Iran in September 1941 and cooperate with the British in building port facilities. This mission, which arrived in February 1942, was the beginning of the Persian Gulf Command, one of the most important units in all of our armies.[19] It has not received the public credit it deserved. The supplies whose movement it made possible helped the Russians to throw back the German armies in the fall, winter, and summer of 1942–1943. In two and a half years it delivered 5,560,000 long tons of supplies, including 150,000 trucks, to the Soviet Union.

Ingenuity and hard work made this achievement possible. The single-track right of way of the Iranian State Railway had to be virtually rebuilt to carry heavy American Delser locomotives. Many of the 3,000 bridges and 225 tunnels needed repair. Operating conditions were more difficult than those in Alaska for, instead of Arctic cold, blistering heat was encountered. Even at night the mercury hovered around 100. Sandfly fever, diarrhea, heat stroke, and respiratory ailments dogged the men. An infinite variety of technical problems had to be overcome, often with improvised means. But the freight moved.

No less arduous and effective was the work of the Motor Transport Service of the PGC. Despite bad roads, mountain passes, dust storms which obliterated vision, and heat which burned out bearings and men, the Motor Transport Service had few accidents. It drove 100 million ton miles with only 6.7 accidents per million miles.

The Persian Gulf Command (PGC) wound up its affairs on June 1, 1945. If generally unrecognized at home, the achievements of the men and their commanding officer, Maj. Gen. Donald W. Connally, attracted the attention of their Commander-in-Chief. In December 1943, when at Tehran for his conference with Marshal Stalin, the President had addressed the troops of the PGC at Camp Mirabar.

"I wish," he said, "that great numbers of our people could see this work of getting equipment through to our ally who has had very heavy losses, but who is licking the Nazi hordes."[20]

I have dwelt at some length upon these problems of supply in the Pacific, in Alaska, and in the Persian Gulf, because they illustrate vividly the interlocking character of all the things that must be done to give effective support to a modern war of global extent. In all of these thorny problems, production was a vital factor. We suffered grave perils in the Pacific because we had not yet produced enough munitions, nor the ships to get them there and the escorts to protect them. We embarked upon the Canol project because we were short of oil production in a critical area of the war, and because we had not produced the means to bring adequate supplies of oil to that area from the more familiar sources of supply. We overcame the myriad difficulties of road and railroad through Iran because supplies, at almost any cost, were vital to the nation which was then bearing the brunt of the war. Even if, as some people believe, we made some supply efforts that proved not altogether necessary, we did so because supply was so vital that we could not afford to take any chances. So far as we could, we had be ready to meet even the most unlikely need, for war is always full of surprises.

In meeting these supply needs, we could not have succeeded but for our production achievements as well as the achievements of skill and fortitude of the men who worked the supply lines. A less productive nation could not have rehabilitated and reequipped the Iranian State Railway or the motor service across Iran. Our weaknesses in supply were frequently grave, but we were always able to dig down into our reserves of productive strength and to repair them before it was too late. Without that, we could not have won the war.

Chapter 8

Assault in Force

One great problem in war is to keep armies engaged.[1] Much of the value of an offensive operation may be lost if it is not pushed to a conclusion before the enemy has time to reorganize. Furthermore, inactive soldiers deteriorate rapidly. But the task of keeping an operation moving depends as much upon the supply situation as it does upon the fighting qualities of the combat divisions. Troops cannot be sent into battle unless they have enough arms and ammunition, and unless they can be fed and clothed. This means, not merely the production of the necessary quantities of supplies, but also an accurate anticipation of the transport conditions which must be met and the provision of whatever special transport equipment may be needed. In this war every major assault was at first an amphibious one which required naval vessels, transports, cargo ships, and landing craft.

In May 1943 the question discussed by the Allied high command was what to do next. The North African campaign had ended, except for negligible pockets of resistance. American war production was soaring, although critical shortages still existed. We had learned many lessons from the North African campaign, however, which assisted us to prepare for further operations. And we could not afford to remain inactive.

But we were not yet strong enough, either in troops or supplies, to cross the Channel. The experience in North Africa had convinced General Eisenhower that about twice the forces originally contemplated would be needed. An invasion in 1943 was no longer regarded as possible. Instead, it was decided to assault Sicily and Italy.

A long-standing defect in American military education was the failure to consider the possibility of offensive invasions or amphibious warfare. The kind of thinking which caused this defect was not limited to Army or Navy leaders. It was inherent in the American people. We had no desire for conquest anywhere. We had no intention of attacking anybody. Why then should we think or train our Army and Navy officers in terms of huge landing operations on some hostile shore?

At Tehran the Combined Chiefs of Staff of the United States and Great Britain were discussing the forthcoming Normandy invasion with Marshal Klementi Voroshiloff[2] and other Russian leaders. The Soviet Marshal agreed that OVERLORD was a serious and difficult operation. Yet he was confident it would go down in history as one of the greatest of all victories. He compared the Channel crossing with the Red Army accomplishments in crossing broad rivers. The American Chief of Staff, on the other hand, pointed out that defeat in an attempt to cross a river was only a military reverse, whereas the failure of a landing operation from the sea was a catastrophe because it meant the utter destruction of landing craft and personnel. Then, General Marshall added that his military training had been based on roads, railroads, and rivers. But, for the last two years, he had acquired an education based on oceans, and now he thought of little else.[3]

World War I had done nothing to dispel the fallacy that had hitherto dogged and limited our military thinking. True, we sent an army to France, but it landed on a friendly coast. We might, of course, have remembered our brief struggle with Spain when we put a few troops ashore at a high and unnecessary cost. But nobody seems to have done so.

In consequence, the shortage of landing craft delayed every amphibious operation of World War II, except the unopposed occupation of Japan.[4] Of course, there were other mistakes also which slowed us up, but General Eisenhower has specified the lack of landing craft as the greatest single obstacle to fighting the war in Europe. If it had not been for this deficiency, the invasions of Normandy and Southern France could have been conducted simultaneously. The original plan had been to have three divisions in the assault on the Normandy Coast, with two more serving as immediate follow-up divisions. General Eisenhower concluded, however, that this did not allow a sufficient margin of safety. A new plan was therefore drafted which specified five assault divisions, retaining the two follow-up divisions. Enough landing craft were in prospect for the first plan, but not for seven divisions. So the Supreme Commander decided to postpone the target date for a month. One cannot but wonder whether an earlier start, and simultaneous attacks on the coasts both of Normandy and Southern France, might not have brought victory more quickly and have saved us several weeks of bitter fighting.[5]

Landing craft of all types, for troops and tanks and the other paraphernalia of war, were given AAA priority in November 1943 in order to meet the needs of D-Day. But even this had to take second place to the secret Manhattan District Project. Friction between branches of the services frequently arose because the manufacture of the atomic bomb could not be explained. In the end, almost sixty-five thousand landing craft were produced for the Navy and over twenty-five thousand for the Army. Most of the latter was the ubiquitous DUKWs.[6] We had these before anybody else, as General Eisenhower has said, and so "beat the world." The DUKW was a two-and-one-half-ton Army truck converted to amphibious use. It was swung over the side of the cargo ship, which waited off shore to be unloaded. Then it swam steadily for the beach where, using its wheels, the DUKW ran as far inshore as might be necessary. No longer did supplies pile up on the beaches, easy targets for marauding aircraft.

Candor compels the admission that the Army is not entitled to initial credit for the DUKW. The idea was born in the Office of Scientific Research and Development (OSRD). It is another illustration of the inestimable value of having civilians, their minds unhampered by military convention, engaged in scientific research and in the development of war materiel. In the spring of 1942, Palmer C. Putnam, an OSRD engineer, decided that the standard two-and-one-half-ton truck could be adapted for amphibious warfare. He consulted Roderick and Olin J. Stephens, the father-son yacht experts. They drew up plans, and General Motors accepted a preliminary production contract. The Army, however, was already worried over the multiplicity of landing craft and little official encouragement was forthcoming.[7] On the word from Maj. Gen. Jacob L. Devers, commanding the armored forces at Fort Knox, that he would try out the new vehicle, OSRD decided to go ahead. Its director, Dr. Vannevar Bush, allocated $250,000 of OSRD funds for the trial models.

About twenty DUKWs were ready for trials by November 1942. Mr. Putnam had trained soldiers in their operation and assembled them at Provincetown, Massachusetts, with their unusual vehicles. But it was not until the OSRD engineer ran one of the trucks through the surf during a gale on December 1, to rescue a Coast Guard crew 150 yards off shore, that the DUKW received the recognition to which it was entitled. But by then the North African invasion, where it might have been used with telling effect, was over.

Neither the DUKW nor any other form of landing craft suffered from neglect after January 1943. By then 7,000 DUKWs were on order. On March 3, General Eisenhower requisitioned 750 for the Sicilian invasion and two months later demanded an additional 300. In all, 1,150 of the amphibious trucks arrived in time for Operation HUSKY. They proved to be the principal facility for discharging cargoes.

The decision to invade Sicily had been made at the Casablanca conference in January 1943 because of the troops which would be available at the end of the Tunisian campaign. Also, General Marshall noted, possession of the North Coast of Africa and of Sicily would liberate the Mediterranean to the extent that 225 ships could be diverted to the Pacific or the Persian Gulf. Airfields in Allied hands would greatly improve air coverage over Mediterranean convoys. At that time, it was assumed that North Africa would be cleared of the enemy by the end of April. The attack on Sicily was set for July.

The continuation of the fighting in North Africa for an additional two weeks complicated the planning and supply problems. HUSKY had to be mounted, in the main, from North African ports, although the 45th Division sailed, combat loaded, from Hampton Roads, Virginia, and regular supply convoys were also dispatched from the United States. Despite high seas, the invasion forces left North Africa on schedule on July 9. They consisted of 160,000 men, over 1,000 guns, and 600 tanks in 3,266 ships. Two days later the beaches on the southeast coast of Sicily were secured.

Losses were light in the landings. Although the Navy counted on the possibility of 300 ships being slink, 2 destroyers, 2 submarine chasers, and a half-dozen landing craft were, in fact, all that we lost. The British lost 4 warships. Supplies came ashore, despite the absence of port facilities, in sufficient quantities. In two days almost 18,000 deadweight tons of cargo and 7,416 vehicles were on the beaches.[8] In thirty-eight days the campaign was over. The Germans contrived to extricate 88,000 troops across the Straits of Messina, but the defeat cost the Axis 100,000 prisoners, mostly Italian, and 12,000 killed and wounded.

Now General Eisenhower could cross the straits and attack the Italian toe. The American Chiefs of Staff, however, were not entirely happy over the invasion, which was destined to be long and costly.[9] At the time of the Quebec conference in August 1943, the Army command felt concern lest the ground forces needed in Italy would make an operation against the continent impossible.[10] Tunisia had sucked in more and more troops. American experts had been inclined to favor instead the occupation of Sardinia, which would further limit Axis air attacks on Mediterranean shipping and would also serve as a stepping-stone for future assaults on either Italy or Southern France. Indeed, it was not until July 20 that General Clark received orders from General Eisenhower to abandon plans for Sardinia. The assault on Italy was to be in the region of the Gulf of Salerno, and General Clark was to develop plans for capturing Naples and nearby airfields.

The logistical difficulties were very great. Without the port of Naples, it was feared, the needed tonnages in supplies could not be landed. That port would at most certainly be virtually destroyed by Allied bombing and by Axis demolitions before evacuation. The Army Service Forces, studying the Italian campaign, concluded that Italy could not be self-supporting at any time during the Allied occupation. This meant that coal, food, medicine, and clothing would have to be shipped to the theater to prevent disease and unrest.[11] The nature of the Italian peninsula was another handicap. It was so narrow that superior forces could not easily be concentrated where they were needed.

As it turned out, the Axis and the Allies were logistically equal until our air strength shattered the enemy communications lines. But it also turned out that the strategic importance of the victory in Italy did not warrant full use of men, shipping, or supplies. They were diverted for the Normandy invasion, and the Italian campaign dragged on until May 1945.

Pessimism alternated with optimism as the Quebec conference of August 1943 ended. The Combined Chiefs of Staff, if somewhat uneasy over the Italian adventure, nonetheless based their planning on the assumption that Germany would be defeated the following year. The deciding factor in the conclusion to invade Italy was the collapse of the Mussolini dictatorship on July 25. Rumors persisted throughout August that unconditional surrender would follow, and it came on September 3, the day the British crossed the Messina Straits. General Clark[12] and his forces were to land at Salerno and press on as rapidly as possible for Naples, which, it was estimated, would fall on D-Day plus 12. But the Fifth Army did not wholly occupy Naples until October 7, and a great amount of salvage had to be done before the port could be used.

Announcement of the surrender was delayed for a week in the hope that the Germans would not seize Italian defense positions. But Hitler's forces acted swiftly. When the Americans landed at 3:30 in the morning on September 9, they were met by heavy fire. Casualties were heavy; no naval bombardment was ordered because of the mistaken theory that the attack would be a surprise. Nearly one hundred ships or landing craft were lost. Then came strong German counterattacks which were not finally beaten off until September 15. An Allied line stretched from the Tyrrhenian Sea across Italy to Bari.

The long, bitter, bloody struggle northward had started. Some conception of the supply problem may be gained from the fact that over 200,000 troops, 45,000 vehicles, and more than 150,000 deadweight tons of stores were landed in the Salerno area during the first month of the fighting. The heroic service troops had done it with inadequate manpower and equipment, under heavy artillery fire and air attack, and in bad weather. A large port was vital to the success of the Italian campaign, however, and engineer and Service troops followed the combat forces into Naples on October 2 and 3, while fighting was still going on.

They found the demolition virtually total. Every building near the port had been blasted. A huge coal dump was on fire. All streets, rail lines, sidings, and other communications facilities were blocked with rubble. Not a vehicle moved. Every pier and every berth was jammed with sunken or otherwise damaged ships. Warehouses, sheds, grain elevators, cranes, and other equipment had been destroyed.[13] But engineer units straightway began clearing roadways to the piers so that landing craft cargoes could be moved. Twenty-two hundred tons were unloaded on the third. The next day the amount doubled.

Not enough service troops were on hand. Italian labor, pressed into service, had no taste for air raids and would leave their posts at the first alert. Others were in such bad health, or so hungry, that they could accomplish little. Yet ten thousand Italians were employed at the Port of Naples during the first two weeks. Among the many essential repair jobs were the ones on oil tanks and pipelines. The Germans had destroyed facilities for 1.5 million barrels of oil. But when the first Allied tanker arrived on October 29, it was able to pump fuel through a four-inch line which had been hastily laid. Similar lines would follow the armies as they advanced north.

The wrecked railroads were repaired with comparable speed. A few Italian locomotives were repaired. On October 23 nine American locomotives, the first to be used in Europe, arrived. Operation of the lines from Salerno to Naples was quickly established. Then, tracks and bridges north of the port were repaired. For a period, until other ports to the north had been captured, Naples was the greatest Allied port of discharge in the world. Between October 4, 1943, and April 1944, it handled 2,375,299 long tons of cargo.

This was possible, of course, only because production in the United States was reaching its peak. By July 1943 General Eisenhower's reports show 750,000 tons of supplies were pouring through United Kingdom ports monthly. This total was increased to 1.9 million tons before the invasion of France. A stockpile of 2.5

million tons was built up, in addition to basic loads and equipment. To handle these huge war supplies, the Communications Zone in England grew to 31,500 officers and 350,000 enlisted men by June 1944. American troops had grown from 241,849 in 1942 to 1,562,000.

The necessary supplies came in floods from the Arsenal of Democracy because, in the main, the factories which produced them were finished and operating.

As. Mr. J. A. Krug[14] observes, "several new industries were built virtually from scratch. Before the war we had no synthetic rubber or aviation gasoline plants of any size, and the explosives, guns and ammunition, aircraft and shipbuilding industries were pygmies when measured against the wartime needs."[15]

Baffling problems continued to worry American industrial management and the war agencies responsible for production. There never was a time, Mr. Krug adds, "when materials, supplies, plant facilities and manpower were in perfect balance. During the war, when demand for manufactured products was virtually insatiable, a surplus of one of two of these elements invariably created a shortage of the other two."[16] This was true, of course, because our situation as to facilities and materials at first, and as to manpower right through the war, was so tight that we almost invariably stepped up our production program for one item only at the expense of at least one, and frequently several other, programs. Thus, a too-generous calculation of what we needed in one direction had to be paid for by shortage in other directions. In view of the multifarious and constantly shifting demands of so vast a war, it was only with the greatest difficulty that we kept our major errors of calculation within moderate limits.[17]

Here are some of the war goods produced in 1943: 85,930 military and transport airplanes costing over $12.5 billion; over 2,500 heavy artillery guns, complete; 98,000 bazookas; 26,000 light and heavy mortars; more than 2.7 million rifles and almost 3 million carbines; 670,000 short tons of ground artillery ammunition and 1.5 million short tons of aircraft bombs; almost 30,000 tanks and over 630,000 trucks; $1,471 million in radio and $913 million in radar equipment; over 1 billion atabrine tablets.

The total of these and everything else would have been far smaller had not the government first spent hundreds of millions for the plants where synthetic rubber, aviation gasoline, ammonia, and chemicals of all kinds were manufactured. It is obvious that our armies would have been slowed to a halt, just as were the German armies in the spring of 1945, had their rubber supplies failed. The AAF would have been grounded as completely as Goering's Luftwaffe.

Japanese victories in the Far East deprived the United States of 90 percent of its normal rubber. We took some action to meet the potential crisis before Pearl Harbor, but not enough was done. The Rubber Reserve Company, a subsidiary of the RFC, was founded in 1940. That year rubber imports increased from 500,000 long tons to 819,000. They reached 1,029,000 long tons in 1941. But our large production of automobiles and other consumer goods combined with expanding military requirements to eat deeply into the stockpiles. These amounted to only 533,000 tons in December 1941. Hurried shipments just prior to Singapore's fall brought the total to 634,000 tons at the end of April 1942. After that the barest trickle of natural rubber reached the United States.

Yet 775,000 long tons had been used in our final year of peace when war production was small. The only possible solution was to cut civilian consumption to the bone and to produce synthetic rubber.[18] German production, it was known, came to about 110,000 tons annually. The United States had produced no synthetic rubber at all until the beginning of 1941, and in that year the total was less than 9,000 tons. The Japanese strategists, we have learned, were certain that the United States could not produce enough artificial rubber in time to make up for the crude rubber supplies which were cut off by the Japanese advance. After the surrender, Admiral Zenishiro Hoshina, Chief of the Japanese navy's bureau of military affairs, so testified.

"We were positive you would suffer from a rubber shortage," Hoshina said. "We were sure you could not solve this problem. The way you did was a source of amazement and a cause of fear in Japan."

The Japanese had some reason for their confidence. The manufacture of synthetic rubber is a complicated technical process. At first, disagreement on methods and on the raw materials to be used delayed the program. To end the confusion, the President delegated

Bernard M. Baruch, Dr. James B. Conant of Harvard University, and Dr. Karl T. Compton of the Massachusetts Institute of Technology as a committee to bring order out of the chaos.

The Baruch Committee's report, submitted in September 1942, is an excellent example of the way civilians, the military, and technical men can work together during a war. The report pulled no punches. Among all critical and strategical materials, it said, "rubber is the one which presents the greatest threat to the safety of our nation and the success of the Allied cause." Civilian tires were wearing down eight times faster than they could be replaced. By 1944 most of the 27 million passenger cars would be off the roads unless driving was sharply curbed.[19] Such a debacle of motor transport would have created an added burden which other forms of transport could not have handled.

The committee agreed that the government's rubber production program was sound. It urged utmost speed. By the middle of 1942, the program called for 877,000 tons of synthetic rubber annually, the prompt erection of fifty new plants at a cost of $700 million, and participation by forty-nine rubber, chemical, petroleum, and other concerns in the work. Some natural rubber, for mixture with the artificial for heavy-duty tires, had to be obtained as well. Sources in Ceylon,[20] India, Mexico, and Latin America were explored. Imports reached a wartime high of 45,000 tons by the first quarter of 1945. By then we were producing synthetic rubber at a rate of almost 1 million long tons a year, and we could have increased the total had it been needed. Mr. William Jeffers—later succeeded by Mr. Bradley Dewey—was Rubber Director, in charge of the whole program.

All this was extremely costly. Rubber might have been made more cheaply from crude oil. But oil was needed for aviation gasoline, so alcohol distilled from grain was used in a ratio of 100 to 1.[21] Such alternatives constantly had to be faced. They even confronted our military leaders, who should have been free to devote all their energies to military matters. The American Joint Chiefs of Staff expressed concern in January 1943 over a decision of the WPB to allocate a doubled amount of construction material to the synthetic rubber program. This, they predicted, would seriously endanger the production of aviation gasoline, for it would mean a loss that year of 5 million gallons.

As has been previously mentioned, this was one of those cases where the giving of the green light to a particular program, which was under able and determined leadership, threatened to solve one problem at the cost of creating another just as bad or worse. It was our feeling in the War Department that the rubber problem could be solved with the help of much more severe rationing of the use of rubber, without risking the adequacy of our supply of aviation gasoline.

However, enough aviation fuel was produced, despite the claims of the rubber program and the enormous requirements of the Allied air forces. Early estimates of the need for high-octane gasoline proved much too low. This was partly because more planes were placed in operation than at first seemed possible. It was discovered, too, that identical types of military aircraft consumed different amounts of fuel in different theaters. Thus, a B-24 in ETO [European Theater of Operations] burned 286 gallons an hour on the average because distances were short, flak was heavy, and the rate of climb was high—which meant full-throttle engines. In the Pacific theater, distances were greater and planes could fly under cruising conditions most of the time since the greater part of their flight was over water and free from flak and other enemy interference. So a B-24 out there used only 215 gallons an hour.

One reason the AAF needed such quantities of fuel was its insistence upon the full training of crews. About 40 percent of the total was burned in the United States; 36 percent in combat; 21 percent in air transport; and 3 percent by the occupational air forces. In 1941 the AAF used 1,750,000 barrels of petroleum products. In March to May 1943, the United Nations air forces burned an average of 19.5 million barrels monthly. This drew heavily on reserves. However, with $233 million invested in high-octane plants by the government and $631 million more by industry, production had increased from 55,000 barrels per day at the end of 1941 to 523,000 per day in July 1945.

A third essential in modern war is industrial alcohol. It had to be used in the synthetic rubber program, for one thing. Before the war American production was principally from molasses imported from Cuba and other Caribbean countries. Submarine activity cut the supplies to a point where there would not be enough alcohol for rubber and also for other war processes such as making smokeless powder, other explosives, dyes, plastics, and photographic film. The distillers of the United States had a capacity of about 120 million gallons of 190-proof alcohol. In September 1942 they were ordered to devote their full capacity to making alcohol, and in 1943 they turned out 228 million gallons. This cut the whisky supplies, of course, with resulting public protests which rose to such a pitch that "holidays" were declared during which stocks were replenished.[22] Sometimes it seemed as though we were not even, as Elmer Davis said, in the war ankle deep.[23]

Scarcely a single American industry was left untouched by the expanding program. The plant capacity of the chemical and allied industries was increased at a cost of $1.7 billion. Nine additional ammonia plants were built. The demand for electric power rose from 161,300 million kilowatt hours in 1939 to 279,500 million in 1944, an increase of 73 percent. Meeting this need was an almost incredible accomplishment in view of the fact that the Navy's requirements for turbines and generators made impossible the construction of new plants. The generators in a single new battleship can produce 225,000 horsepower, enough for a city the size of Dayton, Ohio. The generators installed in naval vessels alone in the last four years have a capacity greater than all other generators, public or private, in the nation.

The seemingly impossible was accomplished by a nationwide pooling of all power resources. Normal competition ceased. One company would turn a customer of long standing over to a competitor and pipe his current to a distant factory, possibly in another state. Typical of the ingenuity shown by the electrical engineers was a crisis which arose when it was decided to build the big Defense Plant Corporation magnesium works at Velasco, Texas. Other conditions were ideal, but synthetic rubber and aviation gasoline plants being built in the area would use all available power. A new power plant would have taken eighteen months to build, even had equipment been procurable. Just as the project was about to be abandoned, power experts located a forty-thousand-kilowatt generator and boilers in New York. Another unused turbine was found in Detroit and a half-finished one in the shops of the General Electric Company. A plant was patched together in Velasco, and magnesium began to flow out of the ocean.

Not all the goods of war are of great size, nor are they made by hundreds of thousands of workers. It is interesting to note that sixty-five thousand employees, about 40 percent of them women, enabled the ball and roller bearing industry to meet the quadrupled demand for anti-friction bearings. It had been a relatively small industry before the war, producing about $100 million a year in bearings which went chiefly to the automobile manufacturers. But no plane could fly without a large variety of bearings, nor could radar, tanks, heavy guns, or other equipment operate. During the war, ball bearing facilities expanded at a cost of $100 million, about 65 percent government financed. Production rose to over $400 million in 1944; thirty-five thousand types and sizes were being made. The problem of getting enough workers for this expanded production was touch and go in 1944, but all the difficulties were finally overcome.

We had a great deal more of everything at the end of 1943 than we had in 1942. But we did not have enough, delivered at the right places, to make the Italian campaign the success that had been hoped. If we had really begun to arm ourselves in earnest in 1941, we might have had enough ships, landing craft, and troops to save a large number of American lives at Anzio and in the fighting which followed. But it must be remembered that shortages at the front do not end the moment war production at home reaches full speed. It takes a long time, weeks and months, to get supplies from the factory to the depots behind the fighting line. Many stages of storage, shipment, transshipment, and distribution must be gone through before anything is placed in the hands of the soldier in the front lines. This process, which is known as filling up the pipe-line, is a very long and complicated one, especially under the far-flung conditions of World War II. But, until all the pipe-lines have been filled, the soldier at the front is immobilized.

Even when they have been filled, he is not yet ready to move forward in decisive fashion. Offensive war is certain, at its climactic moments, to consume supplies at a greater rate, in a given spot, than they can be shipped into that spot. Therefore, to avoid bogging down at the moment when victory threatens, or to avoid finding oneself helpless should unexpected reverses occur, it is necessary to build up a reserve of supplies in the theater. Until this has been done, it is foolhardy to move forward. But building up this reserve takes time. Thus, although we were approaching peak production in most items at the end of 1943, months were to elapse before this productive torrent was to be felt in full force at the front. Generally speaking, one must allow about a year after production is adequate before supply at the front will be equally satisfactory. This is a vital thing to remember when coordinating industrial production with military strategy.

The Anzio attack, twenty-five miles south of Rome, was an attempt to turn the German flank and permit the capture of the Italian capital by the combined Allied forces. Planning for it began in November 1943, with December 20 set for the amphibious invasion. General Eisenhower received permission to retain sixty-eight of the LSTs[24] used against Sicily.

Stubborn German fighting in the Cassino Corridor made it necessary to postpone Anzio. Doubts persisted about the adequacy of landing craft, but the attack was ordered for two o'clock on the morning of January 22, 1944. The Task Force consisted of 376 ships, and it was truly a United Nations fleet. Dutch, Greek, Polish, and French vessels were added to the American and British forces. They carried, in the first assault, 161,000 men, supplies for two days, 700 trucks, and 100 DUKWs. Resistance was not heavy at first. But the Germans rushed reinforcements, including the Hermann Goering Panzer Division. Our 3rd and 45th Divisions fought back stubbornly, and the German attempt to annihilate the forces on the beachhead failed. But enemy guns raked the beaches almost incessantly and we lost 2,781 killed and 10,827 wounded.

The narrow limits of the Anzio beaches and the constant shelling made supply both difficult and dangerous.[25] LSTs were loaded at Nestles and maintained an overnight ferry service to the Allied forces. An LST could carry fifty trucks, which were loaded with ammunition, gasoline, and other supplies at Naples and hurriedly put ashore.[26]

The 488th Port Battalion helped to make Anzio secure. It had loaded four Liberty ships and accompanied them to the assault on D-Day. Then they transferred the cargoes into landing craft and went ashore under fire.[27] German long-range guns bombarded Allied shipping day and night. Nazi planes sowed mines nightly as well.

The United States Sixth Corps pinned down five German divisions in the Anzio section. The Fifth Army and the British Eighth Army, fighting the main battle for Italy, were holding twenty more in that bitter winter of 1943–1944. But it was not until June that Rome fell. In July the third largest port in Italy, Leghorn,[28] was captured, and our supply problems were eased. Leghorn was in worse condition than Naples had been. The northern entrance to the harbor was completely blocked by sunken ships. All quays were badly damaged. Railroads serving the port had been cut at twenty- to thirty-foot intervals by acetylene torches. The streets were heavily mined and almost impassable. So were the harbor waters.

When the Allied forces entered Leghorn, the town was still under artillery fire. The first Liberty ship entered the port on August 20 and discharged its cargo to lighters. By November 24, Allied port battalions had built twelve docks, a collier berth, and two tanker berths. The following month 229,000 long tons of cargo were discharged in Leghorn. By this time it had replaced Naples as the principal supply base for the Allied armies, with a consequent reduction in overland supply routes.

Important lessons, in supply as well as in combat, were learned in Italy. The fighting near Cassino made it clear that ammunition production would have to be increased. Overseas requirements began to soar in the spring of 1944. In September of that year, 225 million rounds of small arms ammunition were fired. In November medium and heavy artillery shells approaching 200,000 tons in weight were consumed. And these totals would be far exceeded, we would learn, in the advance to Berlin. In the fall of 1944, ETO demanded more of every type of heavy artillery and heavy artillery ammunition.

Before the war the Army had been somewhat conservative in estimating the probable need for ammunition. It was believed that mechanized, mobile warfare would prevent, in some measure at least, the prolonged artillery slugging matches which had characterized World War I. But experience, first in Italy and later in France, demonstrated anew that there was no answer so effective as artillery, and lots of it, to prepared fortifications.

Now, to meet the appeals from abroad, shipments were made directly from plants to dockside. Almost ten days were cut from the time it took to get ammunition abroad. Another lesson learned in Italy was that heavy guns would be needed in greater quantities. Gun tubes and recoil mechanisms wore out because of the continued firing. Plant capacity in the United States was heavily strained to supply the replacements.

Ammunition was always a problem. We had no peacetime industry to which we could turn. So, manufacturers of soap, soft drinks, toys, shirts, and other products converted to producing ammunition. New methods of loading were devised. A locomotive company and a railway car manufacturer turned out gun carriages. Material shortages forced the use of steel cartridge cases in place of brass. Ammunition was packed in cardboard and wood when tin and steel were not to be had.

Meanwhile, the Army's ordnance experts constantly strove to improve the quality of American weapons. Notable was a decrease in the weight of the 60-mm mortar so that the base would be eliminated and the mortar fired while being held against the ground. Larger sizes of mortars were perfected.

Thus we entered the closing and decisive phases of the war. Our production was vaulting to new heights, but our estimates of what we would need were just beginning to receive the test of experience. A few months before, in recognition of the fact that our estimates of requirements were often only guesses, and in realization of the fact that a too-generous estimate of one requirement might penalize the fulfillment of another one, we had appointed a board to review requirements.[29] This board worked for several weeks very secretly in the late summer of 1943 and sought to establish some realistic standard for estimating requirements, and to bring actual requirements within the limits of probable need. It did a good job; but in the end, only experience can be a sure teacher, and some requirements which we reduced late in 1943 had to be lifted again when we threw our major forces into action.

It is a serious matter to restore production in a program which has been cut back. That is particularly true while the production effort is still at its peak. If a plant is closed down, the machinery may remain, but the labor force will disperse. Then, if events force the plant to reopen, it is necessary to reassemble the old labor force or create a new one. And it is certain, under such circumstances, that the plants which have absorbed the labor which was previously in the plant where production is about to be restored will be convinced that the workers they are asked to give up are essential to their own success.

Even after the necessary workers are assembled, it takes time to rebuild them into an effective production team. Thus, from the time when the military situation dictates the resumption of production, weeks may elapse before production is back to anything approaching normal. Thus, the problems of production do not end when everything is going full blast. Production, under such circumstances, is like an orchestra. Every instrument is manned and, for the most part, operating efficiently. But it requires constant care on the part of the conductor to see to it that the balance of his ensemble is such as to meet the needs which face him. When we remember that the conductor of the orchestra of war production never knows precisely, until he mounts the podium and opens the book of Fate which lies on the stand before him, just what score his orchestra is going to be required to play, the difficulty of getting the effect he needs for prompt victory is apparent. So it was with us in the recent war. We could never relax, until the very end, lest something go wrong, or get out of balance, and destroy the effect which our strategy demanded.

Chapter 9

The End in Europe

When the chiefs of state of the Big Three gathered at Tehran in November 1943 for final discussion of the Normandy invasion and other phases of the war, production in the United States had reached its peak. This does not mean that all our problems had been solved: far from it. Shortages arose constantly and had to be corrected. But we were able to scale down overall quantity production in 1944. The total munitions to be produced would be $59 billion as compared with $63 billion for 1943.

No serious differences of opinion marred the meetings of the President, the Prime Minister, and the head of the Soviet Union.[1] At a preliminary conference held a few days earlier, on November 23 at Cairo, Mr. Roosevelt said the logistical problem was to undertake OVERLORD in 1944 and keep the Mediterranean ablaze at the same time.

At the time of the Tehran conference over 600,000 tons of materiel, aside from aircraft, had been delivered to Russia, and the monthly totals were rising rapidly.[2] The Red Armies were on the march. The atmosphere at the Russian Legation, where the meetings began on November 28, was warmly cordial. The President, presiding, opened the discussion by outlining the war situation, as he explained, from an American viewpoint. In the Pacific, the United States was following a policy of attrition against the Japanese and was sinking more ships than the enemy could possibly replace. He emphasized the vital need for being able to get at Japan with all possible speed.

Mr. Roosevelt then turned to OVERLORD. Planning for the invasion of France had begun a year and a half before, but transportation problems had forced delay. Now the tentative date was May 1, 1944. The landing-craft bottleneck had prevented the United States from doing all we would have liked. The troops were ready but not the boats. But OVERLORD, even if delayed, would divert the greatest number of German divisions from the eastern front, he felt. Certain other plans might be carried out. Concentration had been given to a stronger offensive in Italy, to operations in the Aegean, or from Turkey. But the main invasion must not be delayed beyond June, in any event.

Marshal Stalin said that the Soviet Union welcomed Allied victories in the Pacific. It was unfortunate that Russia had not been able to help thus far because of German pressure. The Russian forces in the Far East would have to be increased threefold before an attack on Japan was possible. It could not be launched, the Marshal said, until Germany had been defeated. Then, by a common front, would come victory.

Turning to the Soviet offensive against Germany, the Marshal said that sufficient supplies and reserves had been accumulated for its continuation. The best way that the United States and Great Britain could help was by a blow at Germany from some part of France. The Italian campaign, he thought, had been of great value insofar as it had opened the Mediterranean, but he did not believe that further operations there would draw away much German strength.

Logistics as well as military considerations dictated that the main blow against Germany had to be mounted, however fearful the risk, from England. This had been realized from the beginning of the war. It was the core of our basic strategy, which decreed that Germany was to be eliminated first, while operations in the Pacific continued with rising force. Supply lines to Europe were about half the length of those to the Pacific combat zones. This meant that ships could be turned around more quickly, and that troops and supplies could be built up in far less time than in the Pacific. Another factor which guided the early planning was that the forces assembling in England would assist in the protection of the islands in the event of a German attempt at invasion. If the main assault on Germany had been launched from any other point, it would have been necessary to leave a large garrison in the British Isles and thus lose the use of these troops in the offensive operations.

The plain truth is that we had no choice, once the Japanese advances had been halted, in deciding that Germany constituted the greater danger and must be defeated first.[3] We had no reason to fear the technological potential of Japan. Her weapons were inferior, and so were her scientists. But our intelligence reports showed that the boasts by Goebbels of new, secret, and terrible weapons were more than mere propaganda.[4] It was still possible, as the plans for OVERLORD were being carried out, for Hitler to win the war.

General Eisenhower has enlarged on the logistical advantages of the plan for OVERLORD:

> The operation of transporting supplies from the United States to the United Kingdom was facilitated by the fact that cargoes were discharged through established ports and over established rail lines. Additionally, large quantities of materials for the invasion were made directly available ... from British resources within the United Kingdom itself. These conditions could not, of course, exist on the continent and plans were accordingly made to overcome the difficulties envisaged. It was recognized that the major tonnage reception on the continent would be over the beaches during the first two months, with the port of Cherbourg being developed at an early date.[5]

It was also anticipated that Ostend, Antwerp, and other ports to the north would be cleared. But, as General Eisenhower adds, the "expectations did not materialize, due primarily to enemy strategy and the vicissitudes of the campaign."[6] Hitler and his generals did not doubt that Allied armies could land in France. The Germans were wholly confident, on the other hand, that they could win in the war of logistics. The Allied forces, cut off from their supply sources as soon as they got ashore, would steadily grow less effective and would be swept back into the sea.

"The impossible ... was accomplished," General Eisenhower writes, "and supplies came ashore—not afterwards to support a beleaguered army on the beachheads, but actually with the troops as they landed. The Germans were, by virtue of our initial supply, denied the opportunity of dislodging us and were subsequently, throughout the campaign, under sustained attack as the result of the feats of maintenance performed by our administrative organizations."[7]

As our supplies grew to vast proportions in England, the tight little island seemed tight indeed. American port units operated in Southampton, London, Belfast, Londonderry, Glasgow, and wherever else docks existed or could be built. They had their troubles. One ship arrived at Liverpool with one-third of her cargo improperly marked so that it had to be examined piece by piece before shipment to the supply depots.[8] A month before the invasion, thirty-eight vessels reached a clogged British port and had to wait at anchor. For a time, because of the shipping shortage, it looked as though part of the cargoes would have to be dumped behind the port, where exposure to the weather would ruin most of it. By energetic efforts, however, all of these supplies were transported to depots.

In due course, the tonnages accumulated in the United Kingdom would be transported to the Allied forces through the Channel ports. But at first the beaches would have to serve, and they did. By D-Day plus nine, 500,000 men had been landed. On D-Day alone, 1,845 tons of supplies came ashore in addition to those on combat vehicles. Cherbourg was scheduled for capture by June 14 but did not fall until June 27. However, by D-Day plus thirty-eight, a million tons of stores and 300,000 vehicles had been landed. Reversals and delays, such as the postponement of the capture of Cherbourg, had to be assumed. Experience in Italy had made it certain that the port, when captured, would be so thoroughly wrecked that weeks of repair would be necessary. Therefore, measures would have to be taken in order to assure the landing of supplies in sufficient quantity to maintain offensive operations by methods other than the ports, namely, over the beaches.

The fact that this was done successfully was a triumph of organization and skill. But it was also a triumph of production. Initial supply could not have been assured in sufficient quantity but for the DUKWs and other novel landing craft which our industrial genius had produced in such great quantities. Old-fashioned methods and old-fashioned equipment would undoubtedly have failed.

But, to assist the new, but at this time no longer untried, methods of supporting amphibious operations, something totally new had been prepared. It was a project which was as secret as the invasion itself and which was started in London. This was the building of artificial docks, known by code as Mulberry A and B. Without them, General Eisenhower has written, "I do not believe that our operations during the summer could have been successful."[9]

The artificial docks were first approved at the Quebec conference in August 1943. And in the months that followed, according to General Eisenhower, they "occasioned me and my staff many a headache."[10] Test models sank when towed out to sea, although they had behaved perfectly, in miniature, when tried out in tanks. England's labor shortage strained the responsible ministry. The inescapable employment of thousands of Irish raised the possibility that among them might be a few so anti-British that they would reveal what was going on. But the secret was kept. It was not until the middle of July that German reconnaissance uncovered another major reason why the Allies had not been driven out of France.

Nothing remotely like this had ever been attempted. The artificial harbors were to be built in sections in England and floated across the Channel. One was to be located opposite the American target, Omaha Beach, and the other was to serve the British forces. They were to be full-sized harbors, comparable to Dover in capacity. Concrete caissons, two hundred feet long and sixty feet wide with a depth of sixty feet, were to be moored seven miles off the coast to break the force of the waves. Further protection was to be given by breakwaters of 95,000-cubic-foot content, and by sinking freighters.[11] This was to provide an enclosed area about two miles long and one mile wide where Liberty and other ships could be unloaded. Their cargoes would be trucked ashore over pontoon bridge-piers.

The complicated task of towing four hundred units weighing 1.5 million tons across the Channel began on June 7. Completion was scheduled for June 24 and by June 19, both Mulberry A and B were nine-tenths finished. Over two thousand tons of supplies were moving ashore on Mulberry B, the British installation. Then bad weather, which had so hampered the invasion, arose to plague us again. It came in the form of the worst June gale in forty years, and the Mulberries caught it squarely. The storm lasted for four days. During it, except for the work of some unflinching DUKW crews, all unloading had to be abandoned. Two days later, the Mulberries began to fall apart under the beating of the wind and waves. Mulberry A, being more exposed, collapsed first. It looked as if the work of months, tons of critically needed materials, and $100 million would be lost. Mulberry B, however, survived when the winds began to die down on June 22.

This landing of supplies sufficient for continuous and furious offensive operations without the assistance of a port was one of the major strategic surprises of the war. An astonished German general, captured in the campaign, paid tribute to the Allied supply triumph in a document found with his effects, and which is quoted by General Eisenhower:

> I cannot understand those Americans. Each night we know that we have cut them to pieces, inflicted heavy casualties, mowed-down their transport. We know, in some cases, we have almost decimated entire battalions. But—in the morning—we are suddenly faced with fresh battalions, with complete replacements of men, machines, food, tools, and weapons. This happens day after day. If I did not see it with my own eyes, I would say it is impossible to give such kind of support to front line troops.[12]

And yet, until almost the end of July, the beaches were the main source of supply. An average of thirty thousand men and thirty thousand tons of supplies was handled over them daily. It was an operation unique in the history of war.[13]

The three vital components of military supply are food, ammunition, and gasoline. Of the three, fuel is the most important because without it the other two can neither be distributed nor protected from air attack. Few realized how unbelievable the total fuel needs would be. Following our breakthrough at St. Lo, as the Third Army got into full stride across France, 1 million gallons of gasoline a day were required at the front. By then gasoline was far more essential than shells or bullets, for the Axis supermen were not waiting to serve as targets.

Again, radical projects were developed to make certain we would be able to transport enough oil for the invasion and the following operations. Tankers could lie off the coast, of course, and discharge their cargoes into lighters. Gasoline could be transported in cans on dry-cargo ships. But these methods were slow and would be subject to enemy air attacks. They were used, however, in the first few weeks after D-Day. DUKWs brought the cans to the beaches. A marine pipeline reached out from the shore to a tanker anchorage. But such methods were not adequate for a sustained offensive. Some way of supplying fuel had to be devised which would take into account bad weather, shipping shortages, and the still dangerous, if fading, Luftwaffe.

Project PLUTO[14] was the answer.[15] This called for two pipelines under the Channel; the first for a distance of about fifty-six miles from the Isle of Wight to the Cherbourg Peninsula. The second submarine line was to be from Dungeness under the straits of Dover to Boulogne. Under any circumstances, the laying of such lines was an uncertain enterprise. The storms of June, which did so much damage to the Mulberries, and later ones in July, added to the difficulties. Leaks developed. Delays in construction arose. By mid-August, however, both lines were operating with a capacity of 900,000 gallons of gasoline a day. This revolutionary method of delivering oil, General Eisenhower has reported, "provided our main sources of fuel during the winter and fall campaigns."[16]

The lines under the Channel were part of a network of eight hundred miles on which construction began immediately after D-Day. The service troops who went ashore had to contend with concentrated mine fields. One of these was so covered with wreckage that detectors could not be used, but a volunteer party of twelve cleared fifteen hundred mines in four days, at a cost of one killed and five wounded. So great were the obstacles that two and a half weeks of intensive, dangerous labor were needed to get the line slightly over three miles inland.

Yet this did not mean that progress could continue without an established port. Cherbourg fell under the weight of three American divisions on June 27. Hope that it might be operating within three days was dashed immediately. The destruction was almost complete.[17] More than one hundred vessels, one of over twelve thousand tons, had been sunk in the harbor and its estuaries. The docks were a tangle of wrecked freight cars, bridges, sidings, and cranes. The Gare Maritime, where countless carefree American tourists had landed en route to Paris, was a shambles of crumbled concrete. Departing Axis demolition troops had hurled seventy-five tons of this into the slips. The extreme tides at Cherbourg were another problem. An incoming vessel might navigate into a berth at high tide. But unless it could unload and get away in a few hours, it might founder on some sunken barge or other vessel.[18]

Every possible makeshift was used to the full. By June 16 ships were being unloaded by DUKWs. Gasoline was transferred from a Navy tanker. On July 27 two sea trains with crucially needed rolling stock arrived from the United States and discharged their cargoes into barges. It was not until August 9 that the first Liberty ships were berthed at Cherbourg. Meanwhile, the pipeline troops could not get to them by water. The roads from Normandy were choked. So, captured German valves and pipes were used. The lines built on the peninsula linked up with the sub-channel pipes from the Isle of Wight.

Logistics, strategy and tactics can never be separated in war. It was militarily imperative that, while our own communications lines functioned, those of the enemy should be paralyzed. This confronted General Eisenhower and his advisers with one of those decisions which strain the nerves of the strongest men.

Bombing the French railroads, bridges, and highways meant, of course, heavy casualties among the citizens of that long-suffering Ally. Both Prime Minister Churchill and General Pierre Koenig, commander of the French forces of the Interior, asked General Eisenhower to reconsider his decision to bomb these targets. But when this was demonstrated to be impossible, the French commander agreed.

"It is war," he said.[19]

Some conception of the importance of these air attacks may be gained from a comparison of Allied and Axis forces on D-Day. We were far outnumbered. The invasion was made with seven divisions, although ten German divisions were within close reach of our landing points in Normandy. But von Rundstedt[20] was denied mobility because freight yards, railway lines, and bridges had been destroyed. Another German general, who served as transportation officer under von Rundstedt, described his predicament to our intelligence officers. Up to the end of February 1944, when the AAF went out in force against communications targets in France, military rail traffic in the area of Paris had numbered about seventy trains a day. It had been reduced to an average of forty-eight by April and to twenty by the end of May. This had cut off supplies for the Atlantic Wall, and construction work on that fortification had ceased. The prisoner of war said that, in his opinion, von Rundstedt would have been able to rush reinforcements, except for the bombings, and to have opposed the invasion successfully. At a time when production of ammunition and other materiel was increasing in Germany—for it did increase until almost the end of 1944—it was impossible to get them to the front.[21]

During the invasion itself, the German traffic expert said, all railway movements in the Seine and Normandy areas ceased, with resulting diversions and delays. It had been planned to move reinforcement troops at the rate of seventy-two trains daily. Thus the vaunted 15th Army had been scheduled to deploy from Holland to Normandy. But it could not go directly. It had to be moved south to Rheims, further south to Dijon, and then west to Tours. Two divisions of the First Army were based near Bordeaux. Only one small bridge across the Loire was intact, however, and then this was destroyed. The troops and their supplies had to be unloaded, ferried across the river, and then reloaded. The 17th Panzer Division moved slowly to the front, partly by road and partly by rail.

"Everything had ceased to be normal," the prisoner said. "The first trains came through with bearable delays, but as soon as they were recognized, air action against that particular troop movement began. I remember cases where movements which we wanted to bring in at 10 to 12 were actually moved at no more than two to three trains per day."

Energetic efforts were made to keep the trains rolling in France. To replace French trainmen who were showing signs of increasing resistance, he said, seventeen thousand Germans were brought in. But it was in vain. When the retreat toward Paris took place, only 5 percent of all supplies were evacuated.

It might be well to note at this point that American supply organizations, great as were the difficulties and dangers under which they worked, were never confronted with conditions comparable to those which faced the enemy. Had German jet-propulsion, rocket, or atomic research gone further, we too might have had to produce munitions and get them to our armies, despite the enormous handicap of shattered communications lines. It is easy to imagine how slow, in comparison, would have been our progress. Troops bound for overseas embarkation at New York from the south might have had to be routed through Buffalo. A break in our few transcontinental trunk railroads would have paralyzed troop and supply movements to the Pacific. Thousands upon thousands of Americans would have been forced to spend their time repairing railroads, roads, and factories instead of producing the goods of war. And in addition to all this, manpower and materials would have been consumed in moving highly concentrated factories to Kansas, Texas, New Mexico, and other interior points, or underground. But fortunately it didn't happen here, not in World War II.

When describing the brilliant and devastating way in which the AAF ripped up German communications and paralyzed the movements which, could they have been carried out on schedule, might very well have thrown our troops back into the sea before they could establish themselves securely on the French coast, it is well to remember that the basis for this success was laid five and more years earlier. Had it not been for the developmental work in airplanes before 1940, and for the tremendous expansion of the aircraft industry and reorganization of its production methods which began in 1940, we could not have established the practically unchallenged control of the air over the battlefields of Normandy and the communications zones beyond which we actually secured. It detracts in no way from the skill and heroism of those who landed on the beaches on June 6 to say that the successful invasion of Normandy began several years earlier and that the first skirmishes took place in those offices and factories where preparations were made for the immense mass of materiel which, both on the ground and in the air, provided the sinews for this extraordinary victory.

A gigantic burden fell on the Allied supply forces after General Omar N. Bradley, aided by heavy air bombardment, broke the German lines at St. Lo. General Patton's Third Army began the advance which would carry it to the defenses of the Siegfried Line. Miracles in supply were accomplished. The Third Army moved ahead at speeds approaching forty miles per day.

"Our transport services," General Eisenhower writes in analyzing the campaign,

> were taxed to the limit. The incentive offered by the chance of a smashing victory, however, drove the men in whose hands the maintenance of supply rested to feats of super-human accomplishment. In the light of the difficulties they had to overcome, it seems, when one looks back on those amazing days, well-nigh incredible that at no time up to the time we stood upon the threshold of Germany was the momentum of the drive retarded through lack of essential needs. The spectacular nature of the advance was due in as great a measure to the men who drove the supply trucks as to those who drove the tanks.[22]

By September 5 over 2 million Allied troops and almost 3.5 million tons of supplies had been delivered to the armies under General Eisenhower's command. It was not enough to send the scheduled allotments of ammunition, food, and clothing. Demands for replacements were continuous. Trucks bogged down on muddy roads despite the laying of thousands of yards of matting. At Omaha Beach the mud was thigh-deep; no wheeled vehicle could move. The mud and grit wore out truck transmissions. Excessive use of low gear added to the process. Tires were shredded. One truck battalion reported fifty-four flats from a single night's running.

"Losses of ordnance equipment have been extremely high," General Eisenhower reported to the Chief of Staff during the campaign across France. "For instance, we must have [as] replacement items each month: 36,000 small arms, 700 mortars, 500 tanks, 2,400 vehicles, 100 field pieces. Consumption of artillery and mortar ammunition in northwestern Europe averaged 8 million rounds a month."[23]

The production of these great supplies each month in the United States was no longer too difficult. Nor was transporting them across the Atlantic, for the submarine attacks were diminishing. But the wrecking of the French communications systems, without which the invasion might have been a holocaust, now was a liability of major proportions. The modern army, in this age of destruction by air, must build its own communications systems—railroads and roads as well—and then equip and operate them.

The first phase in organized overseas transportation is by truck. On August 25 the Red Ball Express, a new type of super-highway, began operation. It stretched from the Cherbourg Peninsula about 350 miles up to the forward supply dumps. It was a one-way road which returned west by another route, and trucks with trailers traveled at high speed both day and night. During its eighty-one days of operation, traffic on the Red Ball Express averaged over 5,000 tons a day. On one occasion the total rose to 12,000 tons. The Engineer Corps built and maintained the road on which the Military Police, which controlled it, had placed 25,000 signposts in French and English. The Red Ball Express was complete with repair shops and filling stations. This was one of five major highways, opened as other Channel ports fell, over which the bulk of the supplies were carried until the French railroads could be operated again.[24]

Most of the trucks were heavy and difficult to drive over shell-pocked roads without lights. Gasoline was carried in tanker-trailer combinations. Only tough young Americans, many of whom had been driving trucks before they entered the Army, would have so cheerfully survived the hardships incurred day and night on these highways across France. They could never be certain that all the mines had been cleared. Damaged bridges were another danger. Sporadic air attack was always possible. Lt. Col. Randolph Leigh, in his history of supply problems in the ETO, recorded the reactions of one young driver.

"The size of the things makes them hard to handle," the boy said. "The gas splashing inside throws you from side to side. This affects your steering. The 'dolly' (trailer) does not exactly follow the tanker. You have to make allowance for this, especially around curves and where the road is slanted. You have to be careful or they jacknife."[25]

Comparable difficulties and dangers marked operation of the French railroads. American bombings and German demolition had left their marks of ruin again.[26] During the first three months of the invasion, little traffic could be moved. The Military Railways Service of the Chief of Transportation, ETO, had, however, been making plans since 1942 on the assumption that the French railroads would have to be more or less rebuilt following the landings. Continental rail experts assisted in the planning. Designs were drawn for the type of freight, tank, and other cars best suited to the French lines. The cars were manufactured in the United States and shipped to the United Kingdom.

A portion of the French rolling stock had been removed to Germany. Much of the rest were worn out. During the occupation, French resistance forces had hidden essential parts from their German oppressors. These were promptly produced when our transportation troops arrived. But nearly all the stations and freight yards were tangled wreckage. Most of the bridges had to be repaired by the Engineer Corps. A few American diesel engines, some abandoned German ones, and some French locomotives provided what little motive power existed. Among the French engines were twelve which had been turned over by us after World War I. Now they were operated again by their original owners. By the time the French lines were in full operation, nine hundred new American locomotives were being used.

By the end of August 1944, about 750 miles of French railroad were restored. Language difficulties and the difference between French and American equipment sometimes strained amicable relations. It was not infrequent, the records disclose, for a GI trainman and a French railroad employee to be seen gesticulating wildly at each other, or to be heard shouting vehemently in two languages. At that point another American, of Italian or Mexican extraction, would join the fray and shout futile interpretations in a third language. When the new Diesel engines arrived, the French locomotive engineers made fervent pleas to be allowed to drive them. This made the GI engineers highly nervous, but a compromise was usually worked out in which the Frenchman was allowed to ride in the cab and handle the controls under careful supervision.

The trains ran, even if under conditions which would make safety engineers of the Interstate Commerce Commission turn pale.[27] On July 11 operations started between Cherbourg and Carentan, a location that lay between Utah Beach and St. Lo. The Germans had not yet been cleared from the peninsula. For a fortnight the track ran parallel to the front, and most of the trains were fired upon. But this hazard was nothing in contrast to later dangers. All operating rules, even wartime ones, were lifted when the American armies began their advance after July 25. By the end of that month, 333 train runs had been made. The GI engineers demonstrated that Casey Jones was an amateur.

A good many of the Military Railways Service troops had worked for railroads back home. Few, however, were qualified locomotive engineers. Until American rolling stock arrived, these inexperienced soldiers had to run engines and trains which did not have sufficient braking power. Their reverse mechanisms were archaic. The Cherbourg–Le Mans line was without communications of any sort. The GI who took out his train was wholly on his own. Moreover, behind him stretched rickety cars overloaded with highly explosive aviation gasoline, bombs, ammunition, and gunpowder.

"Most of the runs were made at night, and strict blackout rules were in force," Col. Leigh reports.

> Trainmen did not know what curves or grades were ahead. But they did know that there were soft spots in the roadbed and that there were bridges of particularly limited strength. For that reason it was hard to build up on

the level stretches the momentum needed to climb the hills. As a result many trains lost speed and stalled on the upgrades. Then the engineers backed away and took a running start, or else cut their trains, pulling half over the crest to a switch siding and then backing down for the rest....[28]

Local fire departments on the route turned out to pump water for the first trains. When brakes failed to work, the crews could only cling to their posts, as the train careened on through the dark, and hope against hope that nothing was in the way. As on the Persian Gulf lines, where equal dangers had to be faced, the crews worked excessive hours. Sixty hours at the throttle was about the average before being relieved. One crew worked eighty-four hours without resting.

Despite the sweat and the heroism of the GI transportation troops, however, the spectacular sweep across France could not be carried into Germany. Difficulties of supply, General Eisenhower reports, "eventually forced a halt upon us.... Only a miracle of hard work and brilliant improvisation by the supply services carried our armored spearheads so far."

"The Third Army maintenance, in particular, was stretched to the limit ... we had to employ transport aircraft to carry over 2,000 tons a day to keep the spearheads going," he adds. "The enemy's failure to make a stand on any of the river lines freed us momentarily from the necessity for airborne operations which would have taken away the planes from the task of keeping the ground forces supplied, but it was evident that sooner or later such a situation would arise when we came up against the main frontier defenses of the Reich."[29]

The fuel and munitions which flowed into the continent could not all go to the rapidly advancing combat troops. A paradox of war is that supplies must be used to get more supplies. The great port of Antwerp was desperately needed for the continuation of our operations. Cherbourg would only support thirteen divisions; Antwerp fifty. Since the Supreme Allied Commander was planning to have seventy-one divisions ready for combat by January 1945, it was clear that the final assault on the Reich would not be possible until Antwerp was functioning.

Progress to that end was slow. Even after the city was cleared on September 4, Axis forces held the islands which covered the approaches to the port. Shortly after the middle of September, General Eisenhower wrote General Marshall: "Right now our prospects are tied up closely with our success in capturing the approaches to Antwerp. All along the line maintenance is in a bad state—reminiscent of the early days in Tunisia—but if we can only get to using Antwerp it will have the effect of a blood transfusion."

The pockets of resistance were at last cleaned out by November 9. Again, engineer, transportations, signal, and service troops began their herculean task of clearing away the wreckage. This was their hardest and most dangerous assignment. The port was open by November 27. But in January 1945, the vicious V-2 missiles started to fall on Antwerp. They sometimes landed, utterly without warning, at the rate of forty per day. Hundreds of Allied soldiers and civilians were killed. Yet American forces soon received twenty-two thousand tons of supplies a day through Antwerp.

Meanwhile, Operation ANVIL, the invasion of France from the south, had been carried out with a speed which exceeded expectations. General Somervell and his staff in Washington had studied the logistical possibilities of ANVIL in the spring of 1943 and had concluded that it was a feasible venture. It was approved at the Tehran Conference the following December. The shortage of landing craft, as I have already said, prevented a simultaneous attack from the west and south, as then envisioned. The invasion date was first postponed to July and then to August 15.

Like the operation at Anzio, ANVIL was truly a United Nations operation. Among the 700,000 troops were Americans, British, and French. In the French army were Moslems from French Morocco and a few Indo-Chinese. The mixture must have driven our quartermaster officers crazy. French rations were different from the American. Moslems would not eat pork. The Indo-Chinese demanded their own native specialties and would not work when it rained because of an aversion to wet feet. Besides this, Italian labor battalions, if they worked at all, insisted on a wine ration.

The military situation, fortunately, was not quite as complex as the culinary one. The United States Seventh Army under the late Lt. Gen. Alexander M. Patch landed on schedule in the vicinity of Cannes and began a rapid march up the Rhone Valley. German domination of France was about over. The advance of the Allied armies was greatly assisted by the French underground forces, which had long been waiting for their chance to fight. By September 5 more than 2 million Allied soldiers and almost 3.5 million tons of supplies had been landed in France from the west and the south. Paris was free. The *Reichswehr* was falling back to the Siegfried Line.

The supply tasks in southern France paralleled those in the west. The capture and reconstruction of Marseilles was a first essential. When that port fell on August 23, its condition was worse than Cherbourg or Antwerp. Not one of its 121 piers could be used. Seven large vessels had been sunk just outside the harbor and sixty-five in the main harbor. Unexploded mines and wall charges were everywhere. The railroads were, as usual, wrecked. By October 5, however, they were operating as far north as Dijon. By the middle of the month, they were moving fifteen thousand tons daily to the front.

Meanwhile, a special supply crisis, which also became a production crisis, was developing in France. This was the shortage of heavy artillery ammunition, a shortage of an especially critical nature since we were now up against the prepared concrete defenses of the German frontier.

That we would need to increase our supplies of heavy artillery ammunition had been apparent for several months. In March 1944, as a result of combat experience in Italy, the production of this ammunition was sharply increased. New factories were built. Inexperienced industrialists received instruction in the required processes. But it was not until November of that year that the added facilities began to turn out shells in substantial quantities. By then we were in the middle of the final production crisis of World War II.[30]

At the close of August, General Eisenhower cabled a detailed picture of the costs of war. In the campaign in France, he said, United States forces alone had lost three thousand airplanes and nine hundred tanks. Even with "strict rationing," the Supreme Commander continued, 150,000 tons of ammunition a month were being used.

These expenditures would prove to be very small compared with the requirements for the onslaught against Germany. In November 1944 mortar ammunition consumption rose to unprecedented heights.[31]

This had been anticipated at SHAEF [Supreme Headquarters Allied Expeditionary Force]. On September 23 General Eisenhower notified us that his troops were facing the Siegfried Line long before the anticipated date. His field commanders reported that only through the heaviest concentration of artillery fire could the fortifications be reduced without undue casualties. Possibly, it was suggested, ammunition should be diverted from the Mediterranean Theater of Operations.

Two days later General Marshall called attention to the heavy artillery ammunition shortage. The War Department would ship immediately all the shells demanded, he said, but this would exhaust domestic supplies and would put a halt to the training of artillery units in the zone of the interior. On September 30, the War Department estimated a November–December shortage of 300,000 rounds which could not be met.

General Eisenhower's anxiety continued.[32] Any increased shipments within the next ninety days, he cabled on October 21, would have a definite effect on the campaign. But we could promise no larger shipments. On November 22 the Supreme Commander told us that General Bradley estimated that the ammunition on hand or expected could supply the current offensive only up to December 15. Here at home we calculated a deficit of half a million rounds of one important high-explosive category by the end of that month.[33]

None of us will ever forget those anxious months. General Eisenhower sent high-ranking officers home to make still more emphatic the needs in ETO. I toured ammunition plants and told the workers about the rationing of ammunition I had seen on trips of inspection overseas. We sent combat veterans on similar missions to relate their own experiences. We went so far as to furlough soldiers for work in shell plants. We made progress, but the situation continued to be critical. The sizes involved in this shortage were the 8-inch and the 240-mm shells, and also the 155-mm to a somewhat lesser extent.

We could not assume, even in February 1945, that the war would soon be over. The AAF was dropping unprecedented tonnages all over the world. In addition, we had to supply the RAF and our other Allies. Again, shortages faced us. It looked as though a deficit of about 848,000 short tons of bombs, as compared with requirements in all the theaters, would exist by June 1945. The cables from General Eisenhower and General MacArthur continued. The former reported on March 6 that expenditure of bombs by the AAF in February was twice the tonnage received. Unless shipments were increased immediately, "operations will be seriously affected." General MacArthur also said he needed more 105-mm ammunition.

As it turned out, the anticipated expenditures were never reached, and we were able to make production cutbacks in April. Supplies in the theaters were adequate for most of the weapons being used. General Eisenhower tells me that transportation was partly responsible for the shortages which did exist. At one time, he reports, it was necessary to ration some guns to seventeen shells a day, when fifty might have been fired. In the field ordnance experts adapted large stocks of captured German ammunition for use in American guns. And so we got by without the serious drop in the effectiveness of our operations that, at one moment, seemed likely. But the whole incident shows what difficulties can arise, even when war production is at its peak, as a result of the complicated and unforeseen contingencies of war.

The winter of 1944–1945 was one of victory. But it also was marked by bitter fighting, by terrible suffering in rain and mud, in snow and ice. Far too many cases of trench foot arose. The causes of this condition were many. In some organizations, no doubt, the shoepacks designed to prevent it did not arrive. But another reason was the happy-go-lucky optimism of the average American soldier, combined with his distaste for carrying extra equipment. Deceived by the warmth of the day, some would toss away their shoepacks and then regret deeply their carelessness when they lay in freezing foxholes that night. In a few cases, I am told, commanding officers did not enforce the wearing of shoepacks too strictly on the mistaken theory that the war would be over shortly.

The optimism was dispelled, at least temporarily, by the German counteroffensive of December 16, 1944.[34] More enemy forces were involved than our intelligence officers foretold. The movement of these forces had been hidden with considerable skill. As we now know from German sources, the attack was personally ordered by Hitler, who directed that an attempt be made to slash through the Allied armies in the Aachen area, with the port of Antwerp as the goal. Hitler admitted it was a move of great daring, but in no other way could Germany be saved.

To disguise the massing of their troops, the Germans successfully gave the impression, for a month before striking, that new divisions in the Ardennes sector were there for training only. A tentative date set for November was postponed to December while the deceptive maneuvering went on. German deception, however, was not limited to the Allies. Their battalion commanders were ordered to lie to their men. They were told to say that the ground troops would be supported by fifteen thousand aircraft and by V-1, V-2, and V-3 weapons, the last of which were not in use. The tired German soldiers were to be falsely informed that they faced only two badly battered American divisions who had lost the will to fight after the battle for Aachen.

Before the offensive was conclusively checked, ten days after it began, a penetration up to fifty miles had been made. The forward march of the Allied armies had been delayed six weeks. In addition, our bombers had been forced into the battle and so had been unable to attack objectives in Germany for thirty days. But the cost to the Germans had been very heavy. They lost 220,000 men—killed, wounded, or missing. About six thousand tanks and six hundred aircraft had been destroyed, and the Germans had now used their last stores of gasoline and oil. Most important of all, German morale had been shattered.

The German offensive placed, however, a sudden and heavy load on our own supply services in the ETO and also on production facilities in the United States. The Army lost 648 medium tanks, 6 complete field hospitals, 11,000 telephones, 4,000 .30-calibre machine guns, 70,000 bayonets, 24,000 rocket launchers, 10,000 M1 rifles, 2,600 two and a half ton trucks, 288 large guns, 21,000 radio sets, and other items in similar proportion. The total cost was in the neighborhood of $66 million. But we were spending roughly $160,000 every twenty-four hours for munitions in 1944.

The German offensive, combined with the false optimism of the previous summer, was also felt by the Surgeon General's Office of the Army. In the summer plans had been made to curtail hospital expansion, on the theory that the war would soon be over. But the casualties in December 1944, to the end of January 1945, abruptly halted curtailment. Orders were issued for fifty thousand new general hospital beds and twenty thousand convalescent hospital cots. Four regional hospitals in the United States were enlarged into general hospitals as a result of the Battle of the Bulge.

The American dead numbered 7,952 in the period between December 14 and January 28. The wounded came to 42,750, and 19,471 Americans were missing in action or taken prisoner. The losses we suffered at the hands of this German counteroffensive, at a moment when we were tempted to believe that the enemy had lost all capacity for offensive action, served as a sharp reminder that it is never safe to relax one's efforts in war until the enemy has actually capitulated. All during the fall of 1944, when the tide of victory was running strongly, there was a constant temptation to cut back our production efforts in anticipation of the end of the war in Europe. The arguments in favor of doing so were, at first sight, appealing. It would save billions of dollars and would enable us to make a start on the difficult job of reconverting industry to peacetime purposes. But it was necessary to resist this temptation because, as events demonstrated, it never is possible to be sure that the enemy's capacity to strike back has been exhausted. It was our position in the War Department that we were not willing to save dollars at the risk of lives. Furthermore, we had a faith in the capacity of the nation to readjust its industry to peace, even if the start was somewhat delayed, which made us feel that the needs of readjustment did not require risking the prolongation of the war by a single day.

Cleaning the remaining Germans from the west bank of the Rhine was all that now remained before crossing that broad, swiftly flowing river in what General Eisenhower has described as "the largest and most difficult amphibious operation . . . since the landings on the coast of Normandy. . . ."[35] All phases of it were discussed again at the Malta and Yalta conferences in February 1945. A degree of pessimism had replaced the earlier optimism. It was now felt that the Reich would not collapse until July at the earliest, and that the European War might even go on for almost another year. The Allied leaders were apprehensive that improved German submarines, which could operate in shallow waters with slight danger of detection, might cut our supplies. The U-boats were operating in the Channel; one had even penetrated the mouth of the Clyde. Sinkings might rise to 150 ships a quarter. They did rise slightly: from twenty-four thousand tons of American ships in January 1945 to fifty-four thousand in March. But Hitler's new submarines did little to interfere with munitions deliveries.

The Rhine assault included one perplexity which the Allied armies had been spared in the invasion of France. Boats and landing craft had to be transported over the war-torn roads of France, Belgium, Luxembourg, and Germany. But first they had to be manufactured, for special equipment was needed for this crucial operation. The far-flung ramifications of logistical warfare may be seen in the fact that contracts for plywood boats were made with, among others, the Pine Castle Boat and Construction Co. of Pine Castle, Florida, the Minnetonka Boat Works of Wayzata, Minnesota, and the Foster Boat Co. of Charlevoix, Michigan. LCMs (Landing Craft, Mechanized) and LCVPs (Landing Craft, Vehicles and Personnel) were made in Los Angeles; Algonac, Michigan; Erie, Pennsylvania; Kansas City; Warren, Ohio; and North Tonawanda, New York.

The plywood boats were sixteen feet nine inches long, and six feet six inches wide. When equipped with an outboard motor, they could carry twelve infantrymen and three engineers at twenty-five miles an hour. In February 1945 seven hundred of these storm boats were ordered through the French Ministere de la Marine. The French had no plywood, so Army loggers cut the wood and hauled it to the mills. The boats were built from specifications based on photographs of similar boats being manufactured in the United States. They were flown to the battle lines in C-54 planes of the Air Transport Command. The LCMs and LCVPs could not, of course, be flown. An LCM can carry a Sherman tank or sixty men; an LCVP, a bulldozer or thirty-five men. They had to be trucked to the front on twenty-ton trailers specially built to bear their enormous weight. Other special supplies were needed. They included 100,000 tons of bridging materials, 215,000 feet of structural steel, 2,500 outboard motors, 8,000 feet of chain, 5 million board feet of lumber, 315,000 feet of wire rope, and 6,000 pontoon bridge floats. Within an average, per bridge, of nine days and one hour, five railroad bridges were thrown across the Rhine. This was in addition to fifty-seven fixed highway and tactical bridges. Nearly all were constructed under German artillery fire.

The Rhine had already been breached twice before the main crossings. At Remagen, on March 7, occurred what General Eisenhower has described as "one of those rare and fleeting opportunities which occasionally occur in war, and which, if grasped, have incalculable effects in determining future success."[36] The enemy, retreating in haste, failed to demolish the Remagen railroad bridge completely. Alert American troops seized the golden moment. Before the bridge tumbled into the river ten days later, a bridgehead had been firmly established. By the time of the main Rhine crossings, an area twenty-five miles long and ten miles deep was held by the First Army. By then floating bridges had been built by the engineers. The second Rhine crossing was by General Patton's army south of Mainz on March 22.

The Second British Army started across the Rhine in the evening on March 23. The next morning American and British airborne troops were landed, and the United States Ninth Army crossed. The cost, General Eisenhower reported, had been "fantastically small."[37]

Weeks of fighting remained. Men would still die. Supplies of all kinds would continue to be consumed in battle. But no doubt whatever befogged the certain outcome. Indeed, as General Eisenhower has phrased it, the "war was won before the Rhine was crossed."[38] German communications were nonexistent. Even their postal system had ceased to operate, adding to the discouragement of the troops.

"Von Rundstedt," General Eisenhower writes,

> had failed in Normandy and had been removed from his command as the penalty of failure. Later he had been reinstated to conduct the ill-fated offensive in the Ardennes where, in 1940, he had achieved his most spectacular success in the invasion of France. Now, with the Allies over

the Rhine, he was again dismissed; and with him went the last hope of Germany's survival. Kesselring was brought from Italy to assume the forlorn task of holding together the beaten armies in the west in the last month of their existence.[39]

On April 25 the armies under General Eisenhower made contact with those of the Soviet Union. On May 7 the Reich surrendered.

As the American armies, flanked by those of their Allies, rolled across western Germany to that rendezvous with victory, one could not but think what five years had done. The eyes of the German population fairly popped as they saw the almost incredible strength in weapons and equipment of the invading armies. Many of them must have wondered what perverse folly prompted their leaders to court battle with a nation that could put in the field such prodigious quantities of materiel. Yet, on the basis of our munitions situation less than five years earlier, the calculations of Hitler and his colleagues were not fantastic. But alive as they were to our very real weakness in the early stages of the war, they failed to take into account the unprecedented potentiality of American industry when fully geared to the work of war. Even we scarcely knew our own strength until we tried. No nation has ever before approached the power we possessed at that climactic moment. Our democratic weaknesses made us slow to realize our danger, but our democratic strength made us irresistible when aroused to combat. But the breathtaking display of power with which we closed hostilities in Europe must not allow us to forget that we had a terribly close call at the start. Nor can we afford to forget that it took nearly five years from the moment when danger threatened until we reached the pinnacle of our strength in the field. Destiny was generous of time, more generous than we deserved. We cannot count on such generosity again.

Chapter 10

Concentration East

With the surrender of Germany, we were at last able to concentrate all of our forces upon the war in the Pacific. Until that time the necessities of sound strategy had compelled us to subordinate the war against Japan to that against Germany. Through the many long months, during which we were building up for our climactic effort in Europe, General MacArthur utilized to the utmost the limited arms and equipment made available to him. His extraordinary exploitation of terrain and his faculty for getting the most out of the materiel at hand in every campaign constitutes a remarkable achievement.[1]

When the war with Germany ended, the United Nations faced, in one sense, an embarrassment of riches. American production had reached its peak.[2] Great Britain was ready to dispatch a naval task force to the Pacific and to place three divisions under American command. Marshal Stalin, although he had not committed the Soviet Union unreservedly, had made it quite clear at Tehran that the Russian armies in the east would attack Japan when the Reich had fallen. By July 6, 1945—ten days before the atomic bomb test in New Mexico—the Soviet forces were concentrating against the Japanese in Manchuria.

But this tremendous preponderance of power[3] still left us with extremely difficult problems to solve before Japan could be overcome, and some of the most formidable of those problems were logistical. Assuming that the Japanese would fight to the end—and before Hiroshima we had no evidence which justified any other assumption—it was tremendously difficult to plan and carry out the movement of supplies to the theater and to determine the amount of production which would be needed for a one-front war.[4]

Many factors, most of them difficult to determine at all accurately, entered into the calculations and plans we had to make. Until almost the end of the war in Europe, it was not possible to know just when our production needs in that theater would come to an end. Some of those needs, of course, would not stop so long as we had an army of occupation to maintain. It was also nearly impossible to tell how much of the materiel in Europe could be recovered and shipped to the Pacific in time and in condition to be useful there. Estimates on this point varied widely. Furthermore, the requirements in the Pacific differed markedly in a qualitative sense from those in Europe. Differences in climate, in terrain, and in character and equipment of the enemy altered our needs. Also, in so vast a logistical operation as that of this war, with its unprecedented quantities and unheard-of complexities, it was extremely difficult to determine the supply situation at any given moment with sufficient accuracy to enable us to adjust our production plans with precision to our prospective needs.

We began work on our plans for redeployment and for cutting back production many months in advance. However, the constant shifts in the war situation, which persisted almost up to VE-Day, and continued study of problems forced constant changes of plans. Whether our plans were technically as good as they might have been will probably never be known.[5] We assumed, of course, that Japan would fight to the end and that we would not have the assistance of any revolutionary new weapons. During the months of our planning, we had no evidence to indicate a collapse of Japanese determination, nor could we be at all sure that the great atomic experiment would prove a success. We had to assume the war in the Pacific would be won by familiar methods and against an enemy who, up to that point, had distinguished himself by resistance to the last man, even in the most hopeless situation.

The dramatic surrender of Japan shortly after the dropping of the atomic bombs on Hiroshima and Nagasaki deprived us—and happily so—of an opportunity to test thoroughly our techniques for the redeployment of both men and materiel. The cessation of hostilities halted redeployment in mid-career[6] and put an end to our need for production of munitions, except such supplies that were needed to maintain the troops until they could return. But even though our production needs were far fewer than we had originally supposed, and might have been so even had we gone on to defeat Japan by more familiar methods, I have never regretted that we set our production target so high. The dollars we spent brought American boys back safely in return.

But before the sudden ending of the war and even long before the end in Europe, we had worked strenuously to overcome one of the most difficult logistical problems that ever faced a warring nation. The great reaches of the Pacific[7] had the effect of reducing by two-thirds the size of the merchant shipping we transferred there. It took three merchant ships in the Pacific to do the work of one in supplying the European and Mediterranean theaters. The combined theaters in the Far East covered 16 million square miles, an area five times as large as the United States. Yet Allied strategy called for continued blows against Japan, even while we were still short of all we needed for our great effort in Europe. At the Quadrant Conference in Quebec in August 1943, it was agreed that the recapture of Burma, which would make possible land communications with China, was the most useful and feasible. Chinese forces could then be supplied and trained, and air warfare could be conducted from Chinese bases.[8]

Admiral Lord Louis Mountbatten was appointed head of the Southeast Asia Command with Lieutenant General Stilwell as his deputy.[9] The military and logistical problems which faced them were appalling. This was pestilential country where all the weapons of evil nature fought on the side of Japan. Malaria, dysentery, and typhus were prevalent. The steaming jungles sapped men's energy as well as their health and sharply cut fighting efficiency.[10] The torrential rains of the monsoon, between May and October, made ground operations almost impossible. And Allied forces fighting in Burma could be supplied only from India.

The capture of Rangoon by Japan in March 1942 had closed the Burma Road. The China coastal ports were useless because Japan had seized the important ones and dominated the South China Sea. Although the materiel flown over the Himalayan hump increased steadily, big guns, heavy construction equipment, tanks, and large trucks could not reach China by air. For the forthcoming offensive in North Burma, and for the ultimate offensives by the Chinese, a land route was essential.

It was a logistical nightmare.[11] The heavy goods of modern, mechanized war had somehow to be transported from Calcutta to Assam, where airfields to support the operation would be constructed. A single-track railroad wound its erratic route though the sometimes steaming, sometimes mountainous terrain. The monsoon rains made it impossible to bridge the Brahmaputra River, so ferries had to be used.

In no other theater of World War II, perhaps, have tactical operations been so closely linked with logistics. Lines of communication could not be established until fighting units had cleared the way. The fighting units, in turn, depended upon supplies delivered by air,[12] by the rickety railroad, by pipelines, and by new roads hacked through the jungles. The Burma campaign really began with airborne supply, before the campaign itself had been authorized at the Quebec Conference. When, in March 1943, the late Maj. Gen. Orde C. Wingate of the British Army led his forces into the North Burma jungles behind the Japanese lines, a jungle-wise young flier, Col. Philip C. Cochrane, was given as assignment which would help to make possible continued operations in 1944.

Colonel Cochrane was ordered to obtain volunteer fliers for the First Commando Force of the AAF and to train them to give tactical and logistical support to the American and British units in the jungle. They were trained in India to fly bombers, fighters, and gliders. They were to support General Wingate's "Indian Raiders"[13] and Maj. Gen. Frank D. Merrill's "Marauders"[14] by dropping supplies and reinforcements. A suitable spot was picked out in the jungle, and on March 5, 1944, twenty-six transports towing thirty-seven gliders landed five hundred men, including engineers who started to build a landing strip. They also dropped 250 tons of supplies, over one thousand astonished Missouri mules, and bulldozers for the engineers.

Japanese counteroffensives were stopped by American, British, and Chinese forces. Chinese and American troops commanded by General Stilwell covered the construction of the Ledo Road—later renamed the Stilwell Road—as it was built southward into enemy country. The United Nations forces, for the most part from the British and Indian armies, suffered 40,000 battle casualties, and 288,000 men were stricken with disease. But success came.

"The mission . . . given Gen. Stilwell in Asia," General Marshall has reported,

> was one of the most difficult of the war. He was out at the end of the thinnest supply line of all; the demands of the war in Europe and the Pacific campaign, which were clearly the most vital to final victory, exceeded our resources in many items of materiel and equipment and all but absorbed everything else we had. General Stilwell could have only what was left and that was extremely thin. He had a most difficult physical problem of great distances, almost impassable terrain, widespread disease and unfavorable climate; he faced an extremely difficult political problem and his purely military problem of opposing large numbers of enemy with few resources was unmatched in any theater.[15]

In the face of such conditions, it took almost three years to restore communication by land with China. Not until January 28, 1945, did an American convoy cross the Burma border into Yunnan Province. By the end of April almost thirty thousand tons had been transported. A second three-year project was soon finished, the eleven-hundred-mile pipeline from India to Kunming. It, too, had followed the advance of the United Nations troops, had been protected by them, and had supplied them. The end of the Japanese occupation of Burma was at hand. British units entered Rangoon on May 3, 1945.

Thus, even before VE-Day, Japan's defensive position had become perilous.[16] Her leaders knew this. Back in Washington the ASF [Army Service Forces] was at work on plans for a great Chinese counteroffensive which would open the ports at Canton and Hong Kong. But this was only one of the dangers which faced the militarists of the Rising Sun. Danger marched steadily toward them across the islands of the Pacific. Kwajalein in the Marshall Islands was attacked on January 31, 1944.[17] On June 15, 1944, action began to make Saipan in the Marianas a base from which B-29s could operate. On July 21, 1944, Guam was invaded. These actions were led by both Army troops and Marines. Army troops and Seabees soon swarmed ashore and began to convert Guam into a huge mid-ocean supply dump for the invasion of Japan. Japan's doom was sealed, whether her warlords fully realized it or not.[18]

Similarly striking advances had been made in the south. Names which will always stand for American heroism marked the advance of General MacArthur's forces: New Georgia with its airfield at Munda; Bougainville, also in the Solomons; Hollandia; Biak; Mortatai. All these were in Allied hands by September 1944.

"We were determined," General Marshall wrote in his last report as Chief of Staff, "that when the final battle of Japan was fought the armies of the Emperor would find no comfort anywhere on earth."[19]

The Chief of Staff's determination was fulfilled to the letter. I must again point out, however, that it was possible only because maximum production had been reached at home and because the supplies were delivered. The troubles experienced in North Africa, Sicily, Italy, and France had been great. They were even worse in the Pacific. Sometimes our progress seemed slow beyond bearing. It took more than a year to get enough materiel to our bases in New Caledonia and Guadalcanal. The ports of Italy, France, and Belgium had been badly wrecked when we captured them. In the Pacific virtually no ports existed. The goods had to be landed on the beaches. The roads were built through the jungles. Engineer amphibious brigades, trained by the ASF, ran the landing craft in these operations and got the goods of war ashore. Many were air-raid casualties. Many long retained jaundiced complexions produced by atabrine.[20]

Despite the needs of ETO [European Theater of Operations] and the Mediterranean, supplies were ready in the summer of 1944 for another big offensive in the Pacific. A number of plans were being studied at the Pentagon. One called for an attack on Formosa[21] off the China coast. Another was the recapture of the Philippines. It is interesting to note that several influences contributed to the decision to move against the islands which Japan had overrun in those dark, early days of 1942. One factor was the opinion of ASF experts that

Formosa's port facilities were too limited. Luzon, the northernmost island in the Philippines chain, had a greater land area. Its roads were superior to those in Formosa. Better airfields could be built. The ASF planners pointed out that a choice between Formosa and the Philippines had to be made because not enough service troops were available for simultaneous operations.

Meanwhile, Mr. Roosevelt and Mr. Churchill were meeting at the Octagon conference in Quebec. On September 7 and 8, 1944, Admiral Halsey's Third Fleet was sending its planes against Yap and the Palau Islands. During the following two days, the Admiral's planes were over Mindanao, the second-largest island in the Philippines. Task force attacks on Yap, the Palau Islands, and Mindanao had been authorized. On September 13, however, Admiral Halsey recommended through Admiral Nimitz that the next target should be the island of Leyte, southeast of Luzon. In response to inquiries from the military leaders at Quebec, General MacArthur said that he could prepare to land on Leyte on October 20 instead of two months later, as scheduled. This was feasible because bases for the operation had been taken.

The decision to advance the date of the Philippines invasion placed tremendous burdens on General MacArthur's logistical staff. It required radical revision of plans. But General MacArthur agreed heartily with the proposal. He knew that the Japanese, if attacked in the Philippines without delay, would be caught off balance and without adequate defense preparations. A little more than a month before Leyte D-Day, he decided to cancel the Yap and Palau Islands operations.

Some indications of the supply complications may be seen in the fact that the omitted operations were to have been supported from New Guinea. All this had to be changed. The onslaught against Leyte would be mounted from West Coast ports in the United States. Ships had to be unloaded and diverted. When the invasion took place, it was handicapped by insufficient quantities of 105-mm howitzer and 81-mm mortar ammunition because higher priorities were being given the European and Mediterranean theaters. Supplies of this ammunition were scattered through supply bases from Australia up through New Guinea, but locating them, assembling them, and shipping them to the Philippines were done only with the utmost difficulty.

But the capture of the Philippines would confront the enemy with acute supply problems. Our own inability to send reinforcements to the Philippines in 1942 will be recalled. Now the tables were turned. Stores of oil and other essentials in the Netherlands East Indies, Indo-China, and Malaya would no longer be available to the Japanese war machine. General MacArthur's forces landed on Leyte on October 21. Two days later the Japanese began a series of naval engagements which, culminating in the battles off Samar and Leyte Gulf, ended in humiliating defeat for the Japanese navy. It was no longer an effective fighting force. The United States Navy could steam where it chose and when it chose.[22]

It was now clear that Japan had lost both the strategical and logistical phases of World War II by the fall of 1944. Her air force, as well as her navy, was destroyed. Only the Kamikaze, or suicide, attacks would continue to be in any way effective.[23] Japan's merchant fleet, which probably exceeded 10 million tons at the start of the war, had been reduced to not much over 1 million by air and submarine sinkings by the time the war ended. Her war economy was hopelessly shattered.[24] Lack of shipping made it impossible to import rubber, bauxite for aluminum, ferro-alloys, oil, coal, and other necessities.

"By mid-1944" states the concluding report of the United States Strategic Bombing Survey, "those Japanese in possession of the basic information saw with reasonable clarity the economic disaster which was inevitably descending on Japan. . . . Their influence, however, was not sufficient to overcome the influence of the Army, which was confident of its ability to resist invasion."[25]

Plans for the invasion of Japan itself had been under examination for six months. The destruction of Manila by the Japanese imposed pressing obligations, with high priority, on our supply services. The water supply broke down and purification units had to be sent in. Much other material to restore essential civilian services in the stricken city had to be sent in at the very moment when we needed to direct all our resources toward preparation for the invasion of Japan.

Logistical details for the landings in Japan were never fully worked out, since the atomic bomb and the collapse of Japan's war production made them superfluous. But before that sudden ending, troops were being mobilized in the Philippines, in Okinawa, and to the south for what then appeared the most costly amphibious undertaking of the entire war.[26] It was estimated that 2 million Japanese troops and eight thousand planes stood ready to defend the falling Empire. Planning for the hazardous operation began in the fall of 1944. Tentative agreements specified the invasion of Kyushu in the fall of 1945 and of Honshu four months later.

But, in reality, Japan was already defeated when our planning experts were still calculating the method by which it could be done, and the probable cost. Ours was a logistical victory unusual in the annals of war. The enemy was knocked out with his main armies still intact. It is never wise to expect such great fortune, and we did not. Behind all our planning had been certain essential principles. One of these was that the side which could kill the greatest number of its opponents would win. Another was that it was imprudent to assume that enemy leadership would be inferior to our own. A third was that skill in the use of weapons would be about the same on both sides. The deciding factor which would enable us to inflict more casualties on the enemy, then, would be the number of weapons in the hands of our troops and weight of the ammunition. I have always insisted that we should produce on the basis of having five times as much of everything as the enemy.

We did not, however, need to test this theory in ground fighting on the Japanese mainland. It is now clear that we overestimated Japan's capacity for continuing the war.[27] The B-29 attacks from bases in the Marianas, beginning in November 1944, forced a badly organized and ill-managed dispersal program on the part of the Japanese. Because the necessary tunnels, railroad spurs, and power lines were unavailable in time, their aircraft-engine production decreased still further.

The low-level B-29 attacks, inaugurated in the spring of 1945, caused fearful destruction and loss of life in Japan's principal cities. In the first attack on Tokyo, 185,000 casualties were inflicted. Yokohama, with 900,000 people, was almost half destroyed in one hour.

Civilian defense measures were handicapped by a lack of material for shelters. Food shortages were growing serious. About one-quarter of all the people in the cities of Japan fled or were evacuated. The conclusion of the Strategic Bombing Survey, after months of investigation, is as follows:

> Based on a detailed investigation of all the facts, and supported by the testimony of the surviving Japanese leaders involved, it is the Survey's opinion that certainly prior to December 31, 1945, and in all probability prior to November 1, 1945, Japan would have surrendered even if the atomic bombs had not been dropped, even if Russia had not entered the war, and even if no invasion had been planned or contemplated.[28]

That conclusion, however, does not mean that we ought not to have planned an invasion or have dropped the atomic bomb.[29] We were not in a position at the time to know the facts which were later available to the Strategic Bombing Survey.[30] Wars, almost won, have often been lost, or have resulted in drawn or inconclusive contests, because the party who apparently had victory in his grasp relaxed too soon. Even where victory has not been allowed to slip away, premature relaxation has doubled or tripled the cost of finally attaining it. It would have been a criminal risking of needless expenditure in American lives had we not planned, and done everything in our power, to push our advantage to the utmost until the moment that Japan surrendered.

Epilogue

Industry, Science, War, and the Future

Thus ended the greatest war in history.[1] It ended with an outpouring of American military might that made us, by a wide margin, the greatest military and naval power in history.[2] On land, on sea, and in the air, Americans gained victory with a quantity of munitions that staggered the imagination. The abundant equipment of each of our units astonished both friend and foe alike, and the total military production which made this possible was beyond the grasp of the ordinary imagination. If there was satisfaction in our victory, there was also cause for sobering contemplation in the fact that we had created and used more than our minds could comprehend.

But we must never forget the small and perilous beginnings of the creation of this final power. Our inadequacy, when the Second World War began, was fully as astonishing as our abundance at its close. The public may be tempted to forget those anxious moments, but those of us who had responsibility for getting defense production started in 1940 can never forget them. Hitler's belief that he could conquer the world looks fantastic now: the facts supported it in those early days.

In a military sense we achieved victory chiefly in the years 1944 and 1945. We had, to be sure, made some very significant gains before 1944, gains without which the final victory could not have come when and as it did. But those earlier advances were only preliminary; it was still possible for us to fail to win as late as the early months of 1944. Any serious inadequacy in leadership, or in the other factors that bring success in the field, could have snatched potential victory from our hands.

But we won the battle of production even earlier, between the summer of 1940 and the end of 1943.[3] That period, and particularly the early part of it, was critical to our munitions program. We had plenty of difficulty after 1943 in balancing the many demands upon our resources, but we could scarcely have suffered a general failure. Before 1943, however, it was touch and go whether we could equip ourselves and those who fought with us in time to prevent a decisive Axis victory. And then it was uncertain whether we could supply ourselves fast enough to keep the Axis powers from getting so firmly entrenched in their early gains that it would be impossible to dislodge them. Had we started our preparations any later, or proceeded by even a slightly slower pace, defeat might have overtaken us. Or, at best, we should have had to confront ourselves with a costly draw which would only have made certain another and greater war in a few years.

The final judgment upon the wisdom or unwisdom of the measures we took to mobilize American industry for war will doubtless be passed by others than those who carried the responsibility at the time. This appraisal will take years of study and presents tremendous difficulties. In this account I have tried to bring out some of the imperfections, as well as some of the merits, of what we did. Most of us were very imperfectly prepared for our tasks. Had it not been for the industrial mobilization planning in the War Department, and the wise advice of men like Mr. Baruch, our original limitations would been felt more seriously in the final result. We also found ourselves, at times, engaged in serious controversies among ourselves.[4] Controversy in government is never entirely avoidable, and if it represents nothing more than the eagerness of men charged with responsibility to make certain that their particular jobs are well done, it can even have a salutary effect. If, at times, controversy went somewhat beyond that point, one must remember that when a great crisis must be met with half-measures, as we were compelled to do at first, tensions of a serious sort are likely to arise. Where each officer of government wants to do an adequate job in his field, but there is not yet sufficient public support for an adequate overall job, each claimant will inevitably reach for something more than his share of the immediate total.[5]

The answer, of course, is to make the total adequate at the outset. That we were unable to do. There was doubtless some lack of vision in the War and Navy Departments, but it is only fair to army and naval leaders to recognize that the principal fault was the failure of the American people to recognize promptly and fully the magnitude of the emergency which faced us. The will of the nation is the final determinant of policy. The leaders of our armed forces cannot secure our safety unless the nation wills it to be safe. Unfortunately, up to the time of Pearl Harbor, our will was divided and uncertain. We had constantly to compromise between what technically we knew we needed and what it seemed likely the nation would grant us. Those compromises came close to being disastrous. They undoubtedly postponed the ending of the war. Had we gone all out on industrial, as well as military, preparation from the summer of 1940, it is not unreasonable to believe that we might have ended the war almost a year earlier. Had we been able to do so, we would have saved thousands of lives and billions of dollars. Not only that, but it is conceivable that the whole postwar political situation throughout the world might have been profoundly affected. As time goes on, the delay of several months in the maturation of American military power, which was imposed upon us by the limitations which we had to accept in the early stages of our industrial mobilization, may loom larger and larger as a factor in this or our age.

Another great war, if we should be so unfortunate as to suffer one, may strike with far more overwhelming speed and force than the last. Even though the half-hour push-button holocaust which some people envisage is not, as yet, technically ready for being unloosed on an unhappy world, methods whose practicality we have already tested make certain greater destruction and a more rapid culmination of hostilities than was the case in World War II.

Yet, in another and equally important sense, another war would take as long, perhaps even longer, to win. The weapons which may be powerful enough to lay waste a great nation within a few weeks or months cannot themselves be produced in less than a period of several years. They require years for technical development and then years for production on a mass scale. In the Second World War, the United States took nearly five years to reach the peak of its power, including the development of its war production and the movement of munitions and men to the point where they could be brought to bear effectively upon the enemy. With a more complete effort in the opening stages, we might have reduced that period to four years, but certainly not too much less. Most of the fighting, until the climactic year of our effort, was devoted—after the first defensive phase—to placing our forces in a position from which they could bring their full power effectively to bear as soon as that full power was available.

Another great war, even a push-button war, will probably require an industrial preparation just as long, assuming the same intensity of effort and departure from a similar point of initial weakness. In fact, it may well take longer, for many of the processes involved in the new methods of warfare are so intricate and require the extensive use of such unusual skills that the developmental stage of war industry may be considerably longer than in the past. The difference in the length of the struggle will be, not in the scientific and industrial preparation, but only in the final military application of the lethal methods thus prepared. Long-range aircraft, guided missiles, and the other marvels of science may enable a future combatant, when he is prepared industrially, to avoid the long approach marches which we had to make in World War II. Hence, if he manages to conceal his industrial preparations, or if his future victims refuse to credit his aggressive intent even though they watch the rise of his war industry, the first three or four years of the next war may take place without any overt act of hostility, in the sense that we have previously judged overt actions. But this preparatory period, in any realistic sense, is just as surely part of any war as is the period of open hostilities. This is a fact which, as we value our safety, we can never afford to forget.

It is, however, not alone the time needed for organizing the mass production of munitions which will make the real—as distinct from the overt—war of the future as long as war in the past. It may well be that another war will have been won in some laboratory, not merely before the opening of formal hostilities, but perhaps even before the beginning of large-scale industrial mobilization. It may even be won by achievements in the realm of pure science before any serious steps have been taken to apply those advances to specifically military uses.

This requires, perhaps, some explanation. Research in the realm of pure science is exploration into the world of the unknown. It has no concern with developing a new explosive or with improving a weapon. Strictly speaking, pure science does not relate to a specific problem, even to a medical one upon which life or death may depend. It constitutes a search for new knowledge, for new principles. But pure science has, in the long run, a deadly practicality. The atomic bomb which ended the war is, of course, the most striking example. It must be remembered that the scientists who began work on nuclear energy were not seeking to develop this most terrible of weapons. Some, at least, among them would have abandoned their searching had they foreseen where it led.[6]

On this important subject I cannot do better than to quote Dr. Vannevar Bush, whose direction of the Office of Scientific Research and Development did so much to advance our victory. Dr. Bush points out that pure, or basic, research "is performed without thought of practical ends." It results "in general knowledge and an understanding of nature and its laws."[7] He adds:

> This general knowledge provides the means of answering a large number of important practical problems, though it may not give a complete answer to any of them. The function of applied research is to provide such complete answers....
>
> One of the peculiarities of basic science is the variety of paths which lead to productive advance. Many of the most important discoveries have come as a result of experiments undertaken with very different purposes in mind. Statistically it is certain that important and highly useful discoveries will result from some fraction of the undertakings in basic science; but the results of any one particular investigation cannot be predicted with accuracy.[8]

If we are to have any chance whatever of surviving another war, our armed forces must not go back to the scientific lethargy which marked the years between 1918 and 1939.[9] Handicapped by inadequate funds, they perhaps accomplished more than might have been expected of them under the circumstances. But there is a tendency for military minds to think in terms of the weapons already in use; their goal is merely to improve them to the greatest possible degree. The scientist in uniform may be limited in his activities by his superiors whom he cannot question. He may hesitate to venture too far into the unknown because of the possibility that he will discover nothing at all—and thereby damage his chance for promotion. Much more research, both basic and applied, must be undertaken by the Army and Navy.

But this is not enough. Again, I quote from Dr. Bush:

> ... military preparedness requires a permanent, independent, civilian-controlled organization, having a close liaison with the Army and Navy, but with funds direct from Congress and the clear power to initiate military research which will supplement and strengthen that carried on directly or under the control of the Army and Navy....[10]
>
> Some research on military problems should be conducted, in time of peace as well as war, by civilians independently of the military establishment.... There are certain kinds of research—such as on the improvement of existing weapons—which can best be done within the military establishment. However, the job of long-range research involving the application of the newest scientific discoveries to military needs should be the responsibility of those civilian scientists in the universities and in industry who are best trained to discharge it thoroughly and successfully. It is essential that both kinds of research go forward and that there be the closest liaison between the two groups.[11]

The compulsion of the war brought the best minds of the scientific world to the Army, the Navy, and to Dr. Bush's OSRD. Our problem—and the solution is far from easy—is to see that the civilian scientists continue to contribute their talents. The superb staff of the OSRD was liquidated rapidly after the war ended. This was natural.

Epilogue   221

They yearned to return to their university or industrial laboratories. They were weary of the difficulties of working for the government. They had suffered financially from the meager salaries paid to them. If the nation is to be preserved in an age which may see attack by weapons even more destructive than the atomic bomb, government scientific posts must be made more attractive. Compensation equal to that of the universities and foundations, if not of industry, must be provided.

A committee appointed to study the question of scientific personnel in the War Department several months ago submitted a comprehensive report to me. Its findings were far from encouraging. The committee reported that under the present procedure it was "virtually impossible . . . to fill vacancies in any grade with the most capable of available men." It found evidence of "serious conditions endangering the War Department scientific and technical establishment." Existing Civil Service methods were declared partly responsible. "More emphasis is given in classification to administrative or supervisory duties," the report stated, "than to superior performance of professional duties."[12]

Everybody with the slightest knowledge of our governmental system knows that this is true. Promotions are based on the number of subordinates under the individual whose advancement is being considered. Length of service rather than ability is the usual standard. Everybody knows also, the report stated, that "the disparity between salaries in the federal service and outside . . . is too great."[13] The present dismissal procedures allow incompetent personnel to remain in important posts when better men, within and outside the government, might be obtained.

I think that the armed services must make many radical changes if their scientific programs are to be maintained at the essential level. It is true that added compensation is necessary. But scientists do not work for bread alone. They want recognition. I agree, as this committee has recommended, that provision must be made for the publication of scientific papers when security is not involved. Government scientists should be allowed funds with which to attend scientific meetings. It is at these gatherings that they learn about the activities of their colleagues and are stimulated to carry on their important labors.

Another conclusion of the committee must be considered. The War Department's scientific and technical work, it is said, "is handicapped by the supervision of certain types of Army officers."[14] Officers are placed in supervisory positions although they have no familiarity with the project in progress. Officers are sometimes shifted around so frequently that the program is denied continuity. Some officers detailed to technical operations have no talent for working harmoniously with scientific staffs.[15] To put it another way, it does not follow that any officer who has distinguished himself as a field commander can be of value in running a laboratory.[16]

A solution of this problem of maintaining a high standard of scientific research for national defense purposes can be found if the Congress, the Civil Service, and the private scientific institutions of the country work together to find it. We must not fail. It will not do to content ourselves with less than the best, in order not to have to face some of the thorny organizational problems which we must solve in order to get the best. Only the best can win in a war of the future. If we compromise with the best, in order not to arouse the anguished cries of those who have a distorted devotion to existing bureaucratic procedures, we shall ultimately pay for our cowardice in the anguish of the entire nation.

We cannot protect ourselves without the very best scientific research, but we cannot protect ourselves with that alone. We shall also have to prepare for a far more prompt and efficient mobilization of defense industry than we achieved, or even thought of achieving, in the recent war.

In thinking about the techniques of industrial mobilization, we ought to constantly to remind ourselves that we mobilized our industry in the Second World War under very unusual conditions, conditions which are not likely to be repeated. I have already mentioned, and I want to mention again, the fact that the resistance of those nations which ultimately became our allies gave us time, many months of precious time. Napoleon once said of his strategical maneuvers, "I purchase time with men's lives." We purchased time with the lives

Epilogue

of the soldiers of Great Britain, Russia, China, and the other nations which resisted Hitler before we were either ready to fight or willing to do so.

We can count on no such boon in the future. Another great war might not find nations strong enough, without immediate direct aid from us, to resist the aggressor, even if they were inclined to do so. Nor will the oceans, which have so long protected us from the danger of immediate attack, guarantee us immunity in the future. When hostilities begin, we must expect to feel their full weight almost at once. We shall not have time to yawn, stretch ourselves, and arise sleepily from the bed of our illusions. Unless we are armed and equipped, or well on the way to being so, our efforts will be too late.

We must also remember that, in World War II, we mobilized our industry without any direct—and very little indirect—interference from our enemies. No bomb ever fell on an American factory. No American worker ever reported in the morning weary-eyed and half-effective because an air raid had kept him up most of the night. No essential components of production ever failed to arrive at a factory because a bomb had blown an important railroad bridge on the line by which they were being brought. No workers stayed away from work to hunt for new quarters to replace those from which they had been bombed out, or to help dig for members of their families buried in the ruins. The only appreciable damage our war production suffered from enemy action lay in some interference with the flow of supplies which depended upon coastal shipping—such as tanker-borne oil for the industries of the eastern seaboard—and shortages occasioned by enemy naval control of distant areas from which came strategic materials—such as shutting off of our rubber imports. In comparison with the interference suffered by nations whose factories and communications were within bombing range of the enemy, what we suffered was almost invisible.

We can expect no such immunity another time. Even the less fantastic weapons of modern war have been so improved that we must count upon heavy attacks upon our home territory should we again face a great war. If the newest weapons of which the scientists talk about even begin to live up to their advance reputations, we must count upon a degree of direct interference with our domestic economy which will approach, and might surpass, that suffered by the major European and Asiatic combatants in the recent war. Any planning for the industrial side of national defense which fails to take this into account is totally unrealistic.

But that is not all. We often forget that, as soon as we had developed our potential strength, the last war was a one-sided contest. A well-armed pygmy may defeat an unarmed giant if the latter is taken by surprise. But, if the pygmy's first assault fails, his chances are gone. As soon as the giant summons up the power that is potentially his, the outcome can no longer be in doubt.

One need only look at the relative war production figures of the Axis and the Allied nations to see how one-sided the contest was after American war production got really under way. By the end of the war, the United States was producing, not merely as much as all our enemies combined, but almost as much as all our enemies and all our allies together. Once we had reached full speed, no other nation belonged in the same league with us as a military-industrial power.

We cannot count upon the continuation of this one-sided advantage. Other nations, or groups of nations, may develop industrial power as great as ours. The potentiality is there. We may have fought our last war in which it will be feasible to give our armed forces the overwhelming material superiority that they had this last time. We may have to strive, far more desperately and far more skillfully, in the field of war production merely to keep a little distance ahead—or perhaps only to remain equal—to a powerful rival. That situation, of course, has not yet arrived. But it is so definitely possible within a couple of decades that it must figure prominently in our defense planning.

These are the conditions—not those of 1917 or of 1940—which must shape our planning for a future industrial mobilization. Even were we to be adequate to danger on that earlier level, we would need to improve greatly upon our past performances. We cannot move by half-measures into another industrial mobilization. We must decide, promptly and without compromise, the part we are to play in any future world crisis. We shall probably have to make our decision well before the outbreak of hostilities, for if we wait until the shooting begins, it will be too late.

But, no matter how promptly we decide, time will press and we cannot afford a single avoidable delay. That means that our organization for industrial mobilization must be ready to go into action at once. We must know, and be agreed upon, the administrative organization we intend to employ. We cannot experiment first with gross inadequacy, then lesser inadequacy, and finally only slight inadequacy. It must be all, or nothing, at once.

That means, not only organization, but also men. It will be as important, and as difficult, to recruit men to handle the problems of industrial mobilization as it will be to recruit and train those who go into combat. The majority of the key men for this job must be found in industry. They cannot be kept in reserve, as in a sense combat officers are, and constantly practiced in their art as against the brief but terrific months of infrequent emergencies. Men content to spend their lives in purely paper operations of war industry would, for the greatest part, lose touch with the real practices of industry.

But it will not be easy, as it was not easy this time, to get the best men promptly out of private industry into the governmental war production posts where so many of them will be needed. To prepare personnel for this task, to acquaint them with the problems they will have to face, and to do this while they are busy and growing in their peacetime professions, are problems which we have not yet solved but for which we must seek a solution as rapidly as we can.

It is also essential that the nation grow to understand the problems of industrial mobilization. Attention is easily focused upon the combat aspects of preparedness, for they are visible, often glamorous, and ever more appealing to the growing scientific interest of the nation. Also, as combat establishments live a life by themselves, they have to be integrated into the daily life of the nation only to a very modest degree. The practice maneuvers of a fleet, an army, or an air force are seldom bad for business—in fact, often quite the contrary.

But industrial mobilization has little in the way of glamour. It is mostly infinite study and preparation, an endless gathering and analysis of statistics, a study of special ways of doing jobs which, in their peacetime procedures, are thoroughly familiar to us and not easily glamorized. Furthermore, these preparations, if they are to approach adequacy under modern conditions, must inevitably prove bothersome to business. Business firms will have to spend time in supplying information about their capacity. They will be asked to take some preparatory steps for the use of their plants in ways which, in time of peace, have no interest for them. Even communities will be asked to depart from the usual straight line which leads to maximum prosperity in order to make some preparation for playing their industrial role in time of war. Leaders of labor will be asked to contemplate practices which would be inappropriate to the normal relations of capital and labor. Many people will be tempted to say they are too busy to think of all this, and others will take fright at the modification of their usual habits and privileges which they can see industrial mobilization will involve. Demagogues, and some quite sincere but half-informed people, will make use of these fears to accomplish ends of their own, as was done before the Second World War when misrepresentation of the Industrial Mobilization Plan of the thirties played a large part in sidetracking it at the very moment when we most needed it.

Nor will the dangers to industrial mobilization come from the civilian side alone. Obstacles will arise within the armed services. We have just passed an epochal piece of legislation[17] which, within a few months, will unify our national defense organization. It was difficult to overcome tradition and allay the fears of those who suspected the bill was designed to reduce their particular organization to a state of small significance.[18] Concessions were made to overcome these objections, for a unification which receives a reasonable degree of general acceptance is likely to be more effective than a stronger theoretical plan which faces constant opposition. I think the bill just passed will prove a landmark in the development of our national defense.[19]

But it leaves still a danger that the industrial side of our defenses may not be sufficiently emphasized. We have created new agencies to care for this aspect of defense, a National Resources Board to consider the overall resources requirements of defense, and a Munitions Board to coordinate the procurement of the three armed services. In these new instrumentalities we have, not only a structure for peacetime industrial preparedness, but the framework for a wartime structure. It is an enormous advance upon anything we have had previously.

Epilogue

But form does not always guarantee substance. In spite of the sound theory, it would be possible for these new agencies to fail to realize what was expected of them. If neglected, if staffed and supported half-heartedly, they might gradually become supine. If, from within the services, their efforts are resisted, the purposed of unification could be in considerable measure defeated. If starved and neglected by the civilian side of government, these agencies would not have the power to do their job.

For, make no mistake about it, their job is as difficult as any in the whole national defense set-up. Until one goes through the experience, it is almost impossible to grasp the appalling technical difficulties of industrial mobilization. We certainly want brains of the highest order for our combat services, for we can afford nothing less than the best. But it is equally essential—I am almost tempted to say more essential—to have the best brains obtainable to work on the bewildering tasks of industrial mobilization. And we cannot wait until the emergency to enlist those best brains, for the planning period is fully as crucial as the period of execution. First-class men, brought into the war production picture the moment hostilities begin, cannot be expected to produce better than mediocre results for many, many months unless they are given plans and data gathered by first-rate men, by men who understand the complexities of our economic system, men who have the imagination to see what war will do to that system and what modifications are necessary to meet the stupendous demands that another great crisis would put upon the mechanism of the national life.

We must never forget that, if we have another war, it will be nearly won, or nearly lost, on the industrial front before a shot is fired. That front deserves, and must have, in the years of preparation as well as in the months of conflict, the greatest efforts and the ablest minds that the nation can command. If we fail there, we fail everywhere: in combat, and in all those pursuits of peace which depend upon the successful maintenance of our national security.

Notes

Preface

1. Reference to Dean Acheson's memoir, *Present At the Creation: My Years in the State Department.* (New York: W. W. Norton, 1969).

2. Patterson did serve as the president of the Council on Foreign Relations for a time and on the Task Force on National Security Organization as part of the former president Herbert Hoover's Commission on Organization of the Executive Branch of the Government.

3. Virginia Patterson Montgomery is sure this manuscript is her father's own work. She wrote me that her father "was a prolific and efficient writer. We have examples of speeches in the 1940s and early '50s, the WW I manuscript from 1933, and letters. I find the manuscript style consistent with other writings." Email correspondence, Feb. 27, 2013.

4. *The World War I Memoirs of Robert P. Patterson: A Captain in the Great War*, ed. J. Garry Clifford (Knoxville: Univ. of Tennessee Press, 2012).

5. Epilogue, this volume, 227.

6. Ch. 10, 213.

7. Ch. 10, 204.

8. Ch. 4, 72.

9. Keith E. Eiler, *Mobilizing America: Robert P. Patterson and the War Effort, 1940-1945* (Ithaca, NY: Cornell Univ. Press, 1997), 450, 462.

10. Robert M. Morgenthau and Frank Tuerkheimer, "How FDR Helped Save Jews of the Holy Land," *Jewish Daily Forward*, Oct. 12, 2011.

11. Jonathan S. Tobin, "FDR Didn't Try to Save Middle East Jews," *Commentary*, Oct. 12, 2011.

12. Robert M. Morgenthau, Frank Tuerkheimer, and Jonathan S. Tobin, "Did FDR Act to Save the Jews of the Middle East? An Exchange," *Commentary*, October 25, 2011; "Up From El-Alamein," editorial, *New York Sun*, Nov. 23, 2011.

Introduction

For source of epigraph, see Epilogue, this volume, 227.

1. Forrest Davis, "The Toughest Man in Washington," *Saturday Evening Post*, Sept. 5, 1942, 59.

2. Henry L. Stimson and McGeorge Bundy, *On Active Service in Peace and War* (New York: Harper & Brothers, 1947), 342; John D. Millett, *The Organization and Role of the Army Service Forces* (Washington, DC: Historical Div., Dept. of the Army, 1954), 177; J. Garry Clifford, introduction, *The World War I Memoirs of Robert P. Patterson*, ed. Clifford (Knoxville: Univ. of Tennessee Press, 2012), xiii.

3. Eiler, *Mobilizing America*, 23; see also 461.

4. Patterson was also strongly considered for the role of postwar military governor of Germany. See Eiler, *Mobilizing America*, 426.

5. Ibid., 6–7.

6. For background on the Plattsburg camp movement, see esp. J. Garry Clifford, *The Citizen Soldiers: The Plattsburg Training Camp Movement, 1913–1920* (Lexington: Univ. Press of Kentucky, 1972); and J. Garry Clifford and Samuel R. Spencer Jr., *The First Peacetime Draft* (Lawrence: Univ. Press of Kansas, 1986).

7. Eiler, *Mobilizing America*, 18–23 (for quotes, see 20, 23); Forrest Davis, "The Toughest Man in Washington," 60; Clifford, introduction, *Citizen Soldiers*, xiv.

8. Eiler, *Mobilizing America*, 24–28; Eiler, "The Constant Service: A Biography of Robert P. Patterson" (PhD diss., Harvard Univ., 1974), 272.

9. Previous four paragraphs based on Eiler, *Mobilizing America*, 11–12, 28–39; Eiler, "A Return to Action," ch. 10 from "The Constant Service"; Roosevelt quoted in Clifford and Spencer, *First Peacetime Draft*, 123 (see also 24–25, 121–23); for an extended review of Woodring-Johnson feud, see Eliot Janeway, *The Struggle for Survival: A Chronicle of Economic Mobilization in World War II* (New Haven, CT: Yale Univ. Press, 1951), 25–52.

10. Previous two paragraphs based on Eiler, *Mobilizing America*, 40; Brian Waddell, *Toward the National Security State: Civil-Military Relations During World War II* (Westport, CT: Praeger Security International, 2008), 13–19; R. Elberton Smith, *The Army and Economic Mobilization* (Washington, DC: Historical Div., Dept. of the Army, 1959), 39–40, 106–8; Millett, *Army Service Forces*, for quote, see 15 (see also 20–21); Paul A C. Koistinen, *Arsenal of World War II: The Political Economy of American Warfare, 1940–1945* (Lawrence: Univ. Press of Kansas, 2004), 40.

11. Ch. 1, p. 1.

12. Eiler, *Mobilizing America*, 41.

13. Ibid., 41–47; Koistinen, *Arsenal of World War II*, 40–42, 101–5; Waddell, *Towards the National Security State*, 25–42

14. Millett, *Army Service Forces*, 27; Koistinen, *Arsenal of World War II*, 101

15. Patterson quoted by Eiler, *Mobilizing America*, 468; see also ibid., 414, 124–25.

16. Historian Paul Koistinen notes that while their navy counterparts (Secretary of the Navy Frank Knox and Under Secretary James Forrestal) "appeared to maintain their identity as the civilian heads of the Navy Department," Stimson and Patterson "seemed excessively absorbed in and dedicated to military values." Elsewhere Koistinen reports that Stimson and Patterson "came close to being more military than the officer corps": "They argued that civilian mobilization agencies existed to assist the army in carrying out its supply functions. They regularly castigated those agencies for lacking vigilance, for being too soft or too slow, and for being all but unpatriotic." Koistinen charges that "[t]hese talented leaders came close to going through the looking glass; in the passions of war or impending war, they all but lost contact with the essentially civilian nature of American civilization." Of course, Stimson and Patterson were both ex-army men with a front-row seat to the nail-biting task of building, almost from scratch, a force capable of defeating two of the most formidable military machines of the twentieth century, those of Germany and Japan. *Arsenal of World War II*, 125, 244–45; see also 497.

17. Eiler, *Mobilizing America*, 59–60, 124–25, 197, 265, 371; Davis, "The Toughest Man in Washington," 59.

18. Eiler, *Mobilizing America*, 59–60, 124–25, 197, 265, 371; Stimson quoted, 402.

19. Ch. 4, 87.

20. Ibid., 101.

21. Waddell, *Towards the National Security State*, 43–45.

22. Somervell was promoted above many more senior officers. Somervell had an unorthodox military career, coming out of West Point and into the Army Corps of Engineers. He briefly saw action in World War I, earning the Distinguished Service Medal, and then served as a supply officer for the Army of Occupation in Germany. His most memorable service between the wars was a four-year stint (1936–40) as head of the New York City Works Progress Administration office, the largest such office in the nation. He was then tapped in late 1940 to examine, and subsequently to head up, the program for constructing army camps. Somervell excelled in this task

where others had failed, and this success led to his promotion to heading up G-4, the Army's supply command in October 1941. See Millett, *Army Service Forces*, 2–8.

23. As Paul A. C. Koistinen notes, "War Department supply operations had once again converted to military control, despite the intentions of Congress after World War I and over twenty years of effort to bring procurement under civilian control." *The Hammer and the Sword: Labor, the Military, and Industrial Mobilization, 1920-1945* (New York: Arno Press, 1979). See also Eiler, *Mobilizing America*, 240–44; Koistinen, *Arsenal of World War II*, 219–22; and Millett, *Army Service Forces*, 34.

24. Millett, *Army Service Forces*, 36, 35. Donald Nelson, the head of the civilian War Production Board (WPB) was one of many civilians who had a difficult time with Somervell. The official history of the War Production Board and its predecessor agencies relates that Nelson found his job made more difficult by "Somervell's refusal to recognize any degree of subordination to WPB, his insistence on a dominant say-so with respect to matters involving the civilian economy, and his incessant striving to extend the limits of his jurisdiction at the expense of WPB." U.S. Civilian Production Administration (USCPA), *Industrial Mobilization for War: History of the War Production Board and Predecessor Agencies, 1940–1945* (Washington, DC: Government Printing Office, 1947), 216.

25. Eiler, *Mobilizing America*, 245–50; Koistinen, *Arsenal of World War II*, 222, 235–36.

26. Ch. 5, 122, 120.

27. Ch. 9, 201.

28. Eiler, *Mobilizing America*, 391–95; Koistinen, *Arsenal of World War II*, 457–86; Waddell, *Towards the National Security State*, 53–56; Jack Peltason, "The Reconversion Controversy," in *Public Administration and Policy Development*, ed. Herbert Stein, 251–54 (New York: Harcourt, Brace), 1952.

29. Ch. 3, 65.

30. Waddell, *Towards the National Security State*, 123–34; Townsend Hoopes and Douglas Brinkley, *Driven Patriot: The Life and Times of James Forrestal* (New York: Alfred A. Knopf, 1992), 331–51.

31. Robert Patterson, "Address Before the Arkansas Bar Association," *Arkansas Law Review and Bar Association Journal* 4 (1949–50): 305. Patterson testimony quoted in Michael Hogan, *A Cross of Iron: Harry S. Truman and the Origins of the National Security State, 1945–1954* (New York, Cambridge Univ. Press, 1998), 26.

32. Ch. 11, 226.

33. Patterson, "Address," 308; Waddell, *Towards the National Security State*, 133–34; 153–60; Hogan, *A Cross of Iron*, 313; Ernest R. May, "The U.S. Government, a Legacy of the Cold War," in *The End of the Cold War: Its Meanings, and Implications*, ed. Michael J. Hogan, 226–27 (New York: Cambridge Univ. Press, 1992).

34 Patterson, "Address," 308.

1. A Nation without Arms

1. At 174,000 men when the Nazis overran the Low countries in May 1940, the U.S. armed forces ranked eighteenth in the world, smaller than Portugal's and just ahead of Bulgaria's. See Eric Larrabee, *Commander in Chief: Franklin Delano Roosevelt, His Lieutenants, and Their War* (New York: Harper & Row, 1987), 114.

2. As a recent study likewise reports, "Equipment and weaponry were pathetic. Soldiers trained with drain-pipes for antitank guns, stovepipes for mortar tubes, and brooms for rifles. Money was short, and little guns were cheaper than big ones; no guns were cheapest of all. Only six medium tanks had been built in 1939." Rick Atkinson, *An Army at Dawn: The War in North Africa, 1942–1943* (New York: Henry Holt, 2002), 9.

3. Army historian R. Elberton Smith notes that "many individuals and groups felt that the Roosevelt administration was bent on 'socializing' the nation's economy and that it would use the defense program to further this objective." Given this sentiment, "[p]rivate enterprise showed considerable reluctance to begin the [defense] task." Such reluctance is exemplified by a November 1941 *Fortune* magazine poll of corporate executives, which revealed that "businessmen do not like the New Deal [and] that attitude has become a serious concern because it is affecting the management attitude toward the war." R. Elberton Smith, *The Army and Economic Mobilization* (Washington, DC: Historical Division, Department of the Army, 1959), 456-57; "Fortune Survey," *Fortune*, Nov. 1941, 200.

4. Patterson, a Republican appointed in July 1940, forcefully defended Roosevelt's handling of the defense program just before the 1940 presidential election in a network radio address. See Eiler, *Mobilizing America*, 57–58.

5. James B. Reston, *Prelude to Victory* (New York: Alfred A. Knopf, 1942), 48.

6. As Patterson was aware, Americans had come to hold very critical attitudes towards American involvement in World War I, both from the growing postwar belief that Americans had been herded into the war by leaders manipulating public opinion and also from the "Merchants

of Death" hearings held by the U.S. Senate's Nye Committee in 1934–35. Among the many sources available, see Manfred Jonas, *Isolationism in America, 1935–1941* (Ithaca, NY: Cornell Univ. Press, 1966), esp. ch. 5, "The Devil Theory of War." Published in 1934, one of the books that popularized the Nye hearings was H. C. Englebrecht and F. C. Hanighen, *Merchants of Death: A Study of the International Armaments Industry* (New York: Dodd, Mead, 1937). For the best recent account, see Paul A. C. Koistinen, *Planning War, Pursuing Peace: The Political Economy of American Warfare, 1920-1939* (Lawrence: Univ. Press of Kansas, 1998), esp. ch. 14, "The Nye Committee."

7. Few, if any, American armaments made it to the battlefields of Europe during World War I because of the terrible problems of organizing war production in the United States. The difficulties of organizing the American business community were compounded by the internal disarray of the army and navy procurement bureaus. See Brian Waddell, *The War Against the New Deal: World War II and American Democracy* (Dekalb: Northern Illinois Univ. Press, 2001), 20–25; and Paul A. C. Koistinen, *Mobilizing for Modern War: The Political Economy of American Warfare, 1865–1919* (Lawrence: Univ. Press of Kansas, 1997).

8. General Tasker H. Bliss was chief of staff of the U.S. Army from September 22, 1917, until May 18, 1918. Bliss served as an American plenipotentiary at the Paris Peace Conference into 1919.

9. For Patterson's account of his World War I service, see Clifford, *World War I Memoirs of Robert P. Patterson.*

10. Official army historian Mark Skinner Watson, in one of the key books of the War Department's *United States Army in World War II* series, dedicates an early chapter to what he calls "Prewar Sentiment and Its Effect on the Army." In a section titled "The Psychological Effect of Repression," Watson reviews how, "for nearly two decades," repeated congressional rebuffs to army requests for funding took its toll as army leaders who "were reduced to asking not for what was needed but for what they thought they could get." *Chief of Staff: Prewar Plans and Preparations* (Washington, DC: Historical Div., Dept. of the Army, 1950), 36, 37.

11. The best overview of the issues of World War I wartime mobilization problems is provided by Robert D. Cuff, *The War Industries Board: Business-Government Relations during World War I* (Baltimore: Johns Hopkins Univ. Press, 1973).

12. Bernard M. Baruch wrote and spoke extensively about his experiences leading the War Industries Board of World War I precisely to preserve and impart to a reluctant nation the hard lessons learned from

the mobilization experience. See Baruch's *American Industry in the War: A Report of the War Industries Board* (New York: Prentice Hall, 1941). Benedict Crowell also wrote an influential tract about World War I mobilization, *America's Munitions 1917–1918 : Report of Benedict Crowell, the Assistant Secretary of War, Director of Munitions* (Washington, DC: Government Printing Office, 1919). Crowell's postwar advocacy of continued mobilization planning proved instrumental in winning passage of critical parts of the National Defense Act of 1920 that promoted interwar planning for industrial mobilization. As Koistinen writes, "World War I, argued Crowell, had demonstrated that modern warfare made industrial production as important to military success as tactics and strategy. Supply and procurement, therefore, must receive the same emphasis in War Department affairs as traditional military functions." *Planning War, Pursuing Peace*, 6; for Baruch's impact, see 45–50.

13. For a review of these developments, see Brian Waddell, *Toward the National Security State: Civil-Military Relations During World War II* (Westport, CT: Praeger Security International, 2008), 14–19. For a fuller treatment, see Koistinen, *Planning War, Pursuing Peace*, ch. 1, "Procurement Planning, 1920–1939"; and ch. 2, "Industrial Mobilization Planning, 1920–1939."

14. For a thorough review of the developing industrial mobilization plans, see Koistinen, *Planning War, Pursuing Peace*, esp. 54–71.

15. In an official army history, John D. Millet reports, "The officers assigned to [Patterson's office] sometimes felt that they had reached a blind alley in their careers. Often their military rank was too low to permit effective performance of duties." *Army Service Forces*, 27. This attitude, according to another army historian, "made it difficult to get and retain the most capable officers." Smith, *Army and Economic Mobilization*, 111.

16. As noted above, public opinion during the 1930s proved increasingly skeptical of war preparations, believing that the preparations themselves had contributed to American participation in the First World War. Also, the Senate Nye Committee Hearings had exposed the seamy side of past and ongoing military-industry cooperation, thus contributing to the public skepticism of military planning and especially of the profiteering impulses of businessmen during war. Besides sources cited in n6, above, see Arthur A. Ekirch Jr., *The Civilian and the Military: A History of the American Antimilitarist Tradition* (Colorado Springs, CO: Ralph Myles, 1972), 243–53.

17. To be sure, military plans dramatically underestimated what would be required to fight World War II. And it is understandable that the military

services did not accurately understand what would be required. Still, the services failed until late 1941 to reconsider their 1939 Industrial Mobilization Plan, which envisioned a short conflict requiring little disruption to the civilian economy. As Luther Gulick, who served in various civilian and military agencies during the war, writes, "Up until December 7, 1941, in spite of tremendous prodding from the White House, the military leaders could not bring themselves to envision even remotely the extent of the prospective supply needs of a total war waged all over the world." *Administrative Reflections from World War II* (University: Univ. of Alabama Press, 1948), 46. Maj. (later Gen.) Albert C. Wedemeyer, a staff officer in the War Department's General Staff War Plans Division, did produce a Victory Program that envisioned the large U.S. force that would fight in World War II. But, as Keith Eiler notes, the plan was "of little help during the summer of 1941." *Mobilizing America*, 204.

18. Patterson is most likely referring to those in the peace movement who adhered to the idea that the very preparation for war would lead to involvement in war, as seemed to have been true for the First World War, when mobilizations after the Sarajevo assassination proceeded almost automatically. For background on this and related issues, see Bruce Catton, *The War Lords of Washington* (New York: Harcourt, Brace, 1948), 14–22.

19. Baruch was head of the War Industries Board during the latter part of World War I. Baruch proved an ardent advocate of continual military-industrial preparations throughout the interwar period. He successfully sought to insert himself into debates over industrial preparations prior to and during the Second World War, serving as a close confidant to many top-level government officials, including President Roosevelt. Patterson maintained a close relationship with Baruch throughout the war, depending upon him both for his experience and his political connections. Baruch's biographer, Jordan A. Schwarz, reports that Baruch certainly expected that his seeming close relations with Roosevelt and other key Democrats would mean his return to the top job in industrial mobilization. But this did not happen; instead, as Schwarz notes, Baruch "would be mostly an informal power broker in the tall grass of Washington" throughout the war. Baruch nonetheless remained close to key domestic mobilization leaders during and after the war, maintaining a keen desire to reprise his World War I starring role. Schwarz, *The Speculator: Bernard M. Baruch in Washington, 1917–1965* (Chapel Hill: Univ. of North Carolina Press, 1981), 331.

20. Another issue, which Patterson addresses in the next chapter, is the controversy over converting peacetime industry to the production of war materiel during the 1939–41 period. Industrial producers basically refused to convert any of their civilian plant and equipment to wartime produc-

tion. And they refused to reduce in any way their now-booming civilian production so as to divert critically important and increasingly scarce raw materials (steel, aluminum, rubber, and so on) to military production. The auto industry was particularly unwilling to step down any of its own civilian production and had its biggest month in January 1942 before it was completely shut down by government order. As Paul Koistinen has noted, "From 1939 into early 1942, the business community resisted, often refused, converting to defense and war production, despite the offer of more than generous financial terms. Civilian production was too lucrative and defense production too uncertain." *Hammer and the Sword*, 556–57. Of course, some of the big firms agreed to build and operate new government-owned munition plants. See ibid, 59–60, 136–58.

21. The official governmental history of wartime industrial mobilization nicely describes the situation in the spring of 1940: "The success of blitzkrieg warfare . . . stemmed from superior aircraft, superior tanks, mobile units, artillery, antitank and antiaircraft guns—in all of which the United States military were woefully deficient. It was estimated that the German Luftwaffe was composed of some 25,000 planes; the United States Army Air Corps, in the spring of 1940, had 2,665 planes on hand. . . . Six thousand serviceable planes was the maximum authorized by the Congress . . . The United States had no heavy tanks at all. . . . The Nazi Panzer units had swept easily across Europe; the United States was still in the early stages of motorizing its horse cavalry regiments." USCPA, *Industrial Mobilization for War*, 14.

22. Louis A. Johnson had assumed the post of assistant secretary in late June 1937 and quickly began to promote the work and responsibilities of his office to the nation at large. The Office of the Assistant Secretary of War (OASW) did not exist to simply assist the secretary of war but rather had independent powers over industrial mobilization. According to the National Defense Act of 1920, the civilian assistant secretary of war would be responsible for supervising the development of procurement and mobilization planning and would supervise military procurement to provide a semblance of centralized authority over the independent army supply bureaus. For a review of the National Defense Act of 1920 and of the assistant secretary's responsibilities during the 1920s, see Waddell, *Toward the National Security State*, 9–19; and Koistinen, *Planning War, Pursuing Peace*, 5ff. For a recent biography of Louis Johnson's impact on war preparation, see Keith D. McFarland, *Louis Johnson and the Arming of America: The Roosevelt and Truman Years* (Bloomington: Indiana Univ. Press, 2005).

23. As one observer noted, "In 1940 Congress showered $9 billion on the Army, more than all the money spent by the War Department since 1920 [but] It was still $2 billion less than [asked for]." Geoffrey Perret, *There's*

a War to Be Won: The United States Army in World War II (New York: Ivy Books, 1991), 29.

24. Educational orders, used to familiarize key business concerns with military contracting and to build ties between the military and critical war-related industries, were promoted by the Army's Ordnance Department beginning in 1927. Only in 1939 did a law pass allowing such orders to go into operation. The Educational Orders Act of 1939 was the result of intensive prodding by Assistant Secretary of War Louis Johnson, whose efforts also led to appropriations for the stockpiling of strategic materials. See Eliot Janeway, *The Struggle for Survival: A Chronicle of Economic Mobilization in World War II* (New Haven, CT: Yale Univ. Press, 1951), 27–29; and also Koistinen, *Planning War, Pursuing Peace*, 81.

25. The original Neutrality Act, passed in 1935, was partly a result of the Nye Committee hearings into the international arms industry and featured an impartial arms embargo against all belligerent nations, as well as a ban on travel and loans to belligerent nations. The act was extended in 1936 but began to be watered down in a series of extensions in 1937, 1939, and 1941. See Robert A. Divine, *The Reluctant Belligerent: American Entry into World War II*, 2nd ed. (New York: Alfred A. Knopf, 1979), 22–23, 36–39, 72–77, 151–52; and also Jonas, *Isolationism in America*, 150–51.

2. The Slow Beginning

1. It is difficult to imagine how deluded most Americans remained about the prospect of war in early 1940. As army historian Mark S. Watson observes, "The quiet that fell on Europe immediately after the conquest and partition of Poland, and that was prolonged through the winter of the 'phony war,' lulled the fears only of the uninformed, but the uninformed were numerous." *Chief of Staff*, 104. By this logic, Congress, too, remained uninformed. As the official government history of mobilization explains, "When the [military] appropriations requests came before Congress in early 1940, it was evident that Congress had lost the sense of urgency that had moved it to grant increases in the Army the summer before. Repeatedly, Congressmen reported that the aggressors were pretty well occupied with their wars, that they had exhausted their resources for a year, and that to grant the requested appropriations when our national debt stood at $14 billion would mean ultimate chaos." USCPA, *Industrial Mobilization for War*, 40.

2. Still, as journalist I. F. Stone reported, "Five days after the blitzkrieg against the West began, the Senate Naval Affairs Committee reported that it saw no reason to increase naval appropriations. Not until six days before

France surrendered did Congress act on the request made by Admiral Stark, chief of naval operations, for a 25 percent increase in tonnage; it cut the increase to 11 percent." *Business as Usual: The First Year of Defense* (New York: Modern Age Books, 1941), 18.

3. Historian Michael S. Sherry sees Roosevelt's speech as "calculated to shock Americans into rethinking their fundamental assumptions about national security." He also writes, "As dramatization of the primacy of air power, the message was Roosevelt's boldest." *The Rise of American Air Power: The Creation of Armageddon* (New Haven, CT: Yale Univ. Press, 1987), 91.

4. Henry Morgenthau Jr. was President Roosevelt's Hudson Valley neighbor and U.S. secretary of the treasury from January 1934 until July 1945. He was also the father of Robert M. Morgenthau, who wrote the foreword to this volume.

5. The War Resources Board report, issued in October 1939, was buried by Roosevelt because its recommendations were far too controversial at this point. The military's plans essentially called for delegation of authority to someone other than the president—preferably a prominent business leader—and complete reliance on the largest industrial corporations. Going public with such a plan would surely have roused in righteous opposition those forces already suspicious of corporate motives regarding war production. Roosevelt, hemmed in by isolationist sentiment and considered a lame duck, was too politically shrewd to go down this path at this point. See Waddell, *War Against the New Deal*, 68–70.

6. The War Resources Board was a corporate-dominated body—headed by Edward Stettinius Jr., chairman of U.S. Steel—appointed by Roosevelt to study and recommend a course for mobilization based on the military's interwar planning. This planning, heavily influenced by Bernard Baruch's World War I War Industries Board model, assumed that mobilization would require a major reliance upon the nation's largest firms and upon prominent businessmen and their industry associations—exactly what ended up occurring. The board did not survive for long in the highly politicized atmosphere of late 1939, but its recommendations—written essentially by Bernard Baruch and his associate John Hancock of Lehman Brothers—provided the template for the industrial mobilization that followed. See Waddell, *War Against the New Deal*, 68–70. For more contemporary accounts, see Bruce Catton, *War Lords of Washington* (New York: Harcourt, Brace, 1948), 100–104; and Janeway, *Struggle for Survival*, 53–68.

7. William S. Knudsen was president of General Motors. The National Defense Advisory Commission (NDAC) perfectly fit Roosevelt's needs in this situation. It was still authorized under a World War I statute; it was

essentially without any authority; and it had no single administrative leader, leaving authority and initiative with the president. It was revived in response to the renewed Nazi offensives in May 1940. For a full treatment of Knudsen's contribution to wartime mobilization, see Arthur Herman, *Freedom's Forge: How American Business Produced Victory in World War II* (New York: Random House, 2012).

8. M-Day refers to Mobilization Day, or a specific moment when the War Department's planning and operating agencies would merge and begin a full-scale general mobilization. But no M-Day was ever declared. As Koistinen writes, President Roosevelt "rejected the M-Day concept as too limiting because international realities and domestic politics might require gradual, partial, or even secret mobilization." *Planning War, Pursuing Peace*, 68; see also 26.

9. Gen. Charles M. Wesson, chief of ordnance from 1938 to 1942, guided the Ordnance Department during the transition to war production.

10. As it turned out, very few American armaments reached the battlefields of Europe prior to the Armistice in World War I.

11. The Selective Training and Service Act of 1940 was passed on September 16, 1940, and produced the nation's "first peacetime draft." For the most thorough and perceptive account of this precedent-breaking legislation, see Clifford and Spencer, *First Peacetime Draft*. Patterson was part of a key group of civilians known as the "Plattsburgers," so-named after the site in northern New York State where this group set up training camps to ready themselves for military service in World War I, and which they revived after the Nazi offensives in Europe. Patterson himself returned to these camps for military training in the summer of 1940, and it was here, as a simple army trainee, that he received news of his appointment as assistant secretary of war. The civilian Plattsburgers took a lead role in promoting the Selective Service Act, and Patterson was part of this effort. See Clifford and Spencer, *First Peacetime Draft*, 83–88; see also Waddell, *Toward the National Security State,* 97–103; and Eiler, *Mobilizing America,* 11–12.

12. These quotes are from Churchill's speech before the British House of Commons on June 4, 1940. See "Wars Are Not Won by Evacuations," in *Never Give In: The Best of Winston Churchill's Speeches* (New York: Hyperion, 2003), 210–18.

13. Roosevelt had to overrule his own military chiefs in promoting aid to Britain at this time. Army Chief of Staff George Marshall and his planners led a charge against handing over military equipment to the British because of the limited equipment available and because of fears that the

British would soon fall to Nazi aggression, putting any equipment the United States sent into enemy hands. See Waddell, *Toward the National Security State*, 72; Thomas Parrish, *Roosevelt and Marshall: Partners in Politics and War* (New York: William Morrow, 1989), 154–55; and Forrest C. Pogue, *George C. Marshall: Ordeal and Hope, 1939–1942* (New York: Viking, 1966), 51–53, 64–69.

14. The official government history of industrial mobilization reports that British orders served to prepare U.S. industry for military production: "British purchases were by far the largest foreign orders in the United States. They had been invaluable through the first half of 1940, and before sizable United States military appropriations were available, in initiating private American firms into munitions production, and in getting munitions and aircraft plants in place. . . . Great Britain had financed [in 1940] the building of some 61 munitions plants in the United States, at a cost of about $171 million." USCPA, *Industrial Mobilization for War*, 51.

15. Historian Mark A. Stoler explains how difficult these decisions were. "Throughout the early summer [of 1940]," he notes, "[Roosevelt] over ruled army and navy objections to sending England military assistance. By September he had further extended this assistance and U.S. commitments via the 'swap' of fifty overage destroyers for . . . British bases . . . and according to navy rumors he had to threaten [navy chief Harold E.] Stark with relief before winning the CNO's agonized acquiescence in a trade most naval officers opposed." Stoler also quotes an army planner who in mid-June 1940 stated that "if we are required to mobilize after having released guns [to Britain] necessary for this mobilization . . . everyone who was a party to the deal might hope to be found hanging from a lamp post." *Allies and Adversaries: The Joint Chiefs of Staff, the Grand Alliance, and U.S. Strategy in World War II* (Chapel Hill: Univ. of North Carolina Press, 2000), 26, 28.

16. As the official history of industrial mobilization observes, Congress did end "peacetime statutory mandates that all Government contracts had to be let on the basis of advertised bids," but it did not officially terminate adherence to labor laws. In fact, "[Sidney] Hillman [labor representative in the Advisory Commission of the Council of National Defense], had been insistent that the President's policy of preservation of social gains be implemented by the maintenance of fair labor standards under defense contracts," and the Advisory Commission released two statements supporting this policy. In addition, "To give the added prestige of Executive approval to the policy statements, the President submitted both to Congress with his endorsement [in September 1940]." Of course, the history later explains that "there was a feeling, on the part of some members of

Congress, that although defense contractors should be urged to obey labor legislation, defense contracts should not be employed as law enforcement instruments." This attitude certainly would mean nonenforcement of such labor standards. USCPA, *Industrial Mobilization for War*, 58, 82.

17. On cost-plus-fixed-fee contracts, see Irving Brinton Holley Jr., *Buying Aircraft: Materiel Procurement for the Army Air Forces* (Washington, DC: Office of the Chief of Military History, 1964), ch. 16, "The Cost-Plus-Fixed-Fee Contract: Negotiation and Administration."

18. According to the official history of industrial mobilization, "The swift Nazi conquest of Western Europe . . . led to a belief that war would be over in a few months and that any further industrial expansion would be over-expansion before it was completed." USCPA, *Industrial Mobilization for War*, 75.

19. The war was a distraction that most manufacturers, after experiencing years of depressed sales, would not allow to interfere with their now-booming civilian business. As a government report published shortly after the war recounts, "Since war seemed remote to many, it was difficult for industry to pattern its day-to-day behavior on a contingency that might not materialize, while unprecedented civilian and defense demands were creating an exhilarating boom." Edythe W. First, *Industry and Labor Advisory Committees in the National Defense Advisory Commission and the Office of Production Management, May 1940 to January 1942*, United States Civilian Production Administration, Special Study No. 24 (Washington, DC: Government Printing Office, 1946), 145.

20. There were two separate but related issues that are conflated here. One was the hesitation on the part of many firms to take on defense orders in place of their normal civilian orders. The other related issue was the reluctance of firms to build new plants to serve the growing demand for military goods. Many firms would not convert their civilian-oriented plants to military production and also resisted building new capacity they feared would not be needed if the war ended sooner rather than later. It was to overcome this hesitation that the government came up with the innovative plant-financing schemes that Patterson reviews here. In the most sweeping and comprehensive recent review of mobilization, Koistinen explains, "Plant expansion met great resistance. Industry was not anxious to take up munitions production in 1940, for a number of reasons. Expanding capacity after a decade of depression was dangerous; civilian markets at home and abroad were growing; the outcome of the war in Europe was uncertain; and government contracts meant red tape and dealing with the New Deal enemy. For their part the armed services estimated requirements

that were generally low, unreliable, and shifting, which complicated planning for industrial expansion enormously, and often resulted in the military siding with industry in resisting growth, particularly where basic industries such as steel, aluminum, rubber, and copper were involved." *Arsenal of World War II*, 54. For a similar, contemporary view, see USCPA, *Industrial Mobilization for War*, 56.

21. As Koistinen reports, "Despite numerous delays, accelerated amortization still accounted for 57 percent of defense facilities completed before Pearl Harbor." *Arsenal of World War II*, 57.

22. "At least half of DPC investment," Koistinen also relates, "was for plants operated by giant corporations, with the Aluminum Company of America (ALCOA), the General Motors Corporation, U.S. Steel, and the Curtiss-Wright Corporation topping the list." Ibid., 58. See also Gerald T. White, *Billions for Defense: Government Financing by the Defense Plant Corporation During World War II* (Tuscaloosa: Univ. of Alabama Press, 1980).

23. In a 1951 analysis, journalist Eliot Janeway was not so generous about the RFC's Jesse Jones, who, Janeway notes, treated RFC capital as "his money": "From the beginning he [Jones] had prided himself on running the RFC as a dictatorship; and, in fact, it had grown into a one-man empire." So, of course, Knudsen would have to make a personal call to get Jones moving on a War Department request. As Janeway also discerns, "The War Department, by this time [in 1940] was literally machine-gunning requests for money at the RFC. . . . Nevertheless, Jones insisted on sniffing personally at each as if it were a rare and risky banking deal. His subordinates saw that the situation called not for negotiation but for administration. The applications, after all, were being made by but not for private companies; the real applicant in each case was another Executive Department [the War Department]. . . . Jones . . . had become a one-man bottleneck." Janeway explains that it was Jones's immediate subordinates who developed a back-door channel for War Department requests and this opened up RFC financing through its Defense Plants Corporation. Of course, when Jones eventually discovered what his aides were up to, he sent them packing. *Struggle for Survival*, 169–70.

24. In one of the official army studies of wartime mobilization, John D. Millett notes that "Mr. Patterson took office coincidentally with the launching of a huge mobilization program in the summer of 1940. A major difficulty for him was the relatively indifferent caliber and low rank of the military personnel attached to his organization." As Patterson's office expanded fivefold in his first year, a private firm he had employed to study

his organization noted that one of the problems was that "the military personnel often lacked sufficient rank, training, and general ability to perform their assigned duties." *Army Service Forces*, 27.

25. In another official army study, R. Elberton Smith reports that the low prestige of procurement within the army meant a great problem in attracting quality army personnel: "In order to offset this disadvantage and to obtain personnel who could adjust rapidly to the unusual problems faced by his office, Mr. Patterson built up a personal staff of key civilians who became largely responsible for the formulation of policies . . . throughout the defense period. Most of these were lawyers, trained at Harvard and with professional practice in the New York area." *Army and Economic Mobilization*, 111.

26. Congress maintained a steady drumbeat of pressure on the mobilization agencies to distribute more contracts to smaller firms through committees such as Senator James Murray's Special Committee to Study the Problems of American Small Business. See Waddell, *War Against the New Deal*, 80.

27. We can see the connection between the absence of quality procurement officers in Patterson's office and the desire to simply place contracts with the largest companies. As Senator James Murray's investigative committee noted in early 1942, "There was a wealth of testimony that the training and experience which Army and Navy procurement officers have had . . . has incapacitated them from forthright and effective action in wartime. They have learned that a single mistake is liable to wreck a career. . . . Consequently, they feel that the only safe thing to do is to give contracts to big companies with a reputation for performance." U.S. Senate, Special Committee to Study the Problems of American Small Business, *Additional Report*, 77th Congress, 2d sess., 5 Feb. 1942, report no. 479, pt. 2, p. 13.

28. Patterson himself approved an arsenal plant near the coast at Houston, Texas, in December 1941. When his army counterpart, General Brehon Somervell, found out, he immediately shot off a letter saying he hoped that the plant "will not be put out of production by enemy action. It is likewise hoped that, with thousands of square miles and almost unlimited facilities . . . no more production facilities will be located outside the strategic area." Probably realizing he had overreacted, Somervell sent an apology to Patterson the very next day explaining away his reaction and assuring the under secretary that he held him in the highest esteem. Millett, *Army Service Forces*, 35.

29. There were actually plenty of top-level civilians who pressed for a greater distribution of contracts for some very practical reasons, includ-

ing the fact that many large corporations did not have the capacity to get started on the large number of military contracts with which they suddenly found themselves saddled. But the civilians were constantly overruled by military leaders who wanted to control procurement themselves, despite the organizational deficiencies that Patterson worked diligently to rectify. The military's lack of a solid organizational procurement capacity meant that procurement officers took the easy way out and simply dumped contracts with the largest companies as a matter of convenience. The official history of mobilization explains, "Of the more than $11 billion in prime contracts awarded by the Services during the seven months from June to December 1940, 60 percent went to 20 firms and 86.4 percent went to only 100 companies." USCPA, *Industrial Mobilization for War*, 63. The problem with this pattern was that contracts became concentrated in areas experiencing labor shortages. Big contractors did, under intense congressional pressure and because of the need for help in fulfilling their orders, turn to subcontracting to smaller firms. See Waddell, *War Against the New Deal*, 78–79. For contracting and small business, see Koistinen, *Arsenal of World War II*, 172–75, 350–55.

30. See n16, above.

31. As noted above (n16), the labor representative on the National Defense Advisory Committee, Sidney Hillman, sought to have military contractors adhere to existing labor laws. As Koistinen discovered, "Business representatives in the NDAC joined with industrial critics outside the Commission in vehemently denouncing Hillman's interpretation and protesting any 'blacklisting' of firms." Knudsen, speaking before the Army Ordnance Association on October 8, 1940 told 1,500 businessmen that "we don't want any part of the Russian system over here." See Koistinen, *Hammer and Sword*, 135.

32. Ford Motors was one of these companies. As the official history of mobilization explains, "Particularly noteworthy was the award of a large aircraft engine contract to the Ford Motor Co. . . . Ford was, however, under indictment for violation of the National Labor Relations Act, and the contract award called forth violent protests from organized labor." USCPA, *Industrial Mobilization for War*, 59.

33. The auto industry provides the most dramatic example of industry resistance to curtailment of civilian production. In fact, in response to growing demand, the auto industry kept expanding production of private automobiles right up until the attack on Pearl Harbor forced the government to order a halt to all civilian auto production. As Koistinen explains, auto assembly lines "consumed 80 per cent of the nation's rubber, 11 per cent of its tin, 23 per cent of its nickel, 14 per cent of its copper, 19 per

cent of its steel, 12 per cent of its zinc, 34 per cent of its lead, and 10 per cent of its aluminum." Yet, with most of these materials scarce by 1941, "automobile production was one million cars above 1939." *Hammer and Sword*, 585–86. Koistinen also reports that "Knudsen reflected corporate America's resistance to defense conversion and expansion, which the military supported because of its procurement and supply limitations and the desire not to antagonize firms critical to production." *Arsenal of World War II*, 183.

34. Walter Reuther was vice president of the United Auto Workers of the Congress of Industrial Organizations. His plan to convert the auto industry to airplane production received great attention because it was so detailed and workable and because it involved the nation's largest and most critical industry. Reuther's "500 planes a day" plan excited Roosevelt and New Dealers involved in mobilization because of its promise to dramatically increase defense production at a time when private companies showed great reluctance to do so. Reuther recommended that all Detroit-area production facilities be surveyed to determine existing capacity and to plan conversion of currently unused or underutilized plant and equipment. In addition, he proposed to delay retooling the industry for new-model autos, thereby freeing up fifteen thousand skilled machinists to retool instead for the mass production of fighter planes. (Auto plants shut down for six months every year to retool for the next year's new auto models, which Reuther thought was a waste of production potential and skilled labor.) Auto industry leaders, including Knudsen (now co-head of the new mobilization agency, the Office of Production Management), picked on minor details to discredit Reuther's Plan. As I. F. Stone reported at the time, Reuther for his trouble was "assailed . . . as a Communist" and his "plan was never given a hearing." *Business as Usual*, 239; see also Waddell, *War Against the New Deal*, 60–63. For the viability of the Reuther plan from a dispassionate source, see Holley, *Buying Aircraft*, 310–14. Holley argues that Reuther grew to understand that the technical difficulties involved in building aircraft meant that existing auto plants could not produce aircraft. Still, Holley concedes Reuther's point about the necessity of converting those tools that could be used and curtailing the production of new 1942 model automobiles in order to produce the new tools that were needed.

35. The irony was that the auto industry had repeatedly told Patterson that the auto plants were unusable for most military production, especially for aircraft production. Patterson testified to Senator Harry S. Truman's Investigative Committee in the summer of 1941 that, according to the auto companies, the tolerance of existing machine tools was too large to be of

any use in aircraft production. After the attack on Pearl Harbor forced an end to auto production, the industry suddenly announced that, in fact, it could utilize existing plants for war contracts. The Truman Committee thus concluded, "It is quite evident that the information furnished to the Under Secretary of War by the automobile companies . . . was quite inaccurate. We could have and should have made use of automobile plants and tools." U.S. Senate Special Committee Investigating the National Defense Program, *First Annual Report,* 77th Congress, 2d sess., 15 Jan. 1942, report no. 480, pt. 5, p. 34.

36. But as Secretary of War Henry Stimson wrote in his diary, "If you are going to go to war, or to prepare for war, in a capitalist country, you have to let business make money out of the process or business won't work." Quoted in Koistinen, *Hammer and Sword,* 580.

37. There were consequences concerning the necessary reliance on private industry, and it was the resistance to full mobilization that led to calls for a government-owned munitions industry. Bruce Catton, a participant in mobilization battles, remembered "the necessity to bring into the defense effort, as active co-operators, the proprietors of the nation's chief physical assets," explaining, "The job couldn't be done without them, but their fears and suspicions—which, where Franklin Roosevelt was concerned, were deep and beyond number—had to be allayed. For the duration of the defense period, therefore, the game had to be played their way; whatever preparations the nation made had to be within the bounds of territory that was familiar to these men. This meant the rules were not to be changed." *Warlords of Washington,* 29–30.

38. See n14, above.

39. These quotes are from President Roosevelt's press conference, Washington, DC, Dec. 17, 1940. Full transcript available online through the University of California, Santa Barbara's *The American Presidency Project,* http://www.presidency.ucsb.edu/ws/?pid=15913.

40. Roosevelt introduced this concept in his Fireside Chat of December 29, 1940.

41. See n10 for ch. 1, above. As noted there, Army historian Mark Skinner Watson titled a section in his study of General Marshall's prewar command operations "The Psychological Effect of Repression," in which he wrote of how repeated congressional rebuffs to army requests for funding reduced army leaders "to asking not for what was needed but for what they thought they could get." Obviously, lower-level procurement officers would have been all the more hesitant. Watson, *Chief of Staff,* 36, 37.

3. Airplanes Take Five Years

1. Dwight D. Eisenhower, *Eisenhower's Own Story of the War: The Complete Report by the Supreme Commander, General Dwight D. Eisenhower, on the War in Europe from the Day of Invasion to the Day of Victory* (New York: Arco Publishing, 1946), 121.

2. The tests took place in 1921 as part of Billy Mitchell's concerted efforts to convince the nation, and especially the nation's political leadership, that navy battleships were obsolete and no match for bombers, which were also much more cost effective as a first line of defense for the nation. Mitchell was finally court-martialed for insubordination in 1925, and while his reprimand was minor, he decided to resign his commission anyway to continue his seemingly quixotic campaign for air power in civilian garb. See Sherry, *Rise of American Air Power*, 33–38; Allan R. Millett and Peter Maslowski, *For the Common Defense: A Military History of the United States of America* (New York: Free Press, 1984), 368–72; and Major Alfred F. Hurley, *Billy Mitchell: Crusader for Air Power* (New York: Franklin Watts, 1964), 56–70.

3. These were the views of Secretary of War George H. Dern. These quotes can be found in a restricted U.S. Air Force study. It is clear that Patterson is referencing key portions of that report here, despite the fact that the Report was not officially available until 1951. See U.S. Air Force Historical Study No. 6, "The Development of the Heavy Bomber, 1918–1944" (prepared by the USAF Historical Division, Air University, 1951), 12.

4. The Army brass at best equivocated over the role of air power, seeing it primarily as useful in close tactical support of ground troops; at worst they sought to bury the entire air power project. As historian Michael Sherry notes, "Douglas MacArthur, the chief of staff early in the 1930s, followed a shifting course [toward air power]. One moment he allied with pacifists and proponents of disarmament by proposing the abolition of military aviation to the World Disarmament Conference, doing so in hopes of freeing up funds for the ground army. At other times he curried support from aviators by backing the creation of the General Headquarters Air Force and proclaiming the utility of air power." *Rise of American Air Power*, 49. Of course, the navy was certainly not opposed to air power per se. While the army fought the integration and use of air power, the navy did not. "Ever since General Billy Mitchell had demonstrated twenty years before that warships could be bombed successfully from the air," historian Richard Overy writes, "the US navy had been alive to the significance of naval aviation. In the 1920s the navy commissioned the carriers *Lexington* and *Saratoga*, the largest ships afloat until the war. Under Admiral King's

leadership in the 1930s naval aviation made great strides in tactics and training." *Why the Allies Won* (New York: W. W. Norton, 1995), 38.

5. The Baker Board was convened in July 1934 to study future aircraft requirements for the Army Air Corps.

6. In a book published under the auspices of the air force, a retired USAF lieutenant colonel writes, "The B-10 was the pride of the Air Corps. It was the most powerful bomber in the world, and its speed gave it advantage over the pursuits of the day." James P. Tate, *The Army and Its Air Corps: Army Policy toward Aviation, 1919–1941* (Maxwell Air Force Base, AL: Air Univ. Press, 1998), 160.

7. The B-17 "was the most famous plane in the entire history of the Air Corps." Ibid., 164.

8. Roosevelt promoted Henry H. "Hap" Arnold to chief of the Air Corps in September 1938.

9. It is also true that President Roosevelt was at the forefront of efforts to increase the production of military aircraft. As Holley reports, "On 14 November 1938 the President summoned a number of his political and military advisors to the White House. He did not ask for advice, he laid his policies on the line. The Army air arm, he declared, must be built into a heavy striking force." *Buying Aircraft*, 169.

10. As Eiler explains, "Lovett made it an urgent private project . . . to visit all the aircraft factories in the United States and assess firsthand their capacity. His findings were disturbing if not unexpected: by European standards, the American aircraft industry was in the horse-and-buggy age; it was alarmingly small, inadequately capitalized, and technologically backward. Patterson was impressed by this report . . . and he at once asked Lovett to come to Washington for talks with the secretary [Stimson] and himself. As a consequence of this visit, and of Patterson's subsequent urging, Lovett came to the War Department in December as special assistant for air." *Mobilizing America*, 50.

11. "The airplane manufacturers," Lovett told to a reporter in 1943, "were like a lot of custom tailors, and our job was to turn them into Hart Schaffner and Marxes overnight." Quoted in Walter Isaacson and Evan Thomas, *The Wise Men: Six Friends and the World They Made* (New York: Touchstone Book, 1986), 203. Hart Schaffner Marx remained until recently a well-known men's clothing store that sold mass-marketed, off-the-rack, ready-to-wear suits.

12. Walter Reuther of the United Auto Workers publicly promoted a plan to convert the automobile industry (see previous chapter), which was firmly opposed by the auto industry. Lovett wrote to Patterson on November 22, 1940. One study summarizes the letter: "It was essential, [Lovett]

argued, that the automobile companies be 'brought into the game' as subcontractors so that their assembly-line techniques could be applied to the mass production of major components like tail assemblies and aircraft engines." Aircraft industry leaders agreed with Lovett and pressed him to convince the Roosevelt administration. Lovett went to James Forrestal, Patterson's counterpart as under secretary of the navy, who put him in touch with Patterson. A week after Lovett presented his quickly written report, Secretary of War Henry Stimson appointed him as his assistant secretary of war for air. One of Lovett's first reports back to Forrestal stated, "There is so much deadwood in the War Department that it constitutes a positive fire hazard." Hoopes and Brinkly, *Driven Patriot*, 130, 131.

13. The Office of War Information report was widely circulated. See *Army and Navy Journal* 80 (Oct. 24, 1942): 236.

14. According to Secretary of War Stimson, "Lovett possessed incisive judgment and a pertinent wit. He served . . . in all matters affecting the Air Forces as Patterson served in procurement and supply. Both were in a high degree autonomous officers; both combined initiative with loyalty." Henry L. Stimson and McGeorge Bundy, *On Active Service in Peace and War* (New York: Harper & Brothers, 1948), 343. As a prominent critic, I. F. Stone, reported in 1941, "It was characteristic that the heads both of the armed forces and of the OPM [the civilian Office of Production Management] seem to have been opposed to the idea of a big bomber program. Robert A. Lovett, Under-Secretary of War for Air, formerly of the banking firm Brown Brothers, Harriman and Company . . . and one of the best and most public-spirited of the defense program recruits from Wall Street seems to have been the originator of the program [to supply Britain with heavy bombers]." *Business as Usual*, 44.

15. In one of the official army histories, Mark S. Watson quotes a Lovett memo of early 1941 in which Lovett noted the defective organization of the air corps and concluded, "[T]o be fully effective to the General in Command of the Armies, this weapon needs a tight-knit, flexible organization as modern as the instrument itself." *Chief of Staff*, 290.

16. One of the official army histories of the period relates that "the JAC was put in a position to give the aircraft program the kind of co-ordination and control it required. The directive [creating the JAC] vested the committee with power to schedule all deliveries: Army, Navy, British, other foreign orders, and domestic commercial orders." As the study discerns, "That JAC was a successful agency is perhaps best attested by its survival to the end of the war." Holley, *Buying Aircraft*, 266, 268; see 266–73.

17. The official army history recounts that "the directive establishing JAC also provided for the formation of a working echelon, the Air Sched-

uling Unit (ASU), at Wright Field. The ASU was to serve as a central clearinghouse for information from the industry to JAC and from JAC to the industry." The same study explains, "The ASU had to rely upon the existing staff services of the Air Corps Materiel Division." This work was completed by nine hundred civilian and military employees in 1941, and by 1942 this number had grown to more than three thousand, including both army and naval officers. The study concludes, "The task performed for ASU was truly staggering. There were some 6,000 or 7,000 different types of end items to handle." Ibid., 269, 270.

18. The official army history also observes, "About twenty permanent modification centers were opened during the war although not all were in operation at any one time." Another issue requiring modification centers had to do with the fact that "large numbers of aircraft [requiring modification] began to pile up at the end of their production lines" and that "[t]hese seemingly completed aircraft had a depressing effect upon the employees, who were constantly being exhorted to redouble their efforts to increase output. Sending the airplanes to separate modification centers, the morale problem could be solved and the missing parts could be installed without delaying production." Ibid., 530.

19. Karachi is now part of Pakistan.

20. For the development of the B-29, see U.S. Air Force Historical Study No.6, "The Development of the Heavy Bomber, 1918-1944" (prepared by the USAF Historical Division, Air Univ., 1951), 89–93. See also Jacob Vander Meulen, *Building the B-29* (Washington, DC: Smithsonian Institution Press, 1995).

21. Prince Naruhiko Higashikuni, an uncle of the Emperor of Japan, had opposed war with the United States, and subsequetly formed the first postwar Cabinet as prime minister. Samuel Eliot Morison, *History of United States Naval Operations in World War II: Victory in the Pacific* (New York: Atlantic, Little-Brown, 1990), 359. For a critical examination of the planning and execution of the incendiary attacks, see Sherry, *Rise of American Air Power*, 266–300.

22. Project SILVERPLATE ran from 1943 to 1946. See Richard H. Campbell and Paul W. Tibbets, *The Silverplate Bombers: A History and Registry of the Enola Gay and Other B-29s Configured to Carry Atomic Bombs* (Jefferson, NC: McFarland, 2005); and also Fletcher Knebel and Charles W. Bailey II, *No High Ground* (New York: Harper and Brothers, 1960).

23. The B-36 was called the "Flying Battleship" because it boasted sixteen mounted guns. It was also called less flattering names—"Magnesium Monster," "Flying Apartment House," "Sitting Duck," and "Billion-Dollar Blunder"—because, with the arrival of jet aircraft and guided missiles, the

aircraft proved obsolete. As one author reminisced, "The B-36 was the biggest bomber the world ever knew, and it lived and died without having to fly through anything worse than a war of words." See Wesley S. Griswold, "Remember the B-36," *Popular Science,* Sept. 1961, 99, 98.

24. This was part of the final directive released by the Allied leaders at the Casablanca Conference in January 1943.

25. Historian Michael Sherry, drawing on the official military histories, refers to the "Black Week in October, when 148 Flying Fortresses succumbed." He notes, "The Eighth's bomb strikes had been heavy and punishing. . . . Yet the Nazis never suffered seriously from shortages of antifriction ball bearings; fighter output dipped slightly for awhile, then rose again." *Rise of American Air Power,* 158; see also 148–59.

26. On the fate of the P-75, see Irving Brinton Holley Jr., "A Detroit Dream of Mass-Produced Fighter Aircraft: The XP-75 Fiasco," *Technology and Culture* 28 (1987): 578–93.

27. From General Arnold's *Reports of the Commanding General of the Army Air Forces to the Secretary of War* (Washington, DC: U.S. Government Printing Office, 1945).

28. Historian Richard Overy does relate that by April 1944 the Allies had achieved air supremacy over even northern and central Germany: "By the spring [1944] the German fighter force was decimated. Half the fighters and a quarter of the pilots were lost each month." One of the German air force leaders, General Adolf Galland, reported to his superiors, "Things have gone so far that the danger of a collapse of our air arm exists." *Why the Allies Won,* 124.

29. Women piloted these aircraft as well. Operating under the auspices of the Women's Auxillary Ferrying Squadron (WAFS) and the Women's Airforce Service Pilots (WASPS), they provided a valuable service in ferrying aircraft from factories to bases. Over one thousand in number, these women also tested and repaired aircraft, and provided flight training to male students. See Molly Merriman, *Clipped Wings: The Rise and Fall of the Women Airforce Service Pilots (WASPS) of World War II* (New York: New York Univ. Press, 1998).

30. See Daniel Ford, *Flying Tigers: Claire Chennault and His American Volunteers, 1941–1942,* rev. ed. (New York: HarperCollins/Smithsonian Books, 2007).

31. "In October 1944," one of the army's official histories comments, "Air Transport Command (ATC) and other carriers delivered 35,131 short tons to China, dwarfing the 8,632 short tons carried to China in October 1943." Joseph Bykofsky and Harold Larson, *The Transportation Corps: Overseas Operations* (Washington, DC: Center of Military History, 1957), 556.

32. For a discussion of these specific recommendations and postwar issues in general, see Donald M. Pattillo, *Pushing the Envelope: The American Aircraft Industry* (Ann Arbor: Univ. of Michigan Press, 2001), 149–52.

4. A Changing Nation

1. Chaney, an air corps officer for twenty-four years, was chosen to head the Special Observer Group because "the group was to be concerned first of all with planning facilities for future air operations and air defense." Alfred M. Beck, *United States Army in World War II: The Technical Services, the Corps of Engineers* (Washington, DC: U.S. Army Center of Military History, 1985), 7.

2. "ABC" stands for "American-British Conversations." As historian Steven Ross writes regarding the ABC-1 plans, "For the first time in American history, national political and military leaders arrived at basic strategic decisions for the guidance of coalition warfare prior to hostilities." *American War Plans,* vol. 3 (New York, Garland Press, 1992), xiv, quoted in Stoler, *Allies and Adversaries,* 37–40, for discussion of the ABC-1 plans.

3. For a full review and outline of the ABC talks and agreements, see Watson, *Chief of Staff,* ch. 12, "Coordination with Britain."

4. An isolationist senator leaked the ABC-1 plans to the isolationist *Chicago Tribune,* which ran a story on December 4, 1941, titled "FDR's WAR PLANS." As one historian notes, "The political damage to Roosevelt was serious. Alas, for the *Tribune,* the timing was such that, within four days, it had to reverse its editorial line completely and support the President in going to war." Peter Clarke, *The Last Thousand Days of the British Empire: Churchill, Roosevelt, and the Birth of the Pax Americana* (New York: Bloomsbury Press, 2008), 16.

5. The Victory Program resulted from President Roosevelt's letter to the army and navy on July 9, 1941, requesting that they provide information on "the over-all production requirements required to defeat our potential enemies." (Roosevelt's letter contained other language that closely followed a memo Patterson had written to Stimson three months earlier.) The army was much more forthcoming than the navy in responding to this request, and the final document was presented to Roosevelt by Secretary of War Stimson and Secretary of the Navy Knox on September 25. The estimates were the first full statement of combined military requirements. These estimates of munitions and supplies were subsequently translated into production requirements by the civilian Supply Priorities and Allocations Board's Bureau of Research and Statistics, and their document, also called the Victory Program, became an even more crucial contribution to wartime production successes. Roosevelt quoted in Watson, *Chief of Staff,*

338; for background, see ibid., ch. 11, "The Victory Program." For the civilian role, see Catton, *The War Lords of Washington*, 83–90; and Koistinen, *Arsenal of World War II*, 120–21, 187–89.

6. J. A. Krug, *Production: Wartime Achievements and the Reconstruction Outlook* (Washington, DC, 1945). This was a special report prepared for the U.S. War Production Board.

7. "From July 1939 through March 1942," Koistinen reports, "the ANMB [Army-Navy Munitions Board], working directly under the president, became a significant mobilization body, with [its] commodity committees assuming crucial functions. The ANMB was virtually phased out as a mobilization board late in 1942 and early in 1943 when the [civilian] War Production Board and a reorganized War Department began to function effectively." *Planning War, Pursuing Peace*, 19.

8. Historian Jonathan Marshall observes that "on June 7, 1939, Congress enacted administration-backed legislation to authorize $100 million for the acquisition of 'certain strategic and critical materials being deficient or insufficiently developed to supply the industrial, military, and naval needs of the country for common defense ... in times of national emergency.' Although the appropriation was far from sufficient to eliminate the risk of foreign supply disruptions, it represented a huge sum in times of fiscal austerity." *To Have and Have Not: Southeast Asian Raw Materials and the Origins of the Pacific War* (Berkeley: Univ. of California Press, 1995), 36. Koistinen relates, "In the 1938 Naval Appropriations Act, Congress finally earmarked $3.5 million for the navy to accumulate manganese and other strategic materials. [And] national legislators went further with the passage of in June 1939 of the Strategic War Materials Act [referred to by Marshall], which authorized the ANMB, operating through the Treasury Department ... to acquire strategic stockpiles." *Arsenal of World War II*, 116.

9. *Annual Report of the Secretary of the Treasury on the State of the Finances* (Washington, DC: Government Printing Office, 1943), 302.

10. For the collaboration of industry officials with the Nazi state, see Peter Hayes, *Industry and Ideology: I. G. Farben in the Nazi Era* (New York: Cambridge Univ. Press, 2000).

11. See ch. 1, "Hidden Battles: Economic Warfare during World War II," in Matin Lorenz-Meyer, *Safehaven: The Allied Pursuit of Nazi Assets Abroad* (Columbia: Univ. of Missouri Press, 2007).

12. "After U.S. entry into World War II ... the U.S. Justice Department, Alien Property Bureau ... was renamed (December 9, 1941) the Alien Property Division. It was authorized to handle problems of alien property

created by the Second World War as well as liquidate the remaining affairs of the First World War. In March 1942, a new Office of the Alien Property Custodian (OAPC) was established by executive order to handle alien property matters created by World War II, that is to take over most of what the Justice Department (and the Treasury Department) had been doing. The OAPC would last until 1946." Mira Wilkins, "German Chemical Firms in the United States from the Late 19th Century to post-World War II," in *The German Chemical Industry in the Twentieth Century,* ed. John E. Lesch, 320 (Norwell, MA: Kluwar Academic Publishers, 2000).

13. The Army-Navy "E" Production Award was the top award given for "high achievement" in munitions production. The award came with a personal commendation from Robert Patterson as under secretary of war.

14. After the British victory at El Alamein in late 1942, British Prime Minister Winston Churchill noted, "No, this is not the end. It is not even the beginning of the end. But it is, perhaps, the end of the beginning." Historian Warren F. Kimball notes, "By the end of 1942 the fortunes of war would begin to shift. In Russia, Northwest Africa, the desert west of Egypt, and the Pacific, the Axis would be stopped and the Allies would go on the offensive." *Forged in War: Roosevelt, Churchill, and the Second World War* (Lanham, MD: Ivan R. Dee, 2002), 155.

15. Many corporate executives from industrial firms, and some who had little experience in production, served as top-level and line personnel in both military and civilian production agencies. Most of these continued to receive their private-sector salaries, serving the government either for a "dollar-a-year" or "without compensation (w.o.c.)." Their central role in mobilization began to cause problems as members of Congress grew concerned that these men would implicitly put their firms above country. Senator Harry S. Truman, who headed one of the key wartime oversight committees (the Senate Special Committee Investigating the National Defense Program), mentioned this specifically while questioning one such dollar-a-year man: "We can't help but think if a man's whole life has been spent in the creation of an industry, . . . and that he is now receiving a tremendous salary . . . his natural loyalty would come first to the place where his heart has been and where his bread and butter is." Senate Special Committee Investigating the National Defense Program, *Hearings,* 77th Congress, 2d sess., pt. 12, Apr., July1942, p. 5037.

16. When Knudsen, former president of General Motors, was eased out of his civilian mobilization leadership roles with the creation of the War Production Board in early 1942, the army offered him a commission of lieutenant general, which he accepted. This is an indication of the close

relations Knudsen enjoyed with army personnel, including Patterson. Certainly Knudsen was a gifted production man, but dispassionate assessments of his time guiding the prewar civilian agencies have not been so very complimentary. Knudsen relied extensively on his personal contacts with other executives, consultants, and industry advisory committees dominated by the nation's largest firms. As Koistinen conveys, Knudsen never adequately promoted oversight of military procurement, even as military orders began to overwhelm the economy, as they had done in the First World War. For Koistinen, "Knudsen's influence over procurement was never substantial because of his own attitude and the actions of the armed services. He worked closely with and deferred to the military." In addition, Knudsen sided with his colleagues in industry who resisted early expansion of the nation's industrial base out of concern for excess capacity in peacetime markets, and resisted curtailing and converting civilian industry to war production. While there were justifiable grounds for supporting his big business colleagues in these matters, it did mean that Knudsen supported those who, seeing the writing on the wall, resisted the "all-outers," including Patterson, who promoted maximum expansion of military production. Koistinen, *Arsenal of World War II*, 49; see also 22, 54, 74, 97–100, 128, 131. For a general discussion of these issues, see also Waddell, *The War Against the New Deal*, 77–94. For a view that lionizes Knudsen, see Herman, *Freedom's Forge*.

17. The Board of Economic Warfare (BEW) was headed by Vice President Henry A. Wallace. The BEW inherited the powers and responsibilities of the Economic Defense Board (EDB), created in July 1941, after the United States entered World War II and included the secretaries of state, war, navy, agriculture, and commerce, and the attorney general. As Koistinen outlines, "All these departments or offices were concerned about or involved in international economics of defense. EDB [and subsequently the BEW] would direct and coordinate their activity, which was defined to include exports, imports, the purchase and sale of goods (including preclusive buying), foreign exchange, foreign-owned or -controlled property, investments, credits, patents, transportation, communications, and other economic functions." *Arsenal of World War II*, 266–67.

18. Patterson obtained the 1941 number from a report written by Gano Dunn, senior consultant to the Industrial Materials Branch of the National Defense Advisory Commission and its successor, the Office of Production Management. Dunn, who had close ties to the steel industry and was on the payroll of U.S. Steel, worked with the American Iron and Steel Institute (the industry's trade association group) and predicted in February 1941 an excess steel-making capacity of between 10 and 14 million tons.

This forecast was challenged by New Dealers in the Bureau of Research and Statistics (BRS), and Dunn then issued another report showing a deficit of 1.4 million tons for 1941 and 6.4 for 1942. In fact, New Dealers on the BRS calculated that the nation would be short 15.7 million tons in 1941 based on "all-outer" calculations of a much larger army than existed in 1941. But Dunn followed the steel industry's hesitation to report the need for greater steel-making capacity. As the official government history of mobilization concludes, "The [steel] industry, traditionally over-built, hesitated to complicate its post emergency problems by over-building still further, and industry spokesmen ... were dominant in OPM." USCPA, *Industrial Mobilization for War,* 137, 152–53. See also Stone, *Business as Usual,* 151–54; and Koistinen, *Arsenal of World War II,* 40–41.

19. Getting enough aluminum was also a matter of dealing with the monopoly that Alcoa (Aluminum Company of America) had over the production of aluminum in the United States. Investigative journalist I. F. Stone dealt with this issue, finding that those in the prewar mobilization set-up, particularly Edward R. Stettinius Jr., chairman of the board of U.S. Steel, future secretary of state, and then in charge if industrial materials, downplayed the looming shortages of aluminum out of deference to Alcoa. In October 1941 Alcoa's senior vice-president, G. R. Gibbons, testified before Senator Truman's Committee, where he was asked about a Stettinius press release affirming that Alcoa had enough capacity to produce all the aluminum the nation would need at a time when Alcoa could not produce enough aluminum to fill its current orders. Gibbons replied that "I might have seen the release, and thought it was quite correct because I might have thought the war would be over in three months, in which there would be more than enough aluminum." I. F. Stone, "Making Defense Safe for Alcoa, II," in *The War Years: 1939–1945,* 83 (Boston: Little, Brown and Company, 1988). Of course, the government provided loans to help set up a competitor to Alcoa, the Reynolds Metals Company. See George David Smith, *From Monopoly to Competition: The Transformation of Alcoa, 1888–1986* (New York: Cambridge Univ. Press, 1988), 214–24, 236–49.

20. The rubber shortage was so bad by the summer of 1942 that President Roosevelt announced a scrap rubber drive as a last resort before turning to rationing. Richard Polenberg, *War and Society: 1941–1945* (Philadelphia, PA: J. B. Lippincott, 1972), 16; Vernon Herbert and Attilio Bisio, *Synthetic Rubber: A Project That Had to Succeed* (Westport, CT: Greenwood Press, 1985).

21. As it turned out, petroleum-based synthetic oil provided only a small part of the total supply. Koistinen notes that "it was alcohol-based butadiene that saved the day for America's synthetic rubber program. . . .

Eighty-three percent of all butadiene manufactured in 1943 came from alcohol [and not petroleum]; through August 1944, when the alcohol process was intentionally cut back, 80 percent of butadiene was derived from facilities using alcohol and producing at nearly double their rated capacity." And it was farm interests in Congress that pushed through the necessary changes in authority to ensure that agricultural, grain-based alcohol became the basic building block for synthetic rubber. In addition, as Koistinen also states, "Rescheduling the Second Front [the invasion of Europe] from 1943 to 1944 saved the nation from disaster [in terms of avoiding major deficits of synthetic rubber]." Koistinen, *Arsenal of World War II*, 156, 157; see 148–58, for a full treatment of the rubber issue.

22. For Patterson's role in gasoline rationing, see Eiler, *Mobilizing America*, 266–70, 274–77. As reported in a 1942 biographical piece, Patterson also publicly "deplored the use of gasoline for 'petting parties.' No enemy of petting, he merely believes the boys and girls should go afoot down the lovers' lane." Davis, "The Toughest Man in Washington," 59.

23. The problematic priorities situation had two main causes. The largest firms that controlled most of the military contracts wanted to avoid any kind of mandatory allocation or priority controls imposed by government officials, and their representatives were central actors in mobilization, whether in the civilian agencies like the Office of Production Management, as advisors to the military procurement arms, or in their industry advisory committees that worked closely with both the civilian and military mobilization organizations. In addition, the military procurement agencies used their authority to release priorities with brutal inefficiency, creating a chaotic situation reminiscent of World War I. They flooded the economy with priority orders (up to twenty-five thousand a week), undermining any controlling effect these orders might have had. With so many priority claims in use, their value as a rational means to distribute ever-scarcer materials became greatly diminished. The large companies that monopolized contracts and priority orders scoured the markets for scarce materials and then hoarded whatever could be found. As astute observer Eliot Janeway noted soon after the war, "The military's use of this [priority] power quickly demonstrated their own need of civilian control." *Struggle for Survival*, 195. See also Koistinen, *Arsenal of World War II*, 87–88, 99; and Waddell, *War Against the New Deal*, 79–80.

24. The Controlled Materials Plan (CMP) was welcomed because of its relative simplicity. It controlled only three critical materials upon which most production hinged: steel, aluminum, and copper. Materials were allocated by the War Production Board (WPB) to the military services and then from there on to prime contractors. The CMP allowed for the

first time a measure of top-level civilian control, and the WPB Requirements Committee imposed an uneasy balance between expansive military demands and available materials by forcing the military services to live within their allocations. See Waddell, *War Against the New Deal,* 110–14.

25. Fort Bragg, for instance, expanded from 5,400 soldiers in 1940 to 67,000 in 1941. As Doris Kearns Goodwin recounts, "For nine months, a labor force of 28,500 had worked 24-hour days to triple the size of the camp. . . . The hurried pace at Fort Bragg could have been seen at any number of spots across the country." Just to handle the expansion of the U.S. Army from a prewar low of 174,000 (ranked just nineteenth in the world) to the 1941 level of 1.4 million, "42 new camps had to be built. . . . The building of the new camps required 400,000 men, 908,000 gallons of paint, 3,500 carloads of nails, and 10 million square feet of wallboard." *No Ordinary Time: Franklin and Eleanor Roosevelt, The Home Front in World War II* (New York: Simon and Schuster, 1994), 217.

26. Patterson's figures are off here. It is possible that he is referring to total tonnage sunk from the start of the war until this point in early 1942. As one study reports, "The Allies lost 2.6 million tons of shipping between January and April [1942], more than had been lost in the Atlantic in the whole of 1941." Overy, *Why the Allies Won,* 47. And as Uboat.net concludes, "During the war the U-boats sank about 2,779 ships for a total of 14.1 million tons GRT. This figure is roughly 70% of all allied shipping losses in all theatres of the war and to all hostile action. The most successful year was 1942 when over 6 million tons of shipping were sunk in the Atlantic."

5. Altitudinal Goals

1. It is interesting here that Patterson is conceding a major point to his critics who, in the early months of the war, warned about excessive military demands on the economy. What was known as the "feasibility dispute" began when the military services authorized in early 1942 an ambitious program for constructing new processing facilities and manufacturing plants. Civilian planners in the War Production Board (WPB) warned that an unplanned escalation of military requirements would do great harm, as in World War I, by overloading the economy and thereby creating bottlenecks and shortages. Patterson and other military officials had found it perplexing that these same planners had been pressing, before the war began, for an increase in military contracting to spur the conversion from a peacetime to a war economy. Now that they were advocating for pulling in the reins, military officials like Patterson jumped

on the seeming contradiction, thinking it was simply a matter of coddling civilians at home by civilians in the WPB. This ended up becoming a major dispute in the so-called Battle of the Potomac, and the civilians ended up winning a grudging victory of sorts at the time. Patterson did, however, come around to see "the dangers of overprogramming," as Eiler calls it (Mobilizing America, 349). For a succinct review of the "feasibility dispute" and of key sources, see Waddell, *War Against the New Deal*, 104–8. For a recent study of this dispute that credits the civilian economists for providing the heavy lifting that saved the production program from the catastrophic bottlenecks of World War I, see Jim Lacey, *Keep from All Thoughtful Men: How U.S. Economists Won World War II* (Anapolis, MD: Naval Institute Press, 2011).

2. As even Albert Speer, Hitler's minister of armaments and war production, reports, "It remains one of the oddities of this war that Hitler demanded far less from his people than Churchill and Roosevelt did from [theirs]." *Inside the Third Reich: Memoirs* (New York: Macmillan, 1970), 214.

3. In fact, Army representatives at the time proved very obstinate in protecting their plans for constructing new facilities. They agreed to participate in an interagency group that studied the feasibility of constructing new plants while existing plants were idled for want of raw materials. Although their own representative on the group agreed that this was a problem, he was directed to file a dissenting report: "This report opposed any delay in the construction of war plants and also objected to review of War Department projects by an outside agency." USCPA, *Industrial Mobilization for War*, 391.

4. Both the military and corporate officials who joined to oppose the civilian planners on this issue proved highly skeptical at the time about outer limits to the nation's productive potential. As one immediate postwar study found, corporate advisors serving the civilian mobilization agencies opposed the "feasibility concept" because it was advocated "by persons who were regarded as 'academic long hairs.'" And when confronted with the War Production Board Planning Committee's warnings and recommendations regarding excessive military contracting, General Somervell, head of the Army Service Forces and a close colleague of Patterson's, denounced them as "an inchoate mass of words. . . . I am not impressed with either the character or basis of the judgments expressed . . . and recommend they be carefully hidden from the eyes of thoughtful men." See John Brigante, *The Feasibility Dispute* (Washington, DC: Committee on Public Administration Cases, 1950), 53–54, 82–83; and Lacey, *Keep from All Thoughtful Men*.

5. The full quotation is: "The first victory we have to win is to avoid a battle. The second, if we cannot avoid it, to win it. In order to give us the best chances of the first victory we must a) present the maximum appearance of overwhelming strength at the moment of the first attack, and b) attack at as many places as possible." Winston Churchill, "Darlan, Second Secret Speech," *Life,* Feb. 4, 1946, 85.

6. General Eisenhower had been forced to deal with Admiral Jean Darlan, the commander-in-chief of Vichy French forces in North Africa. Darlan finally agreed to cooperate with the Allies in French North Africa now that they had invaded successfully, and he handed over control of Algiers to Allied military control while he retained political control. Of course, Darlan was then immediately sacked by Marshal Petain, who repudiated the deal, although Darlan was by this time under Allied house arrest, remaining so for a few days before declaring his new loyalty to the Allied cause. Darlan had himself just been replaced as premier of Vichy France with "oily, fervently pro-Nazi" Pierre Laval. Roosevelt was immediately confronted with protests from all corners for his willingness to deal with Darlan, especially from prominent British and Free French representatives. Finally losing his patience with two of Gen. Charles de Gaulle's (head of Free French forces) men at a White House meeting, Roosevelt responded, "Of course I'm dealing with Darlan, since Darlan's giving me Algiers! Tomorrow I'd deal with Laval, if Laval were to offer me Paris!" Darlan was assassinated shortly thereafter. Atkinson, *An Army at Dawn,* 119–24, 158–59. See also Kenneth S. Davis, *FDR: The War President, 1940-1943* (New York: Random House, 2000), 464; and Robert Dallek, *Franklin D. Roosevelt and American Foreign Policy, 1932–1945* (New York: Oxford Univ. Press, 1979), 365.

7. Patterson repeatedly stressed the imperative of promoting "industrial morale," including "inspirational parades and rallies in defense plants, speeches by prominent military figures, demonstrations of combat equipment, briefings on world affairs, and so forth." As Eiler notes, "In emphasizing industrial morale, Patterson's primary aim was to increase production." As Patterson put it, the effort was about "narrowing the distance between the firing line and the assembly line." Eiler, *Mobilizing America,* 288.

8. As noted in chapter 2, the NDAC perfectly fit President Roosevelt's need at the time. It was still authorized under a World War I statute, and it was "legally powerless" with no provision for a single authoritative head. Americans were not yet ready for a full-blown mobilization effort, still convinced as they were that the United States could and should avoid involvement in another European war. And the NDAC ensured

that authority would remain in the President's hands; Roosevelt had no intention of abdicating authority over mobilization at this early date. See USCPA, *Industrial Mobilization for War*, 18; and Waddell, *War Against the New Deal*, 70–73.

9. Patterson here sidesteps a central issue of the period. Roosevelt displayed a marked reluctance to go along with the military's plans regarding creation of a civilian board to the extent that those plans meant great reliance upon corporate America. Roosevelt hesitated to centralize authority at this point in any case, given the pronounced isolationist drift of the country, but his reluctance also had to do with the military's plans to defer to the industrial leaders of the nation in any mobilization scheme. New Dealers fought this direction, as did Roosevelt. As Bruce Catton, a first-hand observer of mobilization battles, wrote soon after the war, "It [the plan to centralize authority in the hands of businessmen] proved altogether too much of a dose for President Roosevelt. The New Deal was prepared to co-operate with big business to obtain a defense program, but it wasn't going to hand over title to the old homestead." The irony was that the system began nonetheless to operate in a way designed to place power in the hands of the nation's industrialists. As the military services gained mobilization authority in the resulting administrative vacuum, this power inevitably flowed through them to their prime contractors. As Catton continues, "The War Department had not lost its faith in the idea that broad authorities should be delegated to industrial groups." *War Lords of Washington*, 102, 103.

10. Independent military procurement had a long tradition, but World War I had exposed how the military's anachronistic and often destructive practices could disrupt the civilian economy, and this liability had led to various types of civilian review as mobilization for World War II advanced. Civilian clearance was instituted to bring coherence to disorganized and fragmented military procurement (fragmented not only by service—army, navy, and then air forces—but also within each service as well); civilians were to coordinate War, Navy, and Treasury Department purchases and contract placement to ensure the least disruption to the civilian economy. Military officials, however, forcefully resisted any attempt to regulate their procurement practices, claiming that civilian intervention would interfere with military strategy. The irony was that, as the official history of army economic mobilization relates, the "sequence of . . . [war] planning ran from requirements to strategy"; that is to say, the army waited for armaments and supplies to accumulate before developing strategy. Smith, *Army and Economic Mobilization,* 211. See also Waddell, *War Against the New Deal,* 77–78, 96–99.

11. For a review of the administrative developments during the prewar and early wartime period that covers the evolving mobilization set-up, see Waddell, *Toward the National Security State*, 30–46.

12. It was not simply necessity that forced the changes Patterson refers to here. The domestic battles were truly significant precisely because the combatants understood that wartime decisions would have long-term impacts. An effective alliance of military and corporate personnel sought to counter any and all centralization of civilian authority, and the battles between New Dealers and others on the one hand, and a military-corporate alliance on the other, remain a central reason why mobilization administration continued throughout the war to be a work in progress marked by continual conflicts. For an elaboration of this analysis, see Waddell, *Toward the National Security State*, ch. 2, "Civil-Military Battles Over Domestic Mobilization."

13. For an analysis of the army reorganization, see the introduction to this volume and Waddell, *War Against the New Deal*, 100.

14. This comment dates this manuscript to sometime after the signing of the National Security Act of 1947.

15. As Harry S. Truman wrote in his memoirs, "In my various [Senate] investigations I ran into numerous unnecessary duplications by the Army and the Navy. For example, I found immense air installations located side by side at various points in this country and Panama where the Navy could not land on the Army's airfield, and vice versa. . . . At Pearl Harbor the air bases were as far apart as if they had been on different continents—yet they were practically side by side. Then the Navy had its own 'little army that talks Navy' and is known as the Marine Corps. It also had an air force of its own, and the Army, in turn, had its own little navy, both freshwater and salt." *Memoirs by Harry S. Truman*, vol. 2, *Years of Trial and Hope* (Garden City, NJ: Doubleday, 1956), 47.

16. Paul McNutt, who headed the War Manpower Commission, had to fight hard to keep military leaders from absorbing more of the nation's industrial manpower than could be spared. McNutt and the Selective Service System's head, General Lewis Hershey, continually battled for control of the nation's manpower. Hershey refused to support the occupational deferments that would ensure that skilled tool and die makers, for example, would not be drafted. Hershey also refused to instruct local draft boards about the need for deferments for certain occupations. In fact, fathers and farmers gained deferments much more easily than did skilled workers, and this created scarcities in crucial industries throughout 1943 and 1944. See Waddell, *Toward the National Security State*, 103–4. Furloughs of combat soldiers occurred repeatedly as a result of homefront labor shortages.

As Eiler reports, "In December 1944, 1,987 soldiers were furloughed for the manufacture of rubber tires; 2,500 for artillery ammunition; roughly 1,000 for cotton duck; and about 1,000 more for work in foundries. Additional furloughs of machinists, job setters, toolmakers, and others, to expand the manufacture of heavy-artillery ammunition were ordered in January 1945 and continued into spring." *Mobilizing America,* 417.

17. One can get a true sense of Patterson's sentiment on this matter from his November 1942 letter to Felix Frankfurter: "We are fighting a war for our very existence. It is not any old war; it is the most critical war we have ever faced. The armed forces need ten million men, and war industries need at least twenty million more. These are heavy demands on our manpower, the heaviest we have ever known. They are immediate and pressing." Quoted in Eiler, *Mobilizing America,* 259.

18. Patterson was certainly an enthusiastic supporter of a labor draft, feeling as he did that civilians were being coddled while servicemen bore the major wartime sacrifices. He could reflect back to his own service in the trenches of World War I in this regard. He no doubt also supported the bill out of loyalty to his old Wall Street boss and close associate Grenville Clark, whose pressure had helped secure Patterson his job as assistant secretary of war, and who had in December 1942 organized a Citizens Committee for a National War Service Act, the main force outside of Congress pressing for a labor draft. See Eiler, *Mobilizing America,* 375–77.

19. The Austin-Wadsworth Bill would conscript labor for industry the same way the military services conscripted men for their ranks. Patterson here is being somewhat disingenuous to liken a labor draft to the powers of the government over industry and over profits. The largest companies and their representatives essentially ran mobilization through industry advisory committees and through the use of dollar-a-year men, who flooded into mobilization agencies and into the military's procurement agencies right from the beginning. Labor never gained the kind of clout that industry enjoyed. The government's power to requisition property and force industry to produce what it needed was never used to any real degree, and certainly profits were extraordinary during the war, requiring a postwar renegotiation of war profits. As Koistinen, whose work on labor and industry during the war is unmatched, reports, the proponents of Austin-Wadsworth "would permit industry to operate during the war much as it did during the peace, but regiment labor in order to combat the major dislocations which would inevitably develop. The proposal was not only glaringly biased, it was hopelessly absurd. Efficient economic mobilization must begin with controlling the means of production not just one input of production. England's experience demonstrated that production

controls are fundamental to any manpower program." *Hammer and the Sword,* 467. See also John H. Ohly, *Industrialists in Olive Drab: The Emergency Operation of Private Industries During World War II* (Washington, DC: Center of Military History, 1999).

20. Organized labor was split into two competing camps, the older American Federation of Labor (AFL) and the newer Congress of Industrial organizations (CIO). Fratricidal conflict grew between the two groups before and during the war, as both competed to channel workers into their respective organizations. See Nelson Lichtenstein, *Labor's War At Home: The CIO in World War II* (New York: Cambridge Univ. Press, 1982); and Steven Fraser, *Labor Will Rule: Sidney Hillman and the Rise of American Labor* (Ithaca, NY: Cornell Univ. Press, 1991).

21. The 1947 *Handbook of Labor Statistics* reported that 88,100 workers were killed and 11,112,600 injured during five years of war. See Richard O. Boyer and Herbert M. Morais, *Labor's Untold Story* (New York: United Electrical, Radio, and Machine Workers of America, 1955), 336.

22. Industrial accidents in 1940 resulted in four times the loss of man-hours on the job as work stoppages, and this figure does not include the losses resulting from some eleven thousand deaths on the job. Richard J. Purcell, *Special Study No. 23, Labor Policies of the National Defense Advisory Commission and Office of Production management, May 1940 to April 1942* (Washington, DC: Government Printing Office, 1946), 171.

23. Eiler calls McGrady "a senior statesman in the field," noting, "In some forty years of work in industrial relations, as a representative first of labor, then of the public, and finally of management, 'Ed' McGrady had somehow retained the confidence of all major economic groups." *Mobilizing America,* 51.

24. Historian George Q. Flynn observes that "Secretary Stimson and Undersecretary Patterson of the War Department had little sympathy for protecting labor rights during wartime. They felt that military needs should dictate all manpower decisions and, if these needs led to the curtailment of freedom, that was the price of war. . . . From 1943 to July 1945 the army seized more than twenty-five strike-bound plants. Patterson saw such strikes as close to treason." *The Mess in Washington: Manpower Mobilization in World War II* (Westport, CT: Greenwood Press, 1979), 120.

25. The most celebrated of plant takeovers by the army occurred in mid-1941 at the airframe company North America Aviation in Inglewood, California. It was one of the few times there was a united front within Roosevelt's cabinet to intervene, and on June 9 over twenty-five hundred troops with fixed bayonets moved to break up the picket line and reopen

the plant. As Koistinen reports, "All unions and federations regretted military intervention," and "the North American seizure went as well as it did largely because of the wise counsel of Edward F. McGrady and other labor advisors, who acted to check the military's instinct for crushing opposition." When pressure grew later in 1941 to seize mines closed by United Mine Workers strikes—Secretary of War Stimson himself pushed hard for seizure—McGrady wrote to Patterson warning of the consequences: "The idea is currently widespread that troops are being used as part of a military operation or a campaign to take physical objectives. Such an approach to the problem would be fatal. The miners will not return to work because of any intimidation or because of any overpowering show of force. I know this because I have lived and worked with the miners during many of their struggles, often bloody ones, to gain recognition and strength." Roosevelt did not, in this case, allow the seizure to go forward. Koistinen, *Arsenal of World War II*, 408, 409.

26. "Although Patterson had been little concerned with the scientific aspects of the super-secret 'Manhattan Project' that the Army launched in 1942," notes Eiler, "he was privy to the general nature of the enterprise, and had played a key role in mobilizing the resources that sustained it." *Mobilizing America*, 438.

27. For recent overviews and analyses of the role of women in World War II, see Doris Weatherford, *American Women and World War II* (Edison, NJ: Castle Books, 2009), esp. ch. 9, "Rosie the Riveter Rallies to New Jobs"; and Emily Yellin, *Our Mothers' War: American Women at Home and at the Front During World War II* (New York: The Free Press, 2005), esp. ch. 2, "Soldiers Without Guns: Female Defense Industry Workers."

28. The actress was Veronica Lake. See "Wartime Living: Veronica Lake, by Government Request She Puts up Her Long Hair as a Safety Measure," *Life*, Mar. 8, 1943.

29. As historian Richard Polenberg relates, "As late as 1940 Negroes lived with more insecurity than most whites had known in the worst year of the depression. . . . The surge in defense production failed to improve these conditions. In 1940, of 100,000 aircraft workers, only 240 were Negroes and those mainly janitors. . . . But as the manpower pinch grew tighter in 1943, many of the obstacles to Negro employment collapsed." *War and Society*, 113, 116.

30. A recent book deals with this subject: William M. Tuttle Jr., *"Daddy's Gone to War": The Second World War in the Lives of America's Children* (New York: Oxford Univ. Press, 1995).

31. As military historian Russell Weigley notes, the "American Way of War" involves minimizing the loss of soldiers by emphasizing the use of

overwhelming force, firepower, and technological advantages. Russell F. Weigley, *The American Way of War: A History of United States Military Policy and Strategy* (Bloomington: Indiana Univ. Press, 1973).

6. An Offensive Begins

1. The meeting in London was part of, as historian Mark Stoler puts it, "the worst civil-military and Allied clashes of the war." Roosevelt wanted desperately to immediately engage Nazi forces to help relieve pressure on the Soviets, who, it was feared, were close to collapse, and who might seek a separate peace with the Nazis. The British had agreed to an invasion of Europe in 1943 and then appeared to back off. Whereas U.S. strategy was based on a direct and forceful confrontation with Germany using massed land forces, the British—recalling their disastrous experience in World War I—wanted to avoid land campaigns and instead opt for a strategy based on naval and air power. Pressed, the British sought an invasion of North Africa instead. Army and navy leaders Marshall and King responded to the British hesitancy by arguing for a shift in attention to a Pacific-first strategy of stepping up the war against the Japanese. Roosevelt met this gambit by ordering Marshall and King to London to finalize an agreement with the British for a North Africa invasion; Harry Hopkins, Roosevelt's most trusted lieutenant, accompanied them to ensure their compliance. Even then, Roosevelt had to push Marshall hard to agree with the British. See Stoler, *Allies and Adversaries,* 84–102 (for quote, see 83). See also Waddell, *Toward the National Security State,* 78–81.

2. Somervell was head of the new Army Service Forces. As such he worked closely with Patterson. See introduction, this volume.

3. Operation TORCH depended not just upon secrecy. Like the landings at Normandy in 1944, it also depended upon deception. As one historian notes, "In the case of Torch . . . Churchill dusted off two aborted invasion plans for deception use: Jupiter for northern Norway and Sledgehammer for the 1942 cross-Channel invasion. 'All depends upon secrecy and speed,' he telegraphed Roosevelt. . . . 'Secrecy can only be maintained by deception.'" David Jablonsky, *Churchill, the Great Game and Total War* (London: Routledge, 1991), 171.

4. As Rick Atkinson relates, Roosevelt wanted the invasion to occur before election day. "Please make it before election day," Roosevelt requested of Marshall. But Roosevelt gave his commanders full authority over the invasion date, and Eisenhower set the date for November 8, five days after the midterm elections that would result in serious losses for the president's party. See *Army at Dawn,* 29.

5. "Operation TORCH," one of the official army histories reports, "came at a critical time for supply agencies in both the United States and the United Kingdom. While it was by no means the largest operation undertaken by U.S. forces in World War II, TORCH involved for the first time the organization and equipping of task forces several thousand miles apart; it required for the first time the closest combined planning and implementation by British and American staffs; it came at the beginning of the development of the SOS [Army Services of Supply] in the United Kingdom, when it still lacked adequate personnel and . . . supply procedures and techniques. . . . Moreover the operation had to be prepared in great haste, for the time between conception and execution (three months) precluded long-range planning. As a result, TORCH was not a model of planning and preparation and necessitated many improvisations both in equipment and supply methods." Roland G. Ruppenthal, *Logistical Support of the Armies*, vol. 1, *May 1941–September 1944* (Washington, DC: Office of the Chief of Military History, 1953), 90.

6. The Army Service Forces was one of three army commands (one each for ground forces, air forces, and supply/service forces) created with the 1942 army reorganization. Introduction, this volume; and Waddell, *Toward the National Security State*, 43–44.

7. "Soldiers normally made the Atlantic voyage in swift liners which carried no cargo, and their equipment frequently arrived as much as 80 to 120 days later. Even when troops and equipment departed at the same time, the units had to give up their equipment at least a month before sailing so that it could be crated, shipped to the port, and loaded, thus curtailing the unit's training. Marrying up an organization with its equipment in the United Kingdom was a major task." Ruppenthal, *Logistical Support of the Armies*, 95.

8. "Since the United States was not only to mount and support roughly one third of the attacking force, but was also to be increasingly relied upon to furnish the supplies, equipment, and ships for the forces to be dispatched from the British Isles, Washington became as important a center for plans and operations as Eisenhower's headquarters in London." Bykofsky and Larson, *Transportation Corps*, 145.

9. Problems were legion, including the loss of huge amounts of supplies once they reached England: "As the invasion drew near, the supply picture was characterized by uncertainty and confusion that on occasion bordered on chaos. . . . Early in September the situation became even more alarming when General Eisenhower disclosed that a large part of the supplies and equipment presumed to be in the United Kingdom and available for TORCH

could not be located. And therefore would have to be replaced from the United States." Ibid., 142. Ruppenthal explains that "the most vexing problem arose from the temporary loss of items in the United Kingdom. They had been received but could not be found. In the spring and early summer, when haste in unloading ships and speeding their turn-round were the pressing considerations, and when poor marking made identification and segregation impossible, large quantities of supplies had been thrown into warehouses and open storage without proper identification. Now there was a sudden demand for thousands of items and there were no adequate records indicating their location." Eisenhower, unable to muster the personnel in England to untangle this mess, was forced to simply re-requisition the missing supplies from the United States. *Logistical Support of the Armies*, 96.

10. "In late October 1942, approximately three months after the decision to undertake the invasion, three task forces, totaling some 107,000 American and British troops set sail under naval escort for North Africa. Two forces (the Center and Eastern) were mounted from the United Kingdom to capture, respectively, Oran and Algiers. A third force (the Western) was dispatched from the United States to seize Casablanca." Bykofsky and Larson, *Transportation Corps*, 137.

11. As Bykofsky and Larson note concerning Casablanca: "In the absence of port troops, the Army's poorly organized work details were unequal to the task of cargo handling and had to be assisted by Navy personnel. The docks were piled high with miscellaneous supplies and equipment, literally dumped from the landing craft and lighters in helter-skelter fashion. . . . Because of the disorder on the docks at Casablanca, the Army had to 'forage' for wanted items, and since there were insufficient guards the natives pilfered almost at will." Still, "[d]espite inexperienced personnel, limited facilities, and the constant haste and pressure of war, the U.S.-operated ports in North Africa rolled up an impressive record." Ibid., 154, 161.

12. In a recent study, Rick Atkinson relates that while the seas were calm the first day of the invasion, they "turned nasty with six-foot waves before dawn on November 9. . . . Although 40 percent of the invasion force was ashore, barely one percent of the 15,000 tons of cargo had left [the] ships. Of 378 landing craft and tank lighters, more than half were breached, sunk, or stranded. . . . Sloppy loading at Norfolk, and Patton's chronic neglect of logistics—'Let's do it and think about it afterwards,' in his chief engineer's tart phrase—now cost him dearly." *Army At Dawn*, 138.

13. This can be considered one of many lessons that had to be learned. Although President Roosevelt had to openly buck his military leaders to push for an invasion of North Africa rather than wait a bit longer for a bolder strike into Europe itself—a choice that "provoked dismay, even disgust, and would remain controversial for decades"—the decision made it possible for the American forces to learn in very practical ways the many difficult steps involved in fighting a modern war against a hardened, competent enemy. This wisdom was dramatically missing in 1942, and as Rick Atkinson understands, by opting for a North African campaign, "Roosevelt had saved his countrymen form their own ardor." And Atkinson later concludes, "As for combat, TORCH revealed profound shortcomings in leadership, tactics, equipment, martial élan, and common sense . . . the U.S. Army was simply inept at combined arms—the essence of modern warfare, which requires skillful choreography of infantry, armor, artillery, airpower, and other combat forces." Ibid., 17, 159–60.

14. The bazooka got its name when "Major Zeb Hastings noted the weapon's similarity to an amusing musical instrument called 'bazooka' used by radio comedian Bob Burns, the 'Arkansas Traveler.' The nickname was applied and stuck to what became the M1 rocket launcher (while under development the bazooka was code-named 'The Whip')." Gordon L. Rottman, *FUBAR, F***ed Up Beyond All Recognition: Soldier Slang of World War II* (Oxford, UK: Osprey Publishing, 2007), 23.

15. DUKW, pronounced "duck," was produced by General Motors. Both a truck and a boat, the DUKWs eventually became an indispensable element in the World War II movement of men and materiel from ship to shore. For more on the DUKW, see 280nb.

16. As Rick Atkinson comments, the French naval and coastal battery forces began firing immediately upon the arrival of the American fleet, and the battleship *Jean Bart,* a "ship killer," was one of the first to begin firing: "The *Jean Bart*—France's newest dreadnought, with turrets heavy as a frigate—was still unfinished: she could not leave her slip. [After she started firing on U.S. warships, a] sixteen-inch shell from the *Massachusetts* burrowed through the battleship's forward turret. Another hit the turret's armored apron, immobilizing the guns. After firing just seven rounds, *Jean Bart* fell silent. Three other shells . . . punched through the armored decks, the side, and the keel, and *Jean Bart* settled on the bottom." Her guns were still above the waterline, however; and two days later, with her crew having repaired her damaged turret, the *Jean Bart* fired on the U.S. flagship, the *Augusta,* which was carrying the naval head of the invasion force (Rear Adm. Henry Kent Hewitt) and the army head (Lt.

Gen. George S. Patton Jr.). The *Augusta* narrowly missed being hit and fled while carrier aircraft finally silenced the *Jean Bart* for good. *An Army At Dawn*, 131, 148–49.

17. As Bykofsky and Larson point out concerning the Port Battalions at Casablanca, "The officers and men concerned were subsequently commended by General Patton for doing what at first was thought humanly impossible." *Transportation Corps*, 154.

7. Alaska, Australia, the Persian Gulf

1. As one history discerns, "For Japan to realize the advantages of the economic riches of its empire, a vast, flexible merchant navy was necessary. In scarcely any other department of war was Japanese planning so inefficient. It began the war without a realistic or adequate appreciation of the demands which were likely to be made upon its merchant shipping. ... In 1942 the Japanese lost over a million tons of shipping, and by 1943, the shortage had become acute. ... The losses, by submarine warfare, by mines, and by air attack, were such as to make ridiculous the attempt to weld together the Japanese territories in a single viable empire." Peter Calvocoressi and Guy Wint, *Total War: The Story of World War II* (New York: Pantheon Books, 1972), 784–85.

2. It is interesting that one of the major problems with Japanese war planning and execution, and a major reason for the issue Patterson identifies here, was the dominance of military over civilian forces within Japan. As Calvocoressi and Wint observe, "civilian Ministries were instinctively held in contempt by service [military] Ministries. At joint conferences the requests of civilians for allocations of manpower and materials tended to be overruled, even though the end product might be one of which the services were badly in need. For such reasons ... Japan was never able to utilize its huge economic assets. Japan had risked war for the sake of obtaining raw materials under its flag; but, when this was brought about, it could not transport them. ... The iron, the coal, the bauxite, nickel, tin, manganese, lead, salt, graphite, potash, all the vital materials for war, were all of them technically Japanese, guarded by Japanese troops, but they lay as useless to Japan as though they were in the hands of the enemy, because they could not be transported. They were a kind of fairy gold." Ibid., 785.

3. But replace we did, and then some. As an example of our shipbuilding capacity, historian Richard Overy notes, "In 1943 Japanese shipyards supplied only three more aircraft carriers [for the Imperial navy], and four in in 1944; the United States navy in these two years procured another

ninety." Overy also reports that "[t]he American merchant shipbuilding programme was a production miracle: 794,000 tons of shipping were built in 1941, 21 million tons in the next three years." *Why the Allies Won,* 43, 62.

4. As Mark Watson, in one of the official army histories, reports, "These rapid additions to Philippine defenses, in contrast with the restraints of earlier months, came as a surprise to numerous planning officials." Watson notes the degree to which this was a shift in the U.S. military strategy, coming as it did "less than a week after the MacArthur appointment." MacArthur had been recalled to active duty in the U.S. Army as commanding general of all U.S. Army forces in the Far East in late July 1941, after years serving as U.S. military advisor to the Philippine government, helping prepare the Philippines' armed forces for independence. See Watson, *Chief of Staff,* 438–39. Secretary of State Henry Stimson writes that there were "two leading causes" for the shift in policy: "One was the contagious optimism of General Douglas MacArthur" and "[t]he second reason . . . was the sudden and startling success of American Flying Fortresses [the B-17] in operations from the British Isles." Stimson and Bundy, *On Active Service in Peace and War,* 388. As it turned out, when the Japanese attacked Clark Field in the Philippines on December 8, 1941, "despite many hours' advance warning," the bombers were destroyed on the ground and "Clark Field as a tactical air base had ceased to exist. . . . [T]he Japanese at a single stroke had removed one of the major obstacles to their southward advance." Larrabee, *Commander in Chief,* 316.

5. The full text of this message is reproduced in Ray S. Cline, *Washington Command Post: The Operations Division* (Washington, DC: Office of the Chief of Military History, United States Army, 1951), 76–77. Cline also relates, "The warnings dispatched concerning the Japanese threat in the Pacific did not impress Lt. Gen. Walter C. Short, Commanding General, Hawaiian Department, sufficiently to induce his taking all the precautionary measures it was intended he should take." Ibid., 77.

6. Two new commands were created after the attack on Pearl Harbor. One of these, which operated only briefly, was the American-British-Dutch-Australian (ABDA) Command. The second was "the impromptu Task Force, South Pacific . . . [which] was constituted at sea on 12 December 1941 by Brig. Gen. (later Maj. Gen.) Julian F. Barnes, the senior officer aboard a U.S. Army troop and cargo convoy originally destined for the Philippines but diverted to Australia after America was drawn into the war." Once the convoy reached Brisbane, "General Barnes and his staff went ashore and established Headquarters, U.S. Forces in Australia

(USFIA). USFIA, on 5 January 1942, was redesignated U.S. Army Forces in Australia (USAFIA)." Bykofsky and Larson, *Transportation Corps,* 426.

7. As one of the official army histories reports, "desperate attempts were repeatedly made to bring relief to the defenders of Bataan and Corregidor. Several small vessels were chartered as blockade runners and a few submarines carried critical cargo, but virtually all such efforts were unsuccessful. The Japanese air and sea blockade of the approaches to the Philippines effectively prevented reinforcement whether by ship or airplane." Ibid., 427. As it was, MacArthur was ordered out of the Philippines by presidential telegram on February 22, 1942, and perilously escaped by Navy PT boat through the blockade. The defense of Bataan and Corregidor was vividly re-created in John Ford's classic 1945 film *They Were Expendable,* starring John Wayne and Robert Montgomery.

8. The official army history on the Transportation Corps notes, "The use of local civilian labor was attended by many difficulties, which were most pronounced in Australia. The Australian longshoremen were organized in 'a strong, militant, articulate union,' the Waterfront Workers Federation. Its bargaining position was excellent, both because of political influence and because of the acute wartime labor shortage. The Transportation Corps frequently found the Australian dockers trying, none too efficient, and costly.... On occasion they were described as insolent, thievish, and resentful of the presence of the U.S. Army." Ibid., 471.

9. There were problems associated with the use of African American troops abroad, especially in Australia. As an official army history reveals, "The difficulty of gaining overseas acceptance of Negro troops was so great that ... sparsely populated area[s] [like Alaska] appeared to be one where, if anything, Negroes might be used in increasing numbers." Australia, "whose 'White Australia' immigration policy dated back to the establishment of the Commonwealth ... informed the War Department through the Australian Embassy in Washington that it would not agree to the dispatch of more Negro troops to Australian territory. This position was later modified to permit a limited number to enter, with the stipulation that they were to be withdrawn at the end of the Australian emergency." In addition, the "Australian situation was complicated by clashes between Negro and white soldiers," so much so that "the American commander, Lt. Gen. George H. Brett ... recommended the withdrawal of all Negro troops." In the end, official policy was that "Negro troops should be sent to Australia and New Zealand only in an emergency and for a limited period. 'Their presence,' G-2 felt, 'would undoubtedly build up hostility to the United States throughout Australia.'" Ulysses Lee, *The Employment*

of Negro Troops (Washington, DC: Office of the Chief of Military History, 1966), 440, 429, 436.

10. As one of the official army histories states, "The swift Japanese drive through the Netherlands Indies, New Guinea, and the British Solomons threatened to sever the vital air and sea lanes to Austrialia and New Zealand. In order to avert this possibility, Army, Navy, and Marine forces were organized in the United States and, beginning in January 1942, occupied a series of friendly bases extending from the Society Islands through New Caledonia and thrusting northward into the New Hebrides." Bykofsky and Larson, *Transportation Corps,* 494.

11. One of the marines featured in the Tom Hanks/Steven Spielberg HBO miniseries *The Pacific* wrote, "Atabrine was a malaria preventive. It had been developed after Japan had cornered most of the world's sources of quinine. It had been introduced in the Pacific at the end of 1942, and in early 1944 on New Britain it had kept the incidence of malaria down to a rock-bottom minimum. But the men did not like atabrine. It was the perfection of bitterness. Many men could not swallow atabrine. It also turned a man's skin yellow, a permanent yellow, many men assumed. There were rumors that it made a man sterile. Nothing had more power to make atabrine unpopular than this last rumor, and as the number of atabrine delinquents grew, medical people resorted to an advertising campaign. . . . There were road signs of voluptuous nudes accompanied by the legend: 'Come Back to This—Take Atabrine.'" Robert Leckie, *Strong Men Armed: The United States Marines Against Japan* (Philadelphia, PA: Da Capo Press, 2010), 304. See also May Ellen Condon-Rall and Albert E. Cowdney, *The Medical Department: Medical Service in the War Against Japan* (Washington, DC: United States Army, Dept. of Military History, 1998), 123–24.

12. "Even as efforts to gird Alaska's defenses moved forward, the Japanese launched a two-pronged attack against Midway and Dutch Harbor. . . . The Dutch Harbor attack (3–4 June [1942]) proved diversionary and ended with the withdrawal of Japanese forces and their occupation of Kiska and Attu Islands in the western Aleutians. These enemy bases lacked the strength to threaten seriously Alaska's security or to disrupt the sea lanes in the Bering Sea and the Gulf of Alaska." Bykofsky and Larson, *Transportation Corps,* 33.

13. "Proposals for the construction of a highway were made in the prewar years, but these had consistently received a negative response from the War Department, which believed that such a project would have little military value. . . . Shortly after Pearl Harbor the War Department's attitude shifted to one of active support . . . based on two considerations.

First, a highway to Alaska, if located along the airway placed under development in the winter of 1940–1, would facilitate the latter's supply and expansion; second, the highway would provide an alternative land route in the event of enemy interference with the sea lanes of Alaska. . . . Although the original plans for the Alaska Highway did not contemplate its use as a supply line to Alaska unless the sea lanes were cut, the shipping shortage, increasing ADC [Alaskan Defense Command] supply requirements, and the possibility that Alaska might be developed as an overland route to Siberia lent new emphasis to such a project. . . . By early 1943 the shipping shortage had eased and plans for the use of Alaska as an overland route to Siberia or for offensive operations west of the Aleutians were fading fast. Moreover, the westward shift of strength in Alaska caused the highway to lose much of its potential importance." Ibid., 59, 60.

14. A total of 7,926 lend-lease planes were delivered to the Soviets over the Alaska Highway flyway. The highway was an easily followed route from the air, and pilots in trouble could land on, or bail out near, the highway. As one study reports, "Along the staging route, most of the pilots bailed out close enough to the highway to walk to safety or be found by search parties." The study continues, "No military man appreciated the Alaska Highway more during World War II than General Henry H. 'Hap' Arnold, commander in the USAAF." His assessment of the highway, quoted by Patterson here, was made during an inspection tour in 1943 and reflected Arnold's understanding that the highway had made flying the route so much safer than it would be otherwise. Heath Twichell, "The Wartime Alaska Highway: Boon or Boondoggle?" in *Alaska at War, 1941–1945: The Forgotten War Remembered,* ed. Fern Chandonnet, 170, 171 (Anchorage: Univ. of Alaska Press, 2007). It should be noted that Twichell's father was a white officer in charge of a black engineering regiment sent to help build the highway. This regiment had all its equipment sent to nearby white regiments because of shortages, and yet they managed to build a bridge over a raging river with no major equipment in three days—record time. See interview: http://www.pbs.org/wgbh/americanexperience/features/interview/alaska-interviews/.

15. "Patterson," reports Eiler, "was specifically rapped for his support of the CANOL Project [by the Senate Special Committee to Investigate the National Defense Program, known as the Truman Committee], an undertaking conceived early in the war, at a time when control of the seas were threatened, for developing oil resources in Alaska and the Canadian Northwest. The project was continued for several years—allegedly long after it had become clear, in a changing environment, that it could

contribute little or nothing to the war effort. CANOL produced waste, in the committee's opinion, greater than any known act of enemy sabotage." *Mobilizing America*, 458n.

16. As historian Heath Twichell recounts, "With the Alaska Highway by then a fait accompli, Truman's main focus was on the delays and cost overruns in the Canol project, which was supposed to supply fuel and lubricants for all the trucks and aircraft using the highway and staging route. But his investigators could hardly ignore the disparity between the public's image of the Alcan and the reality. Long stretches of what magazine writers liked to call 'Our Glory Road to Tokyo' were, in fact, not open to through traffic for most of the year following the official ceremony 'opening' the highway on November 20, 1942. . . . Released in January 1944, the Truman Committee's report on Canol was a scathing indictment of the project's futility and waste. (It ultimately produced only 311,145 barrels of gasoline and diesel fuel—at a cost of $7.72 per gallon—before it was shut down in 1945.) It was clear, however, that the senator regarded the Alaska Highway as a comparable boondoggle." Twichell also defends the highway in terms very similar to those Patterson used so many years ago: "Although the fortunes of war dictated (luckily) that it would never serve as Alaska's main supply line, I submit the Alaska Highway was still a bargain: as an insurance policy that gave peace of mind to both the citizens and the defenders of Alaska during a tense and uncertain time; as a combination low-tech navigational aid and fifteen-hundred-mile-long emergency landing strip for the 'young flyers' Governor Gruening worried about; and finally, as the backbone for the U.S. half of the ALSIB [Alaska-Siberia] operation—the conduit for war materiel of vital military and psychological importance to a beleaguered . . . ally." Twichell, "The Wartime Alaska Highway," 169, 171. As one of the army histories reports, "Although the Alaska Highway had contributed little to the supply of Alaska, it had made possible the construction and supply of staging airfields, communications facilities, and distribution pipelines along the route and provided a margin of safety in the event the sea lanes should be cut." Bykofsky and Larson, *Transportation Corps*, 63.

17. Somervell, head of the Army Service Forces, had a stormy relationship with many of the civilians running the mobilization program, and this came out in Senator Truman's Investigative Committee hearings and reports. "Truman," notes one study, "particularly enjoyed roasting General Somervell, whom he described as a man who 'cared absolutely nothing about money.'" And Somervell, in turn, "was especially critical of Truman's committee, which he claimed had been 'formed in iniquity for political purposes.' . . . The struggle between Truman and Somervell came to a head

in December 1943, when the latter was called to testify about the so-called Canol project, one of the most extraordinary, and eccentric, undertakings of the Second World War. The project employed nearly 15,000 men for over two years to drill oil wells in a region about seventy miles south of the Arctic Circle and to construct a 550-mile pipeline across Canada to bring oil to Whitehorse, in the Yukon Territory, to service US airfields in Alaska. The general had approved Canol without consulting key civilian agencies involved in energy or production matters, and without bothering to inquire whether the Navy might be able to transport the oil more cheaply and easily by ship. The committee . . . presented its conclusions on January 8, 1944. The project was described as 'undertaken without adequate consideration or study,' and Somervell's management of the project was assessed as 'inexcusable.'" The general nonetheless pushed the project to completion in May 1944, only to have the whole undertaking scrapped by the Army nine months later, under increasing pressure from Congress." Douglas T. Stuart, *Creating the National Security State: A History of the Law That Transformed America* (Princeton, NJ: Princeton Univ. Press, 2008), 49. As another study understands, "It was subsequently estimated that the entire output of the Canol project could have been supplied by one tanker in a three-month period at a cost considerably lower than that allocated [for Canol] . . . Yet, it is overly simplistic to identify Somervell as the villain in the piece, as the Truman committee did in 1944. The military continued to endorse the project . . . in 1943 and 1944 on the grounds of military necessity . . . [and the] initial decision to proceed with the project was made not by Somervell alone but at a meeting of civilian and military officials that included Brigadier-General Andrew F. Carter and General Walter B. Pyron, both former oil executives with extensive experience, and both active in wartime petroleum planning. Also present were representatives of Standard Oil of California and Imperial Oil." Interestingly, Patterson intervened with his boss, Secretary of War Stimson, after the latter oversaw his own review of Canol in late 1943 and concluded that everything was proceeding according to schedule: "[Patterson] continued to hold some reservations, especially with respect to the long-range development of Canol petroleum and the role of private companies. 'Imperial should not profit unduly,' Patterson wrote later in the year, 'from exploration done at our expense outside the field of its original discovery and development." Stephen J. Randall, *United States Foreign Policy Since World War II: For Profits and Security* (Montreal: McGill-Queen's Univ. Press, 2007), 161.

18. Alaska Governor Ernest Gruening "thought that many of the military construction projects and activities had been wasteful, poorly located,

and poorly planned from the beginning. For example, the construction of neither army nor navy bases took into account the role of air power. At the navy bases at Sitka, Kodiak, Dutch Harbor, and Fort Richardson (the principal army base near Anchorage), structures were crammed together without provision or forethought for concealment, camouflage, or dispersal. . . . Construction had been well underway at the three naval bases 'before it was realized that the Army had to located somewhere' to defend the installations. . . . The case of Dutch Harbor furnished an example. Because it had been made a naval reservation before the advent of air power, 'an entirely new base had to be built on Umnak Island 65 miles to the westward to supply the missing airport.' . . . Everything had to be duplicated on Umnak, including accommodations for ten thousand men together with all the accompanying installations. But Fort Glenn on Umnak had no harbor . . . [so, as Governor Gruening reported in a confidential memo:] 'Dutch Harbor with no airport and Umnak with no seaport, is like a team composed of a lame man and blind man—the lame carrying the blind on his back.'" Claus-M. Naske, *Ernest Gruening: Alaska's Greatest Governor* (Fairbanks: Univ. of Alaska Press, 2004), 98-99.

19. "Critical Lend-Lease supplies . . . passed through the Persian Corridor, with the U.S. Persian Gulf Command (made up of 30,000 servicemen) responsible for the delivery to the Soviets. This lifeline contributed to the Red Army's victory at Stalingrad, a triumph that altered the course of World War II." Marc J. O'Reilly, *Unexceptional: America's Empire in the Persian Gulf, 1941–2007* (Lanham, MD: Lexington Books, 2008), 42.

20. More of Roosevelt's remarks that day: "All of you who are here today, and all of you who are farther south in Iran, can remember always that you have taken a very necessary and very useful part in winning the war. When I woke up this morning in this camp and looked out, I said to myself, 'I am back in Arizona or New Mexico.' And then, suddenly, I realized how far away from home we are. America is proud of you, proud of what you are doing in this distant place. I wish that great numbers of our people could see this work of getting the necessary equipment and supplies through to our ally, who has had very heavy losses, but who is licking the Nazi hordes. And so I am on my way home. I wish I could take all of you with me. The people back home know what you are doing and how well you are doing it. They, too, are proud of you. All I can say is, 'May you get back home to our good America just as soon as you can. Good-by and good luck.'" See full remarks at the online American Presidency Project: http://www.presidency.ucsb.edu/ws/?pid=16347#axzz1QyVHziT4.

8. Assault in Force

1. This was British Prime Minister Winston Churchill's point in pressing the invasion of Italy after Operation HUSKY, the successful conquest of Sicily. As historian Rick Atkinson reports, Churchill, in a May 1943 Washington meeting with Roosevelt, "said it was imperative 'to use our great armies to attack Italy' rather than leave them idle after Sicily." "Some twenty-five Allied divisions . . . would muster in the Mediterranean by the end of Operation HUSKY and [Roosevelt agreed] 'these must be kept employed'" even though Roosevelt, and especially his military leaders, wanted no diversion from the buildup of troops in Britain for a cross-channel invasion of France itself. *The Day of Battle: The War in Sicily and Italy, 1943–1944* (New York, Henry Holt, 2007), 12, 13.

2. Marshal Kliment E. Voroshilov represented the Russian armed forces at the Tehran Conference.

3. These are direct quotations of Marshall's remarks to Voroshilov from the Tehran Conference. See Forrest C. Pogue, *George C. Marshall: Organizer of Victory, 1943–1945* (New York: Viking Press, 1973), 312.

4. Regarding an invasion of continental Europe, historian Richard Overy notes, "The shortage of men was compounded with a serious lack of the means to transport them across the Channel. This could only be done in purpose-built landing craft: large landing ships to transport stores and troops to the invasion zones, and smaller landing craft to carry tanks, guns, and men on to the invasion beaches. Neither ally had attached much significance to the production of landing craft, but during the course of 1943 the issue came to dominate the whole invasion plan. In the spring of 1943 most landing craft were in the Pacific supporting the island-hopping campaign. In the Atlantic theatre, the American navy had only eight converted merchant ships suitable for the task and the British just eighteen. The remaining craft were supporting the Allied forces in the Mediterranean. When the deficiency finally dawned on the Allies a crash programme of production was ordered from American shipyards. By April 1943 8,719 had been built, from 4,000 ton ships to carry eighteen tanks or 33 lorries [trucks], to small beach-craft of 7 tons that could move one lorry or 36 men on to the beaches. Over the following year another 21,500 were procured. . . . It was an extraordinary production achievement, but in the event it only just sufficed." *Why the Allies Won*, 139.

5. "The decision to expand the invasion force," Overy observes, "made unavoidable a further postponement. The extra divisions and the wider front meant more landing craft and larger supplies. So narrow was the

margin in the supply of vessels for amphibious assault that the necessary craft could only be secured by waiting an extra month for the next consignment from American dockyards, and by abandoning the idea of a subsidiary assault on southern France." Ibid., 146.

6. DUKW, pronounced "duck," was produced by General Motors. "D stood for 1942. U for utility. K for front-wheel drive. And W for two rear driving axles." These vehicles were remarkably stable in the water "and the DUKW quickly won converts by its versatility. It could carry 10 tons of cargo when afloat, even though its suspension limited it to 4 tons on the road. To be sure, the vehicle made only 5 knots in the water, but it could do 50 miles per hour on a reasonable road on land. Its low profile in the water made it a difficult target to shoot at, a feature that made the DUKW attractive to its crewmembers. . . . It could transport a total of 36 men or 25 men and all their equipment as assault troops." Interestingly enough, the DUKW managed also to intensify friction between the army and navy: "Is the DUKW a boat or a truck? With considerable reason, the Navy contended that the vehicle was a small craft and, therefore, fell within the Navy jurisdiction. . . . The Army contended that the DUKW primarily was a truck and, therefore, within the Army jurisdiction." I. B. Holley, "Technology and Strategy: A Historical Review," in *Technology, Strategy, and National Security,* ed. Franklin D. Margiotta and Ralph Sanders (Washington, DC: National Defense Univ. Press, 1985), 32–34.

7. "Proud of their new vehicle, the NRDC [National Defense Research Committee, the precursor agency to the OSRD] team took it to the Army Chief of Engineers in search of approval for a production order. To their surprise, they were turned down. The Chief of Engineers said the Army had no requirement for such a vehicle, even after it had performed successfully in demonstrations. To appreciate this rejection, one must recall that the Army was approached repeatedly by inventors and designers with ideas for wonder vehicles, single-purpose, highly specialized pieces of equipment alleged to be the solution of some pressing problem. With an eye on the long history of impractical devices submitted and another eye on anticipated complications imposed on maintenance and supply by the proliferation of special-purpose equipment, Army planners seemed to shy away instinctively from [such ideas]." Ibid., 32.

8. As one of the official army histories notes, "Planning for the Sicilian invasion . . . was far more complete than for TORCH [the invasion of North Africa] and was built on a much sounder foundation. . . . In one way the operation was to resemble the later OVERLORD [the Normandy invasion] operation much more closely because it was to be made across a short stretch of sea, and was not launched from such widely separated points as was

TORCH. . . . HUSKY was also to be a landmark in the development of amphibious logistical support, both in far-shore organization and in equipment. For the first time a naval beach battalion was utilized to achieve a closer co-ordination between the Navy afloat and the Army ashore." Ruppenthal, *Logistical Support of the Armies,* 331

9. At the Trident Conference in Washington (May 1943), Army Chief of Staff George C. Marshall spoke against invading Italy, which he saw "'would establish a vacuum in the Mediterranean' that would suck troops and materiel away from a cross-Channel attack. Operations after Sicily [for Marshall] 'should be limited to the air offensive' or risk a 'prolonged struggle' in the Mediterranean, which was 'not acceptable to the United States.'" As with their response to the British plan to invade North Africa, the American chiefs began to contemplate simply shifting more of their forces to the Pacific struggle against the Japanese. The navy chief, Admiral Ernest J. King, in fact advised his fellow chiefs, "We ought to divert our forces to the Pacific." Fortunately the diversion did not occur. Atkinson, *Day of Battle,* 13–14, 15.

10. At the Quebec Conference (Quadrant), Roosevelt and Churchill "reaffirmed the OVERLORD invasion of western Europe for the following spring, but the British still considered an extended campaign in Italy vital to that cross-Channel attack because it would siphon German reserves from the Atlantic Wall. The Americans disagreed, incessantly reciting Napolean's maxim that Italy, like a boot, should be entered only from the top. Eight hundred miles long, it was the most vertebrate of countries, with a mountainous spine and bony ribs. No consensus existed on what to do if the Germans fought for the entire peninsula [which they did], or whether this was a worthwhile battleground if Italy quit the war." Ibid., 181.

11. As Atkinson reminds us, it was not only military needs that required accounting since "invading armies under international law bore responsibility for the welfare of civilians. . . . Civil affairs authorities calculated that if Italy were to capitulate, the Allies would have another 19 million mouths to feed and bodies to warm south of Rome, requiring 38,000 tons of food and 160,000 tons of coal each month, a huge burden on Allied shipping." Ibid., 59.

12. Lt. Gen. Mark W. Clark commanded the Fifth Army and was the senior American field commander in Italy: "He would remain among the war's most controversial commanders, a man whose very name more than half a century later could cause brows to knit and lips to purse. If his admirers considered him 'clairvoyant and energetic,' in the phrase of General Juin, [the GI cartoonist Bill] Mauldin spoke for many in the lower ranks in observing of Clark: 'He had his limitations. But I think a lot of the

criticism of him occurred because he was associated with a bad time.'" Ibid., 587.

13. German forces attempted to sabotage anything and everything of value in Naples. As Atkinson reports, "Naples itself... had been mutilated ... Wehrmacht sappers had blown up the main aqueduct in seven places and drained municipal reservoirs. Dynamite dropped down manholes wrecked at least forty sewer lines. Explosives also demolished the long-distance telephone exchange, three-quarters of the city's bridges, and electrical generators and substations.... Saboteurs wrecked city trams, repair barns, and even street cleaners. A railroad tunnel into Naples was blocked by crashing two trains head-on.... Even the stairwells in barracks and apartment buildings were dynamited to make the upper floors inaccessible.... Worse yet was the sabotage around the great port.... Not a single vessel remained afloat in the port, a drowned forest of charred booms, masts, and funnels. Thirty major wrecks could be seen, and ten times that number lay submerged. All tugs and harbor craft had been sunk; all grain elevators and warehouses demolished; all three hundred cranes sabotaged or toppled into the water. Vessels had been scuttled at fifty-eight of sixty-one berths, often one atop another." The Allies had their hands full in restoring the city and the harbor to operating condition, and they did it quickly, but the vast damage slowed the supply of Allied forces considerably: "Wool clothing scheduled to arrive in mid-October was delayed until mid-November after ammunition took shipping priority. Shortages of tires, batteries, and spare parts immobilized three of every ten trucks, further hampering quartermasters trying to move materiel from port to battlefront." Ibid., 241–42, 265.

14. Julius A. Krug replaced Donald Nelson as head of the civilian War Production Board in September 1944.

15. Krug, *Production.*

16. Ibid.

17. "When war broke out," historian Richard Overy writes, "the United States was still a predominantly civilian economy, with a small apparatus of state, low taxes, and a military establishment that had only reached the foothills of re-equipment. America faced states that had been arming heavily for eight or nine years.... American leaders were conscious of how much there was to catch up. The giant plans approved by Roosevelt and Congress in the first weeks of war did not just result from America's great wealth of resources, but reflected a genuine fear of military inferiority. In four years these plans turned America from military weakling to military super-power. American industry provided almost two-thirds of

all the Allied military equipment produced during the war: 297,000 aircraft, 193,000 artillery pieces, 86,000 tanks, 2 million trucks. In four years American industrial production, already the world's largest, doubled in size. . . . Where every other major state took four or five years to develop a sizeable military economy, it took America a year. In 1942, long before her enemies had believed it possible, America already out produced the Axis states together." *Why the Allies Won*, 191–92.

18. There was also a presidential effort to collect scrap rubber: "As rubber supplies continued to dwindle [in 1942], the President decided on a scrap drive as a last alternative to rationing. On June 12 he appealed to the people to turn in 'old tires, old rubber raincoats, old garden hose, rubber shows, bathing caps, gloves—whatever you have that is made of rubber.' The petroleum industry managed the drive. Citizens deposited rubber at gasoline stations. . . . In less than four weeks, Americans donated 450,000 tons of scrap rubber in every form imaginable, some of which was mailed directly to the White House. One person sent in a pair of rubber boots which, he said, had been in the family since 1896." Polenberg, *War and Society*, 16.

19. Roosevelt's appointment of the Baruch Committee was forced by congressional passage of a bill that set up an independent rubber supply agency headed by a presidentially appointed czar, subject to Senate confirmation. Rationing gasoline as a way of saving rubber, an issue Roosevelt had little stomach to tackle because of its potential political costs, was firmly proposed by the Baruch Committee. "On the toughest political issue of 1942 the committee was unequivocal. . . . [T]he report exhorted the nation on gasoline rationing in order to conserve rubber. It recommended a speed limit of thirty-five miles per hour, reducing the average mileage per year from 6,700 to 5,000, and enforced rationing of gasoline on the nationwide basis. It assumed the role of national conscience, one that suited Baruch perfectly: 'Let there be no doubt that only actual needs, not fancied wants, can, or should, be satisfied. To dissipate our stocks of rubber is to destroy one of our chief weapons of war. We have no choice!' Roosevelt wasted little time in invoking rationing with the moral authority of the Baruch report. . . . Generally speaking, the report rallied the nation behind rationing, as it was supposed to do. Of course, not everyone liked it." Schwarz, *The Speculator*, 395.

20. Now Sri Lanka.

21. Originally, synthetic rubber was to be overwhelmingly produced from petroleum (over 81 percent), but farm interests in Congress, led by Senator Guy M. Gillette (D-IA), complained noisily. Gillette held hearings

and found no coherent reason why petroleum was preferred over grain alcohol, and so "Gillette charged that Standard [Oil Company] exercised its power in the industrial alcohol field to block the availability of alcohol for butadiene production [and] Subcommittee members argued that 'monopolistic' corporate forces influenced the government to protect their interests." After the Baruch report was released, Roosevelt appointed William M. Jeffers, president of the Union Pacific Railroad, as rubber director. And under his watch, the use of alcohol increased. In the end, "it was alcohol-based butadiene that saved the day for America's synthetic rubber program." In 1943 and 1944, around 80 percent of the synthetic rubber came to be based on alcohol-based butadiene. Koistinen, *Arsenal of World War II*, 156–57.

22. "Drinking [during World War II] soared at such a rate as to produce an unanticipated shortage [of alcohol]: When the whiskey people converted to making industrial alcohol, they thought that they had a five-year supply of whiskey on hand, but consumption rose from 140 million gallons in 1941 to 190 million gallons in 1942. Even though the British filled the returning Lend-Lease ships with scotch whiskey to reduce their unfavorable balance of trade, the shortage persisted. Cans of beer vanished, and bottled beer was sometimes hard to find." Carl J. Schneider and Dorothy Schneider, *World War II* (New York: Facts on File, 2003), 71.

23. In a review of the news in *Life* magazine, it was noted, "Last week Elmer Davis, chief of the Office of War Information, made his first 'review of the general situation.' It was an amazing document—original, simple and truthful. The people pricked up their ears. Nothing like this had come out of Washington since the war began. We are not winning the war yet, Mr. Davis said. . . . We are only ankle-deep in the war. 'We never have lost a war, but . . . We could lose this one.'" Aug. 17, 1942, 24.

24. LST stands for "landing ship, tank," but to sailors, according to Rick Atkinson, it actually meant "large slow target." Atkinson also notes, "The bigger LSTs, originally designed by the British, had caught the fancy of U.S. military logisticians who had seen flat bottoms used to good effect by rumrunners along the Gulf of Mexico in the 1920s. Eleven hundred LSTs would be built during the war, mostly in river yards across the American Midwest. The square bow, with fourteen-foot hinged doors, made the vessel slow and ungainly, and the lack of a keel caused it to roll even in drydock—or so the sailors claimed. But each one could haul twenty tanks." Atkinson, *Day of Battle*, 33, 59–60.

25. It should be noted that Anzio, as one scholar observes, "required massive reinforcement simply to avert total destruction of the isolated

beachhead; by March that reinforcement had made Anzio the fourth largest port in the world." Stoler, *Allies and Adversaries*, 171.

26. As Atkinson reports, "Heavy surf occasionally closed the landing beaches. . . . Enemy raids often disrupted port operations and harassed the cargo fleet. Of greater concern was the imminent return to Britain of most LSTs; as few as a dozen would be left in the Mediterranean after February 10, and at least seventy-two shiploads would be required in Anzio by mid-February. Daily materiel requirements had climbed from 1,500 tons a day to 2,300. Some LCIs [landing craft, infantry] sailing from Naples now carried a hundred tons of ammunition, triple the prudent load, and Navy brokers had begun identifying civilian schooners for use as cargo vessels." *The Day of Battle*, 379.

27. "At first an entire port battalion, the 488th, was sent to Anzio, where its men moved from ship to ship discharging cargo. The unit had a harrowing experience because of enemy aircraft, E-boats, and long-range artillery. Under almost constant harassment, the 488th managed to discharge an average of 1,498 long tons per day in 37 working days. Nevertheless, by 18 February 1944, fatigue, casualties, and illness had greatly lowered the battalion's efficiency. Aboard the ships the men often had no rations." Bykofsky and Larson, *Transportation Corps,* 210–11.

28. Leghorn is the Americanized name of Livorno, Italy.

29. "Early in the summer of 1943, the newly established top-level coordinating agency—the Office of War Mobilization (OWM)—requested each of the major procuring agencies to appoint a board of review to examine the composition of its requirement programs in terms of essentiality and balance and to make recommendations concerning the control and efficiency of procurement as a whole. . . . In general, the board found that the Army's supply operations were successful . . . [but on] the debit side, the board felt that the time had come for a much more adequate screening of requirements, especially for certain categories of supplies." Smith, *Army and Economic Mobilization*, 158–59.

9. The End in Europe

1. There is controversy concerning this view. On the one hand, as historian Richard M. Leighton noted in 1984, "It has become almost commonplace in American interpretations of World War II to say that at Tehran the British were forced to abandon their reservations concerning OVERLORD. Thus, it is asserted, the primacy of OVERLORD vis-à-vis the Mediterranean, and, indeed, its execution were finally assured. Like the classic query,

'When did you stop beating your wife?' this interpretation accepts as fact what is actually the nub of the issue, namely, the American allegation that the British, and Churchill in particular, had never intended to go through with OVERLORD and only resigned themselves to do so under Soviet pressure at Tehran." Leighton clearly thinks that this view does not fit the facts. See Leighton, "OVERLORD Versus the Mediterranean at the Cairo-Tehran Conferences," in *Command Decisions,* ed. Kent Roberts Greenfield, 282 (Washington, DC: United States Army Center of Military History, 1984). On the other hand, in a recent comprehensive study, Mark A. Stoler finds that the British continued to seek delays in OVERLORD in favor of further offensives in the Mediterranean area. As Stoler relates, "The prime minister [Churchill] used all his oratorical powers . . . but to no avail. Russia and the United States had reached a politico-military accord and now simply outvoted and overwhelmed the British, who for the first time in the war lost a strategy debate." *Allies and Adversaries,* 168. Richard Overy provides another recent account of British recalcitrance regarding OVERLORD: "In private, the British deplored the enterprise. Churchill cursed 'this bloody second front'; 'all this "Overlord" folly must be thrown "Overboard,"' wrote . . . the head of the British Foreign Ministry." *Why the Allies Won,* 142.

2. In fact, on the flight from Cairo to Tehran, President Roosevelt could see this for himself. As his official log-keeper noted, "From the air we sighted train loads and motor convoys loaded with U.S. Lend-Lease supplies, bound from the Persian Gulf port of Basra to Russia." Quoted in H. W. Brands, *Traitor to His Class: The Privileged Life and Radical Presidency of Franklin Delano Roosevelt* (New York: Doubleday, 2008), 546.

3. The decision to focus on defeating Germany first was actually made very early by army and navy planners—by 1940—precisely because they saw German military power as the more immediate and dire threat to U.S. security. See Louis Morton, "Germany First: The Basic Concept of Allied Strategy in World War II," in Greenfield, *Command Decisions*; and also Mark Skinner Watson, *Chief of Staff: Prewar Plans and Preparations* (Washington, DC: Historical Div., Dept. of the Army, 1950), 97–125.

4. In a recent study, Richard Overy disagrees and suggests that German pursuit of super weapons seriously handicapped their conventional military needs: "While German scientists pioneered the world's most advanced weapons—rockets, jets, atomic weapons—German forces lacked adequate quantities of the more humdrum petrol-driven equipment. . . . Billions of marks were spent on projects at the very frontiers of military science which brought almost no strategic advantage whatsoever." Overy refers to the "warped outlook of Germany's leaders, who persuaded themselves

as the war began to turn against them that German science could conjure up a new generation of fantastic weaponry that could reverse the war's course at a stroke. . . . At the outbreak of the war they were already at the very starting edge of the world of jets and missiles. When the war came they tried to speed the process of development up, to win the war with the weapons of the 1950s. The result was a technical disaster. . . . German forces got little in terms of performance from the new weapons." Overy, *Why the Allies Won,* 242–43.

    5. Eisenhower, *Eisenhower's Own Story,* 12.

    6. Ibid.

    7. Ibid.

    8. The problem of dock authorities' being in the dark about the contents of cargo ships started as soon as the buildup in Britain began. Supply authorities sought to rectify the problems in various ways and the situation improved in stages. Still, as one official history reports, "the European theater continued to be plagued until well into 1943 by delayed, inadequate, or missing data on inbound cargo." The issue created much frustration. For example, "In March [1943], the theater chief of transportation [in Britain] reported that five cargo ships had arrived without the slightest advance information from the United States. He therefore urged that 'dynamite' be placed under the persons responsible at the ports of Boston and New York." Bykofsky and Larson, *Transportation Corps,* 92.

    9. I was not able to locate this exact quote in Eisenhower's report, but what he does say is this: "Throughout the summer of 1944 they [the Mulberry and the beach supply system] represented an essential factor in the success of our operations. Without them our armies could not have been adequately maintained in the field, and the men who worked them with so much gallantry and devotion deserve the gratitude of liberated Europe for their share in our victory." Eisenhower, *Eisenhower's Own Story,* 55.

    10. Ibid., 53

    11. As Overy recounts, "It was subsequently decided to set up a second breakwater to reduce the tidal strain on the Mulberries. These were known as 'Gooseberries', and were to be made *in situ* from the hulks of old ships. The 55 merchant and naval vessels chosen for sacrifice were gathered together in Scottish ports and sailed to France on D-Day, where they were scuttled in five different places. In all some four hundred separate pieces made up the artificial anchorage. Together they weighed 1.5 million tons; ten thousand men were employed on D-Day towing them to France and building the harbours." *Why the Allies Won,* 147.

    12. Eisenhower, *Eisenhower's Own Story,* 12.

13. Eisenhower himself reports, "At the end of [July 1944] nearly 4,000 men, over 400 vehicles, and over 11,000 tons of supplies were disembarked within its [the Mulberry] shelter during a single period of 24 hours. Throughout the summer and autumn the achievements of the Mulberry exceeded our best hopes." Ibid., 55.

14. PLUTO stood for "pipe line under the ocean."

15. As Eisenhower noted, the PLUTO pipeline project "was second in daring only to the artificial harbors project." *Eisenhower's Own Story*, 56.

16. Ibid.

17. In Eisenhower's words: "The enemy . . . fully appreciated the importance to us of an early seizure of Cherbourg, and when his attempt to defend the city failed he undertook, with typical Teutonic thoroughness, the task of rendering the harbor unusable." Ibid., 56. As one of the official army histories puts it, "Planners had pinned their hopes on Cherbourg; it was the first major objective of the U.S. forces. Because it required an enormous amount of reconstruction, however, the port could not begin operations until 16 July, a full three weeks after its capture." Ruppenthal, *Logistical Support of the Armies*, 464.

18. These problems at the port of Cherbourg meant that much of the cargo unloaded there had to be off-loaded onto smaller ships offshore and then transferred to the port. As Bykofsky and Larson note, "Of the 429,660 long tons of Army cargo discharged at Cherbourg by 13 September, only 38.4 percent was unloaded directly at quayside or at special LST ramps. The remaining tonnage was carried ashore from ships at anchor by DUKW's, barges, and other craft." *Transportation Corps*, 314.

19. In his memoir of the war, Eisenhower writes, "To demolish the key bridges, freight yards, and main rail arteries of France would inevitably result in casualties among the French population . . . [and] some statisticians calculated that the plan would cost at least 80,000 French lives. The Prime Minister [Churchill] was genuinely shaken by the fearful picture presented to him by opponents of our idea, and his appeals to me were correspondingly urgent and appealing. My own air commanders and I challenged the accuracy of the statisticians' figures. . . . In the outcome the efficacy of this preparatory bombing was clearly proved. Moreover, not only were the civilian casualties a mere fraction of those originally estimated, but the French nation as a whole calmly accepted their necessity and developed no antagonisms toward the Allied forces as a result of them." Dwight D. Eisenhower, *Crusade in Europe* (New York: Doubleday, 1948), 232–33.

20. Marshal Gerd von Rundstedt in July 1942 was made Supreme German Commander in the West of Europe. His command was charged with fortifying and defending the coast against the expected Allied invasion.

21. Richard Overy notes the importance of Allied deception in keeping the German command off-balance and unsure as to whether the Normandy invasion was a simple feint or not: "The deception plan, codenamed 'Bodyguard', was drawn up in December 1943. . . . The core of the plot was to persuade the German leadership that the Allies intended to attack across the narrow neck of the English Channel, between Dover and Calais. . . . Credentials for an entire force, one million strong, christened First US Army Group (FUSAG) were fed, piece by piece, into the German intelligence system, where they lodged, until well past the real invasion, as actual fact." *Why the Allies Won,* 151.

22. Eisenhower, *Eisenhower's Own Story,* 59.

23. George Catlett Marshall, *General Marshall's Report: The Winning of the War in Europe and the Pacific, Biennial Report of the Chief of Staff of the United States Army, July 1, 1943 to June 30, 1945, to the Secretary of War* (New York: Simon and Schuster, 1945), 38.

24. The Red Ball Express was one of many different hastily improvised methods of motor transport. As one of the official army histories reports, "Throughout the period of pursuit [of German forces after the breakout from Normandy] motor transport, contrary to all expectations, bore the preponderant burden of supply movement over distances of up to 400 miles. By far the most lavishly publicized for this feat was the Red Ball Express. The campaign by which praise was heaped on the Red Ball driver in such public organs and in commendations from Headquarters . . . undoubtedly served a useful purpose, dramatizing the urgency of moving supplies forward and enhancing the morale of men performing a duty which was monotonous, devoid of glamour, and normally unpublicized. Although his later performance in the XYZ operation, the express service organized to support the final drive into Germany in the spring of 1945, far surpassed that of September 1944, it was for the latter that the Red Ball driver was to be remembered and even memorialized in song in a Broadway musical show entitled 'Call Me Mister.'" Ruppenthal, *Logistical Support of the Armies,* 571. It should also be noted that black troops provided the bulk of the drivers for the Red Ball Express: "The majority of the units were Negro companies. Approximately 73 percent of the truck companies in the Motor Transport Service in the European theater were Negro." Lee, *Employment of Negro Troops,* 633.

25. Randolph Leigh, *American Enterprise in Europe: The Role of the SOS in the Defeat of Germany* (1945; repr., Honolulu: Univ. Press of the Pacific, 2002), 67. Leigh was a lieutenant colonel in the Army Historical Section.

26. In the case of French railroad stock and equipment, U.S. bombing had caused more problems than did German demolition. As Ruppenthal notes, "Enemy destruction of rail lines . . . was not extensive, and rehabilitation was much simpler than expected. . . . Enemy-inflicted damage to equipment was also less than expected, and much rolling stock was captured and put to use. . . . Destruction by the Allied air forces [though] threatened to have a more disastrous effect on the enemy's operations. Beginning late in June supply and transportation officials repeatedly asked that railway bridges, tunnels, and viaducts, whose repair entailed large expenditures of effort, be spared in the hope that the enemy would not destroy them in retreat." *Logistical Support of the Armies*, 550.

27. Ruppenthal notes, "Lack of tools and equipment necessitated a high degree of improvisation. In the absence of a signal system, for example, flagging of trains during darkness was at first accomplished largely with flashlights, cigarette lighters, and even lighted cigarettes." Ibid., 547.

28. Leigh, *American Enterprise in Europe*, 71.

29. Eisenhower, *Eisenhower's Own Story*, 60.

30. In actuality there was little basis for believing that there were any production lags that would affect combat necessities. Patterson's views of any remaining production issues were seriously colored by the ongoing domestic battles relating to reconversion from wartime to peacetime production. As civilians in the War Production Board (led by the WPB head Donald Nelson) pressed for a staged transition away from war production beginning after the Normandy invasion, military officials organized to halt any such reconversion moves. There has been much written about this controversy, and the most exhaustive recent study has noted the following: "A War Department propaganda campaign against the approval of Nelson's [reconversion] program began in June 1944 and intensified in July. . . . For months Robert P. Patterson, and General Brehon B. Somervell, and others made headline news by charging that declining production was threatening the war effort and soldiers' lives, that labor was leaving munitions plants in droves or engaging in strikes, and that, lacking a sense of urgency, the general public was concentrating on peace, not war. . . . On the basis of the data available to him, Nelson realized that the military was misrepresenting the situation. There was no production crisis, workers were not fleeing war plants, and any lags in war production were either in the normal range or created by suddenly increased orders or design changes." Koistinen, *Arsenal of World War II*, 481.

31. Shipping became a key bottleneck contributing to supply problems at the front. As one official military history notes, "During most of the fall of 1944, shipping was the bottleneck. . . . [T]he War Department had cut down on shipping because of the theater's inability to unload. Ships were actually being returned from the ETO [European Theater of Operations] partially unloaded; by mid-November [1944] some 36,000 tons of supplies—the unloaded cargoes of some thirteen to fifteen vessels—were being set up for return to the United States." See Lida Mayo, *The Ordnance Department: On Beachhead and Battlefront* (Washington, DC: Office of the Chief of Military History, 1968), 301–05. For a succinct review of the battlefield supply issues covered here, see Alan J. Levine, *From the Normandy Beaches to the Baltic Sea: The Northwest Europe Campaign, 1944–45* (Westport, CT: Praeger, 2000), esp. 136ff.

32. Historian Stephen E. Ambrose, in his thorough biography of Eisenhower's years as supreme commander of the Allied forces in Europe, calls this period "A Dreary Autumn" and notes, "Since [the port of] Antwerp was not functioning until the end of November, supplies remained inadequate until early 1945. On his visits to the front Eisenhower heard a constant complaint from division commanders—they had neither enough ammunition nor riflemen. In reporting the ammunition shortage to Marshall, Eisenhower said he hoped production of it in the States could be increased, but pointed out that a part of the problem was that the War Department allowances to divisions in combat did not meet minimum requirements. . . . Marshall increased the allowance . . . [but the] shortage of riflemen was a more difficult problem." So, the production issue was but one problem among many (port space, unloading capacity, combat allowances from the War Department, and enough riflemen) that hampered Eisenhower's advance into Germany in late 1944 to early 1945. See Ambrose, *The Supreme Commander: The War Years of Dwight D. Eisenhower* (New York: Doubleday & Company, Inc., 1970), 539–40.

33. Again, the seeming crisis at the front was not one of production lags at home, at least not simply because of any rush to civilian, peacetime production as many in the military inferred. As Koistinen notes, even the "Chief of Ordnance Levin H. Campbell [had] reassured [WPB head Donald Nelson] . . . that any lags in war production were either in the normal range or created by suddenly increased orders or design changes." Koistinen also relates that it was in fact military officials who had trumpeted a very optimistic view as to an early end to the war in Europe: "Moreover, optimism about an impending end to the war came principally from top civilian and military heads of the armed services. Indeed, early in July 1944, General George C. Marshall had informed [Bernard] Baruch that the

Allies had Germany boxed in, and, a month later, Patterson predicted the nation's imminent collapse." After the war, "Nelson ruefully observed that the 'War department deliberately tried to make the people believe' that frontline shortages resulted from home front production failures, 'but the accusation was never once made directly.'" Koistinen, *Arsenal of World War II*, 481.

34. The Battle of the Bulge in the Ardennes.

35. Eisenhower, *Eisenhower's Own Story*, 99.

36. Ibid., 91.

37. Ibid., 102.

38. Ibid., 120.

39. Ibid., 102.

10. Concentration East

1. Unlike his navy counterpart Admiral Chester W. Nimitz, whose strategy involved a series of frontal assaults against seemingly every atoll ("Often those places which occasioned the worst slaughter were incredible small"), MacArthur pursued a strategy of envelopment which involved bypassing strongholds and thereby isolating and denying many enemy garrisons of the supplies necessary for survival. In this manner, MacArthur was thus able "to succeed with weaker strength, as was usually the position in which he found himself, and to succeed with the minimum loss." Calvocoressi and Wint, *Total War*, 776.

2. Koistinen reports, "Munitions production went from about 10 to 40 percent of total output during the period 1940 and 1943–1944. Manufacturing industries trebled their output during the period 1939–1944 [and] the United States in 1944 produced 50 percent more than either all its allies or all its enemies combined." Still, the massive wartime production expansion was "not ... exceptional" since all the warring nations stepped up their military production in similar fashion. It was simply a fact that the United States was easily the world's largest economy and produced in 1944 a proportion of the world's industrial output very close to its proportion before the war. *Arsenal of World War II*, 498.

3. Historian Melvyn P. Leffler in his study of postwar U.S. national security policy. See *A Preponderance of Power: National Security, the Truman Administration, and the Cold War* (Stanford, CA: Stanford Univ. Press, 1992).

4. Observers have noted the degree to which the Allies won because of their greater concern for supply and logistics. For example: "In Germany

and Japan much greater emphasis was placed on operations and combat than on organization and supply. Here were societies where military endeavor ranked as the highest social duty, where military elites dominated the waging of war. The best military brains were at the battlefront, not in the rear.... In both Germany and Japan less emphasis was placed upon the non-combat areas of war: procurement, logistics, military services." Overy, *Why the Allies Won,* 318, 319. See also Calvocoressi and Wint, *Total War,* 784–85.

 5. We must remember the degree of domestic acrimony between the civilian and military officials during this latter period of the war. Donald Nelson, head of the civilian War Production Board (WPB), was forced out in August 1944, replaced by Julius A. Krug, a former WPB official then serving as a lieutenant commander in the navy, who proved acceptable to the top military officials, including Patterson, and who knew that his job depended upon his getting along with his military counterparts. Still, Krug found it necessary to complain to the director of the Office of War Mobilization and Reconversion in May 1945 about the continuing very large military production program: "We suspect also that considerable duplication exists among the procurement plans of the several services. It appears that the Air, Naval, and Army Ground Forces are each developing production plans for winning the war practically single-handed. ... The Navy and Army aircraft programs when taken together seem extremely large for the Japanese war considering the air power used in liquidating the Germans." USCPA, *Industrial Mobilization for War,* 902. For Patterson's good working relationship with Krug, see Eiler, *Mobilizing America,* 412–13.

 6. The abrupt end of the war created serious problems concerning redeployment of servicemen. The army had most of its men in the wrong places. Low-point soldiers from Europe had been transferred home for a one-month leave before their departure for the expected invasion of Japan. Once Japan surrendered, it became extremely difficult to send them back overseas. Meanwhile, the high-point soldiers expecting their tours to be up soon remained stuck in Europe on temporary occupation duty and awaiting available shipping for transport home. Soldiers on leave in the United States grumbled about having to leave again now that the war was over, while soldiers in Europe and in the Pacific complained mightily and seemed on the verge of mutiny. See Waddell, *Toward the National Security State,* 117.

 7. The official history for the Army's Transportation Corps affirms that for the Pacific, "[d]istances were enormous. San Francisco, the main port of embarkation supporting the Southwest pacific, is 6,193 nautical miles

from Brisbane, 5,800 from Milne Bay, 6,299 from Manila. . . . The long turn-around, coupled with the frequent retention of vessels for local service, severely taxed the limited available shipping." Bykofsky and Larson, *Transportation Corps,* 429.

8. As one of the official histories notes, at the Quadrant Conference British and U.S. officials came to see Burma as key to keeping China in the war, and this in turn was key to the eventual defeat of Japan: "At this gathering the Combined Chiefs of Staff planners were able for the first time to submit a combined plan for the defeat of Japan. The planners believed that China offered the best potentialities for bombing Japan, for attacking Japanese communications to the South Seas, and for mounting an invasion of Japan." Charles F. Romanus and Riley Sunderland, *Stillwell's Mission to China* (Washington, DC: Office of the Chief of Military History, U.S. Army, 1953), 357.

9. Known by his troops as "Vinegar Joe," Stilwell became "a new figure in contemporary American legend" in 1942. When his headquarters in northern Burma was about to be overrun by fast-moving Japanese forces, he spurned the C-47 transport aircraft sent to retrieve him. Instead, after sending away as many of his own officers and headquarters staff as the plane would hold and telling the pilots "he preferred to walk," he led a small group of military personnel and civilians through 140 miles of jungles and mountains to India, with Japanese forces in hot pursuit. Romanus and Sunderland, *Stillwell's Mission to China,* 143; Donovan Webster, *The Burma Road: The Epic Story of the China-Burma-India Theater in World War II* (New York: Harper Perennial, 2004), 14. The classic biography of Stilwell is Barbara Tuchman, *Stilwell and the American Experience in China* (New York: Bantam, 1984).

10. One historian notes that "for every Allied combat casualty in the war's China-Burma-India theater of operations, fourteen more soldiers would be evacuated sick or dead from malaria, dysentery, cholera, infections, jungle rot, and a previously unknown infection called brush typhus." Webster, *Burma Road,* 5.

11. Our Chinese allies had little appreciation for the logistical obstacles that faced the United States in supplying them: "Dealing with Chinese officials was extremely difficult . . . because of their utter disregard for logistics. They had no idea of the capabilities of sea and air transport, and they made extravagant demands which they wanted fulfilled immediately. Their pet strategic cure-all was air power, and they were unmoved by the fact that their transport system would not support a tenth of the aircraft they wanted to have in China." Romanus and Sunderland, *Stillwell's Mission to China,* 83.

12. "For two and a half years the only contact China had with America and the Allied world was the fantastic airline that crossed the Hump—the spurs of the Himalayas. . . . Loads carried over the Hump began at the rate of 80 tons a month in the spring of 1942; at the end of the war they were moving at the rate of 80,000 tons a month. In the process the Hump drove men mad, killed them, sent them back to America wasted with tropical fevers and broken for the rest of their lives. Some of the boys called it the Skyway to Hell; it was certainly the most dangerous, terrifying, barbarous aerial transport run in the world." Theodore H. White and Annalee Jacoby, *Thunder Out of China* (1945; repr., Cambridge, MA: Da Capo Press, 1980), 154.

13. As one official army history underscores, Wingate understood that Japanese superiority lay in being able to move much more quickly than Allied forces through jungle areas. He proposed to trump their maneuverability: "Wingate sought to form units stripped of all purely formal equipment, organized into small columns with a base of fire and a maneuvering element and supplied entirely by air. Such units in the jungle would have the mobility of ships at sea, and road blocks would hold no terror for them. Indeed they could attack Japanese lines of communications at will." Romanus and Sunderland, *Stilwell's Mission to China,* 303.

14. As a recent history of the Marauders observes, "The Marauders were the first American infantry force to go into action on the Asian mainland. Their elite status, the nature of their operations behind enemy lines, and their record of victories made headlines back in the United States. In three and a half months of combat, the Marauders materially aided the advance of Stilwell's Chinese divisions into northern Burma. In a daring mission the Marauders captured the vital airstrip at Myitkyina, the goal of Stilwell's campaign, after a march of 100 miles over some of the worst terrain in the world." Edward Young, *Merrill's Marauders* (New York: Osprey Publishing, 2009), 5.

15. The quotation is from Marshall's "Biennial Report of the Chief of Staff of the United States Army: July 1, 1943, to June 30, 1945, to the Secretary of War" (1946, 59–60), which is quoted extensively in Forrest C. Pogue, *George C. Marshall: Statesman, 1945–1959* (New York: Penguin, 1987), 52.

16. According to Richard Overy, "Once the United States brought the weight of its new technology [in weaponry] to bear in the Pacific war the contest became very one-sided. On the ground, in the air, and at sea America enjoyed a wide lead in both quality and quantity. Japanese industry provided obsolescent material in substantial quantities until the blockade began to bite in 1944, but it suffered exceptional levels of attrition, leaving

Japanese forces short of air cover, naval equipment and fuel." Overy, *Why the Allies Won*, 222.

17. One massive study of World War II finds that the successful attack on Kwajalein was because of the lessons learned in the bloody fighting for Tarawa, in which the Marines suffered thirteen hundred dead and two thousand wounded. Taking Tarawa in the Gilbert Islands was necessary to provide a base of operations for attacking Japanese forces in the Marshall Islands (which included Kwajalein). But "much more important [than acquiring this base of operations] were the technical lessons about equipment, tactics, angle of naval fire, and the needed length and nature of bombardment learned in [Tarawa]." Gerhard L. Weinberg, *A World at Arms: A Global History of World War II* (New York: Cambridge Univ. Press, 1994), 648.

18. One study observes, "These were . . . considerable victories, made possible only by mobilization of resources, and their concentration upon tiny islands, which were possibly unique in military history. A feature of all these operations was the disparity of the losses. The Americans should in theory, being attackers, have suffered at least three to one more heavily than the Japanese. But in all three operations [Saipan, Tinian, and Guam], the American dead numbered just over 5,000, while the Japanese lost 42,000." Calvocoressi and Wint, *Total War*, 839.

19. The quotation is from General Marshall's report: *The Winning of the War in Europe and the Pacific*, vol. 3, 62.

20. These are issues covered extensively in the previous chapter.

21. Formosa is now Taiwan.

22. The Japanese had set a trap for MacArthur's forces. "If they had succeeded in their plan, [they] would have achieved a second Pearl Harbor, this time destroying the American army in Asia as formerly they had annihilated the American Asian fleet." They sent a decoy fleet designed to draw Admiral Halsey's main naval forces away from protecting MacArthur's transport fleet of men and materiel. The ploy worked and a larger Japanese fleet moved in to destroy the army transports but came up against a small American naval force left behind to provide some minimal security. This force, ironically made up of battleships sunk by the Japanese at Pearl Harbor that had been "dredged up from the mud of the sea bed" there, effectively destroyed one part of the Japanese attackers. And while a larger part of the attacking Japanese fleet made it through to make contact with the American transports, "the Japanese Admiral did not bombard but sailed away inexplicably." This action at Leyte essentially meant "the death of the [Japanese] navy." Calvocoressi and Wint, *Total War*, 840, 843.

23. For a recent work that focuses on the phenomenon of kamikaze attacks, see Robin L Riely, *Kamikaze Attacks of World War II: A Complete History of Japanese Suicide Strikes on American Ships, by Aircraft and Other Means* (Jefferson, NC: McFarland & Company, 2010).

24. Calvocoressi and Wint report, "By March 1945 Japan had lost 88 per cent of the merchant fleet with which it had begun the war, and it had become almost impossible to import any goods, even the most essential." *Total War*, 858

25. *The United States Strategic Bombing Surveys (European War) (Pacific War)* (1945, 1946; repr., Maxwell Air Force Base, AL: Air Univ. Press, 1987), 82.

26. A recent book cites a Joint Chiefs of Staff study that forecast "half a million lives American lives and many times that wounded" in an invasion of the Japanese home islands. D. M. Giangreco, *Hell to Pay: Operation Downfall and the Invasion of Japan, 1945–1947* (Annapolis, MD: Naval Institute Press, 2009), 188.

27. Gianfranco would at least somewhat disagree with this statement. His recent book argues strongly that Japan retained a great deal of arms and forces to resist any U.S. invasion, although Patterson speaks here of "Japan's capacity for continuing the war," which may refer to Japan's ability to project force outside of its island mainland. Still, Giangreco's very point about Japan's capabilities underlines Patterson's argument about the need to maintain a focus on war production at home. Ibid.

28. *United States Strategic Bombing Surveys*, 107.

29. A recent book examines the role of Patterson's direct superior, Secretary of War Henry Stimson, in the dropping of the atomic bomb: Sean L. Malloy, *Atomic Tragedy: Henry L. Stimson and the Decision to Use the Bomb Against Japan* (Ithaca, NY: Cornell Univ. Press, 2008). See also Michael D. Gordin, *Five Days in August: How World War II Became a Nuclear War* (Princeton, NJ: Princeton Univ. Press, 2007); and Gar Alperovitz, *The Decision to Use the Atomic Bomb* (New York: Vintage, 1996). For a review of sources on the controversy over the use of the atom bomb, see J. Samuel Walker, "The Decision to Use the Bomb: A Historiographical Update," in *Hiroshima in History and Memory*, ed. Michael J. Hogan (New York: Cambridge Univ. Press, 1996), 11–37.

30. For reviews of the strategic bombing campaign against Japan, see Sherry, *Rise of American Air Power*, 166–73; Overy, *Why the Allies Won*, ch. 4, "The Means of Victory: Bombers and Bombing"; and David MacIsaac, *Strategic Bombing in World War Two: The Story of the United States Strategic Bombing Survey* (New York: Garland Publishing, 1976).

Epilogue

1. This epilogue contains Patterson's recommendations for the future, rather than a review of the issues related to the war just ended. In this sense, it encapsulates his thinking of how the United States needed to institutionalize many of the wartime developments relating to war preparation. It thus is much more of a Cold War document than the rest of the manuscript, given its explicit focus on urging permanent military preparation for what Patterson sees as a now more dangerous world. For the turn to Cold War and the rise of the National Security State, see Waddell, *Toward the National Security State,* ch. 5, "The Postwar Synthesis: Building the National Security State"; Hogan, *A Cross of Iron*; Leffler, *Preponderance of Power*; Daniel Yergin, *Shattered Peace: The Origins of the Cold War and the National Security State* (Boston: Houghton Mifflin, 1977); Aaron L. Friedberg, *In the Shadow of the Garrison State: America's Anti-Statism and the Cold War Grand Strategy* (Princeton, NJ: Princeton Univ. Press, 2000); the essays in *The End of the Cold War: Its Meaning and Implications,* ed. Michael J. Hogan (New York: Cambridge Univ. Press, 1992); and Paul A. C. Koistinen, *State of War: The Political Economy of American Warfare, 1945–2011* (Lawrence: Univ. Press of Kansas, 2012).

2. "The United States," notes James William Gibson, "emerged from [World War II] as the only true victor, by far the greatest power in world history." Considering the devastation that even America's allies suffered, Gibson concludes that "the United States won World War II and everybody else lost." *The Perfect War: Technowar in Vietnam* (New York: Atlantic Monthly Press, 1986), 12.

3. As Koistinen elucidates, the production increases were massive: "In November 1943, the nation produced over $5 billion in munitions . . . a level exceeding all future weapons needs. War production . . . went from $3.6 billion in the last half of 1940 to $93.4 billion in 1944. Output for war increased fivefold between 1940 and 1941, over threefold between 1941 and 1942, more than half between 1942 and 1943, and over 8 percent between 1943 and 1944. Where America was devoting around 3.6 percent of its GNP to defense and war in 1940, by 1943–1944 that figure had jumped to just short of 45 percent. . . . In 1943 and 1944 alone, the nation accounted for around 40 percent of the world's munitions output. With Allied output totaling another 31 percent, the United States and its allies far exceeded the logistic strength of their enemies." *Arsenal of World War II,* 342.

4. Patterson refers here to what one scholar has called "World War II's Battle of the Potomac." See Gregory Hooks, *Forging the Military-Industrial*

Complex: World War II's Battle of the Potomac (Urbana: Univ. of Illinois Press, 1991). Besides competition between and within the services, civilians and military representatives became embroiled in a number of controversies before and during the war, including fights over control of procurement and priority power, the feasibility of military requirements, material control and production scheduling, and finally reconversion policies. For a review of these controversies, see Waddell, *Toward the National Security State*, ch. 2, "Civil-Military Battles Over Domestic Mobilization."

5. Patterson, as assistant secretary of war, would have been well aware of the problems of internal coordination of fragmented army supply bureaus (the Supply Arms and Services), and would, in attempting to coordinate army procurement with navy procurement, be aware of how the navy bureaus were even more independent and competitive with one another in terms of procurement and supply. Patterson and his navy counterpart, James Forrestal, were able to bring an admirable degree of coordination within their respective domains and between the army and navy through their sponsorship of a stronger Army-Navy Munitions Board. See Waddell, *War Against the New Deal*, 99–104.

6. Albert Einstein's theoretical work was critical in the development of the atom bomb. When he signed a letter in 1939 that was sent to President Roosevelt urging that the atom bomb be developed, his reasons had everything to do with fears that Hitler's Germany was developing a bomb. Einstein later wrote that "I made one great mistake in my life ... when I signed the letter to President Roosevelt recommending that atom bombs be made; but there was some justification—the danger that the Germans would make them." Silvan S. Schweber, *Einstein and Oppenheimer: The Meaning of Genius* (Cambridge, MA: Harvard Univ. Press, 2010), 60. See also Stuart W. Leslie, *The Cold War and American Science: The Military-Industrial Complex at MIT and Stanford* (New York: Columbia Univ. Press, 1993).

7. Vannevar Bush, *Science: The Endless Frontier, A Report to the President by Vannevar Bush, Director of the Office of Scientific Research and Development* (Washington, DC: Government Printing Office, 1945), section titled "The Importance of Basic Research," 18.

8. Ibid., 18–19.

9. As Bush himself wrote years after the war: "There are two aspects of postwar organization which have since proved to be of great importance. First is the mechanism by which government has supported research in industry and the universities; second is the form of relationship within the Department of Defense between military men and civilians,

and between the armed services, on the development of weapons. After the war ended we might well have gotten ourselves into a serious tangle on this whole matter of government subsidy of research. . . . As we look back I believe we can take pride in the fact that we escaped all these dangers to a truly remarkable extent over the years. And the fact that the momentum of the application of science as the war ended was not lost has had as much to do with our present national strength, in an industrial and military sense." Bush also reports that "[t]he whole program started when President Roosevelt toward the end of the war called on O.S.R.D. [the Office of Scientific Research and Development] for a report and recommendation on postwar science. It was soon possible to gather together committees on various aspects of the problem, for the men who could contribute were already working together. It did not take five years to come to conclusions, as it sometimes does on such matters; it took only a few months, for there was an extraordinary consensus of opinion. The result was entitled *Science: the Endless Frontier.* It called for heavy federal support of the scientific effort in the postwar scene." Bush, *Pieces of the Action* (New York: William Morrow, 1970), 63–64.

10. Bush, *Science,* 33.

11. Ibid., 34.

12. War Department Committee on Scientific Personnel, Feb. 6, 1948. Included in Herbert Hoover, *The Hoover Commission Report on Organization of the Executive Branch of Government (1947–1949)* (Westport, CT: Greenwood Press, 1949).

13. Ibid.

14. Ibid.

15. This situation—the distance Patterson sees between the military and scientists—changed dramatically in the postwar years. As a key observer of the changes perceived in 1960, "The new tasks of the military require that the professional officer develop more and more of the skills and orientations common to civilian administrators and civilian leaders. The narrowing difference in skill between military and civilian society is an outgrowth of the increasing concentration of technical specialists in the military. . . . In fact, the concentration of personnel with 'purely' military occupational specialties has fallen from 93.2 per cent in the Civil War to 28.8 per cent in the post-Korean Army, and to even lower percentages in the Navy and Air Force." And as "the military establishment becomes progressively dependent on more complex technology, the importance of the military manager increases. He does not displace the heroic leader, but he undermines the long-standing traditionalism of the military estab-

lishment, and weakens its opposition to technical innovation. With the growth of the military manager, technological innovation becomes reutilized." Morris Janowitz, *The Professional Soldier: A Social and Political Portrait* (New York: The Free Press, 1960), 9, 22.

16. Vannevar Bush wrote of another side to this issue in his memoirs: "I have written that a military organization must be tightly formed and controlled in order to fight well. But this carries a great disadvantage when it comes to a question such as this one [regarding differences between the Joint Chiefs of Staff and top scientists over the use of the newly developed proximity fuses]. Only officers of relatively junior grade have the technical background, the time, the interest, fully to understand a radically new departure in weapons and methods. The top brass does not. It does not have time to listen and learn. Yet the top brass makes the decisions, and junior officers cannot protest." *Pieces of the Action,* 110.

17. This reference to the National Security Act of 1947 helps date this chapter. President Truman signed the bill on July 26 of that year, and Patterson's remark here, not to mention the content of the manuscript itself, heavily suggests that it was the controversies over this transformational piece of legislation that prompted Patterson to reflect so seriously upon his wartime experiences.

18. Navy leaders, led by Secretary of the Navy James Forrestal (who would go on to become the nation's first secretary of defense), feared that naval aviation would get folded into the soon-to-be independent air force and that the marines would be folded into the army under the army's unification plans. Naval leaders also worried that their status as the nation's first line of defense and offense (and with this status, large and steady budgets) would be appropriated by the new, dashing air force. See Waddell, *Toward the National Security State,* 124–34.

19. The law proved to be even more significant than Patterson thought. As historian Douglas T. Stuart contends, the National Security Act of 1947 "is arguably the second most important piece of legislation in modern American history—surpassed only by the 1964 Civil Rights Act." *Creating the National Security State,* 1.

Index

Page numbers in **boldface** refer to illustrations.

ABC (American-British Conversations) War Plans, 67–70, 253n2, 253n4
Air Coordinating Committee, 64–65
Air Scheduling Unit, 51, 250–51n17
Air Transport Command, 61, 62, 78, 103
aircraft orders and manufacture, 16, 23, 28, 34, 39, 40–65, 79
aircraft, delivery of, 58–59
Alaska, 143, 150–59, 274n12, 277–78n18
ALCAN (Alaska-Canadian) highway, 151–54, 157, 274–75n13, 276n15
alcohol, 81, 172–74, 257–57n21, 283–84nn22–23
alien property, 75, 254–55n12
aluminum, 79, 80
American-British-Dutch-Australian Command, 272n6
ammunition needs, 177–78, 192, 197–99, 200, 210, 291n32
Antwerp, 195–96, 291n32
Anzio, 175–77, 284–85n25, 285n27
Army, U.S., 45, 86, 101, 126, 217
Army Air Forces, 45, 48, 51, 54, 86, 101, 102–3, 199

Army Corps of Engineers, 104–5, 152, 280n7
Army Industrial College, 5, 6
Army Medical Department, 149–50
Army-Navy Munitions Board, 5, 73, 103, 254n7
Army-Navy Petroleum Board, 103
Army-Navy Selective Service Commission, 103
army-navy tensions, 103–4, 165
army reorganization (March 1942), xxxvii–viii, 101–3
Army Service Forces, xxxviii, 89, 102, 106, 125, 126, 127, 132, 167, 209
Arnold, Gen. Henry H. ("Hap"), xli, 45, 53, 54, 57, 61, 65, 96, 153, 249n8, 275n14
arsenals, government, 13, 18, 37, 49, 109, 111, 116
"Arsenal of Democracy", 40, 41, 67, 90, 170
Ascension Island, 58, 254n7
Atabrine, 149–50, 170, 274n11
atomic bomb, xiii, xli, 54, 65, 165, 205–6, 213–14, 219, 297n29, 299n6
Attu, Alaska, 150, 158
Austin-Wadsworth (national service) Act, 108–9, 116, 264n19
Austrailia, 96, 145, 273n9

auto industry, xxxvi, 34, 40–41, 48, 49, 85, 237n20, 245–46n33, 246–47n35
aviation gasoline, 81–82, 170–73

B-10, 45, 249n6
B-17 ("Flying Fortress"), 44, 45, 47, 51, 52, 55, 249n7
B-24 ("Liberator"), 173
B-29 ("Superfortress"), 44, 52, 53, 100, 150, 213, 251n20
B-36 ("Peacemaker"), 55, 251–52n23
Baker Board, 45, 249n5
ball bearings and rollers, 175
Baruch, Bernard M., 4, 9–10, 81, 113, 172, 216, 234–35n12, 236n19, 239n6, 283n19, 291n33
Baruch Committee, 172, 283n19
Bataan, 96, 146, 149, 273n7
Battle of the Bulge, 122, 199–201
bazooka, 130–31, 170, 299n9, 301n16
Bell Aircraft Company, 54
Black troops, 147, 156, 273n9, 289n24
Black workers, 117, 266n29, 275n14
Bliss, Gen. Tasker H., 3, 234n8
Board of Economic Warfare, 74, 78, 256n17
Boeing Aircraft Company, 53, 54
Bradley, Gen. Omar N., 191, 198
British Air Commission, 38
British military orders, importance of, xxxvi, 13, 19–21, 38, 40
Buckner, Emory, xiv
Burma, 207–9, 294n8
Burma Road, 63, 197, 207–8
Bush, Vannevar, 166, 219–20, 299n9
business-military relations, 2, 6–7, 25–26, 34–35, 226, 262n9, 263n12

C-47 "Flying Boxcar", 62
Cairo Conference, 181–82, 285–86n1
Campbell, Lt. Gen. Levin H., 90, 291n33
Canol Project, 154–59, 161, 275–76n15, 276–77n17
cantonments, 84, 104, 259n25
Casablanca, 131, 133, 269n11, 271n17
Casablanca conference, 56, 63, 127, 133, 166
Chaney, Maj. Gen. James, 67, 253n1
chemical industry, 174
Cherbourg, 183, 184, 188, 194, 195, 288n18
child labor, use of, 118
China, 38, 62–63, 64, 207, 294n11, 295n12
Churchill, Winston, 19, 55, 69, 89, 123, 124, 188, 288n19; Operation TORCH, 132, 267n3; quoted, 95, 255n14, 261n5, 286n1; and Roosevelt, xxi, 63, 65, 158, 279n1, 281n10; Teheran Conference, 86–87
Civil Aeronautics Authority, 151
Civil Air Patrol, 60
civilian production, xxxvi, xxxix, 33, 35, 36, 41, 79, 86
civil-military relations, xxvii, xxxii, xxxiii, 98–99, 225, 232n24, 240–41n13
Clark, Gen. Mark, 167, 168, 281n12
Clark, Grenville, xiii, xxviii, xxix, xxx, 264n18
Cochrane, Col. Philip C., 208
Combined Chiefs of Staff, 55, 56, 62–63, 129, 132, 164, 168
Committee for Congested Production Areas, xxvi
Compton, Dr. Karl T., 172

Conant, Dr. James B., 172
Connally, Maj. Gen. Donald W., 160
Consolidated Company, 54, 55
Controlled Materials Plan, 83–84, 258–59n24
contracting problems. See military procurement issues
conversion to war, 8–10, 33–36, 72, 75, 76, 242nn19–20, 246n34
copper, 80, 110, 236–37n20
Coral Sea, 123
cost-plus-fixed-fee contracts, xxxvi, 23, 106
critical materials, stockpiling, 13, 77–78, 79, 254n8
Crowell, Bendict, 4, 235n12
Cunningham, Adm. Andrew, 124
Curtiss-Wright Corporation, 53

Davis, Elmer, 174, 284n23
Darlan, Adm. Jean, 131, 261n6
Defense Plant Corporation, 27, 243n23
de Gaulle, Gen. Charles, 261n6
Demobilization of the Aircraft Industry Subcommittee, 64–65
Devers, Maj. Gen. Jacob L., 166
DeWitt, Maj. Gen. J.L., 152
DUKWs ("Ducks"), 131, 165, 184, 187, 188, 270n15, 280nn6–7, 288n18
Dunkirk, 19, 20
Dutch Harbor, Alaska, 158, 274n12, 277–78n18

educational orders, 13, 18, 238n24
Eglin Field, 53
Eight Air Force, 55, 56, 57
Eisenhower, Dwight D., xliv, xlv, 6, 4, 48, 71, 127, 129, 169; appointment as Supreme Allied Commander, 124; Operation HUSKY, 166–67, 176; Operation OVERLORD, 164–65, 183, 188, 192, 196 197, 198, 288n19; Operation TORCH, 123, 131, 132, 164; quoted, 4, 131, 165, 183, 196
El Alamein, xxii, 89, 91
electric power, expansions of, 174
escort vessels, 130, 132

facilities expansions, industrial, 76, 77, 94–95, 260n3
feasibility issues, 92–94, 259n1, 260nn3–4
Flying Tigers, 63
Forrestal, James, xxvii, xli-xlii, 231n16, 249–50n12, 301n17
France, 21, 37–38, 55, 62, 96, 197
Frankfurter, Felix, xii, xxviii, xxix, xxx, 264n17
Freeman, Adm. Charles S., 152

Garand rifle, 18, 121
gasoline, 93, 186–87, 258n22
Germany, 2, 10–11, 56, 60, 69, 87, 96; Allied strategy towards, 68–70, 74–75, 182–83, 267n1, 281n10, 286n3; bombing of, 44, 54–58, 60, 81–82, 86, 190; military successes, 16, 19; rearmament, 1–2, 11, 73; super weapons, 60–61, 183, 190, 286n4
Gerow, Maj. L.T., 96
Glenn L. Martin Company, 54
Great Britain, 19, 20–21, 37–38, 39–40, 68, 85; controversies over aid to, 20–21, 240–41n13, 241n15
Greenland, 85, 95
Guadalcanal, 156, 210
Guam, 210, 296n18

Halsey, Adm. William, Jr., 211
Henderson, Leon, xxxvi, 85
Hershey, Gen. Lewis, 263n16
Higashikuni, Prince Naruhiko, 54, 251n21
Hillman, Sidney, 100, 241n16, 245n31
Hiroshima, 205, 206, 213–14
Hitler, Adolf, 1, 8, 11, 60, 67, 73, 132
Hopkins, Harry, 123, 153
Hoover, Herbert, xxviii, xxx, 229n2
Hoshina, Adm. Zenishiro, 171
Hull, Cordell, 46, 96
"Hump", the Himalayan, 62, 207, 295n12

Ickes, Harold, 85, 154
I.G. Farben, 74, 75
Italy, 68, 69, 163, 279n1, 281n10; invasion of, 166–69, 175–77, 182
incendiary attacks, 54, 251n21
industrial accidents, numbers, 112
industrial mobilization issues, xxxi, xxxv, xxxviii, 1–2, 5–11, 17, 82, 94, 99; postwar issues, 217–27
industrial mobilization plans, 5, 7, 17, 73, 98, 101, 216, 236n17

Japan, 1, 46, 53, 69, 85, 143, 150, 271nn1–2, 297n27; Allied strategy towards, 54, 69–70, 75, 181–83, 205, 267n1, 281n9, 294n8, 295n16, 296nn17–18; and atom bomb, 54, 214; bombing of, 52–54, 212, 213–14; invasion planning, 205–6, 210–14, 297n27; military successes of, 2, 38, 81, 95, 96, 123, 272n4, 274n10;
Japanese military forces, 38, 47, 63, 81
Jean Bart, 133, 270n16

Jeffers, William, 172, 284n21
Johnson, Louis A., xxx, 12, 237n22, 238n24
Joint Aircraft Committee, 38, 51, 250–51nn16–17
Joint Chiefs of Staff, 69, 95, 96, 103, 125, 158, 159, 167, 172
Jones, Jesse, 27, 243n23

Kamikaze attacks, 212
King, Adm. Ernest, 123, 129, 155, 248–49n4, 267n1, 281n9
Kiska, Alaska, 154, 158
Knox, Frank, xxx, 231n16, 253n5
Knudsen, William S., 17, 33, 64, 80, **136**, **137**, **141**, 239n7, 243n23; quoted, 27, 49, 245n31; role in production expansions, 49, 71, 77, 100, 245–46nn33–34, 255–56n16
Kodiak Island, Alaska, 152, 277–78n18
Krug, J.A., 70, 91, 170, 282n14, 293n5
Kwajalein, 209, 296n17

labor casualties, 112, 265nn21–22
labor hoarding, 106–7, 109
Labor-Management Committees, 111
labor migration, 119
labor relations, 32–33, 114, 245n32, 264n19
labor strikes, 112, 114, 115
labor supply and shortages, 32, 106–110, 115–19
LaGuardia, Fiorella H., 151
landing craft, 17, 95, 123, 131, 164–66, 176, 182, 202, 279n4
Laval, Pierre, 96
LCMs (Landing Craft, Mechanized), 202

LCVPs (Landing Craft, Vehicles and Personnel), 202
Leghorn, Italy, 177, 285n28
Leigh, Lt. Col. Randolph, 193, 194
Lend-Lease, 38, 40, 59, 68, 275n14, 278n19, 284n22, 286n2
Leyte, 211–12, 296n22
Liberty ships, 58, 148, 188
Lockheed Aircraft Corporation, 53, 58
logistics, 143
Lovett, Robert A., 46, 48, 53, 249–50nn10–12, 250n14
LSTs (Landing Ship, Tank), 176, 284n24, 288n18
Luftwaffe, 56, 187, 237n21
lumber, 104–5
Lutes, Lt. Gen. Leroy, 89, 90, 126

M-Day Plan, 17, 240n8
MacArthur, Gen. Douglas, 45, 96, **141**, 146, 199, 205, 210–11, 248n4, 272n4, 292n1, 296n22
machine guns, 181
machine tools, 49, 50
Manhattan Project, 165, 266n26
Marseilles, 197
material shortages, 75, 79, 83, 106, 150, 178
Marshall, Gen. George C., xxvi, xxvii, 46, 87, 96,127, 155, 164, 196, 267n4, 292n33; ammunition shortages, 198, 291n32; army reorganization, xxxvii-viii, 101; on basic strategy, 55, 123, 166, 267n1, 281n9; controversy on supplying the British, 240n13; quoted, 209, 210
McCarthy, Joseph, xv
McGrady, Edward F., 113, 265n23, 266n25

McNair, Lt. Gen. Leslie J., 84
McNutt, Paul V., 263n16
Merrill, Maj. Gen. Frank D. ("Merrill's Marauders"), 208, 295n14
Messerschmitt Me 262, 60, 61
Midway, 123, 158
military-industrial complex, xliv
military procurement, organization of, 28–30, 232n23
military procurement issues, 22–25, 35–37, 41–42, 70–71, 101–4, 234n10, 247n41, 258n23, 262n10
Military Railways Service, 193–94
military unification, 103, 105, 226
Mitchell, Gen. William ("Billy"), 44, 150, 248n2, 248n4
modification centers, 52, 57, 251n18
Montbatten, Adm. Lord Louis, 207
Montgomery, Gen. Bernard L., 90
Montgomery, Virginia Patterson, xviii, xxii
Morgenthau, Henry, Jr., 16
Morgenthau, Robert M., xxi
Munitions Board, xliii, 226
Mulberry docks, 185–86, 287n9, 287n11
munitions industry, Patterson's arguments against, 36–37
Murray, Philip, 111

Naples, 167–69, 282n13
National Defense Act of 1920, xxxi, xxxvii, 5, 235n12, 237n22
National Defense Advisory Commission, 17, 98–100
National Guard, xxxii, 1
National Security Act of 1947, xx, xxvii, xli, xliii, 301n17, 301n19
National Security Resources Board, xlii, 226

National Service legislation (see Austin Wadsworth Act)
Navy, U.S., 45, 102, 123, 147, 152, 212, 217
Nelson, Donald, 100, **138**, 232n24, 282n14, 290n30, 291n33, 293n5
Neutrality laws, xxx, 13, 15, 17, 20, 37, 238n25
New Caledonia, 96, 148, 210, 274n10
New Deal, 233n3
New Guinea, 211, 212
Nimitz, Adm. Chester W., 211, 292n1
Normandy, 164–65, 189, 191
North Africa, 123–34, 163, 166
Nye Committee Hearings, 233–34n6, 235n16, 238n25

Octagon Conference, 211
Office of Price Administration, 85, 98, 113
Office of Production Management, 100
Office of Scientific Research and Development, xlii, 149, 165, 219–21
Office of Strategic Services, 62, 74
Office of War Information, 47
Office of War Mobilization, 100–1, 285n29
Operation ANVIL, 196
Operation HUSKY, 166–67, 279n1, 280–81n8
Operation OVERLORD, 164–65, 181–87, 281n10, 285–86n1, 289n21
Operation SLEDGEHAMMER, 123
Operation TORCH, 123–34, 267n3, 268n5, 268–69nn9–10, 270n13
Ordnance department, 30

P-38 "Lightning", 58
P-47 "Thunderbolt", 57
P-51 "Mustang", 57
P-75 "Eagle", 56–57
Packard Motor Company, 48
Pacific theater, 96, 143, 205ff
paperwork, elimination of, 104–5, 126
Patch, Lt. Gen. Alexander, 197
Patterson, Margaret, **139**
Patterson, Robert P., **135–42**; arguments against government munitions industry, 36–37; defense of President Roosevelt, 233n4; law practice, xiv, xxvii-viii; as federal judge, xiii, xxviii-xxix; manpower and labor draft, 106–19, 264nn17–18, 265n24; reconversion, 290n25; as Secretary of War, 221; as Under Secretary of War, xiii, xxv-vii, xxxi-xl, 77, 100, 103, 235n15, 243–44nn24–25, 261n7; untimely death, xv, xvii; World War I service, xii, xxi, xxviii, 264n18
Patton, Gen. George S., Jr., 120, 125, 128, 130, 191, 203, 269n12
Pearl Harbor, 45, 69, 86, 94, 145, 150
Permanent Joint Board on Defense, 151
Persian Gulf Command, 159, 160, 278n19
Petain, Henri, 20, 40
Philippines, 96, 144–46, 210–12, 272n4
"Phony War" ("Sitzkrieg"), 15, 238n1
plant takeovers, 113–15, 265–66n25
Plattsburgh, N.Y. Professional Men's Training Camp, xi-xiii, 240n11

PLUTO ("Pipe line under the ocean") project, 187, 288nn14–15
Poland, 1–2, 15, 130, 238n1
Pound, Adm. Dudley, 97
priority orders, xxxiii, 82–83, 93, 165, 258n23
Prison Industries Branch, War Production Board, 117
prison labor, use of, 117–18
procurement, see military procurement, organization of; military procurement issues
production numbers, 170, 282–83n17, 292n2, 298n3
Project SILVERPLATE, 54, 251n22
public opinion, 3, 11, 15, 16, 67, 217, 233–34n6, 235n16, 238n1
Putnam, Palmer C., 165–66

Quinine, 149
Quadrant Conference, 294n8
Quebec Conference, 158, 167, 168, 185, 281n10

Reconstruction Finance Corporation, 27
reconversion issues, xxxix, 201, 290n30, 291–92n33
Redball Express, 192, 289n24
Remagen Bridge, 203
Reuther, Walter, 34, 246n34, 249–50n12
Rommel, Gen. Erwin, 89
Roosevelt, Franklin D., xxi, xxv, xxvii, 40, 43, 46, 50, 63, 91, 98, 152, 247n37; announcing production of 50,000 planes, 43, 46, 49, 50, 239n3, 249n9; appointing Patterson a Under Secretary of War xxix-xxxi; Cairo Conference, 181; Casablanca Conference, 63; overruling his military chiefs, 240–41n13, 241n15; Quebec Conference, 158, 211; quoted, 85; reorganization of War Department, xxxviii; Teheran Conference, 86; Trident Conference, 132
Roosevelt, Theodore, xxviii
Root, Elihu, xii, xxviii
rubber, 74, 80–82, 171–74, 257–58nn20–21, 283nn18–19, 283–84n21, 291n31
Rubber Reserve Corporation, 171

Salerno, 168
Schweinfurt raid, 56
Schwellenbach, Lewis B., 115
scientific research, 217–23
Selective Service, xxx, 19, 28, 84, 240n11
Short, Lt. Gen. Walter C., 272n5
shipbuilding, 271–72n3
shipping, shortages and related issues, 59, 86, 124, 128, 131, 144, 158, 184, 212, 259n26, 271–72n3, 274–75n13, 291n31
Sicily, 166–67, 280–81n8
Signal Corps, 71, 103
Sitka, Alaska, 152
small business, concerns for, 30–31, 34, 244nn26–27
Somervell, Lt. Gen. Brehon B., 89, 124, 127, 196, 290n30; Canol project, 156, 158, 276–77n17; pre-war career, 231–32n22; and reconversion, xl, 290n30; relations with civilian mobilization officials, 232n24, 260n4, 276–77n17; relations with Robert Patterson, xxxviii-ix, 244n28; and War Department reorganization, xxxviii-xl, 102

Soviet Union, 21, 64, 85; postwar fears of, xlii, xliv; U.S. supplies to, 40, 71, 96, 153–55, 159–60, 181–82, 275n14, 278n19
supply issues, 159–61; in Burma, 206–8; in European Theater of Operations, 190–92, 195, 197, 210, 291n31; in Italy, 167–68, 175–76, 285n26; for Operation TORCH, 125–30, 131–34; Operation OVERLORD, 185–88, Pacific theater, 147–48, 210–11
Standard Oil, 156, 277n17
Stark, Navy Chief Adm. Harold E., 241n15
steel, xxxvi, 79, 106, 236–37n20, 256–57n18
Stilwell, Lt. Gen. Joseph, 63, 207, 208–9, 294n9
Stimson, Henry L., xiii-iv, xxv-vi, xxx, xxxii, xxxv, 159, 231n16, 247n36, 253n5, 265n24
stockpiling materials, 73, 265n24
strategic bombing, 105, 189, 190, 297n30
Styer, Maj. Gen. W.D., 127
subcontracting, 34
submarine attacks, 144, 155, 174, 202, 259n26
Suez Canal, 38
Supply Arms and Services, U.S. War Department, 30, 101, 299n5

Taft, William Howard, xxx
tanks, orders and manufacture, 39, 40, 89–90, 95, 149, 233n2
tax amortization, xxxvi, 26–27, 29, 243n21
taxes, xv, xliv, 26, 29, 98, 282n17
Tarawa, 296n17

Tehran Conference, 86, 164, 181, 196, 286n1
Thoholte, Lt. Gen. Karl, 120
Thomas, Sen. Elbert, 73
Tito, Josep, 62
Tobruk, xxi
Treaty of Versailles, 1
Trident Conference, 281n9
Truman, Harry S., xiv, xxvii, 246–47n35, 255n15, 263n15, 276n16, 276–77n17
Tunisia, 124, 129, 132, 134, 167, 196

U-Boat attacks, see submarine attacks
Umnak Air Base, 158, 278n18
United Rubber Workers, 115

V-2 rockets, 196
V Loan Program, xxxvi, 28
Vichy, 96
Victory Program, 70, 236n17, 253n5
Von Rundstedt, Field Marshal Gerd, 189, 203, 289n20
Vultee Company, 59

War Department, xxvi, 82, 91; reorganization of, xxvi, xxxvii-ix; war preparations, 4–6, 16, 17, 22, 28
War Industries Board, 234n12, 236n19
War Labor Board 112, 113
War Manpower Commission, 100, 117, 263n16
War Plans Division, General Staff, U.S. Army, 145, 151
War Production Board, xxvi, xxxix, 70, 74, 100, 103, 110–11, 154, 172, 254n7, 258n24, 259–60n1

Index 311

War Resources Board, 17, 239n6
Wesson, Gen. C.M., 18, 19, 240n9
Westover, Brig. Gen. Oscar, 45
Wheeler, Col. Raymond A., 159
Wingate, Maj. Gen. Orde C., 208, 295n13
women, wartime role of, 115–17
Women's Airforce Service Pilots (WASPs), 252n29
Woodring, Harry, xxix-xxx
World War I, 3–5, 12, 16, 18, 164, 234n7
Wright Field, 54

Yalta Conference, 87

www.ingramcontent.com/pod-product-compliance
Lightning Source LLC
Chambersburg PA
CBHW030510080526
44586CB00011B/131